AFTER REPRESSION

## Princeton Studies in Political Behavior

Tali Mendelberg, Series Editor

# After Repression

## How Polarization Derails Democratic Transition

Elizabeth R. Nugent

**PRINCETON UNIVERSITY PRESS**

PRINCETON AND OXFORD

Copyright © 2020 by Princeton University Press

Requests for permission to reproduce material from this work
should be sent to permissions@press.princeton.edu

Published by Princeton University Press
41 William Street, Princeton, New Jersey 08540
6 Oxford Street, Woodstock, Oxfordshire OX20 1TR

press.princeton.edu

All Rights Reserved

ISBN 978-0-691-20306-5
ISBN (pbk.) 978-0-691-20305-8
ISBN (e-book) 978-0-691-20307-2

British Library Cataloging-in-Publication Data is available

Editorial: Bridget Flannery-McCoy
Production Editorial: Jill Harris
Cover Design: Layla Mac Rory
Production: Brigid Ackerman
Publicity: Kate Hensley and Kate Farquhar-Thomson

Cover art by Ganzeer

This book has been composed in Adobe Text and Gotham

Printed on acid-free paper. ∞

Printed in the United States of America

10 9 8 7 6 5 4 3 2 1

*For Nick, Always*

# CONTENTS

# FIGURES

# TABLES

# ACKNOWLEDGMENTS

I began the prospectus for this project in the fall of 2012. At that time, I saved a document on my computer titled "Thank Yous," knowing even before I started my dissertation that I would accrue many debts in writing it. Now that I am finished with the book, I have amassed quite a list; so please bear with me. As always, while this project could not have been completed without the help and support of the many listed here, all errors are my own.

First and foremost, I thank my dissertation committee at Princeton University: chair Amaney Jamal, Christopher Achen, Carles Boix, and Grigore Pop-Eleches. While all four committee members contributed immensely to this book by both encouraging and challenging me, Amaney deserves special mention. Amaney first served as my advisor, and has since become a coauthor, mentor, and friend. I have learned so much by watching her tireless and selfless approach to research, to teaching, to advising her students, and to advancing the field of Middle East politics. I am a better scholar due to her patient encouragement and high standards, as well as the innumerable opportunities she made available to me. I also thank politics faculty members Mark Beissinger, Rory Truex, and Deborah Yashar, as well as Alin Coman from Princeton's psychology department, who provided tremendously helpful feedback on the project at various stages. During my doctoral research, I received financial support from the Center for the Study of Religion, the Fellowship of Woodrow Wilson Scholars, the Fund for Experimental Social Sciences, and the Mamdouha S. Bobst Center for Peace and Justice.

I rewrote my dissertation as a book manuscript while I was a postdoctoral fellow at the Middle East Initiative at the Harvard Kennedy School. My fellow fellows Matthew Buehler, Jonas Draege, Diana Greenwald, Allison Hartnett, and Hind Ahmed Zaki are the stuff colleague dreams are made of; they are wildly intelligent, fiercely supportive, constructively critical, and a whole lot of fun in equal measure. I am indebted to MEI director Tarek Masoud, who has always pushed me to think bigger and to get Egypt right. I am also very grateful to Mohamed Naeem for his thoughts on this project. The Foundations of Human Behavior Initiative at Harvard provided funding for my final round of fieldwork for the project in January 2018.

I finished this book as an assistant professor at Yale University. Lisa Blaydes, Ellen Lust, and Daniel Slater attended my book conference in April 2018, and to have them read the manuscript in its entirety and offer their valued insight was an intellectual dream come true. Steven Wilkinson, then chair of the political science department, made the book conference possible, and he as well as my colleagues Milan Svolik and Daniel Mattingly attended the conference and provided invaluable comments on the manuscript. Dan also permitted me to read parts of his inspiring book manuscript while finishing my own. The brilliant Susan Stokes and Libby Wood offered feedback on a later draft that was tremendously helpful in honing the argument. I thank Kate Baldwin for her sage advice on all things academic and otherwise. James Scott was assigned to me as a mentor during my first year on faculty, and terrified me by actually reading and providing careful feedback on the draft I sent him. I am also grateful for the mentorship of Isabela Mares and Frances Rosenbluth. Thanks are also due to my junior political science colleagues and Yale's Council on Middle East Studies who provided much needed friendship, camaraderie, and community. I benefited from Yale's Coaching for Success initiative in the Scholars as Learners (SAL2) program, which connected me with the unrivaled Dr. Joanna Friedman. This manuscript was published with the assistance of the Frederick W. Hilles Publication Fund of Yale University.

I am grateful to be a part of the broader Middle Eastern politics community, a group of brilliant and kind scholars. Eva Bellin, Josh Stacher, Jillian Schwedler, and Mark Tessler gave me generous feedback on this project at various stages of development. I owe a tremendous debt to the current and former faculty of Georgetown's government department, Arabic department, and Center for Contemporary Arab Studies, including Amin Bonnah, Tamim Barghouti, Rochelle Davis, Michael Hudson, Charles Kiamie, Joseph Sassoon, Samir Shehata, and Hana Zabarah. Their classes and research first piqued my interest in the Arab world as an undergraduate and master's student, and they provided me with the intellectual basis and linguistic tools to be a responsible researcher.

My peers and friends have contributed to this project from its infancy in immeasurable ways. Whether by spending time discussing the project over coffee, wine, and shisha, reading and providing feedback on drafts of all calibers, or reminding me of my larger goals, they have all enhanced and augmented this project beyond what I could have accomplished alone. Carolyn Barnett, Chantal Berman, Alex Blackman, Steven Brooke, James Casey, Killian Clarke, Emine Deniz, Ben Fifield, Michael Hoffman, Marcus Johnson, Adam Lichtenheld, Rebecca Littman, Avital Livny, Katie McCabe, Rohan Mukherjee, Daniel Tavana, Michelle Weitzel, and Yang Yang Zhou are wonderfully supportive and inspiring colleagues, coauthors, and friends. I received helpful comments from audiences at a number of presentations of different parts of this project, including audiences at the 2016 APSA Political Psychology Pre-Conference poster session; the 2016 and 2017 annual meetings of the Middle East Studies Association; the 2017 and 2018 annual meetings of the American Political Science Association; the 2017 APSA MENA Political Science Research and Publication Conference; the 2017 ECPR Joint Sessions Workshop on "The Legacy of Authoritarian Regimes: Political Culture, Institutions, and Democratization"; the 2018 Conference on Democratic Backsliding and Electoral Authoritarianism; and the 2018 annual meeting of the North East Middle East Politics Working Group.

I extend sincere gratitude to the many politicians and activists I interviewed during the course of my research, as well as their staffs. These individuals took hours out of their extremely busy schedules, during an influential period in their countries' histories, to help me make appointments and to share their knowledge and experiences with me. This project would be nothing without their generosity. Though many of these conversations necessarily do not appear in the following pages due to their volume, these individuals shared stories about how their political activism affected their lives, their livelihoods, their bodies, and their families. I remain inspired by their perseverance and poise under the most difficult of situations. I thank Intissar Samarat for research assistance in Tunisia. Her unrelenting persistence opened many doors, and her sense of humor made each interview all the more enjoyable. Ahmed Fixthi Ebada, Hamza Mighri, and Osama al-Sayyed also contributed invaluable research assistance. I thank the fantastic staff of One-to-One for Research and Polling for their hard work and attention to detail on the experimental component of this project. Many thanks are also due to the *Centre d'Etudes Maghrébines à Tunis* (CEMAT) for my research affiliation in Tunis, and to its outstanding director, Laryssa Chomiak.

At Princeton University Press, Bridget Flannery-McCoy and her predecessor Eric Crahan, as well as their teams, have been wonderful to work with and continue to demonstrate heroic patience with this first-time author. I thank Tali Mendelberg for supporting the manuscript, including it in the Political Behavior Series, and suggesting careful edits that sharpened its contribution. The brilliant and talented artist Ganzeer created the cover art for the book.

Finally and most importantly, I thank my family. Claire, DJ, Maggie, Patrick, and Vivian are my most favorite people, and their support through this long process has meant everything. Leonard diligently sat on my desk through nearly a decade of analyzing, translating, reading, writing, and editing. My grandparents Mary and George Anderson were elementary school teachers for most of their lives, and fostered in me a love of learning from a young age. My parents Patty and Michael have provided me with every opportunity and support possible, and reminded me of my goals when I needed to be newly encouraged and refocused. I like to think that my career as an academic and researcher combines two of their many strengths: my mother's curiosity and warmth towards new people, and my father's talent as a writer. I am eternally grateful to them for so much, and I hope they consider this finished piece an accomplishment of their own.

And to Nick, to whom this book is dedicated. It is difficult to express what my husband means to me, so let me just say that the beautiful life we have built together is beyond anything I dared hope for. In addition to the constant support he provides to me and our family, Nick's helpful comments, critiques, and corrections have directly contributed to the improvement of this book.

The completion of this manuscript was measured on a timeline dictated by our daughter, Juliette. Wanting her in our life spurred additional fieldwork and furious revisions during my postdoctoral fellowship. Her April 2019 due date motivated me to submit the manuscript weeks before her arrival. I received reviewers' comments on her one-month birthday, and sleepily drafted a response during her naps. Her dramatic entrance into our life gave me a perspective on work, career, partnership, and community I didn't know I needed. Becoming Juliette's mother also provided deeper insight into the sacrifices of my interview subjects. While I don't necessarily agree with many of their political positions, I now understand wanting to create a better world for my child.

# A NOTE ON TRANSLATION AND TRANSLITERATION

The research presented in this book relied on extensive Arabic-language interviews and texts published in Arabic. I recorded interviews with the permission of interview subjects and translated them into English. This was sometimes difficult, given the many differences in linguistic styles and cultural references between the two languages, but I have tried to maintain the original meaning of the subjects' words. The transliteration method I used is based on that adopted by the *International Journal of Middle East Studies*. However, I dropped diacritical marks that indicate long vowels and emphatic consonants in line with contemporary Arabic-language transliteration practice. I used local common transliterations for names, places, and events, which differ systematically but significantly in Egyptian and Tunisian dialects.

# PART I

# Theoretical Perspectives

# 1

# Introduction

2011 unleashed an unprecedented level of mass mobilization that swept the Middle East and made the inconceivable—a democratic transition of power—finally seem possible. Prior to the wave of protests that became known as the Arab Spring, Middle Eastern dictators typically held onto power for decades. Most had managed to survive the Third Wave of democratization that had dislodged several of their peers in Asia, Latin America, and sub-Saharan Africa. The region's authoritarian regimes appeared to be as entrenched as ever on the eve of the uprisings. Starting in Tunisia and quickly spreading to Egypt, Libya, Bahrain, Yemen, and Syria, the Arab Spring protests dislodged two long-ruling authoritarian presidents from office and threatened the stability of dozens of others. Though highly divided by political, social, ethnic, and economic differences, the masses came together to demand autonomy and to hold their governments accountable. The rallying cry of the uprisings was "the people want the fall of the regime!" Individuals from all classes, walks of life, and political persuasions who were equally fed up with authoritarian rule joined in the protests.[1] Demonstrators proudly displayed their national flags while camping in main squares, and Muslims and Christians took turns linking

---

1. The diversity of protesters would later be confirmed by survey data (Mark R. Beissinger, Amaney A. Jamal, and Kevin Mazur, "Explaining Divergent Revolutionary Coalitions: Regime Strategies and the Structuring of Participation in the Tunisian and Egyptian Revolutions," *Comparative Politics* 48, no. 1 [2015]: 1–24).

hands to protect each other from the security forces as they prayed in protest spaces.

Democratic opposition parties joined their fellow citizens in protest. Political figures representing competing political ideologies—communists, socialists, leftists, centrists, Islamists, and even quietist Salafists—demonstrated a remarkable unity of purpose. Many of these politicians had spent their lives challenging authoritarian rule, and their small victories had been hard-won through significant struggle and sacrifice. Watching the systems they had so long resisted teetering on the brink of collapse, they appeared to sense that this unprecedented opportunity could not be squandered. They put aside their past disagreements to join their voices and hands in protest. One Muslim Brotherhood leader described the camaraderie he felt during the eighteen days of protest in downtown Cairo as "like a dream."[2] As the first Arab Spring protests gained traction in Tunisia, Rachid Ghannouchi, head of the country's banned Islamist opposition group, Ennahda, called Ahmed Najib Chebbi of the legalized opposition party *Parti Démocrate Progressiste* from exile in London. "The boat is threatened with sinking," Ghannouchi said. The two men agreed that the democratic opposition, including both secular and Islamist groups, would need to work together to capture the momentum of the protests, offer a viable alternative to the old regime, and move the transition forward.[3]

But the hopeful unity from the early days of the uprisings quickly dissipated, and the paths of transition in each country soon diverged.[4] Regimes in Algeria, Iraq, Kuwait, and Morocco granted a number of concessions, such as lifting emergency laws, dissolving parliaments, holding new elections, expanding suffrage, and increasing social welfare spending. Such measures appeared to respond to protesters' demands, but ultimately helped the authoritarian leaders undermine the opposition and demobilize protesters—and stay in power. Elsewhere, the uprisings descended into violent conflict. The Bahraini revolt ended with a brutal regime crackdown supported by Saudi Arabia in March 2013. The Syrian uprising descended into a still-ongoing civil war, dividing the country into regions controlled by the Assad government, opposition rebel groups, and the *jihadi* group known as the Islamic State amidst the meddling involvement of various

2. Amr Darrag. Interview with the author. June 13, 2016. Istanbul, Turkey.

3. Ahmed Najib Chebbi. Interview with the author. January 19, 2017. Tunis, Tunisia.

4. Jason Brownlee, Tarek E. Masoud, and Andrew Reynolds, *The Arab Spring: Pathways of Repression and Reform* (New York: Oxford University Press, 2015).

foreign actors. Similarly, the Libyan uprising soon degenerated into a civil war between forces affiliated with two rival transitional regimes.

Egypt and Tunisia, the first two countries to witness protests, initially experienced similar transitions. Egypt's Hosni Mubarak and Tunisia's Zine al-Abidine Ben Ali stepped down from the offices they had held for thirty and twenty-three years, respectively, after weeks of unrelenting protests. Their resignations swiftly empowered alternative political elites, the vast majority of whom constituted the democratic opposition to the regime. As the crowds of protesters thinned, these elites faced the formidable challenge of replacing an authoritarian state with a democratic one. Within a year of the presidents' resignations, former opposition leaders were finally elected to national constituent assemblies in both countries, and charged with drafting new constitutions, putting in place the rules and timelines for holding first legislative and then presidential elections, and deciding how to hold the previous regimes accountable for their repressive behavior. In both countries, the religious-secular cleavage represented the most important divide in these early elections, and Islamist parties, which were influential members of the previous regimes' opposition, won 37 percent of the vote.

Yet despite these important similarities, Egypt and Tunisia were in vastly different situations just three years later. In Egypt, tensions between elites were palpable under the Muslim Brotherhood-dominated government. The Brotherhood-affiliated Freedom and Justice Party (FJP) won a plurality in the 2011–2012 Constituent Assembly elections, and Mohamed Morsi, a former member of the group's Guidance Bureau, was elected president in June 2012. Morsi's opponents accused him of being heavy-handed and dictatorial, and secular parties walked out of the December 2012 constitutional drafting process in protest after significant disagreements over the text and its content. This gave the FJP and its allies significant control over the draft constitution, which they approved in a quickly held referendum marred by a low turnout. In late June 2013, Murad Ali, a spokesman for the FJP, remarked, "with the current state of polarization and without reaching an understanding or working together, we will reach hell and kill each other in the streets."[5] Massive anti-Morsi protests organized on the first anniversary of his inauguration were followed by a military coup d'état on July 3. Members of the Brotherhood's rival political movements, including former Director General of the International Atomic Energy Agency, Nobel Peace Prize recipient, and rival politician Mohamed al-Baradei,

5. Quoted in *New York Times*, June 30, 2013. https://nyti.ms/2x1ufyZ.

youth leaders from prominent protest movements, and a representative of the Salafist Nour Party, sat in symbolic support behind Army General Abdel Fattah al-Sisi as he announced the forced change in government on national television. By the year's end, the Brotherhood was banned from politics and named a terrorist organization after a brutal regime crackdown on the group and its supporters. The violent campaign peaked with the August 2013 massacre of pro-Brotherhood demonstrators in Cairo's al-Nahda and Rabaa al-Adawiya squares, in which nearly 1,400 were killed and 16,000 detained. The authoritarian relapse gained momentum; by May 15, 2014, 41,163 individuals had been arrested and prosecuted, the majority accused of ties to the Brotherhood.[6] In the same month, General al-Sisi won the presidency with over 96 percent of the votes cast in a typical authoritarian election, which was boycotted by the opposition.

Meanwhile, Tunisia progressed towards democratic consolidation despite significant challenges. Elections for the 217-seat National Constituent Assembly (NCA) were held on October 23, 2011. The former Islamist opposition party Ennahda placed first with 37 percent of the vote. Ennahda leaders formed a Troika government to run the NCA, working with leaders from the formerly banned center-left opposition group *Congrès pour la République* (al-Mu'tamar min ajl al-Jumhuriyya) and formerly legalized secular opposition group the Democratic Forum for Labor and Liberties (known as Ettakatol from its Arabic name, *at-Takattul ad-Dimuqrati min ajl al-'Amal wal-Hurriyyat*). To streamline the constitution-building process, the Troika formed six 22-person committees. Each was tasked with drafting a principle component of the constitution, and each was staffed by members of different parties, including Islamists, leftists, secularists, and independents in proportion to the number of seats they held in the NCA. The NCA approved an inclusive constitution in January 2014 with support from all major political groups. This was a major achievement given a number of false starts, difficult debates, and the terrifying assassinations of two leftist politicians, all of which contributed to the extension of the assembly's mandate from one to three years. Between October 2014 and January 2015, the country held its first post-authoritarian legislative and presidential elections. Tunisia experienced its first successful transfer of power through the ballot box when Ennahda lost these contests to Nidaa

---

6. As detailed by the independent statistical database Wiki Thawra in a report titled "Report on the Detained and Prosecuted during the Sisi/Adly Mansour Period." Available in Arabic at https://wikithawra.wordpress.com/2014/01/09/sisi-mansour-detainees/.

Tounes, a newly formed party including many former regime members united under an anti-Islamist platform.

By 2014, it was evident that for all the hope inspired by the 2011–2012 protests, the Arab Spring would result in very little democratic change, with the glaring exception of Tunisia. What went wrong in many countries, and what went right in Tunisia?

## The Puzzle

The examples of Egypt and Tunisia confirm a central lesson of past transitions: the collapse of an authoritarian regime may trigger a transition, but it does not always lead to successful democratic consolidation. A transition might instead result in reentrenched authoritarianism or any number of revolutionary alternatives.[7] Decisions made by elite actors during critical moments of potential political transition matter immensely. The successful progression from authoritarian breakdown to democratic consolidation is highly contingent on whether elites can compromise and cooperate during the transition, and make the necessary decisions and sacrifices to establish democratic norms and processes.[8]

Elite actors' ability to compromise and cooperate in turn depends on the level of polarization among them.[9] Higher levels of polarization make

7. Guillermo O'Donnell, Philippe C. Schmitter, and Cynthia J. Arnson, *Transitions from Authoritarian Rule: Tentative Conclusions about Uncertain Democracies* (Johns Hopkins University Press, 2013 (1986)), 5.

8. Dankwart A. Rustow, "Transitions to Democracy: Toward a Dynamic Model," *Comparative politics* 2, no. 3 (1970): 337–363; Guillermo O'Donnell, Philippe C. Schmitter, and Laurence Whitehead, *Transitions from Authoritarian Rule: Southern Europe* (Johns Hopkins University Press, 1986); Scott Mainwaring, *Transitions to Democracy and Democratic Consolidation: Theoretical and Comparative Issues* (University of Notre Dame, Helen Kellogg Institute for International Studies, 1989); Giuseppe Di Palma, *To Craft Democracies: An Essay on Democratic Transitions* (University of California Press, 1990); Herbert Kitschelt, "Political Regime Change: Structure and Process-driven Explanations?," *American Political Science Review* 86, no. 4 (1992): 1028–1034; Philippe C. Schmitter, "Transitology: The Science or the Art of Democratization?," in *The Consolidation of Democracy in Latin America*, ed. Joseph S. Tulchin and Bernice Romero (Boulder, Colorado: Lynne Rienner, 1995), 11–41; John Higley and Gyorgy Lengyel, *Elites after State Socialism: Theories and Analysis* (Latham: Rowman & Littlefield, 2000); John Higley and Michael Burton, *Elite Foundations of Liberal Democracy* (Latham: Rowman & Littlefield, 2006).

9. Samuel P. Huntington, "Will More Countries Become Democratic?," *Political Science Quarterly* 99, no. 2 (1984): 193–218; O'Donnell, Schmitter, and Arnson, *Conclusions*; Mainwaring, *Transitions to Democracy and Democratic Consolidation: Theoretical and Comparative Issues*; Adam Przeworski, *Democracy and the Market: Political and Economic Reforms in Eastern Europe and Latin America* (Cambridge: Cambridge University Press, 1991); Stephan Haggard and Robert R. Kaufman, *The Political Economy of Democratic Transitions* (Princeton: Princeton

it less likely that actors will reach a consensus during critical moments of democratic consolidation, as these differences can prevent coalitions from forming and make compromises harder to reach. While the comparative politics literature often invokes polarization as an important concept, it is more precisely defined in studies of American politics as the distance between parties on dimensions that matter for political compromise and cooperation. Polarization includes two components: (1) affective distance in the realm of emotions, feelings, and attitudes (the extent to which groups *dislike* each other) and (2) distance in policy preferences on salient political issues (the extent to which groups *disagree* with each other).

First, *affective* polarization is based on the nature of an individual's psychological attachment to a group, which can include positive in-group assessments as well as negative evaluations of the out-group.[10] As Achen and Bartels explain, "identities are not primarily about adherence to a group ideology or creed. They are emotional attachments [to groups] that transcend thinking."[11] In the United States and Western Europe, partisan identities such as Democrat and Republican or liberal and conservative often form the salient political cleavage, whereas in other contexts, politicized religious identities such as Islamist and secularist or ethnic identities such as Kurdish and Arab serve as the basis of these divisions. Affective polarization occurs when group members distrust and hold negative views of out-group members and perceive a greater social distance between their in-group and the out-group.

---

University Press, 1995); Juan J. Linz and Alfred Stepan, *Problems of Democratic Transition and Consolidation: Southern Europe, South America, and Post-Communist Europe* (Johns Hopkins University Press, 1996); Herbert Kitschelt et al., *Post-Communist Party Systems: Competition, Representation, and Inter-party Cooperation* (Cambridge: Cambridge University Press, 1999); Michael McFaul, "The Fourth Wave of Democracy and Dictatorship: Noncooperative Transitions in the Postcommunist World," *World Politics* 54, no. 2 (2002): 212–244; Brownlee, Masoud, and Reynolds, *The Arab Spring.*

10. Christopher Ellis and James A. Stimson, *Ideology in America* (Cambridge University Press, 2012); Shanto Iyengar, Gaurav Sood, and Yphtach Lelkes, "Affect, Not Ideology: A Social Identity Perspective on Polarization," *Public Opinion Quarterly* 76, no. 3 (2012): 405–431; Shanto Iyengar and Sean J. Westwood, "Fear and Loathing Across Party Lines: New Evidence on Group Polarization," *American Journal of Political Science* 59, no. 3 (2015): 690–707; Lilliana Mason, "'I Disrespectfully Agree': The Differential Effects of Partisan Sorting on Social and Issue Polarization," *American Journal of Political Science* 59, no. 1 (2015): 128–145.

11. Christopher H. Achen and Larry M. Bartels, *Democracy for Realists: Why Elections Do Not Produce Responsive Government* (Princeton University Press, 2017), 228.

Second, *preference* polarization reflects distance in policy preferences.[12] Polarization increases when group members perceive greater disagreement with other groups on central policy questions. This does not necessarily imply a change in their motivating ideology, but rather a shift in how the group presents their policy positions. For example, the US Democratic Party's motivating ideology is centered on creating an interventionist government that regulates society and the economy to foster certain protections and equality. While that ideology has not changed, the party's policy preferences have shifted as it redefines what falls under the scope of government responsibility, the nature of that responsibility, and what programs are needed to achieve this goal—and how these policies differ from those of their Republican counterparts.

The polarization that matters for democratic transitions is *between* parties; this type has long been theorized to exert significant influence over the nature and civility of political competition.[13] I analyze polarization between parties of the democratic opposition in electoral authoritarian regimes.[14] Opposition parties contest the regime's political program and demand reform through peaceful means, primarily through electoral representation if this is available. These elite actors contest elections rather than seek political change through violence or upheaval.[15] During a transition, these opposition parties become key actors when their presence at the bargaining table—and their compliance with the terms—is necessary to ensure a successful agreement.[16]

Returning to the cases of Egypt and Tunisia, opposition parties emerged from the authoritarian period in 2011 differently polarized both in affect

12. Lloyd A. Free and Hadley Cantril, *Political Beliefs of Americans: A Study of Public Opinion* (Rutgers University Press, 1967); Ellis and Stimson, *Ideology in America*; Morris P. Fiorina and Samuel L. Abrams, "Political Polarization in the American Public," *Annual Review of Political Science* 11 (2008): 563–588; Alan L. Abramowitz, *The Disappearing Center: Engaged Citizens, Polarization, and American Democracy* (New Haven: Yale University Press, 2010).

13. Adam Przeworski, *Capitalism and Social Democracy* (Cambridge University Press, 1986), 99–101.

14. Holger Albrecht, "Political Opposition and Arab Authoritarianism: Some Conceptual Remarks," in *Contentious Politics in the Middle East: Political Opposition under Authoritarianism*, ed. Holger Albrecht (Gainesville: University Press of Florida, 2010), 3.

15. For examples, see Andreas Schedler, *Electoral Authoritarianism: The Dynamics of Unfree Competition* (Boulder: Lynne Rienner Publishers, 2006); Larry J. Diamond, "Thinking about Hybrid Regimes," *Journal of Democracy* 13, no. 2 (2002): 21–35; Steven Levitsky and Lucan Way, "The Rise of Competitive Authoritarianism," *Journal of Democracy* 2, no. 13 (2002): 51–65.

16. Elisabeth Jean Wood, *Forging Democracy from Below: Insurgent Transitions in South Africa and El Salvador* (Cambridge University Press, 2000).

towards other groups and in their preferences over key political issues, as I outline in further detail in subsequent chapters. In Egypt, political parties distrusted their counterparts and held extremely negative opinions about them. In contrast, Tunisian party leaders identified as a united opposition that had suffered together under the previous regime and felt positively about the other political groups with which they were required to co-operate and negotiate. In addition, Egypt's political parties had more extreme policy preferences compared to those in Tunisia, which held more centrist views regarding the role of religion in politics and the public sphere.

While past studies have mainly focused on institutional or socioeconomic explanations of democratization, this book investigates how the personal experiences and shared history of the opposition contribute to the success of a democratic transition. The groups that work together to bring down authoritarian regimes often fail to establish democracy because they are highly polarized and cannot sustain unity, cooperation, and compromise after the regime collapses. This general dynamic helps to explain the divergence between Egypt and Tunisia as well as the long-term failure of many other Arab Spring uprisings. I explore what explains the level of polarization among political parties at the start of each country's transition, and what determines how polarized an authoritarian party system will be after a democratic transition.

## The Argument

I argue that the political identities of opposition groups are shaped by their experiences of authoritarian repression; these identities in turn determine the levels of political polarization at the moment of transition. I focus heavily on the repressive tactics of authoritarian regimes to explore the effect of the physical suffering, psychological humiliation, and trauma experienced by regime opponents who were repressed. I draw on social identity theory to understand how this pain and trauma influences opposition members' subsequent preferences and actions. This foundational theory provides social-psychological explanations for the causes and consequences of group identity formation, and has important implications for understanding polarization in group-based political interactions. Before I outline my explanation, I summarize prior studies' approaches to polarization. While these theories identify important components of political contestation, they fail to fully explain polarization because they do not sufficiently incorporate an understanding of preference formation and the centrality of identity in this process.

## EXISTING EXPLANATIONS: STRUCTURE, STRATEGY, AND IDEOLOGY

While previous research on polarization treats affective and preference polarization separately, explanations for both phenomena fall into three categories: structural, strategic, and ideological. According to these studies, either the structural characteristics of the political system or the strategies or ideologies of the political actors determine political affect and preferences, the distance between groups on these dimensions, and the resulting level of polarization in the system.

In *structural* explanations, polarization reflects factors external to the political system, such as a society's underlying social, political, and economic cleavages, or the demographic distribution of society according to class, sector, region, ethnicity, or conceptions of religion and state. These accounts assume that polarization is a more or less objective representation of structural differences in society, as parties seek to maximize their vote share by mobilizing based on causes and identities relevant to the electorate.[17] Broader historical processes such as nation-building, state consolidation, development, modernization, industrialization, and incorporation of territory create meaningful underlying divisions within society. These divisions, in turn, dictate the political placement of parties as well as the relative distance between the actors who mobilize and represent these interests in political competition.[18]

Previous studies have proposed structural explanations for both the affective and preference dimensions of political polarization. For instance,

17. Stephan Haggard and Robert R. Kaufman, "Democratization During the Third Wave," *Annual Review of Political Science* 19 (2016): 125–144.

18. Seymour M. Lipset and Stein Rokkan, "Cleavage Structures, Party Systems, and Voter Alignments: An Introduction," in *Party Systems and Voter Alignments: Cross-National Perspectives*, ed. Seymour M. Lipset and Stein Rokkan (Toronto: Free Press, 1967), 1–64; Geoffrey Evans and Stephen Whitefield, "Explaining the Formation of Electoral Cleavages in Post-Communist Democracies," *Elections in Central and Eastern Europe: The First Wave*, 2000, 36–70; Kevin Deegan-Krause, "New Dimensions of Political Cleavage," in *Oxford Handbook of Political Science*, ed. R. Dalton and H.-D. Klingemann (Oxford: Oxford University Press, 2006).

scholars have explained differences in the distribution of policy prefer-ences across cases through variation in underlying cleavage structures, and increased polarization in policy preferences within cases as the result of shifts in these underlying cleavages.[19] Similarly, the level of affective polar-ization is a natural outgrowth of social group membership, and changes in affect towards the out-group occur as the result of exogenous shocks, such as unfavorable demographic changes or cross-national variation in historical processes. Increasingly homogeneous interpersonal networks create situations in which partisan group members become more isolated from each other and from competing viewpoints, which in turn exacerbates and increases negative affect.[20]

In *strategic* explanations, polarization reflects the internal aspects of a political system, as parties create platforms and other kinds of political appeals to maximize their vote share. While the preferences reflected in these platforms and groups' affect towards others generally reflect cleav-ages within society, internal aspects of the political system shape how the distribution of societal cleavages is aggregated to create political polariza-tion. The features that define the internal workings of the political system, primarily electoral rules and institutions, have the most influence over this process. Electoral systems complicate the translation of interests into polit-ical competition and enhance or diminish polarization. For example, the electoral rules in some countries might require certain thresholds for par-ticipation, and thus force elites to strategically form partnerships and mod-ify their policy preferences accordingly. The argument for affective polar-ization is similarly rooted in party strategies: in attempts to win support and votes, elites strategically create information environments that prime partisan identity, which in turn exacerbates negative intergroup feelings. In the American context, attention has turned to the way in which media and political campaigns create this dynamic. Increasingly partisan news dis-seminated through both partisan outlets and mainstream media activates

19. Lee Sigelman and Syng Nam Yough, "Left-right Polarization in National Party Sys-tems: A Cross-National Analysis," *Comparative Political Studies* 11, no. 3 (1978): 355–379; Nolan McCarty, Keith T. Poole, and Howard Rosenthal, *Polarized America: The Dance of Ideology and Unequal Riches* (Cambridge: MIT Press, 2006); Joseph Daniel Ura and Christopher R. Ellis, "Partisan Moods: Polarization and the Dynamics of Mass Party Preferences," *Comparative Polit-ical Studies* 74, no. 1 (2011): 277–291; Noam Lupu and Rachel Beatty Riedl, "Political Parties and Uncertainty in Developing Democracies," *Comparative Political Studies* 46, no. 11 (2013): 1339–1365.

20. Shanto Iyengar et al., "The Origins and Consequences of Affective Polarization in the United States," *Annual Review of Political Science*, 2018.

partisan identities and strengthens negative feelings towards other parties.[21] Political campaigns similarly make partisan identities more salient.[22] Both components ultimately contribute to the increasingly negative affect towards political out-groups and higher aggregate levels of affective polarization.

A third and final set of explanations for polarization focuses on parties' motivating ideologies to describe the two types of polarization discussed above: affective and preference. These theories often focus on parties with religious or radical ideologies, such as the Islamist parties analyzed in this book.[23] First, in these explanations, ideology is a key aspect of affective polarization. The idea of "party sorting" suggests that partisans have deeply held worldviews that steer them towards political affiliations in alignment with these views. Here, the underlying ideologies motivating both individual partisans and political groups determine who is considered an opponent, and to what extent in-group members should have a negative opinion of opponents.[24] Second, ideological placement is also theorized to determine preference polarization.[25] According to this line of thinking, ideology is fairly constant and changes only as a result of parties' participation in electoral competition. Inclusion exposes these previously excluded

21. Giovanni Sartori, "Politics, Ideology, and Belief Systems," *American Political Science Review* 63, no. 2 (1969): 398–411; Gary W. Cox, "Electoral Equilibria Under Alternative Voting Institutions," *American Journal of Political Science* 31, no. 1 (1987): 82–108; James Adams and Zeynep Somer-Topcu, "Do Parties Adjust Their Policies in Response to Rival Parties' Policy Shifts? Spatial Theory and the Dynamics of Party Competition in Twenty-Five Postwar Democracies," *British Journal of Political Science* 39 (2009): 825–846.

22. Iyengar et al., "The Origins and Consequences of Affective Polarization in the United States."

23. Ideology constitutes much of the explanation underpinning inclusion–moderation theories that seek to explain changes in Islamist parties' behavior over time and the evolution of their participation in electoral institutions, however limited, in the Middle East and other parts of the Muslim world.

24. Mason, " 'I Disrespectfully Agree': The Differential Effects of Partisan Sorting on Social and Issue Polarization"; Jon C. Rogowski and Joseph L. Sutherland, "How Ideology Fuels Affective Polarization," *Political Behavior* 38, no. 2 (2016): 485–508; Lori D. Bougher, "The Correlates of Discord: Identity, Issue Alignment, and Political Hostility in Polarized America," *Political Behavior* 39, no. 3 (2017): 731–762.

25. Samuel Huntington, *The Third Wave: Democratization in the Late Twentieth Century* (Norman, Oklahoma: University of Oklahoma Press, 1993); Adam Przeworski and John Sprague, *Paper Stones: A History of Electoral Socialism* (University of Chicago Press: Chicago, 1986); Scott Mainwaring, Guillermo O'Donnell, and J. Samuel Valenzuela, *Issues in Democratic Consolidation: The New South American Democracies in Comparative Perspective* (South Bend, Indiana: University of Notre Dame Press, 1992).

actors to other ideologies and democratic procedures, which updates their preferences and changes their behavior.[26]

While these explanations explore a number of important components of polarization, they often fail to tell the whole story for four reasons. First, structural accounts of preference polarization often fail to explicitly define the causal link between these two phenomena—a country's ethnic make-up, for example, and the distance between politics parties' policy preferences. Katznelson and Weingast observe, "people and their preferences tended to be collapsed into categories established by the interplay of theory and history. Once defined, say, as peasants, kings, Protestants, bureaucrats, or other such positions in the social order, agents were, of course, recognized as the bearers of preferences, but their content almost could be taken for granted."[27] It remains even less clear why these identities might be politically salient in the first place, and how underlying structural conditions translate into negative perceptions of out-groups. Second, strategic accounts that analyze polarization as the result of internal factors of political systems find little or no effect; electoral laws and institutions generally do not exacerbate preference polarization.[28] This may be because the majority of studies analyze democracies, which by definition grant elites a high level of autonomy to mobilize underlying cleavages, or because these institutions do not function as theorized. Third, structural accounts do not help us determine whether certain campaign and media environments are necessary for affective polarization. Fourth, parties that are assumed to be ideologically motivated often update their preferences regarding policies and other actors. However, this may be because they shift their emphasis to different aspects or interpretations of their ideology to reflect changes in affect and preferences rather than a response to increased liberalization within a system or an underlying shift in

26. Janine Astrid Clark, "The Conditions of Islamist Moderation: Unpacking Cross-Ideological Cooperation in Jordan," *International Journal of Middle East Studies* 38, no. 4 (2006): 539–60; Carrie Wickham, "The Path to Moderation: Strategy and Learning in the Formation of Egypt's *Wasat* Party," *Comparative Politics* 36, no. 2 (2004): 205–228.

27. Ira Katznelson and Barry R. Weingast, "Intersections Between Historical and Rational Choice Institutionalism," in *Preferences and Situations: Points of Intersection Between Historical and Rational Choice Institutionalism*, ed. Ira Katznelson and Barry R. Weingast (New York: Russell Sage Foundation, 2005), 13.

28. Nolan McCarty, "Measuring Legislative Preferences," in *The Oxford Handbook of the American Congress*, ed. George C. Edwards III and and Eric Schickler Frances E. Lee (Oxford: Oxford University Press, 2011).

ideology.[29] Thus, while these theories identify important elements of political contestation, they underestimate the importance and centrality of preference formation and identity in this process. Perhaps most importantly, they fail to take into account how regimes might use repressive tactics and manipulate parties' structures, strategies, and ideology.

## REPRESSION, IDENTITY, AND POLARIZATION

I advance an original theory of the two-stage process through which repression conditions levels of polarization in authoritarian political systems. The first stage entails regime repression. In contrast to previous accounts of polarization, I argue that parties are less polarized when their individual members suffered repression together under an authoritarian regime. The nature of political repression in an autocracy influences how opposition actors identify themselves. Regimes that brutalize a large segment of opposition create a common identity among these groups: the shared experience of repression instills a shared identity among opposition leaders from all factions.

Repression conditions political identities via three mutually reinforcing mechanisms. First, it affects the *psychological* processes through which actors learn about their group: repression provides important information to political actors about who is a member of their group, what status their group holds relative to other groups, and whether they share similarities with other groups. In the second mechanism, repression alters groups' *social* environment by determining whether political prisoners are exposed to prison or exile, and whether these spaces are shared with members of other political groups. In the third mechanism, repression changes the *organizational* structure of opposition groups as they struggle to survive. Previous studies have identified the second and third mechanisms as possible effects of repression and imprisonment but have not always assigned them an important role in identity formation as a function of repression. Together, these three mechanisms significantly influence identity formation.

In the second stage, political identities shape the landscape of affective bonds and articulated preferences among actors following established

29. Jillian Schwedler, *Faith in Moderation: Islamist Parties in Jordan and Yemen* (Cambridge University Press, 2006).

processes of preference formation.[30] The extent to which identities are in conflict determines the nature of the preferences they produce. The perception of identity differences among actors determines the extent to which each group's related affective and preference positioning is in conflict and distant. This occurs through the psychological process of group differentiation, wherein differences in affective and preference positioning naturally flow from variations in identities. In general, individuals unconsciously seek to reduce cognitive dissonance, and group differentiation processes reconcile discrepancies in identities with differences in feelings and opinions. As a result, when group identities are highly polarized, group-related affect and preferences will be as well.[31]

I explore the effects of two types of repression. All authoritarian regimes repress their political opposition to some degree, yet some single out a specific opposition group (targeted repression) while others repress all mobilized political opponents (widespread repression). The important factor for the current study is the extent to which groups experience repression in the same way as their competitors, since those that do develop a shared, bridging political identity as victims of the regime that cuts across other political divisions such as ethnic, religious, or liberal versus conservative. Widespread repression in effect levels the playing field, as all groups are weakened equally, and members of different groups often increase their interactions in prison or exile.

In contrast, a targeted repressive environment creates different conditions and experiences across groups. Psychologically, a targeted repressive environment reveals to the opposition that only one group is being victimized. In addition, members of a singularly or differently repressed group experience increased social interaction only with other members of their in-group in repressive spaces of prison and exile. And while regimes intend for repression to weaken the organizational strength of a targeted group, this tactic can also force a group to adapt by putting in place defensive structures that protect and further isolate the group from both

30. For a concise overview of how identities condition related preferences, see James N. Druckman and Arthur Lupia, "Preference Formation," *American Review of Political Science* 3, no. 1 (2000): 1–24.

31. Henri Tajfel and John C. Turner, "An Integrative Theory of Intergroup Conflict," in *The Social Psychology of Intergroup Relations*, ed. William G. Austin and Stephen Worchel (Monterey, CA: Brooks/Cole, 1979); Marilynn B. Brewer and Rupert J. Brown, "Intergroup Conflict," in *The Handbook of Social Psychology: Fourth Edition*, ed. Daniel T. Gilbert, Susan T. Fiske, and Gardner Lindzey (Boston: McGraw-Hill, 1998), 554–594.

the regime and other opposition groups. Thus, targeted experiences of repression will heighten individuals' identification with other members of the in-group.

The dynamics of repression condition the level of polarization within a political system. Where repression is widespread, the opposition becomes less polarized as identities—and related affect and preferences—converge over time. In a targeted repressive environment, heightened in-group identification within the targeted group increases intergroup distance over time. The result is a more highly polarized political system characterized by negative affect between groups and widely divergent policy preferences.

## SCOPE CONDITIONS

Many of the psychological processes related to identity formation and polarization described in this book are universal and may be relevant in a variety of settings (i.e., during controlled liberalization under authoritarianism rather than a democratic transition) and in response to several types of violence (i.e., civil war instead of state repression). However, I note three scope conditions here to make my argument more precise, while encouraging readers to consider other situations to which the argument may apply.

First, depending on the type of transition, studies of democratization focus either on polarization between the regime and the opposition, or within the opposition.[32] Polarization between the regime and opposition is most relevant when studying the gradual transitions that defined the Third Wave of democratization in Asia, Latin America, and Eastern Europe; these processes were characterized by negotiated pacts, based on a power-sharing formula slowly initiated and implemented by undemocratic leaders.[33] However, the Arab Spring transitions more closely resemble a rupture in the old order.[34] Rapid mass mobilization quickly removed authoritarian leaders and ruling parties from power. Former regime actors were thus largely absent from the transition; the former opposition dominated the interim government charged with navigating the early transition

---

32. Arguably, polarization between the regime and the opposition also largely depends on how cohesive the opposition is, and whether there is polarization among these groups.

33. Huntington, *The Third Wave: Democratization in the Late Twentieth Century*.

34. Rustow, "Transitions to Democracy"; Donald Share, "Transitions to Democracy and Transition through Transaction," *Comparative Political Studies* 19, no. 4 (1987): 525–548.

period.[35] Therefore, given the nature of the Arab Spring transitions, I seek to explain polarization *within* the opposition.

Second, I define the opposition as a special type of elite political actor found in electoral authoritarian regimes, which Albrecht describes as "an institution located within a political system but outside the realm of governance that has decisive organizational capacities and engages in competitive interactions with the incumbents of a political regime based on a minimum degree of mutual acceptance."[36] According to Albrecht, the opposition must be institutionalized in formal political parties, which challenge the regime's political program and peacefully demand reform primarily through electoral representation where possible. In electoral autocracies, these are the non-regime elite actors who contest elections.[37] Defining the opposition in this way excludes the two types of domestic threats that theories of authoritarian repression typically focus on[38]—mass-based threats and risks from regime elites (who are defined as having at least some degree of participation in political leadership).[39]

Existing theories largely neglect the democratic opposition, which is distinct from both the ruling cadre and the broader regime. Instead of desiring to change the ruling party leader or reform ruling party structures, such as intra-regime threats that emanate from within the ruling coalition, the opposition seeks broader and more meaningful reforms. Opposition elites are thus unique in how they relate to the regime, as they are decidedly not aligned with the ruling party or coalition nor committed to its continued existence.[40] The formal opposition is also different from mass movements

35. Rustow, "Transitions to Democracy"; James Loxton, *Authoritarian Successor Parties Worldwide: A Framework For Analysis* (South Bend, IN: University of Notre Dame, Helen Kellogg Institute for International Studies, 2016); Haggard and Kaufman, *The Political Economy of Democratic Transitions*.

36. Albrecht, "Political Opposition and Arab Authoritarianism: Some Conceptual Remarks," 3.

37. For examples, see Schedler, *Electoral Authoritarianism: The Dynamics of Unfree Competition*; Diamond, "Thinking about Hybrid Regimes"; Levitsky and Way, "The Rise of Competitive Authoritarianism."

38. Ronald Wintrobe, *The Political Economy of Dictatorship* (New York: Cambridge University Press, 1998); Sheena Chestnut Greitens, *Dictators and their Secret Police: Coercive Institutions and State Violence* (New York: Cambridge University Press, 2016).

39. Milan W. Svolik, *The Politics of Authoritarian Rule* (Cambridge: Cambridge University Press, 2012); Jason Brownlee, *Authoritarianism in an Age of Democratization* (New York: Cambridge University Press, 2007).

40. Jean Blondel and Ferdinand Müller-Rommel, "Political Elites," in *The Oxford Handbook of Political Behavior*, ed. Russell J. Dalton and Hans-Dieter Klingemann (Oxford University Press, 2007).

that resist and dissent either generally (i.e., the fall of the regime) or regarding specific issues (i.e., calling for an increase or repeal of subsidies). Unlike mass-based threats, opposition parties put forward a comprehensive, alternative program of governance to that exercised by the regime; they do not focus on a singular political issue or the general structure of the regime, and do not seek to achieve their aims primarily through protests. The opposition challenges the regime and its policies via formal democratic institutions such as elections. Some scholars differentiate between opposition groups based on whether the state grants them legal status and permits them to officially contest elections. Yet as real-world examples demonstrate, the repression of a group is unrelated to its legal status; regimes target both legally recognized and illegal (officially unrecognized) groups in other ways.[41] I therefore refer to the opposition as comprising both legal and illegal groups.

The third scope condition is that my argument most directly applies to explaining the dynamics of polarization in electoral authoritarian regimes. Repression under electoral authoritarianism is categorically different than that carried out in fully exclusive regimes that limit all participation and stifle any mobilization.[42] Electoral authoritarian regimes use repression as part of a larger collection of survival tactics, which also includes institutionalizing semi-competitive electoral systems, legislatures, and ruling parties in order to create a veneer of democratization or liberalization.[43] There is the possibility of political participation in electoral authoritarian regimes, despite heavy control over elections and related institutions. The presence of various political institutions permits opposition actors to perceive themselves as either included in or excluded from political contestation, which is an important component of the identity portion of my argument. In addition, the opposition's ability to regularly contest the regime politically, in however substantively limited a way, allows observers to analyze changes in various parties' affective relationships and articulated policy

41. Ellen Lust, *Structuring Conflict in the Arab World: Incumbents, Opponents, and Institutions* (Cambridge: Cambridge University Press, 2005).

42. Hannah Arendt, *The Origins of Totalitarianism* (New York: Harcourt, Brace/World, 1966); Juan Linz, *Totalitarian and Authoritarian Regimes* (New York: Lynne Rienner Publishers, 2000).

43. Baghat Korany, Rex Brynen, and Paul Noble, *Political Liberalization and Democratization in the Arab World: Comparative Experiences, Volume 1* (Boulder, Colorado: Lynne Rienner Publishers, 1995); Diamond, "Thinking about Hybrid Regimes"; Levitsky and Way, "The Rise of Competitive Authoritarianism"; Andreas Schedler, "The Menu of Manipulation," *Journal of Democracy* 13, no. 2 (2002): 36–50; Schedler, *Electoral Authoritarianism: The Dynamics of Unfree Competition.*

preferences based on their public interactions as well as their political platforms, manifestos, and official statements.

## The Evidence

### CASE SELECTION

This book examines two authoritarian regimes and transitions in the Middle East—Egypt and Tunisia. The study of transitions from authoritarian rule has long excluded the Middle East, because despite some superficial liberalization the region has remained staunchly authoritarian during previous waves of democratization.[44] While the Arab Spring uprisings have had only limited democratizing effects, the few transitions that were initiated permit the expansion of the scope of cases included in broader transitology studies and theories to include those in the region. My argument highlights and analyzes a new type of legacy that must be considered during transitions—the long-lasting psychological and identity effects of repressive authoritarian institutions. Tunisia serves as a case of widespread repression of the opposition and decreasing polarization among these groups, while in Egypt one group was targeted for repression (the Muslim Brotherhood), resulting in increasing polarization within the opposition. These different experiences of repression created varying levels of polarization among the opposition groups that emerged during the 2011 transition period and influenced each country's subsequent trajectory towards either democratic consolidation or authoritarian reentrenchment.

I selected Egypt and Tunisia as the book's primary comparative case studies to minimize differences in order to isolate, as much as possible, variation on important causal and mediator variables. While they share many important similarities, I do not mean to imply that they are "the perfect pair of structures or processes, exquisitely matched on every variable except for the purported cause and the purported effect."[45] Indeed, social science research cannot account for 100 percent of the variance between cases.

44. Korany, Brynen, and Noble, *Political Liberalization and Democratization in the Arab World: Comparative Experiences, Volume 1*; Eva Bellin, "The Robustness of Authoritarianism in the Middle East: Exceptionalism in Comparative Perspective," *Comparative Politics* 36, no. 2 (2004): 139–157; Eva Bellin, "Reconsidering the Robustness of Authoritarianism in the Middle East: Lessons from the Arab Spring," *Comparative Politics* 44, no. 2 (2012): 127–149.

45. Charles Tilly, *Big Structures, Large Processes, Huge Comparisons* (New York: Russell Sage Foundation, 1984), 80.

Instead, I compare two sets of processes, noting important relevant similarities and differences, and where measurable variation in state repression, identities among the opposition, and resulting polarization among these groups may contribute to explaining my outcome of interest.

The cases share three main similarities: time period, regime type, and the political salience of the Islamist-secular divide. First, they have comparable historical eras—1981–2011 for Egypt (Hosni Mubarak's period of rule) and 1987–2011 for Tunisia (Zine al-Abidine Ben Ali's leadership). Both countries adopted tightly controlled multiparty elections at a similar historical and temporal moment in an attempt to diffuse demands for reform from the mobilized opposition following economic crises.[46] Though parliamentary elections were held somewhat regularly in Egypt by Mubarak's predecessors, the 1984 elections were the first true multiparty contest. Similarly, Tunisia's first president, Habib Bourguiba, introduced multiparty elections in 1981, but the 1989 elections were hailed as the first semi-competitive contest. The majority of leaders charged with governing each country after 2011 came of age politically during this period, and experienced or witnessed repression in ways that, I argue, shaped their subsequent political behavior.[47]

The second similarity is that both countries were classified as electoral authoritarian regimes on the eve of the 2010–2011 uprisings. Moreover, both regimes were similarly structured around a single ruling party, the National Democratic Party in Egypt and the Democratic Constitutional Rally in Tunisia. These parties regularly won inflated percentages in national elections and served as an institution for governing, channeling and demobilizing dissent, and gathering surveillance on citizens. As I discuss in more detail in chapter 4, differences across the party systems were endogenous to each regime's repressive system. For example, the Islamist opposition was permitted to contest elections in Egypt but not in Tunisia, but this difference reflects how the regime controlled its opposition. Relatedly, Egypt and Tunisia experienced in rapid succession the unexpected and unprecedented exogenous shock of mass mobilization, which quickly

46. Jillian Schwedler and Laryssa Chomiak, "And the Winner Is…: Authoritarian Elections in the Arab World," *Middle East Report*, 2006, 12–19.

47. This is an elite riff on political socialization theory. See Angus Campbell et al., *The American Voter* (New York: John Wiley, 1960); Donald D. Searing, "The Comparative Study of Elite Socialization," *Comparative Politics Studies* 1, no. 4 (1969): 471–500; Virginia Sapiro, "Not Your Parents' Political Socialization: Introduction for a New Generation," *Annual Review of Political Science* 7 (2004): 1–23.

destabilized the long-ruling regimes and created transitions by rupture.[48] As chapter 8 explains in more detail, former regime actors were not entirely eliminated but were largely absent from central negotiations during the transition period after each country's ruling party was legally disbanded and its members barred from participating in the 2011 elections for the constituent assemblies. In both countries, the political parties that fared well in the early post-transition elections were drawn from the former organized opposition to the regime. These groups were put in charge of negotiating the central political aspects of the transition period.

Finally, the Islamist-secular axis of competition was salient within the opposition under successive authoritarian regimes as well as during the transition period in both countries. Islamists won by considerable and comparable margins: both the Muslim Brotherhood in Egypt and Ennahda in Tunisia won roughly 37 percent of the vote in the first free and fair elections of 2011 for the national constituent bodies charged with drafting constitutions and negotiating the immediate transition period. Competing parties presented themselves as secular opposition to these Islamist groups, and public debates during the transition period centered on whether Islamists would work cooperatively in newly democratized institutions and whether they would force the codification of a more conservative interpretation of Islam in reformed legislation. Differences emerged from competing notions of the countries' identities: whether the country would prioritize its Islamic heritage and its obligation to facilitate the Islamization of public and political life, or whether it would be secular and keep religion and politics separate.

## STRUCTURE, STRATEGY, AND IDEOLOGY IN EGYPT AND TUNISIA

Explanations rooted in structural, strategic, and ideological considerations do not fully explain the different trends of polarization in Egypt and Tunisia for three reasons. First, structural explanations for the variation in polarization would suggest that underlying societal cleavages were different in the two countries at the moment of transition. On the eve of the 2010–2011 uprisings, they measured similarly on socio-economic, development, and public opinion indicators that are often linked to the success of and support

---

48. Rustow, "Transitions to Democracy"; Share, "Transitions to Democracy and Transition through Transaction."

TABLE 1.1. Structural Comparison of Egypt and Tunisia

|  | Egypt | Tunisia |
| --- | --- | --- |
| Percent urban | 44 | 66 |
| Urbanization rate (2005–2010) | 1.68 | 1.38 |
| Gross National Income (2011) | $10,512.40 | $10,404.50 |
| Human Development Index (2010) | 0.69 | 0.71 |

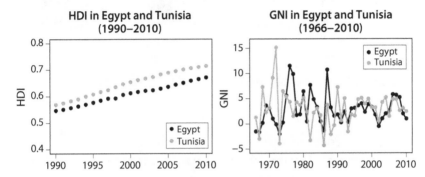

FIGURE 1.1. Comparison of HDI and GNI in Egypt and Tunisia

for Islamist parties.[49] While Tunisia is somewhat more urban than Egypt, the two countries had a similar urbanization rate during the study period (2005–2010). In addition, the countries' gross national incomes (GNI) were nearly equal in 2010, as were their Human Development Index (HDI) scores (see table I.I). Figure I.I illustrates that the countries' changes in GNI and HDI are somewhat erratic but track each other over time, particularly in more recent years. These broad similarities do not appear to fully explain why Egypt was much more polarized than Tunisia in 2010–2011.

In addition, Egyptians did not measure as significantly more "Islamist" or "Muslim" than Tunisians on a number of different indicators. Egyptian and Tunisian respondents to the 2010 Arab Barometer reported high—and nearly equal—levels of private prayer and listening to the Qur'an. They differed in attendance at Friday services, but this is likely because Friday is not part of the weekend in Tunisia and this makes it more difficult for

49. Melani Cammett and Pauline Jones Luong, "Is There an Islamist Political Advantage?," *Annual Review of Political Science* 17 (2014): 187–206; Sharan Grewal et al., "Poverty and Divine Rewards: The Electoral Advantage of Islamist Politics Parties," *American Journal of Political Science*, 2019,

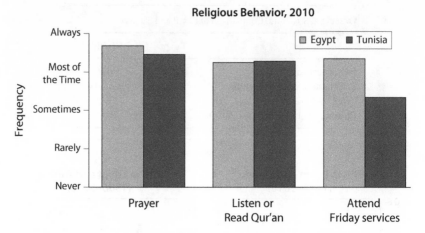

FIGURE 1.2. Frequency of Religious Behaviors in Egypt and Tunisia, 2010 (Source: Arab Barometer)

individuals to attend that service. Historical evidence of trends in religiosity also support the idea that Islamist parties' change in positioning was not fully related to changes within their constituencies. Religiosity was visibly increasing in Tunisia beginning in the early 2000s[50] as Ennahda became more centrist. Egypt's "Islamic Revival" during the 1970s to 1990s predated the Brotherhood's increased polarization, and the increased practice and public expression of Islam was firmly entrenched by the 2000s, when there were changes in the Brotherhood's articulated preferences.[51] Similarly, the data do not capture significant differences in social cleavages that might have polarized the political systems differently.

Second, strategic arguments would suggest that the internal aspects of the political system, namely the formal electoral rules of the Mubarak and Ben Ali regimes, were either different or changed differently during the period under analysis. However, both regimes largely limited electoral participation during the study period.

As I noted above, both Egypt and Tunisia were electoral authoritarian regimes with a single ruling party in 2010. They also had similar party systems: the main Islamist parties in each country were more effective at mobilizing support than their secular counterparts. Although Ennahda

50. Anne Wolf, *Political Islam in Tunisia: The History of Ennahda* (Oxford University Press, 2017), 108.

51. Leila Ahmed, *A Quiet Revolution* (New Haven: Yale University Press, 2012); John L. Esposito, *Islam and Politics* (Syracuse University Press, 1998); Saba Mahmood, *Politics of Piety: The Islamic Revival and the Feminist Subject* (Princeton University Press, 2011).

was largely absent from Tunisian society and politics between 1990 and the 2010–2011 uprising, and was thus unable to provide social services to mobilize supporters, a recent historical corrective suggests that the party was still much stronger than secular parties in 2011, similar to the Brotherhood's relative position in Egypt.[52] Ennahda began to remobilize after party leaders Hamadi Jebali and Abdelhamid Jlassi were released from prison in 2006 and 2007, respectively, and began to rebuild the Executive Bureau in secret. The political systems were most different with regards to the regular presence of Islamists in elections; Mubarak permitted the Brotherhood to participate in controlled contests, while Ben Ali sidelined Islamists entirely in the early 1990s. Existing arguments based on the inclusion–moderation thesis[53] would predict that the Brotherhood's participation in elections and parliament would result in convergence on issues of central importance, but we instead observe the opposite.

Finally, ideological explanations would suggest that the Islamist parties' motivating ideologies were different from the start, or shifted in different ways during the study period, which caused their political positioning to diverge. Nathan Brown helpfully distils "two different levels of abstraction" with regards to ideology.[54] The first, abstract level refers to the worldview and mission of a group, while the second level refers to programmatic commitments and statements, or how a group translates its motivating ideology into concrete, practical goals. I focus here on the first level. Ennahda and the Brotherhood's motivating ideologies were largely similar during this period. The missions of both groups are guided by a commitment to the central components of reformist political Islam, which promotes a gradualist approach with a long-time horizon, in contrast to quietist or revolutionary approaches to Islamizing public and political life. Both organizations sought to promote Muslim values through proselytizing (da'wa), religious education (tarbiyya), and charity. These activities comprise elements of a larger mission to reform the country's political, economic, and social life in order to reverse its moral and related economic and political decline through the correct application of Islamic law. However, Ennahda is not simply the Tunisian chapter of the Muslim Brotherhood, though its founders were inspired by Brotherhood ideology and ideologues, and early public statements as well as its newspaper al-Ma'rifa focused on moralizing

---

52. Wolf, *Political Islam*.

53. Jillian Schwedler, "Can Islamists Become Moderates? Rethinking the Inclusion-Moderation Hypothesis," *World Politics* 63, no. 2f (2011): 347–376.

54. Nathan J. Brown, *When Victory is Not an Option: Islamist Movements in Arab Politics* (Cornell University Press, 2012).

and propagating religious values.[55] Important differences did exist between the two groups' motivating missions. Ennahda differed from the Brotherhood most significantly in its incorporation of aspects of Tunisia's national Islamic tradition, specifically the Zaytouna approach to reform influenced by the Mu'tazila school of Islamic theology.[56]

While different motivating ideologies may explain differences in the starting preferences of a group, in part, they cannot fully account for the shift in each group's preferences over time. Indeed, the motivating ideology of a group can remain the same while its preferences shift. Indeed, Asad describes Islam as a "historically evolving set of discourses, embodied in the practices and institutions of Islamic societies and hence deeply imbricated in the material life of those inhabiting them."[57] Tunisian and Egyptian Islamists emphasized different aspects of their ideologies over time as they translated them into concrete goals and political preferences, particularly as they related to the application of shari'a. As Kalyvas warns, "the actions of political actors should not be inferred solely on the basis of either religious scriptures or religious ideology. Religious doctrine, like all doctrines, is a contested and malleable field of meaning, amenable to multiple interpretations. Islam has been used to support both democracy and dictatorship, while Islamists creatively deploy selected elements of Islamic tradition to justify their actions."[58] At different times, both groups shifted the emphasis in their ideology to justify participation in elections and increased democracy within both the organizations and the broader political system, as well as undemocratic behaviors and the use of violence.

How did the ideology of the regimes that these Islamist movements sought to reform differ? Though they relied on a legitimacy derived from popular, political, and economic sources, both regimes also sought religious legitimacy in various ways, and sought to ensure that religion was not the exclusive domain of Islamists. During his early years, Mubarak permitted Islamists to rebuild their political and social institutions as part of a broader appeal to populist legitimacy cultivated through tolerance of opposition and the reinstatement of elections. He also developed a closer

---

55. Wolf, *Political Islam*, 40–41.

56. The Mu'tazila school of theology is defined by a belief in the compatibility of Islam with reason and rational thought. Mu'tazilites believe the Qur'an was created by men, and preach an interpretive approach to the text rather than blind adherence to scripture.

57. Talal Asad, *Formations of the Secular: Christianity, Islam, Modernity* (Stanford, California: Stanford University Press, 2003).

58. Stathis N. Kalyvas, "Commitment Problems in Emerging Democracies: The Case of Religious Parties," *Comparative Politics*, 2000, 395.

relationship with al-Azhar, the pre-eminent Sunni institution in the Muslim world, and met frequently with its leader Sheikh Gad al-Haqq Ali in an effort to co-opt the institution to publicly legitimize the version of Islam formally recognized by the state. Over time, the state-controlled press and media Islamized; the regime launched newspapers such as *al-Liwa* and *Aqidati* that presented its own interpretation of Islam's role in public and political life, and significantly increased the number of hours of religious programming on state television. The regime justified its increasingly religious policies and rhetoric as an important tool to counter Egypt's growing extremism and jihadı problems. When al-Azhar's leadership became more critical of the regime as it increasingly repressed Islamists in the mid-1990s, Mubarak began to rely on Dar al-Ifta, considered to be the second-most important religious institution in Egypt after al-Azhar. The head of Dar al-Ifta' was mufti Mohammed Sayyid Tantawi, and the regime perceived him to be politically flexible and willing to support the state. For example, Tantawi issued a fatwa in which he ruled that savings certificates issued by state-owned banks did not violate the Qur'anic ban on usury, which helped the regime undermine increasingly popular Islamic banks and restore public confidence in state banks.[59]

While the Tunisian state has been credited with successfully secularizing its population, both Bourguiba and Ben Ali tried to co-opt Islam to enhance their own legitimacy. For instance, Ben Ali broadcast the call for prayers on television and on the radio, reopened Zaytouna University as a state institution (rather than an independent university and religious institution), established a Ministry of Religious Affairs, and created a Supreme Islamic Council tasked with ensuring that state legislation was compatible with Islam. However, to assert state control over religion, Ben Ali's regime also passed a law in 1988 that required all religious gatherings to be supervised by an employee of the Ministry of Religious Affairs.[60] While there are important (if subtle) differences in how the Mubarak and Ben Ali regimes attempted to co-opt religion to bolster their own legitimacy, their different approaches to state secularization do not appear to account for the variation in polarization we observe between the two countries. If anything, historical developments suggest that Tunisia should have been more polarized on the eve of the uprisings, with a portion of the population displaying higher levels of support for secularism generated by the regime's policies.

59. Hesham al-Awadi, *In Pursuit of Legitimacy: The Muslim Brothers and Mubarak, 1982–2000* (London: Taurus, 2004), 120–121.

60. Wolf, *Political Islam*, 39.

## DATA AND METHODS

It is challenging to conduct research in a data-scarce region like the Middle East. In an ideal world, I would have had full access to both regimes' archives to construct a list of political prisoners and had honest conversations with the regime officials responsible for repression in order to construct a more objective measurement of my independent variable, repressive contexts. I would also have been able to time travel in order to observe and interview political actors victimized by repression, to document changes and developments in group identification in real time, and to collect additional primary documents before they were destroyed or lost. However, I was unable to access government archives, so I relied on the documents I was able to access that survived decades of regime repression as well as subsequent tumultuous political changes. I asked interviewees to reflect on events that happened decades in the past rather than observing them myself.

To address these data limitations, I employ a mixed-methods approach that combines qualitative and quantitative data and analyses. The strengths of each approach offset the weaknesses of the other, and the large number of data sources and types of analyses included in this book should be treated as complements rather than substitutes. The empirical evidence comes from a variety of primary and secondary sources that I collected during a year of fieldwork based in Tunis, Tunisia, and Cairo, Egypt. The bulk of original data was gathered in over one hundred semi-structured interviews with members of the former opposition. For additional primary source evidence, I reference political memoirs written by members of the former opposition; reports, internal documents, and public documents generated by former opposition parties; and documents, statements, and reports issued by local and international human rights organizations. I also rely on secondary Arabic-, English-, and French-language sources about the history of each country's political system and opposition groups written by both local and foreign experts and scholars.

The set of interviews presented in this book is a representative sample of important actors who constituted the democratic opposition under the Ben Ali and Mubarak regimes. The democratic opposition under authoritarianism are the groups whose demands and leadership must be incorporated by democratization.[61] During transitions, opposition actors necessarily

---

61. Ruth Berins Collier, *Paths toward Democracy: The Working Class and Elites in Western Europe and South America* (Cambridge University Press, 1999), 4–8.

needed to be included in the negotiation process in order for any final agreement to be meaningful and have teeth.[62] The roles and perspectives of other key actors involved in the transition, such as institutional representatives and newly mobilized political groups, are discussed in the final section of the book. Interviewees were recruited through a combination of strategic and snowball sampling. To define the pool of all potential interviewees, I first identified which opposition parties were active under the previous authoritarian regime and remained relevant during the transition; there were no more than twenty parties per country. The third section of chapter 4 lists the specific groups. I then identified key leaders within each of these groups and contacted as many as I could, persistently following up on my requests until either the interview was scheduled or the interviewee declined to meet. Although I did not find this citation until after completing my fieldwork, I took an approach that mirrors Mosley's advice, in that I continued to contact members of the same party and sought out additional members of the opposition until I felt that I had captured all perspectives and constructed a complete narrative that was echoed by each additional interviewee.[63]

I conducted most interviews in-country between 2012 and 2018. In Egypt, I accessed the relevant population through personal and professional networks I have developed over time since beginning my research in Egypt in 2005. As a result of developments following the 2013 coup, I also met additional members of the Egyptian opposition in London, Istanbul, and New York. In Tunisia, I worked with a talented and personable local research assistant to contact individuals I wished to interview. This was particularly helpful, given that I was less familiar with Tunisia and its dialect than I was with Egypt at the beginning of the project. Tunisia offered a more welcoming research environment, and I was often able to contact political actors through their public offices using publicly available contact information. At the end of each interview, I asked the interviewee if there were additional people they thought I should speak with and whether they would be willing to put me in contact with them. Tunisian politicians of different ideological persuasions often had each other's personal cell phone

62. Wood, *Forging Democracy from Below: Insurgent Transitions in South Africa and El Salvador*, 6.

63. Layna Mosley, "Just Talk to People? Interviews in Contemporary Political Science," in *Interview Research in Political Science*, ed. Layna Mosley (Ithaca, NY: Cornell University Press, 2013), 1–28.

numbers, and would call in my presence to confirm they could share this information with me. In contrast, I was only offered names and numbers from each of my Egyptian interviewees' political groups.

My interviews took the form of a life history.[64] During these conversations, which lasted from forty-five minutes to three hours, I asked interviewees chronologically and in detail about their personal history, focusing on their political activism and their personal and shared experiences of state repression. The semi-structured nature of the interviews allowed me to ask about specific topics, but also permitted participants to focus on the events and experiences they considered important for their own political development. All interviews took place in a location chosen by the interviewee, usually a private office or residence. I respected all requests from interview subjects not to repeat their accounts of how their political activism had affected their families, bodies, and mental health. Others were comfortable speaking on background but not on the record; these details and conversations informed my research, but I do not directly reference them in the book or include them in my count. Some interviewees showed me old pictures, from before or after serving their prison sentences, or from cameras smuggled into a cell. Others gave me books and clippings of writings they felt would illuminate their experience, some of which they insisted I keep. All interviews were recorded with the oral consent of the interviewees and saved to password-protected computers and cloud storage sites. I took notes during the interviews and transcribed the conversations after they were completed. I later used NVivo software to code the recordings, using markers to indicate relevant snippets pertaining to the components of my argument (for example, "experience of repression," "affective polarization," "preference polarization," "in-group identification," and "opposition identification").

To analyze the case study evidence,[65] I use a methodology known as within-case process tracing, which involves assessing diagnostic evidence from processes, sequences, and conjunctures of events within a single

---

64. Tom Wengraf, *Qualitative Research Interviewing: Biographic Narrative and Semi-Structured Methods* (London: Sage, 2001).

65. I follow John Gerring, *Case Study Research: Principles and Practices* (New York: Cambridge University Press, 2007), in his definition of a case study as "the intensive study of a single unit for the purpose of understanding a larger class of similar units." George and Bennett (*Case Studies and Theory Development in the Social Sciences*, 17) similarly refer to a case study as "an instance of a class of events."

case.[66] The result is what Geertz calls a "thick description,"[67] which helps establish causal links and the trend data needed to make cross-case comparisons.[68]

Process tracing is the most appropriate approach to use since it lets the researcher create comparable evidence-based narratives to help generate causal inferences across cases. This method ultimately allows the researcher to examine the specific mechanism through which an independent variable affects a dependent variable over time.[69] When investigating how repression affects levels of polarization through individual experiences of it, the ability to combine individual stories with aggregated evidence is a powerful way to understand broader causal mechanisms and relationships, and to unpack highly complex phenomena. Using this method to compare the two cases, I demonstrate the complex relationship between the nature of repression and polarization. In the conclusion, I offer two additional illustrative case studies with evidence from secondary sources.

Chapter 7 presents quantitative experimental data generated through lab experiments designed to test the central psychological mechanism through which I argue repression alters political identities, and ultimately levels of affective and preference polarization. I conducted the experiments in May 2016 with a sample of 434 adult Tunisian citizens in an effort to eliminate potential confounding factors—such as a regime's strategic choice of repressive strategy, relative group size, pre-existing relationships between groups, or group membership selection bias—from consideration by testing the theory in a controlled environment. The bulk of the fieldwork and

66. Andrew Bennett and Jeffrey T. Checkel, *Process Tracing: From Metaphor to Analytic Tool* (Cambridge: Cambridge University Press, 2014); James Mahoney and Kathleen Thelen, *Explaining Institutional Change: Ambiguity, Agency, and Power* (New York: Cambridge University Press, 2010).

67. Clifford Geertz, *The Interpretation of Cultures: Selected Essays* (New York: Basic Books, 1973), 5–10.

68. Tilly, *Big Structures, Large Processes, Huge Comparisons*. According to David Collier, "Understanding Process Tracing," *PS: Political Science and Politics* 44, no. 4 (2011): 824, this description starts "not with observing change or sequence, but rather with taking good snapshots at a series of specific moments." These "snapshots" document important variation and changes in a manner that suggests causality.

69. Alexander L. George and Timothy J. McKeown, "Case Studies and Theories of Organizational Decision Making," *Advances in Information Processing in Organizations* 2, no. 1 (1985): 21–58; David Collier, Henry R. Brady, and Jason Seawright, "Sources of Leverage in Causal Inference: Toward an Alternative View of Methodology," in *Rethinking Social Inquiry: Diverse Tools, Shared Standards*, ed. Henry E. Brady and David Collier (Lanham, Maryland: Rowman/Littlefield, 2010).

case study components of the project were conducted first, and informed the design of the lab experiments. While the observational case study evidence from Egypt and Tunisia addresses issues of internal and measurement validity, the experimental set-up helps assuage endogeneity and external validity concerns. For example, I am often asked whether the fact that the Muslim Brotherhood was much stronger and larger than its opponents in various ways may have contributed to the collapse of the transition in Egypt, with the assumption that this was not the case in Tunisia. While I do not think this is the case (both parties won similar percentages in early elections, and the mobilizational imbalance was similar across both cases), the results from the lab experiment provide additional evidence that these dynamics can apply regardless of group size or strength. The conclusion of the book also presents descriptive statistics of public opinion data in an effort to explore whether elite polarization is related to similar levels of mass polarization witnessed during the transition period.

## Plan of the Book

The book proceeds as follows. Chapter 2 presents the argument in more detail. I begin by reviewing existing work on three central concepts—polarization, preference formation, and repression. I also highlight insights from social psychology on shared trauma, identity formation, and the causes and consequences of group identification, which are fundamental to understanding where and how my argument builds on (and where and how it differs from) existing approaches to polarization. I then put forward an original argument that the repressive conditions within an authoritarian regime can help predict polarization levels during a transition period. I argue that the nature of the regime's political repression affects how opposition groups come to identify themselves, which in turn shapes differences in affect and preferences among the opposition groups. In this way, the nature of repression in authoritarian systems shapes the levels of political polarization observed during transitions.

The remaining chapters are divided into three parts. Part 2, "Repertoires of Repression," contains chapters 3 and 4. In order to be confident that it is variation in repressive environments that is causing the variations in levels of polarization, the source of the repression must be unrelated to polarization among opposition groups. Previous studies on repression have assumed that authoritarian leaders start from scratch when designing repressive institutions based on perceived threats, and that all available options are open to them. However, historical approaches demonstrate that contemporary authoritarian leaders inherit certain coercive institutions and states with a pre-defined capacity. As a result, variation in repressive environments is largely determined by the state-building projects that preceded independence. These efforts and institutions shaped the state's capacity to collect intelligence and accurately use force, as well as the nature of coercive institutions over the course of the authoritarian period. Chapter 3 first outlines this broader argument, and then traces the historical development and significant path dependence of coercive institutions in Egypt and Tunisia. It also delineates which institutions carried out repression in each country. Chapter 4 then documents the widespread nature of political repression in Tunisia under Ben Ali and the targeted nature of political repression in Egypt under Mubarak. It also outlines which parties constituted the democratic opposition during the study period.

Part 3, "Repression, Identity, and Polarization," chronicles how repression conditioned divergent patterns of affective and preference polarization across the two countries through the three mechanisms outlined in my theory. This part also details the coding and variation of the main variables—comparative repressive environments, processes and levels of polarization, and development of group identifications in both countries. These variables establish an internally valid causal relationship between repression and polarization in specific real-world instances. In chapters 5 and 6, I document how widespread repression in Tunisia decreased polarization within the opposition between 1987 and 2010, and how targeted repression in Egypt increased polarization within the opposition between 1981 and 2011. These two chapters follow the same structure for ease of comparison: they first document the effects of repression on group identities, and then link these identities to subsequent political polarization.

In chapter 5, I demonstrate the effects of widespread repression on Tunisian opposition groups through psychological, social, and organizational mechanisms. Psychologically, a widespread repressive environment made Tunisian opposition members aware that they were not the only targets of harsh state repression. It also altered socialization patterns among opposition groups by imprisoning Islamist and secular opposition members together, and by exiling members of these same groups together abroad, where they exchanged ideas about how to best combat the regime. Exile in European countries also exposed members of both Islamist and secular opposition groups to Western democratic values, which they incorporated into their preferences. Finally, widespread repression altered the organizational structures of individual opposition groups by creating cross-group human rights organizations that advocated the freedoms of political prisoners of different ideological persuasions. As experiences of repression became increasingly ubiquitous among the Tunisian opposition over time, members of individual parties more strongly identified with a collective opposition identity and demonstrated more positive feelings towards members of other opposition groups. In addition, two major collaborative initiatives in the early 2000s solidified an agreement among opposition leaders about how religion and politics would be dealt with should authoritarianism end.

Chapter 6 begins by documenting the effects of a targeted repressive environment on the Egyptian opposition through psychological, social, and organizational mechanisms. Psychologically, a targeted repressive environment revealed to Brotherhood members that they were being uniquely victimized by the state, and that other groups were at best tacitly—and at worst explicitly—in support of this harsh treatment. In addition, targeted repression altered the social environment for opposition members; Islamists were imprisoned together, away from the few secular activists who were also detained, and thus discussed political ideas among themselves rather than with other groups that had different ideas about reform. Finally, targeted repression altered the Brotherhood's organizational structure by creating an increasingly secretive, exclusive, and isolated organization as it sought to survive regime repression. The targeted nature of repression against the Brotherhood primed in-group identification, as the group was uniquely treated in a brutal way and identified as the regime's main victim. As a result, the identity of the larger opposition became increasingly fractured between opposition groups that were co-opted, tolerated, or targeted by the regime. Consequently, negative perceptions of the out-group permeated the political system and levels of affective polarization increased. At the same time, the Egyptian opposition was increasingly divided on how to define the nature of the state with regards to religion and politics. Following waves of targeted repression, the Brotherhood grew stronger in its preferences for religious influence over the state and the public sphere, and what little collaboration that did occur between opposition groups under Mubarak never addressed issues related to religion and politics due to fears of infighting.

Chapter 7 presents experimental data generated by lab experiments designed to test the psychological mechanism through which I argue repression alters political identities, and ultimately levels of affective and preference polarization. While the two previous case study chapters demonstrate how repression and polarization unfolded in the complicated real world, the lab experiments provide a clean (if hard) test of the book's theory, focusing on the central psychological mechanism. The results demonstrate how repression shapes levels of polarization among groups through identity formation.

The fourth and final part of the book, "After Authoritarianism," returns to the transition period to further consider the central role of polarization in elite decisions critical to continued progress towards democratic consolidation. In chapter 8, I synthesize the literature on polarization during authoritarian transitions to highlight how polarization prevents the compromise and cooperation that is vital to successful transitions. I then discuss the timeline of events between 2011 and 2014 in Egypt and Tunisia to chart how these transitions progressed, and document where affective and preference polarization contributed to the divergence. I focus on the debates and decisions related to drafting and approving a new constitution, holding the first elections, and creating a transitional justice initiative. High levels of polarization derailed Egypt's transition, while significantly more agreement in Tunisia facilitated cooperation and compromise in parallel processes. However, as with any social phenomenon, the divergence in these transitions is likely due to multiple causes. While affective and preference polarization among elite actors clearly played a major role in this divergence, I also highlight other factors, such as structural predecessors, continued protests, the emergence of new political actors, and ongoing events in other countries, that were important for political developments.

Chapter 9 concludes by reviewing the book's key findings and discussing their broader implications for the literatures on polarization, repression, and elite behavior during authoritarian transitions. I also demonstrate the generalizability of my argument beyond Egypt, Tunisia, elites, and authoritarian contexts in three ways. First, I discuss transitions in Algeria and Indonesia, two other countries with a salient Islamist–secular cleavage where similar identity dynamics determined by repression appear to have affected the success of transitional outcomes. Second, I explore the relationship between elite and mass polarization, and demonstrate with a variety of original public opinion data how comparative levels of elite polarization in Egypt and Tunisia appear to have conditioned levels of mass polarization in each country between 2011 and 2014. Finally, I explicate the implications of my work on authoritarianism for other regime types.

# 2

# A Theory of Polarization in Authoritarian Regimes

This chapter presents the book's argument. I first synthesize existing understandings of political polarization, preference formation, and repression, three concepts central to my argument. I also highlight the insights from social psychology on shared trauma, identity formation, and the causes and consequences of group identification that are fundamental to understanding how my argument differs from existing approaches to polarization. I then outline an argument about polarization in authoritarian regimes in which repression shapes identities and identities condition levels of political polarization among competing actors. I conclude the chapter with a brief discussion of how polarization affects cooperative behavioral outcomes, foreshadowing the fourth part of the book.

## Preference Formation in Polarization

Political polarization is the distance between political groups on dimensions that matter for political competition. Polarization includes affective distance in the realm of emotions, feelings, and attitudes, and distance in policy preferences on salient political issues. As detailed in the previous chapter, existing explanations for polarization focus on structural, strategic, and ideological variables, but fail to fully explain why opposition in authoritarian regimes, such as Tunisia and Egypt, demonstrate different levels of polarization over time. The issues with existing explanations for polarization stem from a common problem: these theories tend to neglect the process by which political preferences form. Well-established psychological research demonstrates that preferences do not flow directly from structure, strategy, or ideology, but instead are created and updated through a cognitive process. The contemporary study of political behavior has increasingly incorporated social psychology in order to understand the micro-foundational cognitive pathways through which individuals form and update preferences about politics. In psychological processes of preference formation, the lived experience of *context* and *resulting group identities* matter for the way individuals form and update preferences.

## CONTEXT AND IDENTITY

Preference formation is the process by which people establish and update attitudes through what they experience and what they feel, an "equilibrium between brain, body, and world."[1] The individual-level, cognitive process of preference formation is an iterative causal chain through which lived experiences give rise to identities, which create or update related beliefs and evaluations, and ultimately form or update preferences. What political scientists call preferences, psychologists call attitudes, defined as "a person's general evaluation of an object."[2] The object can be any of a broad array of people, events, products, policies, and institutions, while attitudes capture people's orientations towards these objects. In the realm of political preferences, these objects often include politicians, political events, policies, and governmental institutions, which are either currently in existence or have the potential to exist. Attitudes indicate the valence of the evaluation, indicating support or dislike.

Identities are the central source of information in the formation of attitudes and preferences. In forming a preference, individuals draw on information, or "any data potentially relevant to" future choices.[3] Which identities one holds and prioritizes determines how new information is evaluated and ultimately which information is adopted or discarded. How one identifies oneself, and who else one considers to be a part of that

1. Druckman and Lupia, "Preference Formation," 3.

2. Daniel J. O'Keefe, *Persuasian: Theory and Research* (Safe: Oxford University Press, 1990), 18.

3. Druckman and Lupia, "Preference Formation," 5.

identity group, has a significant effect on how an individual processes new information and, subsequently, updates attitudes and preferences. For example, information endorsed by a member of a trusted in-group makes that information more important and reliable, while information provided by a member of an out-group is downgraded and discarded. In short, identity ultimately determines attitudes by providing a heuristic marking certain information as more important or of better quality than other information.[4]

The focus on internal cognitive processes within preference formation should not detract from the individual's broader context, the "world" component mentioned above. Context clearly matters; while individuals may have idiosyncratic tendencies, they also form opinions about other people and their ideas within certain external structures, and identity is generally constructed relative to other groups.[5] The institutional settings, political systems, and ideologies that constitute context provide a baseline for identities, creating groups divided along specific dimensions of cleavage with potential for political contestation. However, as scholars of polarization and political cleavage formation have been careful to note, while patterns of polarization are clearly derived in some way from the social, political, economic, and historical contexts in which political actors find themselves, contextual differences are not deterministic of political preferences and cannot fully explain variation in the distribution of preferences without engaging psychological theories focused on the individual.[6] The same levels of inequality can result in varying levels of contentious politics and polarized preferences; the way in which the translation of these differences into political contestation occurs is conditional on the broader context in

---

4. Arthur Lupia and Mathew D. McCubbins, *The Democratic Dilemma: Can Citizens Learn What They Need to Know?* (Cambridge: Cambridge University Press, 1998).

5. Katznelson and Weingast, "Intersections Between Historical and Rational Choice Institutionalism," 3–4 write that the best contemporary approach to institutions and preference formation requires that an understanding of the "building blocks of preferences—including interests, desires, values, opinions, tastes, and morals—be located inside thickly inscribed temporal and spatial contexts."

6. See Peter A. Hall, *Some Reflections on Preference Formation* (Memorandum for the Workshop on Rational Choice/Historical Institutionalism, 2000); Peter A. Hall, "Historical Institutionalism in Rationalist and Sociological Perspective," in *Explaining Institutional Change: Ambiguity, Agency, and Power*, ed. James Mahoney and Kathleen Thelen (New York: Cambridge University Press, 2010), 204–224 for a more in-depth discussion of the strengths and weaknesses of literature linking institutions and context with preference formation.

which they are formed and on which elites mobilize these preferences.[7] The preferences people hold "cannot be inferred from their 'objective' circumstances; political action is contextual and strategic, but it also reflects the ideologies, values, and perceptions of actors."[8] The missing link in many existing theories of polarization is identity as a major influence on preference formation. Structure, strategies, and ideology do not matter in and of themselves, but rather in the way individuals and groups experience these constitutive components of context. Lived political experiences are therefore the basis for translating structural conditions, institutional norms, and ideologies into political preferences.

In modern politics, one lived experience of immense consequence for political identity formation is interaction with the state. The state is the major realm of political contestation, political identities are constructed with relation to the state, and state behavior makes certain categories politically relevant.[9] Interactions with the state are particularly influential when they reveal information about the nature of society, and both an individual's and group's role and relative position therein. Through repeated interactions with the state and its representatives, an individual receives indicators about who she is, which group she belongs to, and what attributes her group claims. When state treatment is unequal, an individual learns where her group stands relative to other groups; when it is equal, an individual learns about commonality with groups that have similar experiences. The iterative lived experience of the state induces learning and the updating of identities, which in turn updates affect towards others and the preferences one holds relative to other groups.

Theories of polarization must ultimately be grounded in individuals and thus require a deeper investigation into the contextual and identity sources

7. For example, comparative essays in Ira Katznelson and Aristide R. Zolberg, *Working-Class Formation: Nineteenth-century Patterns in Western Europe and the United States* (Princeton, NJ: Princeton University Press, 1986), argue that similar structural conditions produced very different notions of class formation across European countries. They explain this variation by engaging the historical realities of the daily lives of groups of working people.

8. Mainwaring, *Transitions to Democracy and Democratic Consolidation: Theoretical and Comparative Issues*, 16.

9. Donald Horowitz, *Ethnic Groups in Conflict* (Berkeley: University of California Press, 1985); David D. Laitin, *Identity in Formation: The Russian-Speaking Populations in the Near Abroad* (Ithaca, NY: Cornell University Press, 1998); Daniel N. Posner, *Institutions and Ethnic Politics in Africa* (New York: Cambridge University Press, 2005); Richard Mansbach and Edward Rhodes, "The National State and Identity Politics: State Institutionalisation and Markers of National Identity," Geopolitics 12, no. 3 (2007): 426–458; Kanchan Chandra, *Constructivist Theories of Ethnic Politics* (New York: Oxford University Press, 2012).

of preferences through a social psychological lens. If levels of polarization within a political system are closely related to the preferences of political actors, and these preferences are meaningfully shaped by actors' identities as formed through experiences of the state and its institutions, then scholars must locate the origins of polarization in these experiences and more fully investigate the differential experience of political actors. Groups come to see themselves as either in conflict or in harmony as a result of comparative lived political experiences of a given context, and then automatically form and adjust their affect towards other political groups and their relative political preferences accordingly. The psychological literature would suggest that the level of political polarization is specific to group experiences within a given system, which helps to explain how similar objective structures can produce divergent political outcomes.

By failing to take the process of preference formation into account, existing theories do not fully account for how variation in context matters for processes of polarization through identity formation. Two important questions remain: first, which aspects of context matter most? And by what mechanisms does context create conflicting or consonant identities and preferences?

## RECONSIDERING REPRESSION

The polarization that matters for democratic transitions occurs under authoritarianism, and authoritarian contexts are characterized by repression, or severe state control of both society and politics.[10] Scholars have applied the label "repression" to a number of state behaviors which seek to demobilize actors who challenge regimes' beliefs, institutions, and actions. The most evident aspect of repression is the *physical* coercive actions undertaken by regimes against opposition actors. The physicality refers to tactics regimes utilize against opposition actors' bodies, including arrests, beatings, harassment, targeted assassinations, raids, torture, disappearances, mass killings, and forced exile. Physical repression is not the only strategy available to authoritarian regimes to confront mobilized opposition, but it is the most common tactic, and the one most feared by opposition activists. Accordingly, violent repression has received the most attention from academics, policy makers, and political activists, not least because it demonstrates the way a regime exploits the state's monopoly on

10. Linz, *Totalitarian and Authoritarian Regimes.*

violence to demobilize challengers.[11] While authoritarian regimes can and do repress both citizens and opposition elites, I focus my analysis on repression of opposition, who are most acutely affected and regularly targeted by state repression as a policy of regime maintenance and survival. The democratic opposition is a prime candidate for repression as a non-violent, visible, and organized institution mobilizing against authoritarian regimes.

Regimes also rely on non-physical forms of repression to demobilize the opposition. Many regimes adopt long-term state policies of economic reward and punishment to redistribute benefits to loyal supporters, as identified through electoral outcomes.[12] While the co-optation of opposition groups into ruling coalitions or institutions is often considered separately, as an alternative repression, it is similarly intended to control, marginalize, and ultimately demobilize parts of the opposition.[13] Regimes often employ co-optation in combination with other tactics, repressing some opposition groups while co-opting others into formal and informal institutions and alliances in order to divide and weaken the larger opposition's resistance.[14] In addition, regimes impose legal restrictions on permitted political opposition when they participate in electoral contests.[15] However, in many authoritarian regimes, an opposition party's legal status is unrelated to whether the regime will repress or harass it in other ways.[16]

Existing studies have focused great attention on understanding the form and function of repression, with an eye towards the regimes which employ repression as a defensive or survival strategy. The form of repression utilized by authoritarian regimes is defined in terms of which opposition groups are affected by repression. In an early formative book on totalitarianism, Arendt argued that regimes utilize repression with the intention

---

11. Christian Davenport, *How Social Movements Die: Repression and Demobilization of the Republic of New Africa* (New York: Cambridge University Press, 2015), 29.

12. Lisa Blaydes, *Elections and Distributive Politics in Mubarak's Egypt* (New York: Cambridge University Press, 2011); Tarek Masoud, *Counting Islam: Religion, Class, and Elections in Egypt* (New York: Cambridge University Press, 2014).

13. Levitsky and Way, "The Rise of Competitive Authoritarianism."

14. Lust, *Structuring Conflict in the Arab World: Incumbents, Opponents, and Institutions*; Holger Albrecht, "How Can Opposition Support Authoritarianism? Lessons from Egypt," *Democratization* 12, no. 3 (2006): 378–397.

15. Glenn E. Robinson, "Defensive Democratization in Jordan," *International Journal of Middle East Studies* 30, no. 3 (1998): 387–410; Marsha Pripstein Posusney, "Multi-party Elections in the Arab World: Institutional Engineering and Oppositional Strategies," *Studies in Comparative and International Development* 36, no. 4 (2002): 34–62.

16. Lust, *Structuring Conflict in the Arab World: Incumbents, Opponents, and Institutions*.

of demobilizing entire societies.[17] Similarly, a seminal piece on the exceptional nature of the Middle East's authoritarian regimes by Bellin suggests that regime repression will target any and all challengers in the hopes of demobilizing them.[18] However, most contemporary authoritarian regimes rely on selective repression, with the relative balance and choice of targets varying across cases.[19]

Research on repression has overwhelmingly focused on explaining dependent variables related to the longevity of regimes when they utilize repression in different forms. The "success" of repression is similarly defined from the perspective of the regime, as favorable outcomes that minimize any reforms, concessions, changes in the regime, or electoral outcomes that award more seats to the opposition. Repression is more likely to be "successful" when it takes certain forms. More specifically, repression that is targeted, affecting certain groups and not others, is most effective because it divides the opposition and pits groups against each other. This resonates with the robust finding that the opposition is most effective at combating and winning reforms and concessions from authoritarian regimes when it can unite and form a broad-based coalition, often based on a single issue. In these studies, scholars maintain that repression affects political opportunity structures. The opposition is assumed to act strategically, in response to favorable structures as created by and through repressive tactics used by the regime. Repression alters the opposition groups' calculus by changing constraints and opportunities in a manner which hinders their ability to individually mobilize and contest the regime. This then changes the probability of cooperation across groups when contesting the regime through elections, protest mobilization, or general demands of reform.[20]

---

17. Arendt, *The Origins of Totalitarianism.*

18. Bellin, "Robustness of Authoritarianism."

19. Sidney Tarrow, *Power in Movement: Social Movements and Contentious Politics* (Cambridge: Cambridge University Press, 1998).

20. Lust, *Structuring Conflict in the Arab World: Incumbents, Opponents, and Institutions;* Albrecht, "How Can Opposition Support Authoritarianism? Lessons from Egypt"; Marc Morje Howard and Philip G. Roessler, "Liberalizing Electoral Outcomes in Competitive Authoritarian Regimes," *American Journal of Political Science* 50, no. 2 (2006): 365–381; Jillian Schwedler and Janine A. Clark, "Islamist-Leftist Cooperation in the Arab World," *ISIM Review* 18 (2006): 10–11; Deena Shehata, *Islamists and Secularists in Egypt: Opposition, Conflict and Cooperation* (London: Routledge, 2009); Nicholas van de Walle, "Tipping Games: When Do Opposition Parties Coalesce?," in *Electoral Authoritarianism: The Dynamics of Unfree Competition,* ed. Andreas Schedler (Boulder, Colorado: Lynne Rienner, 2006).

However, personal accounts of repression reveal that it is not simply a behavioral constraint, but rather an influential lived experience—an
emotional, psychological, and physical trauma. A Tunisian politician interviewed for this book described the psychological effects of repression, in
which he described feelings of shame, embarrassment, and helplessness
caused by acts of repression. He said, "when I was brought into the Ministry of the Interior, they stripped all my clothes off me and paraded me up
and down the four floors, in front of male and female police officers. They
laughed at me. It felt like a great injustice, an attack on my being, on my
existence. And I wasn't able to do a thing."[21] Moreover, repression does
not always result in increased cooperation, as many theories would lead us
to expect, or to decreased mobilization, as regimes might hope. Instead,
different forms can lead to increased resistance and opposition, increased
commitment to group goals and fellow group members, and the radicaliza-
tion of those targeted for specific beliefs or actions depending on the targets
of repression and personal reactions to these traumatic experiences.[22]

As a result of a myopic focus on regime survival, the repression literature
has generally tended "to neglect the targets and victims of state repression ... this leaves us in a situation where comparatively little effort is
extended to understanding what impact repression has on the individuals
subjected to it or on the broader society in which these actions take place."[23]
More recent work begins to address this lacuna by unpacking political
effects of repression explicitly *not* related to the longevity of regimes. Balcells finds that those who were victimized during the Spanish Civil War
and Franco dictatorship rejected a nationalist identity along the salient axis
of contestation during the war (i.e., left-right).[24] Blaydes demonstrates
that Saddam Hussein and his regime used collective punishment of certain social groups. Over time, repression cemented sectarian divisions in
society, with disastrous consequences for Iraqi politics post-2003.[25] Lupu
and Peisakhin find that the descendants of individuals who suffered the

21. Abdelfattah Mourou. Interview with the author. January 16, 2017. Tunis, Tunisia.

22. Edward Peters, *Torture* (New York: Basil Blackwell, 1985); Neil MacMaster, "Torture:
From Algiers to Abu Ghraib," *Race and Class* 46, no. 2 (2004): 1–21.

23. Davenport, *How Social Movements Die: Repression and Demobilization of the Republic of
New Africa*, 9.

24. Laia Balcells, "The Consequences of Victimization on Political Identities: Evidence from
Spain," *Politics & Society* 40, no. 3 (2012): 311–347.

25. Lisa Blaydes, *State of Repression: Iraq under Saddam Hussein* (Princeton University Press,
2018).

Soviet deportation of Crimean Tatars in 1944 identify more strongly with their ethnic group and hold stronger pro-Crimean attitudes.[26] Similarly, Rozenas, Schutte, and Zhukov find that Ukrainian communities subjected to greater intensity of Soviet deportation in the 1940s are now significantly less likely to vote for pro-Russian parties.[27] These studies suggest a causal link rooted in identity formation for the way in which repression affects various outcomes. However, given the difficulty in obtaining the proper evidence, the authors are hard-pressed to conclusively argue that identity is the causal mechanism. Moreover, they do not convincingly explain the microfoundations of how and why identities are transformed by repression, or the manner in which these identities are transmitted throughout the repressed group and over time.

## How Repression Shapes Identity

I posit a two-stage theory of the process through which repression conditions levels of political polarization. In the first stage of the causal process, the nature of repression conditions political identities. The important variation here is in how the repressive environment affects groups differently with a given authoritarian context. While some regimes use targeted repression, singling out a specific opposition group, others employ widespread repression against the entire spectrum of political opposition actors. Differential experiences of repression shape groups' political identities to be in either more or less conflict with others' identities. Widespread experiences of repression will decrease in-group identification, as the groups targeted form a bridging collective identity of victimized opposition sharing experiences of repression across multiple groups. In contrast, targeted experiences of repression will heighten in-group identification for the singularly targeted group, as only in-group members share experiences of repression.

In the second stage, the nature of political identities condition group-related affect and political preferences. In widespread repressive environments, stronger intergroup identity and decreased in-group identification leads to lower levels of political polarization. This is measured both in higher levels of positive affect and lower levels of preference disagreement

---

26. Noam Lupu and Leonid Peisakhin, "The Legacy of Political Violence across Generations," *American Journal of Political Science* 61, no. 4 (2017): 836–851.

27. Arturas Rozenas, Sebastian Schutte, and Yuri Zhukov, "The Political Legacy of Violence: The Long-Term Impact of Stalin's Repression in Ukraine," *Journal of Politics 79*, no. 4 (2017): 1147–1161.

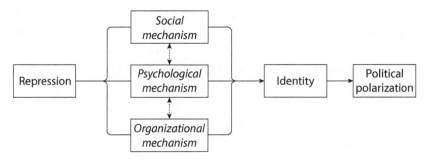

**FIGURE 2.1.** Visualization of Theoretical Argument

among groups who identify with each other. In contrast, targeted repressive environments increase political polarization. Targeted groups experience stronger in-group identification, resulting in higher levels of negative affect and preference disagreement with other groups, and creating a political system characterized by higher levels of political polarization.

The following sections walk sequentially through the logic underpinning this argument. First, I discuss how repression conditions political identities through three mutually reinforcing pathways. Because repression is, in essence, a bundled treatment of experiences, it affects identity formation through multiple mechanisms. First, experiences of repression affect *psychological* processes, providing information on group membership and relative group status, and how actors should define themselves vis-à-vis competing groups. This critical mechanism, supported by original experimental evidence presented in chapter 7, has been neglected in previous studies of the political effects of repression. Second, repression alters *social* environments determining whether political prisoners are exposed to prison or exile, whether these spaces are shared and, if so, with whom. Third, repression alters the *organizational* structure of opposition groups as they struggle to survive repressive conditions. I address each of these mechanisms in turn, as well as their mutually reinforcing interaction, in shaping identities. I then link how identities created in this manner condition levels of affect and preference polarization among opposition groups.

## A PSYCHOLOGICAL MECHANISM

First, repression alters identities through a psychological mechanism. The existence of a group requires entitativity, a quality approximating "groupness," or the perception that individuals together constitute a group. Experiences of repression adjust an individual's existing feelings of groupness. Group identification necessitates an individual's awareness of belonging to a certain group and having a psychological attachment to that group based on a perception of shared experiences, interests, and beliefs with other group members.[28] Full identification includes not only categorizing oneself as part of the group, but thinking and feeling positively about the group.[29] An in-group is always contrasted with the out-group, which is by definition a group with which one does not identify.

Psychological studies have firmly established the importance of shared experiences in creating identities.[30] Standard feelings of groupness and the ability to differentiate between one's in- and out-groups emerge from even the most arbitrary of group membership assignments and in basic group interactions.[31] But experiences of repression significantly adjust an individual's feelings of groupness. Trauma is a particularly effective collective experience in identity formation, as it very clearly and viscerally reveals information about what attributes and experiences individuals have in common. Durkheim first observed that painful experiences promote cohesion and solidarity within pre-existing groups,[32] and more recent studies have tested and confirmed this relationship experimentally.[33] Shared traumatic experiences can also create new identities by exposing previously unconnected individuals to the same suffering and pain, recategorizing group boundaries and creating new, bridging identities that bring individuals together based on a common experience.[34] Traumatic experiences

28. Arthur H. Miller et al., "Group Consciousness and Political Participation," *American Journal of Political Science* 25, no. (1981): 494–511.

29. Naomi Ellemers, Russell Spears, and Bertjan Doosje, "Self and Social Identity," *Annual Review of Psychology* 53, no. 1 (2002): 161–186.

30. Brewer and Brown, "Intergroup Conflict."

31. Henri Tajfel, M. B. Billig, R. P. Bundy, and Claude Flament, "Social Categorization and Intergroup Behaviour," *European Journal of Social Psychology* 2, no. 1 (1971): 149–178; John C. Turner, "Social Categorization and Social Discrimination in the Minimal Group Paradigm," in *Differentiation Between Social Groups: Studies in the Social Psychology of Intergroup Relations*, ed. Henry Tajfel (London: Academic Press, 1978), 101–140; Michelle B. Brewer, "Ingroup Bias in the Minimal Intergroup Situation: A Cognitive Motivational Analysis," *Psychological Bulletin* 82, no. 2 (1979): 475–482.

32. Émile Durkheim, *The Elementary Forms of Religious Life* (New York: Oxford University Press, 2001 (1912)).

33. Brock Bastian, Jolanda Jetten, and Laura J. Ferris, "Pain as Social Glue: Shared Pain Increases Cooperation," *Psychological Science*, 2014, 1–7.

34. Donald T. Campbell, "Common Fate, Similarity, and Other Indices of the State of Aggregates of Persons as Social Entities," *Behavioral Science* 1, no. 3 (1958): 14–25; Howard Schuman and Jacqueline Scott, "Generations and Collective Memories," *American Sociological Review* 54, no. 3 (1989): 359–381; N. R. Brown et al., "Living in History: How War, Terrorism, and Natural

are particularly influential by further enhancing the nature of pre-existing identities and creating new ones because shared trauma places emphasis on shared attributes.[35] In the study of collective memory, emotional and traumatic memories are found to spread deeper into networks because an individual is more likely to talk about an emotional experience than a regular one with others, and particularly with those who also experienced a traumatic event.[36]

To put these findings in terms related to the question at hand, the nature of repression affects how actors come to identify themselves in the same manner as shared trauma more broadly. The shared trauma of repressive acts reveals important information about who constitutes a fellow in-group member and strongly primes feelings of groupness with common victims. When a group is targeted exclusively, the isolating experience of repression serves to strengthen in-group identification. In contrast, when multiple groups are collectively affected within a widespread repressive environment, repressive experiences are shared and do not increase identification with the narrower in-group. By exposing multiple groups to the same trauma, widespread repression serves to change the reference group for identity formation from the particular in-group to the larger collective of opposition groups, strengthening inter group identity. Said differently, widespread repression creates feelings of groupness that permeate previously constructed boundaries, with the "opposition" as a larger concept serving as the basis of identity, while targeted repression reinforces divisions, with individual opposition groups (for example, the Muslim Brotherhood) serving as the basis of identity.

Disaster Affect the Organization of Autobiographical Memory," *Psychological Science* 20 (2009): 399–405; Howard Schuman, Robert F. Belli, and Katherine Bischoping, "The Generational Basis of Historical Knowledge," in *Collective Memories of Political Events: Social Psychological Perspectives*, ed. J. W. Pennebaker, D. Paez, and B. Rime (New York: Lawrence Erlbaum Publishers, 1997); Wolfgang Wagner, Nicole Kronberger, and Franz Seifert, "Collective Symbolic Coping with New Technology: Knowledge, Images, and Public Discourse," *British Journal of Social Psychology* 3, no. 41 (2002): 323–343.

35. Marilynn B. Brewer, "When Contact is Not Enough: Social Identity and Intergroup Cooperation," *International Journal of Intercultural Relations* 20, nos. 3/4 (1996): 291–303.

36. Jonah Berger and Katherine L. Milkman, "What Makes Online Content Viral?," *Journal of Marketing Research* 2, no. 49 (2012): 192–205; Kent D. Harber and Dov J. Cohen, "The Emotional Broadcaster Theory of Social Sharing," *Journal of Language and Social Psychology* 4, no. 24 (2005): 382–400; Dan Sperber and Lawrence A. Hirschfeld, "The Cognitive Foundations of Cultural Stability and Diversity," *Trends in Cognitive Sciences* 8, no. 1 (2004): 40–46.

## A SOCIAL MECHANISM

Second, repression creates identities through a social mechanism, as repression alters the social environment in which opposition groups operate. My conceptualization of this mechanism refers to a group's external socialization, or whether and how the group interacts socially with other groups and settings, and is thus exposed to other kinds of people and competing ideas (within-group, or internal socialization, is discussed in more detail in the next section on the organizational effects of repression). When a state represses the opposition, members of affected groups are forced into certain physical spaces, most notably prisons and exile.[37] In a widespread form, repression brings together members of multiple opposition groups in prison and exile. Meanwhile, in a targeted form, repression isolates a group in these same spaces and insulates them from exposure to other opposition groups.

Repression alters individual opposition group's exposure to other groups. Competing opposition groups are brought into close proximity in repressive spaces in a widespread repressive environment. The social mechanism with regards to other groups is akin to that suggested by contact theory: under the right set of circumstances, more exposure to different people increases familiarity with them and typically reduces prejudice among groups.[38] Certain configurations of repression can plausibly lead to reevaluations of both the in-group and the out-group, with positive implications for intergroup affect and cooperation. Widespread repression is more likely to create the right set of conditions by creating equal group status within the repressive environment (i.e., identifying all parties present as victims) and facilitating the creation of common goals (i.e., continued opposition against a common enemy).

Similarly, repression alters opposition groups' exposure to certain kinds of people, with implications for modifications in political preferences. Influential social groups such as peers of various kinds and families further exert important influence on socializing individuals into certain political

37. Liisa H. Malkki (*Purity and Exile: Violence, Memory, and National Cosmology among Hutu Refugees in Tanzania* (University of Chicago Press, 2012)) masterfully demonstrates how the experience of exile facilitates identity formation among Hutu refugees exiled in Tanzania.

38. Gordon W. Allport, *The Nature of Prejudice* (Reading, Massachusetts: Addison-Wesley, 1979); Thomas F. Pettigrew, "Intergroup Contact Theory," *Annual Review of Psychology* 49, no. 1 (1998): 65–85.

preferences and behaviors.[39] By influencing one's physical location and space, repression controls the social groups with which one socializes, and may even create new social groups through forced interaction. It is possible that this may be an unintended by-product of repression, but an important one nonetheless. When repression only targets a certain kind of opposition member, social experiences in exile and prison spaces will reinforce the in-group network. In contrast, when multiple groups are imprisoned or exiled together, they will be forced to socialize with individuals from groups not their own. Relatedly, the nature of the political contexts in which exiled political opposition find themselves when repressed should matter for their political ideas and behavior. There is a long-standing literature on political socialization, wherein the norms and ideas of an established political system influence the ideas and behaviors of those living under it. Sometimes, this occurs through an active state role, in which states indoctrinate their citizens with certain attitudes in an effort to gain increased support and compliance.[40] In this sense, socialization results from prolonged and intense exposure to different state projects. Here, individuals are socialized by the political systems to which they are exposed.[41] Prolonged exposure to democratic political systems might socialize these groups to be more tolerant and open in their political preferences. In contrast, continued exposure to authoritarian systems where repression, dominance, and intolerance is the name of the game may socialize groups into even more intolerant affect and preferences.

## AN ORGANIZATIONAL MECHANISM

Third, repression alters the organizational structure of opposition groups as they cope to survive under restrictive conditions. Many scholars have

39. Herbert Hyman, *Political Socialization* (New York: Free Press, 1959); Michael McDevitt and Steven Chaffee, "From Topdown to Trickle-up Influence: Revisiting Assumptions about the Family in Political Socialization," *Political Communication* 19, no. 3 (2002): 281–301.

40. Fred I. Greenstein, *Children and Politics* (New Haven: Yale University Press, 1969).

41. Grigore Pop-Eleches and Joshua A.Tucker, "Communism's Shadow: Postcommunist Legacies, Values, and Behavior," *Comparative Politics* 43, no. 4 (2011): 379–408; Romana Careja and Patrick Emmenegger, "Making Democratic Citizens: The Effects of Migration Experience on Political Attitudes in Central and Eastern Europe," *Comparative Political Studies* 45, no. 7 (2012): 875–902; Thomas Gift and Daniel Krcmaric, "Democracy and Foreign Education," *Journal of Conflict Resolution*, 2015; Lisa Chauvet, Flore Gubert, and Sandrine Mesplé-Somps, "Do Migrants Adopt New Political Attitudes from Abroad? Evidence using a multi-sited exit-poll survey during the 2013 Malian elections," *Comparative Migration Studies* 4, no. 1 (2016): 19.

noted that analyses of the relationship between repression and continued mobilization is inconclusive, having found robust support for both mobilizing and demobilizing effects.[42] This seemingly contradictory finding can be explained by thinking through how repression alters organizations. More specifically, repression may cause changes in individual membership and group institutions following an incident or repeated incidents of repression, leading to either mobilization or demobilization. At the institutional level, repression demobilizes organizations that lack a robust infrastructure to prepare their members to withstand repression and to create and sustain organizational trust. Groups either have these characteristics prior to experiencing repression or adopt them in response to repression. When first targeted by repression, most groups lack this capacity, but their continued survival forces them to adapt.

Three sets of organizational features help groups survive repression. First, groups can update the substantive content of their membership, the processes of joining, and the requirements of staying. Groups can update their procedures and structures to actively promote loyalty and vigorous commitment as an important and necessary trait for qualified new members and those who remain under repression. At the individual level, it is logical that when faced with repression, many members will experience fear and tire of continued punitive treatment. In this case, they may cease doing the acts and promoting the ideas which led to their suffering, and leave the group.[43] When this happens en masse, it can lead to factionalization, which weakens the group. However, groups are often strengthened by the "radical flank effect," when less committed members exit the group and leave behind only die-hard members.[44] These members are those individuals who are likely to respond to repression with anger, and thus are more likely to be mobilized or radicalized by repression.[45] Repression may foster within them the belief that the government's activity is unjustified, further committing and mobilizing them for their cause, and strengthening the division between the activists and the non-activists.

42. See Christian Davenport, "State Repression and Political Order," *Annual Review of Political Science* 10 (2007): 1–23, for a summary of the literature on repression and inconclusive results regarding its (de)mobilizing effects.

43. Davenport, *How Social Movements Die: Repression and Demobilization of the Republic of New Africa*, 29.

44. Herbert H Haines, "Radical Flank Effects," *The Wiley-Blackwell Encyclopedia of Social and Political Movements*, 2013.

45. Ted Gurr, *Why Men Rebel* (Princeton: Princeton University Press, 1970).

In addition, groups can strengthen their internal socialization processes in the face of repression to further strengthen members' resolve in pursuing group goals. The idea underpinning this effect is that if members are well socialized into a group, and there are strong group social and material sanctions for non-participation, members will be more likely to stay in the group. An individual's normative commitment to a group depends on long-term processes of socialization into said group. Groups strengthen the socialization process to maintain continued commitment by incorporating rituals demanding stronger levels of commitment and investment, derogating alternative groups, and convincing members of the superiority of the organization. One way in which this occurs is through frame alignment, wherein groups work to increase the degree of congruence between an individual's identity and goals and those of the group through internal socialization processes.[46]

Finally, the structure of the group can also be adapted as groups struggle to survive different types of repression. Structure is typically measured through a group's level of centralization. A natural response to an external attack is to close in on oneself defensively, and political groups often become more centralized, tight-knit, or rigid in the face of repression. Davenport sees increased centralization as a potential negative, leading to rigidity and ultimately a group's demise, though al-Anani demonstrates how increased centralization may, in fact, permit the survival of groups facing extreme pressure.[47] Other groups adapt to repression by becoming more diffuse. Decentralization in the face of repression may also lead to increased chances of survival by permitting an organization of many layers and cells to persist under extremely repressive conditions. Whether a group becomes more centralized or diffuse in response to repression may be conditioned by whether the broader repressive environment is targeted or widespread.

## THREE MECHANISMS IN INTERACTION

Psychological, social, and organizational mechanisms work together to create and shape identities. First, the psychological mechanism outlined above is a necessary and primary component of the broader process through which repression shapes identity. Group entitativity is an important,

---

46. David A. Snow et al., "Frame Alignment Processes, Micromobilization, and Movement Participation," *American Sociological Review*, 1986, 464–481.

47. Davenport, *How Social Movements Die*; al-Anani, *Inside the Muslim Brotherhood*.

causally prior condition for group identification; one cannot become more attached to a group without an awareness of the group's existence and her membership in said group. Repression creates this awareness by revealing information about the existence of groups, the relative status of groups, and to which group an individual belongs. Changes to the social environment and the structure of the organization then reinforce the groupness created through the psychological mechanism and strengthen identity ties. Structural changes influenced by repression alter the content and requirements of membership, the processes of joining and staying in the group, and the demographics of the group. But the psychological mechanism determines whether a group identifies as hostile or accommodating towards other groups, and thus whether the content, processes, and membership become more or less exclusive. Similarly, the social mechanism dictates the ideas and people to which opposition groups are exposed, but the way in which a group adopts or rejects these new ideas and people has to do with how they define their in-group and who is included as a member.

Over time, the three mechanisms interact with each other, creating group identities and updating them over time. The psychological process provides information on an individual's group and its relative status vis-à-vis other opposition groups, and the organizational and social mechanisms reinforce this identity. When repression targets a group exclusively, traumatic experiences borne of repression serve to strengthen in-group identification through a more exclusive identity, social environment, and organizational structure. By contrast, when multiple groups are collectively affected within a widespread repressive environment, repressive experiences are shared and do not increase identification with the narrower in-group. By exposing multiple groups to the same trauma, widespread repression serves to change the reference group for identity from the particular in-group to the larger collective of opposition groups, strengthening inter group identity. Over time, as repression reveals more information about one's group, and identities update and strengthen by incorporating that information, the psychological mechanism may have downstream effects for the social and organizational mechanisms, and vice versa.

## Group Identities and Group Differentiation

In the first step of my argument, repression alters the nature and salience of identities. In the second step, the nature and salience of identities condition levels of political polarization among opposition groups by initiating processes of group differentiation. Social identity theory holds that individuals maximize differences between their in-group and the out-group at all times to reduce cognitive dissonance, and strengthened in-group identity necessarily induces higher levels of group differentiation.[48] Group differentiation occurs through in-group favoritism, in which group members exaggerate inter-group differences and emphasize intra group similarities.[49] Groups highlight their defining shared features and attitudes in contrast to those of the out-group. Shared characteristics that are more central to the definition of group identity are highlighted while more peripheral traits are downplayed.[50]

The strength of group differentiation is directly related to the strength of in-group identification. Group differentiation is strongest when in-group identification is, and is exacerbated by situations in which in-group identity is primed through differential treatment or experiences, such as combative situations, when groups are pitted against each other in conflict, or situations of relative deprivation, when a group is disproportionately discriminated against by a third party.[51] The stronger levels of group identification resulting from these situations lead to higher levels of group differentiation.

Processes of group differentiation cause individuals to become more extreme on in-group attitudes and preferences.[52] With groups based on ascriptive characteristics such as ethnicity or gender, the emphasized difference may be a shared physical feature, and preferences change with regards to in-group-favoring policies. However, in political groups formed on the basis of common political ideologies, policy preferences related to group ideology and goals are the group's defining characteristic and thus becomes the characteristic on which groups differentiate themselves when the strength of in-group identification increases. For example, for Greene, processes of group differentiation "create a bipolar partisanship

48. Henri Tajfel and John C.Turner, "The Social Identity Theory of Intergroup Behavior," in *Psychology of Integroup Relations*, ed. Stephen Worchel and William G. Austin (Chicago: Nelson-Hall Publishers, 1986).

49. Brewer and Brown, "Intergroup Conflict," 58.

50. Caroline Kelly, "Political Identity and Perceived Intragroup Homogeneity," *British Journal of Social Psychology* 28 (1989): 239–250; Bernd Simon, "Intragroup Differentiation in Terms of Ingroup and Outgroup Attributes," *European Journal of Social Psychology* 22 (1992): 407–413; Michael A. Hogg and John C. Turner, "Intergroup Behaviour, Self Stereotyping and the Salience of Social Categories," *British Journal of Social Psychology* 26 (1987): 325–340.

51. Murray Horwitz and Jacob M. Rabbie, "Individuality and Membership in the Intergroup System," in *Social Identity and Intergroup Relations*, ed. Henry Tajfel (Cambridge: Cambridge University Press, 1982), 271–274.

52. David M. Mackie, "Social Identification Effects in Group Polarization," *Journal of Personality and Social Psychology* 50 (1986): 720–728.

where individuals characterize the political parties into 'us' and 'them' and exaggerate perceived differences," manifested in social distance and differences in policy preferences between groups.[53] The resulting political polarization, including differences both in affect and in preferences, is then an indication of political distance between groups.

To explicitly relate these psychological processes to the question under analysis here, the comparatively decreased in-group identification resulting from widespread experiences of repression leads groups to recategorize boundaries, identifying less with their individual group and more with a larger collective of opposition groups. By perceiving themselves as part of a broader opposition, parties do not differentiate between themselves, feel more positively about out-groups they previously considered to be competition, and converge on central policy preferences. In contrast, the increased in-group identification resulting from targeted repression activates processes of group differentiation and the targeted group maximizes distance from others as in-group identity increases. Increasing the strength of in-group identification increases the distance in affect and preferences between groups.

## Consequences for Compromise

Repression's effect on identities and political polarization has important behavioral implications. Both affective and preference polarization have consequences for compromise and cooperation between groups. Social psychological accounts confirm that both attitudes towards others and policy preferences resulting from processes of group differentiation precede— and indeed, determine—cooperation.[54] Thus, if group conflict is at its core fighting over real or perceived differences, the distance between groups on dimensions that matter for cooperation is an important causal variable in explaining why these groups cooperate.[55] As Brewer and Brown write, "where group interests are incompatible, where what one group gains is at the expense of another, the social psychological response is likely to be negative. Where they are compatible or complementary, the reaction should be

53. Steven Greene, "Social Identity Theory and Party Identification," *Social Science Quarterly* 85, no. 1 (2004): 136–153.

54. Naomi Struch and Shalon H. Schwartz, "Intergroup Aggression: Its Predictors and Distinctness from In-group Bias," *Journal of Personality and Social Psychology* 56 (1989): 364–373.

55. Donald Campbell, *Ethnocentric and Other Altruistic Motives* (Lincoln, Nebraska: University of Nebraska Press, 1965).

more positive."[56] Positive behavior suggests compromise and cooperation, while hostile behavior implies the opposite.

Group interests both incorporate and are conditioned by distance from out-groups in the realm of affect and preferences. Indeed, both negative affect and divergent preferences are important for why political polarization leads to subpar cooperative behavioral outcomes. High levels of negative affect dictates when groups cannot cooperate because they refuse to work together.[57] This is on full display in the vast literature on ethnicity and redistribution; when individuals strongly identify with their in-group, they display high levels of in-group favoritism with detrimental effects for cross-group cooperative outcomes. High levels of difference in preferences prohibit compromise when groups cannot agree. This assumption, in which higher levels of disagreement make the finding of common solutions much more difficult, underpins the literatures on transitology, political polarization in developed democracy, and bargaining.

## Conclusion

In this chapter, I have outlined a theory of polarization in authoritarian regimes, which assigns significant predictive power to variation in repressive conditions. Building on established research in social psychology on shared trauma, identity formation, and group identification, I argue that the nature of political repression under a given authoritarian regime dictates how actors come to identify themselves, thereby shaping their attitudes towards competing opposition groups and related policy preferences. In the chapters that follow, I explore this theory empirically. Chapters 5 and 6 present sequential evidence from Egypt and Tunisia, which documents the relationship outlined here between repression, identity formation, and polarization obtains. Chapter 7 undertakes a similar endeavor in a lab experimental context. Chapter 8 links the polarization conditioned by authoritarian repression to the divergent cooperative behavioral outcomes witnessed during each country's transition period. In the next section, I start at the beginning of the causal chain, exploring why and how Egyptian and Tunisian authoritarian regimes came to repress their opposition in systematically different ways.

56. Brewer and Brown, "Intergroup Conflict," 565.

57. Iyengar et al., "The Origins and Consequences of Affective Polarization in the United States"; Daniel Balliet, Junhui Wu, and Carsten K. W. De Dreu, "Ingroup Favoritism in Cooperation: A Meta-Analysis." *Psychological Bulletin* 140, no. 6 (2014): 1556.

# PART II

# Repertoires of Repression

# 3

# The Historical Origins of Authoritarian Repression

In this chapter, I discuss how regimes come to repress their opposition in different ways. Though an analysis of the determinants of how an authoritarian regime comes to utilize a specific repressive strategy (i.e., an analysis in which repressive regime type is the *dependent* variable) is temporally and logically prior to the main subject of inquiry in this book (i.e., an analysis in which repressive regime type is the *independent* variable), an understanding of the origins of repression is centrally important to analyzing the effects of repression. In order for variation in repression to have meaningful explanatory power for the questions assessed in this book, the source of this variation must be plausibly exogenous and unrelated to the dependent variable under analysis (here, the level of polarization among opposition groups).

Political scientists tend to conceptualize repression as a strategic choice; when a leader comes to power, he assesses threats and then adopts the appropriate repressive policies and related institutions to combat them. As I document in the next chapter, the nature of repression under Mubarak and Ben Ali was qualitatively different. Many political scientists would chalk this up to different strategies undertaken by each ruler. However, the so-called repressive "strategies" of both countries' post-colonial leaders were quite consistent over time, and did not change in response to shifts among the opposition, raising the question of just how strategic these policies were.

In contrast to the strategic approach, historically minded research details the extent to which institutional baggage determines states' repressive behavior and leaders' strategic choices. This historical approach documents how the repressive environments of independent authoritarian regimes are largely determined by previous state-building projects, many of which precede independence in post-colonial states. These projects shaped the state's capacity to collect intelligence, the organization of policing and other coercive institutions, and had path-dependent implications for the nature of the coercive apparatus during the subsequent authoritarian period. While colonial state-building projects certainly do not explain the entirety of the variation in post-colonial repression, historical evidence suggests leaders' strategic considerations have a smaller influence than institutional legacies for the nature of authoritarian repression, and there is more consistency than change in repression over time and across regimes within the same national context.

In this chapter, I offer evidence for how differences in colonial coercive institutions in the Middle East conditioned coercive institutions in their independent counterparts in the post-colonial period, and thus how this specific type of colonial legacy influences the nature of repression used by the regimes that follow. The chapter theorizes the colonial origins of coercive institutions, the path dependence of these institutions, and the constraining nature of inherited institutions for leader behavior and the prospects of institutional reform. In the following two sections, I discuss how the interaction between the centrality of coercion and variation in the nature of colonial projects provides significant explanatory power for the coercive institutions inherited by Middle East political leaders in the mid-twentieth century upon independence, and then lay out a typology of coercive institutions and the nature of state repression. I then trace the historical development of coercive institutions in Egypt and Tunisia to demonstrate institutional continuity and path dependence through independence before concluding the chapter.

## Repression as a Strategic Choice

Existing work on the origins of coercion attribute observable variation in repression under authoritarian regimes to choices made by authoritarian leaders when they come to power. While existing theories differ in the details, they all assign significant autonomy to leaders and their strategic choice of coercive institutions. More specifically, scholars argue that authoritarian leaders construct coercive institutions based on the dominant perceived threat when they assume power. Leaders face at least two types of threats (foreign and domestic)[1] and more likely three kinds of threats (external, internal mass-based, and internal elite-based)[2] that could dislodge them from power. When designing an internal security apparatus, leaders face organizational trade-offs in preparing either to face down a popular threat or to protect themselves against rival elites. In short, the type of perceived threat faced by a ruler when coming to power determines the nature of all types of institutions adopted by authoritarian leaders for coercion, co-optation, and survival.

The choices made by leaders in response to perceived threats create coercive institutions that vary on a number of different attributes, such as exclusivity, measured by the social and demographic composition of the organization, as well as the level of organizational centralization. Coercive institutions are more violent when they are fragmented and unable to adequately collect intelligence on their populations because they are constructed to monitor and defend against rival elites, and less violent because they better penetrate society and thus can preemptively address possible mass mobilization, having been constructed to defend the regime against mass uprisings. Embedded in these arguments is a sense of path dependence conditioned by decisions made in an initial period. Institutional stickiness[3] then makes it difficult for regimes to adapt as new threats arise, resulting in predictable patterns of state coercive institutions and repressive behavior over time.

However, these existing studies rely on two mistaken assumptions when making claims about the origins of coercive institutions. First, scholars analyze the military as the repressive institution of interest, whereas it is actually the police, a domestically-focused institution, that defends the regime in regular moments of authoritarian governance, carrying out everyday repression of both elite and mass-based political opposition. In reality, the military is seldom deployed to the streets except in infrequent moments of extraordinary mass mobilization,[4] and military-led coups have become increasingly rare events in contemporary authoritarian regimes like those

1. Wintrobe, *The Political Economy of Dictatorship*; Greitens, *Dictators and their Secret Police: Coercive Institutions and State Violence*.

2. Svolik, *The Politics of Authoritarian Rule*; Brownlee, *Authoritarianism in an Age of Democratization*.

3. Mahoney and Thelen, *Explaining Institutional Change: Ambiguity, Agency, and Power*.

4. Nicholas J. Lotito, *Soldiers and Societies in Revolt: Military Doctrine in the Arab Spring* (PhD diss., Columbia University, 2018).

in the Middle East.[5] While much of the literature on authoritarian repression focuses on militaries, there is reason to think similar arguments apply to the police. The police are similarly tasked with political control, constitute coercive institutions which are politically and economically costly to change, and are centrally important for the state's monopoly of violence.

Second, theories of political repression often rely on mistaken assumptions about the origins and historical development of the instruments of coercion. Existing explanations are *demand*-driven: the type of challenge the regime faces when it comes to power determines its strategic response and subsequently the design of coercive institutions. New leaders assess potential domestic threats and construct the corresponding coercive institution while weighing various organizational trade-offs. Once created, these organizations are subject to institutional stickiness, which constrains regimes' adaptability as new threats arise and results in predictable patterns of political repression in each regime. A more accurate explanation of regimes' use of repression must be *supply*-driven. Historical reality undermines the assumption that contemporary authoritarian leaders have full autonomy to design and construct coercive institutions. Instead, contemporary authoritarian leaders inherit certain coercive institutions and states with a given predetermined capacity. This is particularly true for leaders coming to power in the mid- or late-twentieth century, after the conclusion of major state-building projects. Contemporary leaders take charge of states with predetermined resource endowments and institutional capacities. While the path dependence of existing arguments holds up to empirical scrutiny, the idea that authoritarian leaders have full autonomy in constructing coercive institutions does not. Instead, the path dependence of the coercive apparatus extends back further in history than previously acknowledged, often predating the birth of a political regime.

## The Origins of Coercive Institutions in Contemporary Authoritarian Regimes

Historical work on the origins of coercive institutions departs from strategic accounts summarized above. Instead of making choices at independence with downstream implications for the nature of established coercive institutions and patterns of state repression, leaders inherit

5. Holger Albrecht, "The Myth of Coup-Proofing: Risk and Instances of Military Coups d'État in the Middle East and North Africa, 1950–2013," *Armed Forces & Society* 41, no. 4 (2015): 659–687.

institutions, particularly when it comes to national and domestic security. In post-colonial states, such as those in the Middle East, independence leaders take control of a country with certain pre-established capabilities and are highly constrained in creating new institutions. In this way, post-independence authoritarian coercive capabilities are shaped by pre-independence institution-building.[6]

In the Middle East, a consequential period of modern state-building coincided with the European colonial period. The state-building projects significantly shaped the institutions of Middle Eastern states, but were guided by an overarching colonial strategy that favored the interests of the colonizer rather than addressing threats perceived by local actors.[7] This had implications for state capacity and the nature of coercive institutions central to governance at independence and in subsequent periods. Though there is much debate about how different types of colonizers were, and thus how meaningful a distinction exists between, say, British and French colonial legacies for subsequent economic, political, and social developments, a country's colonial experience should logically hold predictive power for the nature of coercive institutions inherited at independence. The difference between colonial systems of control is not a simple difference between indirect and direct rule, but rather a categorical difference in the nature of the relationship between the colonizer and the colonized.[8]

Coercion was at the center of European colonial projects. Foreign actors asserted their authority over local populations in many ways and through different institutions, but none was as visible as the colonial police officer, a metaphor of the power imbalance inherent in the colonial relationship.[9] Police were the main coercive arm of the colonial state and focused on internal security in colonial holdings. The police were charged with identifying and eliminating domestic political threats, many of which took on a nationalist tone towards the end of the colonial period. The right to control and shape national security forces was explicitly denied to local

6. Allison Spencer Hartnett, Nicholas J. Lotito, and Elizabeth R. Nugent, "The Origins of Coercive Institutions in the Middle East: Preliminary Evidence from Egypt" (working paper, 2018).

7. Joan Ricart-Huguet, "The Origins of Colonial Investments in Former British and French Africa" (working paper, 2019).

8. Michael Crowder, "Indirect rule—French and British style," *Africa* 34, no. 3 (1964): 197.

9. David Arnold, *Police Power and Colonial Rule: Madras, 1859–1947* (Oxford University Press, 1986), 2.

entities under European control because of its centrality in colonialism. Instead, domestic police forces were established by colonial powers, serving and shaped by their interests. Because they were not accountable to the populations which they policed, colonial police "tended to ingrain the coercive character of policing"[10] against disturbances the political and criminal in nature.

Intelligence collection is central to the effective use of coercion. In the words of Ferris, "intelligence is not a form of power but a means to guide its use, whether as a combat multiplier, or by helping one to understand one's environment and options."[11] Undoubtedly, the two are closely related. Intelligence collection by foreign powers in their colonies served two political purposes: most immediately, to allow the foreign power to effectively control political participation and mobilization, and ultimately, to remain in charge of the colonial holding. Foreign powers relied on locally recruited personnel, indigenous bureaucracies, and existing social groups to monitor indigenous society and collect and interpret collected intelligence. Thomas coined the term "intelligence states" as a way of making sense of what role the colonial state, which he characterizes as an unequal partnership between colonial rulers and local networks, played during this period.[12]

While all foreign powers relied on local populations for intelligence and policing, they did so to different extents and in systematically different ways. The British and the French differed in their approach to colonial intelligence collection. These two powers governed significant amounts of territory in the Middle East during the late colonial period, and both did so through forms of indirect rule. During this period, France and Britain were "obliged to construct at least the facades of independent administrations" as the result of waning domestic support for colonialism and economic hardships following the World War I. The resulting mandate

10. David M. Anderson and David Killingray, "Consent, Coercion and Colonial Control: Policing the Empire, 1830–1940," in *Policing the Empire: Government, Authority, and Control, 1830-1940*, ed. David M. Anderson and David Killingray (Manchester University Press, 1991), 9.

11. John Ferris, "Intelligence," in *The Origins of World War Two: The Debate Continues*, ed. Robert Boyce and Joseph A. Maiolo (Basingstoke: Palgrave, 2003), 308.

12. Martin Thomas, "Colonial States as Intelligence States: Security Policing and the Limits of Colonial Rule in France's Muslim Territories, 1920–40," *Journal of Strategic Studies* 28, no. 6 (2005): 1033–1060; Martin Thomas, *Empires of Intelligence: Security Services and Colonial Disorder After 1914* (Berkeley: University of California Press, 2008).

states were somewhat of a "hybrid, a half-way house between colonial rule and independence," and built on initial state-centralization projects that had developed under the Ottoman Empire.[13]

This period left indelible marks on state institutions and served as an anchor for their subsequent development after European forces departed. Colonial legacies affected post-colonial variation in state capacity[14] and both the nature and subsequent performance of national economies.[15] Colonial legacies determined variation in the strength and professionalization of post-independence bureaucracies, with implications for successful consolidation following independence.[16] In addition, the type of colonialism experienced correlates with post-independence electoral strategies in the Middle East, suggesting the way in which colonial powers co-opted local opposition has explanatory power for making sense of post-colonial authoritarian regimes' policies of political control.[17] Given the effect this period had on other institutions, there is reason to think colonial legacies matter for coercive institutions as well.

The historical approach to the origins of coercive institutions outlined here is based on two central assumptions. The first is that of institutional path dependence. As noted above, existing literature agrees that choices leaders make create coercive institutions that are difficult to reform, resulting in predictable patterns of state violence and control. Here, the starting point is moved back in time, to institutions adopted by colonial powers who oversaw the initial creation of modern coercive institutions, instead of by post-independence authoritarian leaders. Colonial coercive institutions then determined subsequent independent authoritarian regimes' coercive institutions and policies. Post-independence authoritarian leaders

13. Nadine Méouchy and Peter Sluglett, eds., "General Introduction" in *The British and French Mandates in Comparative Perspectives (Les Mandats Français et Anglais dans une Perspective Comparative)* (Leiden: Brill, 2004), 9–11.

14. Jeffrey Herbst, *States and Power in Africa: Comparative Lessons in Authority and Control* (Princeton University Press, 2000).

15. Daron Acemoglu, Simon Johnson, and James A. Robinson, "The Colonial Origins of Comparative Development: An Empirical Investigation," *National Bureau of Economic Research*, 2000.

16. Lisa Anderson, *The State and Social Transformation in Tunisia and Libya, 1830–1980* (Princeton: Princeton University Press, 1986).

17. Ellen Lust-Okar and Amaney Jamal, "Rulers and Rules: Reassessing the Influence of Regime Type on Electoral Law Formation," *Comparative Political Studies* 35, no. 2 (2002): 337–366.

did not fully remake states and their institutions, but rather appropriated pre-existing institutions nearly intact for their own protection and survival.

Evidence from a variety of countries demonstrates that the reform of coercive institutions predating a leader's tenure will be challenging, if not impossible, barring significant exogenous economic or security shocks. Historical research on coercive institutions in countries as diverse as post-Soviet Russia, Burma, Taiwan, the Philippines, Zimbabwe, Egypt, Algeria, and Turkey document coercive agencies that are particularly sticky and very successful at resisting reform due to the high financial costs as well as the security instability such a disruptive reform might cause.[18] As a result, "many a policing institution has been passed on, almost 'as is,' to newly independent states."[19]

The second assumption in the historical approach is that institutions constrain leaders' choices surrounding repressive behaviors; it is "ultimately *the institutions* that provide scripts for political processes."[20] Institutions and the constraints they impose guide the behavior of political actors when making decisions and policies. In contrast to theories wherein a leader has full autonomy to construct coercive institutions at late stages of state development, the historical approach emphasizes that leaders inherit certain institutional tools, and these tools guide what they see as threats and how they respond. To bastardize a well-known idiom, this argument rests on the belief that if a leader starts off with a hammer, all encountered threats will be treated as nails, rather than in the ability of a leader to develop a hammer in response to encountering nails.

18. Julie Anderson, *Intelligence and Democracy: A Russian case study of secret police transformation in the post-Soviet context* (PhD diss., City University of New York, 2008); Mary Callahan, *Making Enemies: War and State-Building in Burma* (Ithaca: Cornell University Press, 2003); Steven A. Cook, *Ruling But Not Governing: The Military and Political Development in Egypt, Algeria, and Turkey* (Baltimore: Johns Hopkins University Press, 2007); Elizabeth J. Perry, *Patrolling the Revolution: Worker Militias, Citizenship, and the Modern Chinese State* (Lanham: Rowman/Littlefield, 2006); Reo Matsuzaki, *Institutions by Imposition: Colonial Lessons for Contemporary State-building* (2011); Ronald J. Weitzer, *Transforming Settler States: Communal Conflict and Internal Security in Northern Ireland and Zimbabwe* (Berkeley: University of California Press, 1990).

19. Emmanuel Blanchard, "French Colonial Police," in *Encyclopedia of Criminology and Criminal Justice*, ed. Gerben Bruinsma and David Weisburd (New York: Springer, 2014), 1846.

20. Kenneth A. Shepsle, "Rational Choice Institutionalism," in *The Oxford Handbook of Political Institutions*, ed. Sarah A. Binder, R.A.W. Rhodes, and Bert A. Rockman (Oxford: Oxford University Press, 2006), 24. Emphasis added.

## French and British Colonial Projects in the Middle East

While the utility of comparing French and British colonialism has rightfully been questioned as a helpful simplifying heuristic representing variation in colonial experience, there nonetheless existed important systematic differences in the way the two powers approached colonialism. France's colonial projects in the region were ideologically imbued with a sense of moral purpose. French colonial involvement was justified by the concept of *mission civilisatrice* (in English, civilizing mission) and the idea that France had a moral duty to extend the benefits of its civilization, education program, and language in order to improve the wider world. Moreover, during the late colonial period when the Middle East was being colonized, French colonial missions were also driven by a nationalistic desire to restore France as a major world power: during the 1890s, French leaders and bureaucrats came to firmly believe that "(more) colonies—whether in the Middle East and North Africa or elsewhere—would contribute to the revival of France as a great power."[21]

For the Middle East in particular, the French maintained three semi-religious motivations for colonial involvement: the French had long been the protectors of the Catholics of the Levant under the Ottoman Empire; France's historical connection with the area went back to the Crusades; and the claim, which was popular in France, that Syrians desired French protection and civilizing. All three claims cast the French as a savior figure. These feelings of superiority gave the French brand of colonialism a "racial coloration"[22] with implications for the policies undertaken by the French. The French systems "sought to maintain the radical and juridical hierarchies upon which colonial rule was founded."[23] To accomplish this task, colonized populations were to be fully dominated and subdued, then remade in the image of the ideal French citizen.

In contrast, the British were less ideologically motivated and more focused on economic and security issues. The British did not employ any of the religious and civilizational ideological concepts used by the French

21. Peter Sluglett, "Some reflections on the nature of the British presence in Iraq (1914–1932) and the French presence in Syria (1918–1946)" in Méouchy and Sluglett, *British and French Mandates*, 111.

22. Georges Balandier, *The Sociology of Black Africa: Social Dynamics in Central Africa* (New York: Praeger, 1970).

23. Florence Bernault, *A History of Prison and Confinement in Africa* (Portsmouth, New Hampshire: Heinemann, 2003).

to justify their colonial holdings. Instead, local populations' "inferiority and lack of capacity for self-rule (rather than their potential for becoming good Englishmen) were regularly invoked as justifications for subjugating them."[24] British interests in the Middle East were generally less abstract than French ones and focused on securing new capital, raw materials, and markets. The British maintained a healthy fear of Russian and French territorial and trade encroachment, and valued territory for what it permitted in terms of access to major trade routes and India. In addition, the British colonial project worked to shore up the country's exclusive access to the oil necessary for its naval and merchant shipping fleets. Furthermore, the British were motivated to maintain an economic efficiency in governing colonial territories. From the beginning of colonial expansion, the British were concerned with maximizing resources and creating colonies that paid for themselves. This was in direct contrast to French colonial projects which frequently overspent allotted funds.[25] The difference manifested in less direct colonial interference, more strategic local partnerships, such as those between the British and tribes and families in the Gulf, and less settler colonialism than the French.

## COERCION AND THE COLONIAL PROJECT

The way in which British and French colonial projects differed in nature was reflected in a variety of institutions created to carry out these projects. The differences in European approaches to colonialism were cemented in the nature of local coercive institutions, created with heavy foreign influence. More specifically, the difference in the motivating goals and ideologies of French and British colonialism was institutionalized in colonial police and intelligence forces in three interrelated ways: the nature and level of indigenization, the intelligence gathering capabilities, and the institutional centralization of the local coercive apparatus.

First, local police forces were differently indigenized under British and French colonial rule. In French colonial systems, the local police force was never fully indigenized. Many colonies held by different European powers witnessed the evolution of foreign pacification into overt coercion into collaborative governance between locals and colonizers at the tail end of

---

24. Sluglett, "Some reflections," in Méouchy and Sluglett, *British and French Mandates*, 112.
25. Sluglett, "Some reflections," in Méouchy and Sluglett, *British and French Mandates*, 120.

colonization. But in the French empire, "no movement of indigenization proper has ever taken place in the higher ranks of policing hierarchy" due to feelings of French superiority, making the French approach closer to the Belgian than the British model.[26] In contrast, the British heavily indigenized local police forces and did so early in the colonial period. The cost-efficient approach by the British to colonial administration guided the nature of the coercive institutions created to surveil, police, and control local populations. British economic and strategic interests led to the prioritization of stability over the full domination and civilizing of local populations. As a result, British colonial forces relied more heavily on local populations and actively worked to divide, conquer, and co-opt local partners.

Second, the extent to which local coercive institutions relied on intensive intelligence gathering differed across British and French colonial rule. Intelligence gathering is a function of indigenization, which determines the supply and quality of locally gathered intelligence. French intelligence gathering lacked the meaningful connection with local informants. Instead, the French relied both on models and institutions imported or adapted from metropolitan France to the colonies—such as the gendarmerie and Paris prefecture of police designed to subdue populations of North African migrants back home[27]—as well as local hierarchies and authorities, particularly in rural areas, to police colonial populations. Even when relying on local informants, French colonial officers did not fully trust them and often undertook actions which further distanced these individuals from the local population. For example, many Maghrebi junior officers expressed frustration at the lack of promotion prospects within the racially codified hierarchy of the officer corps. In response, the French imposed even stricter segregation of Armee d'Afrique garrisons (composed of members of the French army recruited from and stationed in French North Africa) from the surrounding civilian population, further weakening local ties and thus intelligence collection abilities.[28] The racism and feelings of superiority inherent to the French colonial project created preconceived notions of what constituted a threat, and the French did not distinguish between local groups in their policing or intelligence gathering, seeing all denizens as potential enemies.

26. Blanchard, "French Colonial Police," 1842.
27. Ibid.
28. Thomas, "Intelligence States," 1053.

A feeling of superiority of French civilization contributed to a lack of understanding of local contexts, evident in surveillance reports. As Blanchard writes, "indeed, the chasm from local circles was such that intelligence services often had to resort to broad, hackneyed ideological patterns (the Communist threat, pan Arabism, the influence of foreign nations ...) which actually stood in the way of taking the full measure of protests or local separatist movements."[29] French intelligence was rife with imposed ideas driven by interactions between authorities and North African migrants in metropolitan France, and "the political polarization of metropolitan France and the spectre of Communist infiltration were super-imposed onto the entirely different political context of North Africa."[30] Thus, while the French appeared to gather extensive information about their colonial subjects,

> in times of acute political crisis, however, security personnel reverted to a simpler typology. When the colonial order was under threat, indige-nous subjects were again viewed monolithically as potentially, if not actually, hostile, rather than as differentiated, heterogenous national population among whom only a tiny minority of individuals were sedi-tious. This conflation of the dependent population into the category of potential enemy—a classic case of "othering" in the language of post-modernist scholarship—reflected the underlying structural weakness of [French] colonial states.[31]

While the intelligence gathering institutions put in place by the British were far from perfect, they were significantly more discerning and more effective at uncovering threats to colonial rule than similar institutions in their French counterparts. Before involving themselves in the Middle East, the British developed and expertly honed their intelligence gather-ing and policing skills in India. In the British Raj, effective control of the colony rested heavily on an "information order."[32] The order relied heavily on successfully tapping into pre-existing networks of informants to gather information, and thus colonial officers spent extensive time and effort cul-tivating strategic relationships with local allies. British colonial strategy further centralized and bureaucratized the intelligence gathering of local,

29. Blanchard, "French Colonial Police," 1843.
30. Thomas, "Intelligence States," 1038, 1048.
31. Ibid., 1052.
32. Christopher A. Bayly, *Empire and Information: Intelligence Gathering and Social Commu-nication in India, 1780–1870* (Cambridge: Cambridge University Press, 1999), 3–6, 365.

regional, and national governments over time to develop a more cost- and time-efficient organization.

The British used the Indian model as an example for later colonial holdings. For example, the British recruited a class of Iraqi client collaborators, which both depended upon Britain and upon which Britain depended, though the balance was obviously unequal. The strength of these relationships may have been facilitated by the length of the British presence and governance in Iraq. British colonial officers were fully integrated into Baghdad and Mosul before being granted an official mandate in 1920. By then, "Basra had been under British control for well over five years. Taxes had been collected, a modicum of civil order had been maintained, courts had been in session, and children had gone to school, all under British supervision."[33] British colonial officers viewed local collaborators as strategically important not only for governing during the mandate period, but also to ensure British interests once they inevitably departed from the region.

While main differences in intelligence gathering are evident across British and French colonies, some generalizations emerge for explaining variation *within* a given colonial type. The increased presence of European settlers in a colony led foreign powers to establish more direct rule and thus a more penetrative intelligence force relative to other colonies held by the same power. Colonial officers of all nationalities believed that indigenous populations were more likely to revolt against more invasive forms of colonialism, associated with a higher presence of foreigners, and thus both British and French coercive institutions relied relatively more heavily on existing structures to govern and gather intelligence on potential opposition in these contexts.[34]

Third and finally, colonial coercive institutions varied by level of centralization across British and French colonies as the result of and with further implications for the effectiveness of intelligence gathering and policing. Intelligence collection agencies in British territories were highly centralized at the national level, often directly under the control of an executive such as the British colonial governor who had the authority to mobilize the police against credible threats. The British also established the Colonial Police Service (CPS) to coordinate and centralize intelligence gathering across territorial holdings. In contrast, the process of analyzing intelligence was not centralized in the late French empire. Instead, local *Service de*

---

33. Bayly, *Empire and Information: Intelligence Gathering and Social Communication in India, 1780–1870*, 114.

34. Blanchard, "French Colonial Police."

*Renseignements* (SR) military intelligence services and the special police branch, the *Sûreté Générale,* worked in isolation at both the local and country levels. Multiple national institutions arose with overlap in their official duties. Often, these redundancies were intentionally institutionalized to keep checks on other intelligence collection agencies. These bodies were charged with collecting significant amounts of anthropological information to categorize the colonized, but were unable to discern whether that information was helpful for controlling the population and addressing potential threats.

The nature of French coercive institutions led to multiple threats being lumped together by the French come from North Africa. During the early 1930s in Tunisia, colonial officials linked the threat of local nationalists and pan-Arab militants with that of German and Italian propagandists, Communist International agents, and European arms traffickers. This mistake appears to have originated through the organization of colonial intelligence collection in Tunisia and its implications for collecting reliable intelligence. In the words of Thomas, "little wonder that an agency assigned to monitor illegal immigration, the loyalties of Tunisia's large Italian community, and the politics of Destourian nationalism should conflate all three into a single threat to French rule ... the supposed connections between these activities were more the product of fertile SR imagination than of hard evidence."[35]

Similarly, the systems put in place by French colonial officials to gather intelligence in Algeria fell short repeatedly. The SR's reliance on informants' reports, compounded by the diffuse nature of the intelligence community's structure and its related inability to authenticate or evaluate said reports, meant that SR and Sûreté personnel frequently sent contradictory messages to Paris about the probability of revolt in Algeria. The conclusions made by colonial officials were further convoluted by "a mixture of racial and class stereotyping" as well as French domestic political concerns regarding a growing North African migrant population.[36] In sum, the nature and structure of the French colonial intelligence system rendered it unable to distinguish between potential threats, overemphasizing minor threats as existential ones while failing to address real threats due to inefficiencies in intelligence collection and processing.

---

35. Thomas, "Intelligence States," 1050.

36. Ibid., 1049–1050, 1052. See also Thomas, *Empires of Intelligence: Security Services and Colonial Disorder After* 1914.

The interaction of levels of early indigenization, intelligence collection, and decentralization led to the creation of coercive institutions that committed predictable patterns of coercive behavior and related violence. More generally, decentralized and fragmented security apparatuses have a decreased ability to effectively collect and analyze intelligence, and this produces repression which is reactive when threats have already emerged, and which is more indiscriminate, because exact threats cannot be pinpointed. In contrast, centralized security apparatuses permit regimes to use more targeted violence against actual threats and only when necessary. Regimes with this kind of intelligence institution can identify what is a real threat and act preemptively to apprehend threatening groups before their actions escalate.[37]

The implications of institutional differences across British and French coercive institutions is evident in the nature of state violence against local populations. The decentralized nature of French institutions, creating indiscernible intelligence and a less accurate understanding of local threats, meant that the French were more violent in their policing during the late colonial period than were the British.[38] In some colonies, the French employed a "terrorization policy" through air policing, affecting whole populations instead of credibly threatening subgroups.[39] Meanwhile, the British more accurately targeted those subgroups that threatened British interests and the stability of colonial rule.

## INHERITED INSTITUTIONS AND POST-COLONIAL REPRESSION

As noted above, the existing literature agrees that choices leaders make create coercive institutions that are difficult to reform; path dependence is central to arguments about authoritarian strategies of repression and the resulting predictable patterns of state violence and control. Historical accounts simply move the starting point back in time to strategies adopted by colonial powers who oversaw the initial creation of modern coercive institutions, instead of by post-independence authoritarian leaders. Colonial coercive institutions and strategies directly determined

37. Greitens, *Dictators and their Secret Police: Coercive Institutions and State Violence.*

38. As Blanchard, "French Colonial Police," 1843 writes, "[French] colonial police forces were never known to put a strong emphasis on discipline and educating their personnel. Thus, restraining the use of force was never considered a priority, or even a reality."

39. Ibid., 1844.

subsequent independent authoritarian regimes' coercive institutions and strategies. Specifically, colonial institutional legacies account for cross-national variation in the institutional structure and level of centralization of intelligence collection, the capability to effectively collect and process intelligence, and relatedly the nature of the violence deployed against oppositional threats. This is because post-independence authoritarian leaders, like those in the Middle East, did not remake coercive and intelligence gathering institutions, but rather appropriated these institutions nearly intact for their own protection and survival.

Through this causal pathway, patterns of repression should vary by former colonial status. The nature of repression under authoritarian regimes can be divided into three ideal types. In a widespread repressive environment, a regime treats all opposition the same, and all groups are similarly exposed to state repression. In a targeted repressive environment, the regime represses only one portion of the opposition. A targeted environment may see either one or multiple parties repressed, so long as there is at least one meaningful opposition group that is not affected by state repression. Finally, an authoritarian regime may have a third option: to not use physical repression against opposition, and instead rely exclusively on controlling masses through other institutions of control, such as elections, ruling parties, and legislatures. While possible in theory, this kind of authoritarian regime does not exist in practice.

If the types of institutions adopted by colonial regimes are too entrenched for post-colonial independence leaders to reform, and a model holds in which colonial experience predicts the nature and type of state survival strategies and the shape of related institutions, then colonial legacies should account for the observable variation in post-independence authoritarian regimes' use of repression. Moreover, former French and British colonies should demonstrate meaningful variation in post-colonial patterns of state repression of opposition. Coercive institutions in former French colonies should will be more decentralized, violent, and reactionary, resulting in widespread repression, while coercive institutions in former British colonies will be more centralized, constrained in their targets, and preemptive, resulting in targeted repression. And indeed, this appears to be the case within the population of post-independent Arab republics colonized by the British and the French, outlined in table 3.1.

The notable exception in the table is Algeria, which was under French colonial influence between 1827 and 1962 but resulted in the targeted state repressive policy typical of former British colonies. In Algeria, the French

TABLE 3.1. Colonial Legacies and Repression in Arab Republics

| Country | Colonial history | Post-colonial politics | State repressive policy |
|---------|------------------|------------------------|-------------------------|
| Egypt | British | One-party state | Targeted |
| Iraq | British | One-party state | Targeted |
| Palestine | British | One-party state | Targeted |
| *Algeria* | *French* | *One-party state* | *Targeted* |
| Lebanon | French | Multi-party republic | – |
| Syria | French | One-party state | Widespread |
| Tunisia | French | One-party state | Widespread |

sought not only to implement their typical civilizing mission and to maintain strategic interests but also to extract significant economic resources, and thus administered the colony differently than their other holdings. Algeria was considered to be a part of France and incorporated more directly into the French economy, and it became a major French settler colony.[40] Both of these policies contrasted sharply from French policy in other colonies with implications for the country's resulting institutions and repressive environment.

Predictable patterns of state repression—correlated with former colony status, beginning at independence, and continuing over the course of the following decades—suggest that these institutional legacies shape leaders' use of repression against opposition as a survival strategy. Ultimately, targeted or widespread coercive institutions prevailed and are evident when viewing the full course of each country's post-independence repressive histories as a unit. Thus, the comparison of Tunisia, a former French colony, and Egypt, a former British colony, as the main cases in this book captures inherited variation in repressive strategies. In the cases under consideration here, Egypt displays a pattern of targeted state repression between independence and the 2011 uprisings, while in Tunisia, a pattern of widespread state repression emerges during the same time period. The remainder of the chapter outlines the history of Egypt's and Tunisia's coercive institutions to demonstrate their origins, path dependence, and continuity through independence.

40. John Ruedy, *Modern Algeria: The Origins and Development of a Nation* (Bloomington: Indiana University Press, 1992); Fiona Barclay, Charlotte Ann Chopin, and Martin Evans, "Introduction: Settler Colonialism and French Algeria," *Settler Colonial Studies* 8, no. 2 (2018): 115–130.

## Coercive Institutions in Tunisia

Prior to the 2010–2011 uprisings, Tunisia possessed three institutions responsible for monitoring and repressing domestic political opposition. The first was the Directorate of State Security housed under the Ministry of the Interior, which relied on human intelligence to monitor domestic political threats. The second was the National Guard. The National Guard's Directorate of Intelligence and Investigations (DII) was primarily in charge of monitoring external threats, although the regime used its intelligence to inform domestic repression as well. The third and final agency was the Presidential Security Sub-Directorate of Intelligence (PSSDI). After coming to power in a 1987 coup, Ben Ali separated the Presidential Security Guard from the Minister of the Interior to strengthen the organization's attachment and loyalty directly to the president. The PSG was in charge of the General Directorate of Presidential Security and Protection of Prominent Officials (GDPSPPO), and the PSSDI had its own system of intelligence gathering focused on domestic threats deemed critical to the regime's survival.

### HISTORICAL DEVELOPMENT

French influence on Tunisian coercive institutions began with the official protectorate, established in 1881. In May of that year, representatives of the French republic and the Tunisian bey, Mohamed as-Sadiq, signed the Treaty of Bardo. Prior to the treaty, a French expeditionary force numbering 36,000 invaded Tunisia in reaction to a raid by one of its tribes into Algeria. This was an early demonstration of how French interests in Tunisia were driven by its strategic location and the importance of Algeria in the larger French empire. The French withdrew these troops at the conclusion of the first treaty.[41] The 1883 Convention of al-Marsa, signed by the same parties, extended the initial agreement. The treaties maintained the bey as absolute monarch and an independent structure for the local government, but contained a central clause which obligated the bey to undertake "such administrative, judicial, and financial reforms as the French government may deem useful."

41. Noureddine Jebnoun, *Tunisia's National Intelligence: Why "Rogue Elephants" Fail to Reform* (Washington, D. C.: New Academic Publishing, 2017).

Through these agreements, the French remade the Tunisian coercive apparatus in its image. The French reorganized the Tunisian military along the lines of the French standing army. A general census was conducted in 1883 in order to begin conscription into the military. However, these conscripts were not to be employed in high-level posts but rather as field soldiers, a practice that would continue throughout the protectorate period.[42] As for local policing, the French replicated the gendarmerie of Paris, a highly militarized police unit largely focused on protest policing, in its North African holdings, which was similarly dominated by French citizens in higher ranks.

As the protectorate continued, the Tunisian monarchy increasingly ceded more control of national defense and internal security to the French colonial and military authorities. The French Resident General was the top colonial administrator and civil authority in charge of internal security, in both its criminal and its political aspects. Tunisia's first modern police force was established as a section of the French police (*Sûreté Générale*, later *Sûreté Nationale*) and paramiliary gendarmerie (*Garde Républicaine*). Staffed almost entirely by mainland French officers, these forces struggled to gather relevant and reliable information from reluctant Tunisian informants, their communications often limited to phrasebook Arabic.[43] From 1929, the gendarmerie was reorganized to correspond to Tunisia's existing administrative divisions, and reassigned to focus on rural policing and the needs of the *contrôleurs civils*, French military governors assigned to each of Tunisia's five regions.[44]

The increasing decentralization and institutional overlap that came to define the Tunisian coercive apparatus corresponded with the way in which the French policed other parts of their empire, notably Indochina. Coercive institutions in French colonies were constantly reorganized based on an overarching desire to govern rather than simply occupy or administer colonial territories. By 1916, the colonial inspectorate of the Indochina federation had nine distinct institutions in addition to the indigenous

---

42. Anderson, *State and Social Transformation*, 5.

43. Martin Thomas, *Violence and Colonial Order: Police, Workers and Protest in the European Colonial Empires, 1918–1940. Critical Perspectives on Empire* (Cambridge: Cambridge University Press, 2012), 108.

44. Martin Thomas, "The Gendarmerie, Information Collection, and Colonial Violence in French North Africa Between the Wars," *Historical Reflections/Réflexions Historiques* 36, no. 2 (2010): 85.

police operating at a local level, which proved to be a logistical hindrance for effective policing. As a result, "the lines separating civil police from gendarmeries and paramilitary militias from regular army units, let alone workplace security guards and armed overseers, were often crossed."[45]

Tunisia's first dedicated intelligence agencies were established in the early 1930s in response to mounting political and labor activism. In an attempt to improve the situation, a general intelligence section (*Section de Centralisation du Renseignement*) was established in Tunis in May 1930, plus regional surveillance posts "at Tunisia's most sensitive strategic points: Bizerta, La Goulette, Ghardimaou, Ben Gardane, Sfax, and Sousse," which focused on frontier surveillance.[46] In July 1932, the Tunis Residency created a *police spéciale* (secret police) to coordinate with French and Algerian *Sûreté*. These intelligence agencies focused less on gathering accurate information about indigenous Tunisian political activism and more on counterespionage, especially regarding international conspiracies connecting Tunisian nationalists to foreign agents.[47] In the interwar period, policing in Tunisia became increasingly focused on domestic political repression. The depression struck Tunisia hard, and the post-WWI rise of nationalism saw the rise to prominence of the pro-independence Destour movement. Colonial authorities responded to nationalist protests and labor action with violent repression, crushing demonstrations with the police and a new motorized riot control force (*Garde Républicaine Mobile*, or GRM), as well as French Army troops.[48] From its inception, the colonial police were dominated by French citizens, but increasingly incorporated indigenous Tunisians over time, who would continue in service after independence. Both gendarmes and police began to incorporate more indigenous recruits during the 1930s, though they remained subordinate to French officers. In the 1930s, the French administration increasingly recruited native Tunisian gendarmes and special auxiliaries to improve its efficacy in rural areas where French fluency was uncommon.[49]

45. Thomas, *Violence and Colonial Order*, 146.
46. Thomas, *Empires of Intelligence: Security Services and Colonial Disorder After* 1914, 283.
47. Ibid., 267, 283–285.
48. Blanchard, "French Colonial Police," 1840.
49. Thomas, "Gendarmerie," 85.

## COERCIVE INSTITUTIONAL PATH DEPENDENCE
## AFTER COLONIALISM

France maintained control of policing and intelligence gathering until independence in 1956, when Habib Bourguiba became the first president of independent Tunisia and created a Tunisian Ministry of Interior to command the security forces. Bourguiba did not have any "rational or planned policy" plans for reforming the intelligence and security apparatus he inherited from the French. Instead, the nascent regime relied on "personnel who served under the French colonial rulers … French civil servants, like many other Europeans who belonged to the French administration under the protectorate's colonial regime, consented to work in Tunisia's different departments within the framework of 'technical cooperation.'"[50] Bourguiba formally reorganized the Signals Intelligence service, which was attached to the new Office of the Minister of Interior, but did not fundamentally change the structure or mandate of the institution, and relied on the legal framework put in place by the French.[51]

Significantly, the colonial security forces constituted under French authority provided a direct model for the new Tunisian police, which adopted the organizational structures and tactics of the colonial forces and continued to receive "technical assistance" from French advisers embedded in Tunisian institutions. Within the Ministry's purview were the national police force and gendarmerie, as well as the secret police, renamed the *Direction de la Sûreté de l'État* (DSE), which would be abolished only after the revolution in 2011. The DSE was the clear inheritance of the French colonial secret police, adopting its methods and tactics, as well as its legacy of the extensive and widespread use of torture. At independence, among the first tasks of the Tunisian police was to carry out an aggressive campaign of repression against the supporters of Bourguiba's rival, Salah Ben Youssef. The campaign was assisted by French security officials and supplemented by militias affiliated with the ruling party, legally authorized to conduct vigilante operations by beylical decree. Far from a clean break with the past, Tunisia's police instead represented a "Tunisification" of the existing colonial coercive apparatus.

50. Jebnoun, *Rogue Elephants*, 14.

51. Final report of the Tunisian Commission for Truth and Dignity, *Tafkik Munthumat al-Istibdad (Dismantling the System of Repression)* 2019, 63. http://www.ivd.tn/rapport/doc/11.pdf.

In 1967, the regime undertook a second reorganization which uni-fied the police and national guard into one organization called the Gen-eral Directorate of National Security (GDNS) within the Ministry of the Interior. However, it further decentralized intelligence collection when it established a second set of anti-riot police, the Brigade of Public Order (BOP), which became critical for repressing students and organized labor demonstrations. The BOP drew officers from the police established under the French. Al-Tahir Balkhujah, tasked with undertaking the establishment of the BOP, acknowledged that one of the most important challenges he faced during his tenure was the need to improve security officers' analysis and reporting assessment skills; he was quoted as saying, "Tunisia's security apparatus draws its illegitimate legitimacy from the regime itself by target-ing its perceived and imaginary opponents, tailoring intelligence reports that reflect the authoritarian mindset of the leadership, and supporting its preconceived policy,"[52] suggesting that Tunisia had inherited problematic intelligence and police institutions.

The inefficient collection and use of intelligence continued to plague Tunisia under Bourguiba. In 1978, a crisis erupting from a general strike[53] "showed the failure of the intelligence services and the security appa-ratus to better understand and assess society's demands and to provide the government with relevant information with regard to policymaking in order to ease tension and prevent social upheaval."[54] A second major intelligence failure occurred in January 1980 and demonstrates that the supposed "police state" was not collecting effective intelligence: the state failed to detect Libyan insurgents who spent three weeks in the coun-try before launching their assault and mobilizing an insurrection in the mining city of Gafsa. In response to these failures, the Bourguiba regime undertook a final superficial reorganizing of the Interior Ministry in 1984, creating the Coordination Directorate of Specialized Services (CDSS), charged with monitoring and policing elite-based mobilized opposition. However, rather that improving the capabilities of the coercive apparatus, this move appears to have simply added another layer of bureaucracy to an already crowded chain of command.

52. Jebnoun, *Rogue Elephants*, 17.

53. On January 25, 1978, state security forces and workers violently clashed during a general strike and demonstrations organized by the General Union of Tunisian Workers, resulting in the death or injury of hundreds of civilians. The incident became known as "Black Friday."

54. Jebnoun, *Rogue Elephants*, 19.

Bourguiba's successor Ben Ali had served as the head of intelligence under the former president beginning in 1984. During his presidency, he relied heavily on overlapping and opaque intelligence agencies, while further decentralizing and creating redundancies within the state's coercive apparatus. One of Ben Ali's first acts as president was to dissolve the National Defense Council and replace it with a National Security Council (NSC). The mission of the NSC was "to collect, study, analyze, and assess all information and security data related to national security within the realms of domestic policy, foreign affairs, and defense policy in order to protect the state's internal and external security and consolidate its foundations." This brought together the Cabinet of Ministers and created seven special intelligence committees to aid the president in decision making. While in theory this decision should have centralized intelligence collection, it did not. Ben Ali's "reforms" further decentralized an already decentralized system.

Ben Ali relied on three separate agencies for intelligence on domestic threats and political opposition. The first was the Directorate of State Security (DSS), a direct descendant of the BOP. The DSS was housed in the CDSS, under the GDSS in the GDNS, in the MoI. The DSS collected intelligence which then the General Intelligence Directorate (GID) used to act.[55] The second was the General Director of the National Guard's Directorate of Intelligence and Investigations (DII). Though officially the DII was primarily in charge of external threats, Ben Ali used the information it collected abroad to inform his regime's approach to domestic threats such as Islamism as well. The third and final agency was the Presidential Security Sub-Directorate of Intelligence (PSSDI). After coming to power in a coup, Ben Ali separated the Presidential Security Guard from the Minister of the Interior. The PSG was in charge of the General Directorate of Presidential Security and Protection of Prominent Officials (GDPSPPO), and the PSSDI served as its own system of intelligence, gathering what it deemed critical for the regime's survival.[56]

55. As noted in Jebnoun *Rogue Elephants* 57, "the DSS had its own sophisticated informers' networks also known as Human intelligence (HUMINT), which penetrated the country's social fabric as well as the bureaucracy. The recruitment and motivations of informers discredited the value of the information.... Moreover, the DSS's reliance on torture and heavy-handed treatment distorted the information process."

56. Jebnoun, *Rogue Elephants*. See also Amnesty International, *Tunisia: Prolonged Incommunicado Detension and Torture* (AI Index: MDE 30/40/92) March 1992, available at https://www.amnesty.org/download/Documents/192000/mde300041992en.pdf.

To collect intelligence on domestic oppositional threats, the regime relied heavily on spies—here, meaning individuals unaffiliated with opposition groups whose role is to gather information in a covert manner—and citizens policing each other, which differed significantly in practice from relying on informants embedded within groups. In addition to the CDSS, the tourist security directorate within the National Guard was also tasked with collecting information on the legally recognized members of the opposition. To monitor these actors, local intelligence operatives recruited the waiters, restaurant owners, and staff employed in the cafes and hotels frequented by the opposition for meetings. The intelligence provided by these spies was then incorporated into intelligence reports.[57] The RCD Party structure served a similar purpose, as a means through which to collect intelligence on party members through reports and surveillance from other party members.[58] In short, the purpose of the RCD was to infiltrate and surveil "opponents, everywhere, and at all times."[59]

The intelligence failures that challenged the Bourguiba regime continued to plague Ben Ali as "the failure to assess and understand the threats within Tunisia's geopolitical regional context became a constant characteristic."[60] These failures were a function of the continued decentralization and institutional overlap of the coercive apparatus. Significant "manipulation of intelligence" resulted from "mistrust between services and failure to produce professional assessments. The lack of information sharing between different services and the vertical siloing of these services weakened their understanding of the intelligence dynamism and its inherent risks and uncertainties." Ben Ali further manipulated the inherited divisions among the country's various intelligence agencies. For example, he turned military security intelligence into "a tool tasked with monitoring the Tunisian Armed Forces' internal security and with gathering information on the private lives of military personnel, including his comrades, with the purpose of blackmailing them when Ben Ali thought it would be to his advantage to do so."[61] The similarly decentralized nature of the RCD

57. Jebnoun *Rogue Elephants*, 37.

58. Béatrice Hibou, *The Force of Obedience: The Political Economy of Repression in Tunisia* (Malden, MA: Polity Press, 2011).

59. The final report of Tunisia's Truth and Dignity Commission outlines the decentralized and hierarchical organization of the RCD's role in informing on private citizens in great detail. http://www.ivd.tn/rapport/doc/11.pdf, pages 13–46.

60. Jebnoun, *Rogue Elephants*, 24–25.

61. Ibid., 30.

Party apparatus did not create good intelligence. Instead, as Hibou has noted more generally about the regime's approach, these diffuse organizations permitted the appearance of constant surveillance while the regime was simultaneously unable to penetrate society in order to collect useful intelligence and identify credible threats.[62]

In summary, the decentralized intelligence institutions which were inherited from the French and persisted under Tunisia's two post-independent authoritarian rulers were defined by three characteristics. First, the system relied on the appearance of constant surveillance rather than accurate information gathering. Second and relatedly, the system relied on ineffective spies drawn from the local population instead of informants embedded with in groups. Finally, the Tunisian coercive apparatus was plagued by infighting among multiple, overlapping agencies, rather than a centralized intelligence and policing supervisory body. All of this created ineffective intelligence for the country's repressive institutions, and forced both Bourguiba and Ben Ali to strike at any perceived threat, not just the credible ones. In line with existing theories of how institutional organization conditions the nature of state violence, the "increasing [and widespread] oppression went hand in hand with the constant reorganization"[63] of the Tunisian coercive apparatus, which was diffuse, decentralized, and included many redundancies.

## Coercive Institutions in Egypt

In contemporary Egypt, repression of domestic political opposition is performed by the State Security Investigations Services (in Arabic *Mabahith Amn al-Dawla*, known as SSIS.). The organization is the main security and intelligence apparatus of Egypt's Minister of the Interior and is headquartered in Cairo, Egypt. Though it was officially dissolved in March 2011 following the uprisings, it is unclear whether the institution was meaningfully dismantled. After the 2013 coup, the organization was renamed Egyptian Homeland Security.

SSIS's intelligence and policing, focused on domestic threats, constituted one third of the Egyptian intelligence community. In addition, the General Intelligence Directorate (*Jihaz al-Mukhabarat al-'Amma*, popularly referred to as *al-Mukhabarat*) was responsible for national security intelligence, which includes both domestic and foreign targets due to a

---

62. Hibou, *Force of Obedience.*
63. Jebnoun, *Rogue Elephants*, 35.

focus on counterterrorism broadly defined. Because of the way in which terrorism labels are often politically motivated, there exists some overlap in the missions of SSIS and the GID. The third agency is the Military Intelligence Services, which largely focuses on foreign threats.

## HISTORICAL DEVELOPMENT

The British occupied Egypt in 1882 with the expressed goal of securing the Suez Canal route to India, and nearly immediately declared the police system desperately inadequate and in need of reform.[64] At the same time, the British dissolved the standing 100,000-man-strong Egyptian army, lowering its standing power to 10,000 for several decades. British garrisons also returned to the barracks, only to be brought out in moments of crisis, like the 1919 revolution. The Ministry of Interior would become the most important coercive institution in Egypt. The British occupation elevated security concerns from a local or provincial issue into a matter of national policy and introduced the phrase *al-amn al-'amm* (public security).[65] As colonial authorities worked to extend the power of the state deeper into Egyptian society, the responsibilities of the Ministry of Interior grew. The MoI's expansive mandate included "the police and the local and provincial officials, the mamurs [provincial governors] and the mudirs [district administrators] ... public health and many features of the urban life of the country."[66]

In 1890, British reforms targeted the *ghaffir*, or village guard, seeking to emulate the village policing model in use in India.[67] Notably, British administrators called for arming all ghaffirs, ensuring that the encroaching hand of the state would be an armed one. Next, a major reorganization of the MoI in 1894 established powerful British oversight of the police. Yet despite these and other measures intended to expand the police force, the performance of the Egyptian police remained abysmal by typical policing output measurements: "Under British control, defects in the police such as low pay, harsh discipline, and maltreatment of suspects persisted, and ordinary

64. Harold Tollefson, *Policing Islam: The British Occupation of Egypt and the Anglo-Egyptian Struggle over Control of the Police, 1882–1914* (Greenwood Publishing Group, 1999), 1.

65. Nathan Brown, "Brigands and State Building: The Invention of Banditry inModern Egypt," *Comparative Studies in Society and History* 32, no. 2 (1990): 267.

66. Robert L. Tignor, *Modernisation and British Colonial Rule in Egypt, 1882–1914.* (Princeton University Press, 1966), 70.

67. Tollefson, *Policing Islam*, 53.

crime increased."[68] Rather than reducing crime and improving public security, the effect of British reforms was simply to strengthen colonial oversight over local populations.

By the turn of the twentieth century, Egypt's nationalist movement had developed into a serious threat, and the British discovered a critical new mission for the police: collecting political intelligence. In September 1910, the colonial administration created the Central Special Office (CSO) as the country's first official secret police and intelligence organization. Official documents described the unit as "a thoroughly organized service for the collection of all information regarding Political Secret Societies— individuals known, or believed to be, Political Agitators."[69] The CSO relied on data collected from informant networks managed by plainclothes police officers employed by the department. Over the remainder of the British period, the collection and analysis of intelligence relevant to the CSO's work was increasingly centralized. After the 1919 revolution, the CSO came under the jurisdiction of the MoI, and a new ministry-level Special Section was created to oversee the collection and analysis of police intelligence.

Unlike the regular police, the political police found success by employing an informant-based intelligence gathering approach that produced reliable data about opposition threats. For example, in January 1911, only five months after its creation, the CSO issued a comprehensive report on secret organizations. In 1912, it successfully monitored and apprehended an assassination plot against the British consul general, Lord Kitchener, and the Egyptian prime minister. And in July 1914, it foiled a murder plot against the Egyptian monarch.[70] The CSO even recruited an informant in the elusive Vengeance Society, the secret movement of the nationalist Wafd Party, and was able to monitor its activities.

Despite Egypt's formal independence in 1922, British domination of domestic politics persisted. In this period, the *mukhabarat* remained focused on the threats to the Egyptian government that would also challenge British influence. The case of Egypt's nascent Islamist movement exemplifies the CSO's ability fo effectively monitor political opposition forces. Around 1930, the CSO began to monitor a new Islamist movement

68. Tollefson, *Policing Islam*, 553–554.

69. As cited in Owen L. Sirrs, *A History of the Egyptian Intelligence Service: A History of the Mukhabarat*, 1910–2009 (Routledge, 2010), 8.

70. Eliezer Tauber, "Egyptian Secret Societies, 1911," *Middle Eastern Studies* 42, no. 3 (2006): 605–610; Malak Badrawi, *Political Violence in Egypt 1910–1925: Secret Societies, Plots and Assassinations* (Routledge, 2014), 86.

called the Society of Muslim Brothers. As the society's clandestine Special Organization laid plans to infiltrate the government, solidify contacts with sympathetic military officers, and establish the foundations for an eventual coup, there were CSO informants watching at every turn. In November 1948, the police moved preemptively against the group: the movement was officially banned; its cadres were arrested, interrogated, and tortured; its assets were confiscated; and its leaders, including Hassan al-Banna, were subjected to heightened surveillance. A large part of the efficacy of Egypt's political police derives from its form and level of indigenization. From the beginning, the political police had relied on local informants and plainclothes Egyptian police. After the Anglo-Egyptian Treaty of 1936, the Interior Ministry and political police were further Egyptianized. These thousands of Egyptians employed in the state coercive apparatus, first by the British and later by the nascent post-independence government, ensured the institutional continuity of Egyptian policing after the British withdrawal. The bureaucrats, spies, and policemen of the Ministry of Interior formed a technical elite who were "responsible for installing the structure of the modern state under the mandate period" and "carry[ing] the state through the independence period."[71]

World War II was a defining moment for the Egyptian Ministry of Interior. The contemporary mode of governing via continual constitutional state of emergency was first established at this time when the Egyptian government emulated a long-standing colonial policing practice. The state of emergency extended extraordinary powers to the central government in the name of national security and interest, and the MoI was central to the carrying out of a continual state of emergency. Indeed, the army was sidelined after the fall of Ali Mahir's government in 1940, leaving the MoI as "the key institution in the Egyptian government's conception and enforcement of public security"; though the military would play an important political role, there was a clear bureaucratic hierarchy for domestic intelligence and policing. The emergency framework became routine during and after the war as a consequence of the "increased pace of commerce and political life throughout Egypt and particularly in urban areas before and during the war prompted the Egyptian state to expand its intelligence collection and police presence."

---

71. Méouchy and Sluglett, "General Introduction," in *British and French Mandates,* 17.

## INSTITUTIONAL PATH DEPENDENCE
## AFTER COLONIALISM

The Free Officers' Revolution of 1952 formally ended the monarchy, established Egypt as an independent republic, and led to the eviction of the British from Egyptian lands. This moment represented a potential turning point for the coercive apparatus. Before seizing power, the Free Officers had consistently called for the dismantling of the political police, already detested by Egyptians, and they reiterated this policy demand after taking power. For example, two days after the coup "on July 25, the new civilian prime minister declared the army would 'terminate the system of political police and informers' because it was 'unhealthy' and produced 'bogus information.'"[72] Later that year, the new regime announced the abolition of the political police at the governorate level (Special Branches) and within the Interior Ministry (Special Section).

However, and perhaps unsurprisingly, internal security soon proved to be just as great a concern for the Free Officers as it had been for the British. Moreover, the new regime attracted its most threatening opposition from many of the same sources faced by the former regime: dissident military officers, communists, and the Muslim Brotherhood, with the added bonus of loyalists to the old regime. Thus, instead of following through with the announced dismantling of the coercive apparatus, the Free Officers expanded and enhanced existing institutions, further centralizing intelligence collection and analysis. While publicly discussing the termination of the political police, the new "prime minister told a journalist that the political police was a 'remarkable instrument of government'—an instrument apparently worth preserving."[73] Behind the scenes, the regime set to work strengthening the capabilities of the *mukhabarat*.

One of the new regime's earliest decisions was to reincarnate the political police apparatus under its modern name, the GID (in Arabic *Mabahith al-Amn*). While covering the same missions as its predecessor, the GID enjoyed expanded security powers and capabilities, and more direct control of the intelligence collection process. The new organization was led by Zakaria Muhi al-Din and supervised by a cadre of military intelligence officers, all trained under British supervision in Egyptian war colleges. The GID was characterized as quite similar to the preceeding CSO, as there was

72. Sirrs, *Egyptian Intelligence Service*, 25.
73. Ibid.

"continuity between the old political police and the GID in organizational structure, mission, and staffing. The GID also assumed control over the archives of the old Special Section."[74] The GID continued many CSO practices and expanded its use of torture against a growing number of political detainees.[75]

Nasser's successors further strengthened and centralized the coercive apparatus, while retaining its two characteristic features: first, that of gathering intelligence through a large network of informants, and second, that of significant targeted police repression, including harassment, arrest, interrogation, prolonged detention, and torture. Under Sadat the GID took its current name. However, the reorganization did not affect its core mission, which was mainly fighting "political crime."[76] Sadat reinforced the SSIS's orientation toward internal security, while strengthening the capabilities that made the GID a potent political force.

Trends in the security sector continued in like manner under president Hosni Mubarak. In the 1980s and '90s, domestic intelligence capabilities were further enhanced and centralized, but retained their modus operandi. Informants pervaded "all levels of government and the public sector," and the "harassment and intimidation of political opponents continued."[77] The coercive apparatus faced a series of tests, beginning in 1986 with the mutiny of thousands of conscripted riot police from the Central Security Forces (CSF, in Arabic *Quwwat al-Amn al-Markazi*).[78] Mubarak crushed the revolt with military airstrikes and artillery bombardments, and consolidated his control over the institutions of state repression through purges across the MoI. Beginning in 1992, the regime faced an unprecedented urban and rural insurgency. The regime's counterinsurgency strategy relied heavily on the SSIS, with its brutal interrogation tactics and network of informers. Intelligence successes, tied to the intensive use of informants, were soon credited with turning the tide against the militants.[79]

---

74. Sirrs, *Egyptian Intelligence Service*, 31.

75. Barbara Zollner, "Prison Talk: the Muslim Brotherhood's Internal Struggle during Gamal Abdel Nasser's Persecution, 1954 to 1971," *International Journal of Middle East Studies* 39, no. 3 (2007): 413.

76. Sirrs, *Egyptian Intelligence Service*, 163.

77. Ibid., 162, 182.

78. The CSF includes approximately 325,000 short-term conscripts, used primarily for riot control and intimidation. As Sirrs (*Egyptian Intelligence Service*, 162) writes, "if the SSIS comprised the eyes, ears, and interrogator of the regime, the CSF was its instrument of brute force."

79. Sirrs, *Egyptian Intelligence Service*, 158–168.

In short, Egypt's coercive apparatus has shown a striking resilience across leaders and regimes, from the colonial period through independence and across multiple presidencies. Today, the Egyptian police remain a formidable instrument of state repression. Its size, in terms of budget and personnel, is a state secret, but it is clear that this organization has a nationwide presence with an officer cadre numbering in the many thousands. Egyptians from all walks of life serve as informants, and these informants remain vital to the pervasive domestic intelligence system. Torture remains in widespread use across the security forces, as documented by human rights organizations, journalists, and even Egypt's high court. The regime uses its vast but centralized intelligence operation to target meaningful political threats, though developments since 2011 demonstrate it is possible for the state to expand its use of force.

Central to this continuity is the institutional path dependence of the MoI and security forces, which have remained largely intact for the last one hundred years. Organizational continuity has created path dependence in police personnel, organization, and methods. Moreover, the coercive apparatus has maintained a consistent approach to political control, based on pervasive human intelligence operations and a divide-and-rule strategy for countering potential threats. Unfortunately, the lasting legacy of Britain's seventy-year occupation was not deliverance from the scourges of criminality and public disorder, but rather "the creation of a secret police system to monitor, harass, intimidate torture and even extort money from the Egyptian population."[80]

## Conclusion

This chapter outlined a historical approach for understanding how contemporary authoritarian regimes come to repress in different ways, rooted in coercive institutions inherited from the colonial period. In the next chapter, I document how variation in coercive institutions translated into targeted and widespread repression of political opposition groups in contemporary Egypt and Tunisia. While the inherited nature of institutions renders repression somewhat exogenous to the strategies of post-independence authoritarian leaders, it does not fully strip rulers of agency, nor does it preclude shifts in regime ideology or targets. For example, rulers in both Egypt and Tunisia were able to decrease the level of repression during periods

80. Ibid., 194–195.

of strategic liberalization. For both the Mubarak and Ben Ali regimes, this occurred most noticeably when the rulers came to power, following moments of heightened repression under their predecessors. In addition, the victims of targeted repression shifted in Egypt under different rulers; Nasser and Mubarak targeted the Brotherhood while co-opting secular opposition, while Sadat co-opted the Brotherhood and attacked their competition. However, as Brownlee observed in Egypt, whatever deviations might occur during a given period "easily slipped away. And they easily slipped away because the 'openings' of that earlier decade had no institutional basis, coming as they did solely at the discretion of the regime."[81] The history of coercive institutions in Egypt and Tunisia confirms that inherited institutions significantly constrain authoritarian leaders' behaviors in important and predictable ways, with more continuity than change over time and across regimes.

81. Jason Brownlee, "The Decline of Pluralism in Mubarak's Egypt," *Journal of Democracy* 13, no. 4 (2002): 8.

# 4

# Targeted and Widespread Repression in Authoritarian Regimes

This chapter focuses on the book's main independent variable: the nature of repression under authoritarian regimes. It also introduces the main political players in the stories that follow. I first present a typology of authoritarian repertoires of repression, as a generalizable way of thinking about variation in repression. Next, the chapter turns to the authoritarian party systems in Egypt and Tunisia. I outline the ruling parties in Tunisia and Egypt and what constituted the democratic opposition under the Ben Ali and Mubarak regimes. The opposition categories I use serve to simplify presentation of an otherwise unwieldy collection of opposition actors, and differ slightly across cases; for example, Tunisia had significantly more parties that were directly descendant from the ruling party than in Egypt. Most importantly, the categories are intended to demonstrate that both countries' opposition included parties representing a wide array of political platforms across the religious-secular axis. I then document the different repertoires of repression used by each regime against its democratic opposition. The divergences have important implications for my categorizing of Tunisia as a widespread repressive regime and of Egypt as a targeted repressive regime. Chapters 5 and 6 cover implications of the variation in repressive regimes for polarization among opposition actors.

TABLE 4.1. A Typology of Authoritarian Repression

| Targeted | | Widespread |
|---|---|---|
| Different experiences of repression between groups | | Similar experiences of repression across multiple opposition groups |
| *More Targeted* | *Less Targeted* | |
| 1 of 10 groups repressed | 4–6 of 10 groups repressed | 10 out of 10 groups repressed |

## A Typology of Authoritarian Repression

By definition, all authoritarian regimes repress their opposition, but the way in which they do so varied across cases. I define the form of repression utilized by authoritarian regimes in terms of how many opposition groups are affected by the regime's behavior, as a function of the total number of mobilized opposition parties. What is important about this for the first stage of my argument is how a given repressive environment affects groups differently within the same authoritarian regime, shedding light on context in a manner which influences politically relevant identities.

Some authoritarian regimes employ widespread repression against the entire spectrum of political opposition actors. Tunisia serves as an example of widespread repression, as all mobilized opposition groups were affected by repression in a similar manner. Other authoritarian regimes use what I term targeted repression, in which they single out some opposition groups while permitting others to exist largely undisturbed and even possibly compete for a small and highly controlled slice of the electorate. In the case studies that follow, Egypt serves as a case of targeted repression, in which one opposition group is targeted while others are not. The analytical importance of these categories is that they measure the extent to which repressive experiences are shared across opposition groups, or whether they are concentrated within a subset of the opposition. In a widespread repressive environment, members of all opposition groups are arrested, exiled, and put under surveillance. In a targeted environment, members of only some groups experience this treatment.

While I use a coarse typology in this book between targeted and widespread regimes, we might also think of a number of subcategories of targeted repressive regimes, where different combinations of some (but not all) opposition groups are repressed. For example, imagine an authoritarian regime in which there are ten opposition parties. In a widespread system, all ten of these parties will be repressed. In a highly targeted system, perhaps one of ten parties will be repressed. In a less targeted system, four, five, or six parties might be repressed.

## Authoritarian Party Systems in Tunisia and Egypt

### RULING PARTIES

Prior to the 2010–2011 uprisings, both Tunisia and Egypt constituted electoral authoritarian regimes.[1] As such, both regimes were concentrated around a single ruling party which was closely affiliated if not synonymous with the regime. In each country, the ruling party regularly won inflated percentages in national elections and functioned as a regime-serving institution for governance, the co-optation of dissent, and the surveillance of citizens. In Tunisia, this party was the *Rassemblement Constitutionnel Démocratique* (RCD). The party was founded in 1934 by a group of Tunisian nationalists under the French protectorate.[2] In 2010, the party had 7,500 local cells, 2,200 professional cells, and two million members, incorporating nearly one in every five Tunisians.[3] The RCD's decentralized, diffuse structure was effective at projecting the appearance of an omnipresent party-state throughout the country, but complicated the funneling of locally collected surveillance on members and opposition activities to higher intelligence institutions through party institutions, as demonstrated in the previous chapter. On March 9, 2011, a court order officially dissolved the party and liquidated its assets following the uprising.

In Egypt, the National Democratic Party (NDP) served as the country's ruling party. The NDP emerged from the country's first ruling party, the Arab Socialist Union (*al-Ittihad al-Ishtiraki al-'Arabi*; ASU).[4] The ruling party was conceived as an institution to create a popular base for the regime and to bring together political dissent within one framework, which it essentially did until the advent of semi-political pluralism in 1976. In 1977, then-president Anwar Sadat passed Law 40 regulating the formulation of political parties. The law legalized the establishment of opposition parties and carved the ASU into three smaller parties created from different "platforms" contained within the larger organization. The NDP was

1. Schedler, "The Menu of Manipulation."

2. The RCD was first known as the *Nouveau Parti Libéral Constitutionnel*, or Neo-Destour (from the Arabic *dustur* for constitution), from 1934 to 1964, and then as the *Parti Socialiste Destourien* (PSD) until 1988.

3. Hibou, *Force of Obedience*, 86–93.

4. The ASU was first known as the Liberation Rally from 1952 to 1956 and the National Union from 1956 to 1962.

drawn from the centrist platform and became the country's new ruling party. The ASU's right platform became the Liberal Socialist Union (*Hizb al-ʿAhrar al-Ishtirakiyyin*), and its left platform became the National Progressive Unionist Party known as *Hizb al-Tagammu* (known as Tagammu) and headed by former Free Officer Khaled Mohieddin.

## THE DEMOCRATIC OPPOSITION

Beginning in the late 1970s, the regimes of many Middle East countries initiated controlled political liberalization. This period was notable for the establishment of regular, semi-competitive elections and political opposition groups tolerated by the regime. However, these developments did not signal an impending democratization.[5] Instead, authoritarian elections were intended to release pressure for reform. Following economic crises and the anti-regime mass mobilizations they engendered, organized opposition emerged across the region in the mid-1970s. Controlled liberalization promised to streamline and co-opt these opposition groups through tightly controlled campaigns and fraudulent ballots. As regimes experimented with liberalization, democratic opposition parties became more visible in the regional political sphere, though many parties predated liberalization and simply began to participate formally at this time.

As outlined in chapter 1, I define the opposition as "an institution located within a political system but outside the realm of governance that has decisive organizational capacities and engages in competitive interactions with the incumbents of a political regime based on a minimum degree of mutual acceptance."[6] As defined, the opposition takes a specific organizational form, that of political parties. In authoritarian regimes, opposition parties challenge the ruling party and regime's political platform through democratic means, participating in elections when possible and rejecting the use of violence.[7] I use the terms opposition and democratic opposition interchangeably. In the following two sections, I outline which parties constituted the democratic opposition under the Ben Ali and Mubarak regimes in Egypt and Tunisia, respectively, between the 1980s and 2010–2011 uprising.

5. Korany, Brynen, and Noble, *Political Liberalization and Democratization in the Arab World: Comparative Experiences*, Volume 1.

6. Albrecht, "Political Opposition and Arab Authoritarianism: Some Conceptual Remarks," 3.

7. Diamond, "Thinking about Hybrid Regimes"; Levitsky and Way, "The Rise of Competitive Authoritarianism"; Schedler, *Electoral Authoritarianism: The Dynamics of Unfree Competition*.

## Tunisia

Tunisia's formal opposition came into being when President Habib Bourguiba amended the constitution to legalize political opposition parties ahead of the 1981 elections. Three opposition parties entered these first contests. However, an alliance headed by the ruling RCD won 94.2 percent of the vote and all 136 seats in the Chamber of Deputies. On November 7, 1987, Ben Ali came to power through a bloodless coup by declaring Bourguiba medically incompetent and unfit to lead the country. Upon seizing power, the new president initially promised a number of democratic reforms to Tunisia's political sphere. In December 1987, he released thousands of political prisoners who had been held under Bourguiba. Constitutional amendments and the National Pact of 1988 inaugurated in the early years of the Ben Ali period furthered the appearance of a pluralistic, multiparty electoral system; however, these reforms also outlawed parties organized on the basis of religion. The 1989 legislative contest held under Ben Ali was labeled the country's first competitive multiparty election, though it was not until 1994 that opposition parties were formally represented in parliament.

The RCD faced a number of opposition parties from across the ideological spectrum which can be organized into three broad, informal categories: leftists, Islamists, and splinters from the ruling party. These groupings do not imply any formal coordination or automatic affinity within each category. Rather, I find that organizing the parties in this way helps to elucidate their initial goals and policy preferences, to make sense of subsequent changes in preference positioning and related cooperative behavior, and to demonstrate that Tunisian opposition parties represented a broad spectrum of alternative political programs.

The first group of opposition parties was of a leftist orientation and advocated reform towards a democratic and modern civil state divorced from religion. The leftist opposition included two generations of activists. The first, older generation was comprised of the country's original opposition parties of various communist, Arab nationalist, and other leftist ideologies, mobilized against Bourguiba. This included the Tunisian Communist Party (*al-Hizb al-Shuyu'i al-Tunsi*), founded in 1934;[8] the Tunisian branch of the Ba'ath Party, formed in 1955; *Harakat al-Tajammu al-Qawmi al-'Arabi*, an Arab nationalist, Nasserist party known simply as *Tajammu*,

---

8. The Communist Party went through periods of legalization. It was banned by the Vichy regime in 1939–1943, and under Bourguiba from 1963 through 1981. Mohamed Nafaa served as its first secretary general from 1946 to 1981, and Mohamed Harmel served as its second.

founded by lawyer Bechir Essid ahead of the 1981 elections; and *Harakat at-Tahrir ash-Sha'biyya al-'Arabiyya Tunis*, which emerged from political mobilization in Tunisia's industrial sectors ahead of economic protests in the late 1970s.

The second generation of leftists included parties formed later in the twentieth century. In 1983, Ahmed Najib Chebbi founded the *Rassemblement Socialiste Progressiste* (later renamed the *Parti Démocrate Progressiste*, known as the PDP), which was legalized in 1988. The Tunisian Communist Workers Party (*Hizb al-'Ummal al-Shuyu'i al-Tunsi*, known as PCOT) was founded in 1986 with Hamma Hammami as Secretary General. The Social Liberal Party (*Parti Social-Libéral*, PSL) was founded in 1988 as the Social Party for Progress under the chairmanship of Mondher Thabet. The Renewal Movement (*Harakat al-Tajdid*, known simply as *Ettajdid*) was formed in 1993 by the remnants of the Tunisian Communist Party, which abandoned its communist ideology and adopted a center-left, secularist platform. Ahmed Ibrahim served as the party's First Secretary from 1993 through the 2010 uprising, and the party was legalized in November 1993.

During the same period, more center parties also emerged promoting secular platforms. In April 1994, the Democratic Forum for Labour and Liberties (*Forum Démocratique Pour le Travail et les Libertés*, known by the Arabic word for Forum, *Ettakatol*), was founded with Mustapha Ben Jaafar as Secretary General as a social democratic party and officially recognized by the state in October 2002. Finally, the *Congrés pour la République* (*al-Mu'tamar min ajl al-Jumhuriya* known as CPR) was established on July 2001 through a declaration with 31 signatories including prominent human rights activists Moncef Marzouki, Naziha Rejiba, Mohamed Abbou Abberraoud Ayadi, and Samir Ben Amor. CPR advocated a secular state in its program but had a heterogeneous leadership, combining self-identified secularists and Islamists. The regime banned the party in 2002. Many leaders of second generation parties had previously participated in the student opposition movement of the 1960s and 1970s, and were repressed by the Bourguiba regime for their activism. Known as *Perspectives*, this student movement was established in 1963 and brought together individuals from a number of leftist ideologies, including those from the communist, Marxist, Trotskyist, Maoist, and Ba'athist trends.[9] In addition, some members of

9. Tawfiq al-Madini, *Tarikh al-Mu'arida al-Tunsiyya min al-nisha' ila al-thawra* (Tunis: Sotupresse, 2012), 209–210.

the older generation remobilized during the second generation: for example, Essid established a second socialist and Arab nationalist political party, *Mouvement Unionistes Nassériens*, in 2005, though it was not legalized until after the revolution.

The second group of Tunisian opposition was Islamist, represented politically by Ennahda. The Islamist movement grew out of the clandestine Islamic Association in Tunisia (*al-Jama'a al-Islamiyya fi Tunis*), which had propagated religious activism in Tunisia in the late 1960s and 1970s in response to the state's aggressive secularization program. Members of the *jama'a* discreetly gave lectures, sponsored conferences, and created a cell of activists by preaching. They preached an Islam that was not simply "prayers and rituals" but which also addressed Tunisia's specific spiritual, economic, and political problems, prescribing a return to Islam as the solution.[10] Ahead of the 1981 elections, leaders applied for a government license to operate a political party under the name *Mouvement de la Tendance Islamique* or *Harakat al-Ittijah al-Islami* (the Movement of the Islamic Tendency, known as MTI). Their request was denied, and the party ultimately did not contest the elections. Nevertheless, the group released its founding manifesto in June 1981 under the leadership of Rachid al-Ghannouchi and Abdelfattah Mourou. The movement re-branded itself *Harakat Ennahda* (Renaissance Movement) during the 1989 elections under Ben Ali. This name was chosen because it did not include overt religious references in an effort to comply with the ban on religious-based parties, but Ennahda was denied formal recognition. The party was only legalized after the uprising, on March 1, 2011.

The third group of opposition was comprised of opposition parties which emerged as direct splinters from the ruling party. This includes the *Mouvement d'Unité Populaire* (MUP), the *Mouvement des Démocrates Socialistes* (MDS), the *Union Démocratique Unioniste* (UDU), and the *Parti de l'Unité Populaire* (PUP), all legalized in 1988. The parties were not created to represent emerging social constituencies, new social groups, or major reform initiatives, but rather were formed as the product of personal rivalries within the RCD.[11] The parties maintained the RCD's vaguely socialist ideology, differing only slightly in the specifics of policies that

10. Linda G. Jones, "Portrait of Rashid al-Ghannouchi," *Middle East Report* 153 (1988): 22.

11. Rikke Hostrup Haugbolle and Francesco Cavatorta, "Will the Real Tunisian Opposition Please Stand Up? Opposition Coordination Failures under Authoritarian Constraints," *British Journal of Middle Eastern Studies* 3, no. 38 (2011): 330.

should be implemented. In addition, the splinter parties called for more oversight of the presidency and the RCD. Members of the groups were sometimes kept on a meager state payroll.[12] Perhaps the most telling sign that these parties might better be considered an extension of the ruling party was how quickly they became irrelevant to political life after the uprisings: all faded away with the dissolution of the RCD in 2011. While the parties' legality was never threatened by the regime in the same way it was for the other opposition groups, these groups referred to themselves as opposition and party leaders sincerely believed they contributed to Tunisia's democratization by participating in governing institutions as loyal opposition. Most importantly for my inquiry here, these parties were also repressed by the regime for their opposition despite their legal status, and the regime often tried to infiltrate these parties to collect intelligence.[13] As a result, the stories of these parties appear throughout the Tunisian opposition's historical narrative of repression.

### Egypt

Egyptian president Anwar Sadat paved the way for multiparty elections in 1977 by passing Law 40 to regulate the formation of political parties and establishing the Political Parties Committee. As mentioned previously, the immediate effect of the law was to restructure the ruling ASU into three "platforms," which became the NDP, Hizb al-Ahrar, and Tagammu, representing the centrist, right, and left trends of the party, respectively. The 1979 parliamentary elections were a contest between the three former platforms of the ASU, with the NDP taking 92 percent of seats. The 1984 elections under Mubarak were the first to permit independent opposition parties to participate and can be considered Egypt's first multiparty elections.

Parties mobilizing in opposition to the NDP were numerous, but the regime denied legal status to the majority of these groups. Ahead of the 2011 uprisings, twenty-four opposition parties operated legally in the country. According to Human Rights Watch, between 1977 and 2004, the regime's Political Parties Committee rejected sixty-three applications for legal status and approved only two small parties that never achieved

---

12. Mohamed Moncef Chebbi. Interview with the author, December 5, 2014. Tunis, Tunisia. Chebbi was one of the founders of the UDU and former mid-ranking leader of the RCD.

13. Final report of the Tunisian Commission for Truth and Dignity, *Tafkik Munthumat al-Istibdad* (*Dismantling the System of Repression*) 2019, 45–46. http://www.ivd.tn/rapport/doc/11.pdf.

national competitiveness.[14] The remainder of parties were legalized through presidential decrees or court orders, though they represented only a fraction of opposition choices on offer.[15]

The Egyptian democratic opposition can be divided into three camps based on their motivating ideology and institutional origins. At one end of the spectrum lay parties mobilizing on state reform programs inspired by leftist—whether socialist, Arab nationalist, or Nasserist—ideologies, while at the other were parties espousing Islamist ideologies, with secular groups possessing liberal economic ideologies in between. Similar to my categorization of the Tunisian opposition, the categories outlined here imply neither ideological unity nor cooperation. Rather, they demonstrate that Egypt's party system hosted a full spectrum of ideological offerings along the secularist-Islamist axis of competition, and that a party's legal status did not exempt it from targeted repression by the state.

Among the first group of leftists, a number of opposition parties mobilized on secular notions of Arab socialism closely related to Nasserist ideologies following the ideas of the country's first president. The motivating ideologies of these parties were not intrinsically opposed to religion, and actively acknowledged the contributions of Islam to Arab civilization. However, their reform programs sought to create a state based on secular principles in which religion was considered a private matter and thus had no place in governance. Tagammu, formed from the left flank of the ASU, stated its goal as maintaining the accomplishments of the 1952 revolution. The party vehemently rejected religious extremism, a term which in the party's usage not only included terrorism but also the heavy influence of religion in the public sphere. In terms of economic policy, the party advocated a strong state socialism to address political and social issues, a negative reaction to the increasing privatization programs of the state under Sadat. Mobilizing on a similar platform, the Egyptian Arab Socialist Party (*Hizb Misr al-ʿArabi al-Ishtiraki*) was established in 1976 by Mamdouh Salem (prime minister from 1975–1978) during the onset of political liberalization under Sadat. Its platforms articulated a

14. These were the National Accord Party (*al-Hizb al-Watani al-Dimuqrati*) and the Democratic Generation Party (*Hizb al-Jil al-Dimuqrati*), though it suspended the activities of the former in 2001 citing a dispute within the leadership of the party.

15. For example, in 2004, the Mubarak regime legalized eleven parties in response to international pressure to democratize, in the context of the post-9/11 "War on Terror" and ahead of the 2005 parliamentary elections Maye Kassem (*Egyptian Politics: The Dynamics of Authoritarian Rule* (Boulder, Colorado: Lynne Reiner, 2004), 57).

commitment to preserving the gains of the 1952 revolution and, with that, a secular state.

The Arab Democratic Nasserist Party (*Al-Hizb al-'Arabi ad-Dimuqrati al-Nasseri*) was formed by former members of the ASU who left the party to form Tagammu. They had realized early that "Nasser intended to allow them to participate in the political system only under state control and supervision" and questioned this undemocratic application of his political vision.[16] They were further disillusioned with economic changes implemented by the ASU under Sadat and were disappointed with the cooperation between Tagammu and the regime. Initially, these Nasserists joined organizations such as the Socialist Vanguard (*Tali'at al-Ishtirakiyyin*), a secret Nasserist group established in 1963, and affiliated youth organizations, both loosely under the umbrella of ASU leadership.[17] In the early 1980s, they joined a number of similar illegal organizations such as *Thawrat Misri* to advocate a platform closer to Nasser's original ideology. The Nasserist Party received official accreditation in April 1992 under the leadership of Diya al-Din Dawud. The party won three seats during the 2000 parliamentary elections, but failed to win any seats in the following two parliamentary elections. The momentum of the Nasserist Party dissipated when a younger faction defected from the group in 1986 to form the *Karama* Party (meaning dignity in Arabic) as a separate Arab nationalist party calling for a return to Nasserist principles. Similar to the Nasserist Party, Karama put forward a reform platform which aimed to create a strong, state-led socialist program addressing political and social issues, guided by secular principles.

The Egyptian opposition also included a number of communist movements. In 1975, the Egyptian Communist Party was established, using the name of a then-defunct party previously founded in 1921. Its leadership was repressed severely in 1977 during the Bread Riots and neither Sadat nor Mubarak recognized the party. As a result, communists largely operated underground. Members who continued to be politically active either worked within some of the existing leftist parties, such as Tagammu, or worked in other leftist opposition spaces such as student and workers unions. After 2011, individuals from these movements founded

16. Hamied Ansari, *Egpt: The Stalled Society* (SUNY Press, 1986), 94.

17. See Amin Iskandar, *Al-Tanzim al-sirri li-Jamal 'Abd al-Nasir: Tali'at al-Ishtirakıyın: al-Mawlid, al-Masar, al-Masir* (Markaz Mahrousa lil-Nashr, 2016) for a detailed history of the organization's founding, development, and relationship with a for a detailed history of the organization's founding, development, and relationship with above-ground Nasserist organizations.

a number of small left-wing parties and entered the 2011 parliamentary elections through the Coalition of Socialist Forces (*al-Tahaluf al-Qawiyya al-Ishtirakiyya*).

Towards the center of the political spectrum was a group of secular parties advocating liberal economic policies. Though only a couple originated from within the ruling party, this group of parties as a whole closely aligned ideologically with the NDP. The New Wafd Party was established in 1978, though briefly dissolved under Sadat, as a revival of the original Wafd Party. The Wafd Party was a nationalist party founded in 1919. It was instrumental in creating a constitutional monarchy and national parliament in Egypt before being dissolved in 1952.[18] The party's platform a liberal motivating ideology somewhere between state-driven Arab socialism and private capitalism, assigning the state a moderate role in alleviating social and political problems. New Wafd policy preferences about religion reflected the sentiment of a statement made by original founder Saad Zaghloul: "religion is for God and the nation is for all." While recognizing the importance of Islam in Egyptian culture, the platform supported a strong secular state in which Coptic Christians and religious minorities were protected. Its presidential candidate, Numan Gomaa, won 2.8 percent of the vote during the 2005 elections. In 2001, Ayman Nour left the New Wafd Party to form the *Ghad* (meaning tomorrow in Arabic) Party and was granted a license in October 2004. The party similarly advanced a liberal economic program with a secular program. Nour also contested the 2005 presidential elections, winning 7.3 percent of the vote. In 2007, a number of businessmen closely associated with the NDP founded the Democratic Front Party, known as *Gabha* (front in Egyptian Arabic), and quickly received legal accreditation. Its founders were regime loyalists who were nonetheless concerned with preparations being made within the ruling party for the political inheritance of Mubarak's son, Gamal; they founded the party in response to a constitutional amendment which appeared to pave the way for Gamal to legally succeed his father.[19] The party claimed to represent the silent majority (i.e., the 77 percent who did not vote in the 2005 parliamentary elections) who they believed wanted a secular state.

---

18. Joel Gordon, *Nasser's Blessed Movement: Egypt's Free Officers and the July Revolution* (Oxford University Press, 1992), 134.

19. The founding leadership included the likes of Yehyia al-Gamal, a former minister and a member of the People's Assembly, and Osama Ghazali Harb, a former NDP member and a member of the Shura Council from 1995 to 2010.

The party's platforms also called for further development of the private sector.[20]

The Islamist end of the political spectrum was dominated by the Muslim Brotherhood (*al-Ikhwan al-Muslimun*), the largest of Egyptian opposition groups denied legal status. It was founded in 1928 by Hassan al-Banna and combined political activism with community building. The initial activities of the organization focused on Islamic education and charity, and the organization became integrated into communities by providing schools, health clinics, and other social services, particularly to those left out of state patronage systems.[21] The organization considered its Islamic *da'wa* (preaching) and *tarbiyya* (education) programs to be closely related to its political mission, in that these activities were intended to prepare society to demand from its leaders or forcibly undertake reform to install a shari'a guided state. The Muslim Brotherhood never became a legally licensed party under Mubarak, but in 2011 the Freedom and Justice Party (*Hizb al-Hurriya wal-'Adala*) gained accreditation and operated as a party nominally independent from the Brotherhood. In 1996, members of the organization's reformist generation broke away from the Brotherhood when Abul Ela Madi founded the *Wasat* (Center) Party. Those members and leaders who left to join Wasat disagreed with the Brotherhood's leadership about the party's tactics in achieving reform.[22] Like its parent organization, the Wasat Party was denied a party license each of the four times it applied for one under Mubarak.

In addition to the Brotherhood, there were a number of smaller Islamist parties that mobilized as political opposition in the 1980s. The Socialist Labor Party, later known as the Egyptian Islamic Labor Party, was formed in 1978, succeeding the earlier *Masr al-Fattah* movement. It was originally founded as a socialist movement and adopted an Islamist approach to economic reform, calling for a socialist economic system based on principles of the shari'a while competing in elections in the late 1980s. The Liberal Socialists Party was established in 1976 on a platform promoting privatization and shari'a as the main source of legislation. The Umma Party was established in 1983 and was one of the few parties to receive an official

20. Much of the historical description of the party system under Mubarak derives from the thorough history written by Amro Hashim Rabia, *Al-Ahzab al-Saghira wal-Nizam al-Hizbi fi Masr* (Cairo: Al-Ahram Center for Political/Strategic Studies, 2003).

21. Masoud, *Counting Islam: Religion, Class, and Elections in Egypt*.

22. Wickham, "The Path to Moderation: Strategy and Learning in the Formation of Egypt's *Wasat* Party," 205–228.

state license. However, none of these parties attracted a significant following; in the 2000 parliamentary elections, the Liberal Socialists Party won one out of 444 seats, and the Umma Party fielded a single losing candidate.

## Differing Repertoires of Repression

Tunisia and Egypt each had an estimated 30,000 political prisoners under Mubarak and Ben Ali[23] These figures suggest a sizable political prisoner population, as well as different levels of saturation of experiences of repression within each country; Egypt's population totaled 79.39 million in 2011, while Tunisia's population was only 10.67 million in the same year. However, while these numbers reveal something about repression in comparative perspective, there is more to be understood from the demographics of these political prisoner populations, and the extent to which repressive experiences were shared across political opposition groups in each country.

### REPRESSION IN TUNISIA, 1987–2010

Tunisia represents a case of widespread repression, meaning that over the course of the Ben Ali regime, repression came to affect nearly all opposition groups, regardless of whether they held legal or illegal status. When Ben Ali came to power in November 1987, he promised a political opening intended to depart from the staunch authoritarianism of Bourguiba. In December, he released the thousands of political prisoners who had been held under Bourguiba as a gesture of goodwill. Initially, opposition parties truly believed that the change in leader would bring political change, and all significant opposition parties signed the 1988 National Pact, a document put forward by the regime as a vision for increased pluralism and political participation. Signatories, which included Islamist opposition Ennahda, assumed that their participation in the pact guaranteed the

---

23. These numbers were cited to me separately in nearly all interviews I conducted with former political prisoners, activists, and members of human rights organizations, though individuals were quick to mention that this figure was based on commonly accepted knowledge and did not rely on firm documentation. These figures also appear in other reports on political prisoners in Egypt (for example, R. Clemente Holder, "Egyptian Lawyer's Death Triggers Cairo Protests," *Washington Report on Middle East Affairs*, July/August (1994): 60–62) and Tunisia (for example, Andrea Khalil, "Tunisia's Women: Partners in Revolution," *Journal of North African Studies* 19, no. 2 (2014): 186–199).

right to participate in the democratization of the country and the upcoming elections. However, Ben Ali moved to ban Ennahda as a party based on religion over the following year. Secular opposition parties largely supported this move, revealing a polarized political system divided over the appropriate role of religion and religious parties in politics. As described in the final report of Tunisia's Truth and Dignity Commission, exposure to repression "in all its forms of cruel and inhumane treatment, was not limited to a limited political period, but rather was an organized and continuous act by the political authority towards anyone who differed in opinion and every political opponent."[24]

### Islamist Opposition

Ennahda became the first victims of the Ben Ali regime, despite their agreement to the National Pact. A number of events preceded the crackdown on the group and, together, appear to have triggered and provided the regime public justification for a wave of repression against the group. First, Ennahda candidates ran as independents in the 1989 elections due to the ban on religious parties and performed remarkably well, even in spite of significant interference from the regime. Official—and most likely, altered—tallies released by the government saw the movement win roughly 17 percent of votes nationally, and between 20 and 30 percent in both Tunis electoral districts, Bizerte, Gabes, Kebili, Sousse, and Tozeur.[25] However, due to regime manipulation of seat assignment formulas, Ennahda was not assigned a single seat.

The next year saw an increase in Ennahda supporters taking to the streets to voice their frustration with the regime, and clashes between Islamist university students and members of the security forces were frequent. The Ben Ali regime accused Ennahda sympathizers of attacking police with stones and Molotov cocktails. In response, the police formed anti-riot squads to attack Islamists' peaceful meetings and non-violent occupations of universities. In September 1990, an Ennahda student supporter named Tayeb Khammasi was shot by the police during one such demonstration. The shooting triggered another series of protests by

24. 2019, 94. http://www.ivd.tn/rapport/doc/11.pdf.

25. In a September 6, 2006, classified cable from the U.S. Embassy in Tunis, Ennahda leader Hamadi Jebali claimed that a journalist from French newspaper *Le Monde* had heard from French Embassy sources that Ennahda had actually won the election with over 60 percent of the vote. Jebali repeated this to me in an interview on December 10, 2014, in Sousse, Tunisia, and many other Ennahda leaders referenced the same information when I asked about the 1989 election.

Ennahda supporters, which resulted in early arrests of the group's members, which were in turn followed by more demonstrations.[26]

Two additional incidents involving alleged or potential Islamist violence against state targets preceded the crackdown on Ennahda. Both events appear to have either been fabricated or exaggerated by the regime. In February 1991, armed militants attacked RCD headquarters located in the Bab Souika neighborhood of Tunis. The militants were not affiliated with Ennahda, but leader Rachid Ghannouchi issued a lukewarm condemnation of the attack that tacitly linked the two Islamist groups.[27] Then in May 1991, Minister of the Interior Abdallah Kallel announced that the regime had thwarted a coup attempt in which military officers had conspired with Ennahda members to overthrow the president. This became known as the Barraket Essahel affair, named after the town near Sousse where the alleged coup plotting had taken place. To date, no evidence has been produced to substantiate the claims put forward by the regime surrounding the alleged coup. In addition, at least two members of Ennahda charged with involvement in the coup and in attendance at preparatory meetings were already being held in prisons by the regime at the time of the alleged plotting.

The regime began to arrest Ennahda members and leaders on various charges in the weeks and months after the 1989 elections. In June 1990, Hamadi Jebali, a member of Ennahda's executive council and the editor of the movement's paper, *al-Fajr*, received a six-month suspended sentence and a fine of TND 1500 for publishing an article titled, "The People of the State, or the State of the People?"[28] Jebali was rearrested shortly thereafter for publishing an article written by Tunisian human rights lawyer Mohammed Nouri, titled, "When will military courts, serving as special courts, be abolished?" in *al-Fajr* in October 1990. Both Jebali and

26. Amnesty International, "Tunisia: Heavy Sentences After Unfair Trials" (AI Index: 30/023/1992) September 1992, available at https://www.amnesty.org/download/Documents/192000/mde300231992en.pdf.

27. Ghannouchi said that although the party leadership had neither planned the attack nor had any awareness of the plot, he thought it was an "understandable reaction undertaken by a group of Muslim youth activists against the tyrannical and oppressive politics of the regime." This trumped all other condemnations issued by Ennahda. Daniel Ritter, *The Iron Cage of Liberalism: International Politics and Unarmed Revolutions in the Middle East and North Africa* (Oxford: Oxford University Press, 2015), 116.

28. Amnesty International, "Tunisia: Imprisonment of a Journalist" (AI Index: MDE 30/06/91) February 1991, available at https://www.amnesty.org/download/Documents/196000/mde300061991en.pdf.

Nouri were tried in a military court and found guilty of "defamation of a judicial institution."[29] In January 1991, Jebali received a sentence of one-year imprisonment, while Nouri was sentenced to six months' imprisonment. *Al-Fajr* was ordered closed on February 8, 1991. Other Ennahda members were rounded up for the purpose of *interpellation* (interrogation). Ali Lareydh, then spokesperson for Ennahda, and Ziad Doulatli, a prominent member of the group, were arrested in December 1990. Lareydh had been arrested and tortured in October 1990 as well, and was released after three days without having been formally charged.[30] Many of the hundreds of student sympathizers arrested in connection with university protests were released uncharged, but only after having been held in prolonged detention for up to forty days and often tortured.

In addition to individual trials of Ennahda members, the regime tried the group and its leadership in three mass cases. In May 1991, twenty-eight Ennahda supporters, including one juvenile, were tried in criminal court for their involvement in the Bab Souika attack. The twenty-seven adults were convicted and given sentences ranging from two years' suspended sentences to life imprisonment. Three of those convicted had their sentences strengthened on appeal; their life sentences were upgraded to the death penalty, and they were executed by hanging in October 1991. In 1992, 279 Ennahda members and alleged sympathizers from the military were tried in two cases in the Bouchoucha and Bab Saadoun military tribunals for the Barraket Essahel incident. The defendants were arbitrarily divided into two groups and tried separately, the majority in absentia. Forty-five defendants received life sentences and 220 others received sentences of between one and twenty-four years imprisonment.[31]

29. The irony of being tried in a military court for a piece criticizing the military courts was not lost on the two men, as each recounted to me in personal interviews.

30. Amnesty International, "Tunisia: Political Detainees' Rights Violated; Lawyer's Action" (AI Index: MDE 30/08/91) March 1991, available at https://www.amnesty.org/download/Documents/196000/mde300081991en.pdf.

31. Amnesty International, "Tunisia: Heavy Sentences after Unfair Trials" (AI Index: MDE 30/23/92) September 1992, available at https://www.amnesty.org/download/Documents/192000/mde300231992en.pdf. The report suggested that there was no logic to how the defendants were divided between the two latter trials: "the Bouchoucha trial involved mostly civilians and most of the leadership of al-Nahda, including Rachid Ghannouchi, who was one of those tried in absentia, but the defendants also included about 50 members or former members of the military, police or prison services. A higher number of such military or other service personnel

From 1990 to 1992, between 8,000[32] and 10,000[33] Ennahda members and leaders were arrested and charged with capital offenses such as belonging to an illegal organization, attending unauthorized meetings, or seeking to change the nature of the state. A number of Ennahda members fled the country for Europe due to health and safety concerns ahead of the crackdown or by escaping during it. This included Ennahda leader Ghannouchi, who had been released from prison on May 14, 1987 and left for Europe through Algeria due to health issues.

While some low-ranking Ennahda members and supporters were arrested, held for short periods of time, and released without charges, the majority of members were held through 1999, when Ben Ali undertook a number of reforms under the watchful eye of the international community ahead of negotiations with the International Monetary Fund and the European Union. The movement's leadership served longer sentences. In 2004, 100 of the 265 high-ranking Ennahda members convicted in the 1991 Barraket Essahel trial remained in prison, 40 of them in prolonged solitary confinement.[34] In October of the same year, Ben Ali granted a conditional release through presidential pardon to nearly eighty political prisoners after winning a fifth term with 94.5 percent of the vote. The last 21 leaders of Ennahda being held in Tunisian prisons were conditionally released by presidential pardon on November 5, 2008 ahead of the November 7 anniversary of Ben Ali's ascension to the

---

or former personnel appears in the Bab Saadoun trial at which other leading civilian members of al-Nahda, such as Ali Laaridh [*sic*] and Ziad Doulatli, were also among the accused."

32. This figure was consistently recited to me in interviews with Ennahda and former secular opposition leadership, and appears to be a commonly accepted tally despite scant documentation of individual arrests. See also Amnesty International, "Prolonged Incommunicado Detention and Torture" (AI Index: MDE 30/04/92) March 1992, 8. Available at https://www.amnesty.org/download/Documents/192000/mde300041992en.pdf.

33. To my knowledge, the first reference to this figure is an April 1993 press release issued by Amnesty International regarding the health of Thameur Jaoua, an Ennahda supporter who had been arrested and tortured while recovering from back surgery (Amnesty International, "Health concern: Thameur Jaoua, Tunisia" (AI Index: MDE 30/01/93) April 8, 1993, available at https://www.amnesty.org/download/Documents/188000/mde300011993en.pdf. Subsequent reports from domestic and international human rights organizations vary between 8,000 and 10,000 when referring to arrests during the 1990–1992 period.

34. Human Rights Watch, "Tunisia: Long-term Solitary Confinement of Political Prisoners," (16.3) July 2004, available at https://www.hrw.org/reports/2004/tunisia0704/tunisia0704.pdf. Internal records held by *L'Association Internationale de Soutien aux Prisonniers Politiques* (AISPP), a human rights organization working closely with Ennahda lawyers, confirmed these numbers.

presidency.[35] Nahdawis exiled abroad remained there through the 2010 uprising.

### Non-Islamist Opposition

The beginning of regime repression of non-Islamist opposition groups coincided with the tail end of the major crackdown on Ennahda. Members of both illegal leftist parties as well as legalized opposition parties with socialist and center-left motivating ideologies became the next victims of the regime. Beginning as early as 1991, thousands of individuals were arrested, and not all were charged in connection with Ennahda—suggesting the regime had already begun to repress other groups at this time. A human rights report further indicated that there was a noticeable uptick in repression of "known or suspected political activists across the political spectrum" ahead of the 1994 presidential elections.[36]

Illegal leftist opposition bore a significant amount of regime repression. Nasserist Essid, then of Tajammu, was sentenced in October 1990 to four years' imprisonment on charges of defaming the president and other offenses for material he had allegedly written in opposition newspapers. He was released by pardon at the end of 1992. The regime banned the activities of the Tunisian Ba'athist Movement after the 1991 Gulf War and arrested its known active leadership, essentially ending the movement's political activity in the country.[37] Members and leadership of the illegal PCOT were repeatedly repressed by the Ben Ali regime. A group of student members was arrested in November 1992, charged with maintaining an unauthorized association, holding unauthorized meetings, and distributing leaflets. Another wave of arrests against PCOT members followed student protests in Tunis and other cities calling for better economic, political, and social conditions in February 1998. PCOT members faced charges of belonging to a criminal and terrorist gang, holding unauthorized meetings, inciting rebellion, insulting the president, spreading false information aiming to disturb public order, defamation against the authorities, and distributing leaflets. In July 1999, sixteen students, in addition to PCOT leader Hamma Hammami, trade unionist Abdelmajir Sahraoui, journalist Fahem Boukaddous, and Hammami's wife, human rights lawyer Radhia Nasraoui, received

35. Though Ennahda's Sadok Chorou was rearrested a few weeks after his release for expressing his political views to the media in an interview. He was held in Nadhour prison.

36. Amnesty International, "Human Rights Defenders in the Line of Fire" (AI Index: MDE 30/20/98) November 1, 1998, available at https://www.refworld.org/docid/3ae6a9a918.html.

37. Al-Madini, *Tarikh al-Mu'arida al-Tunsiyya min al-nisha' ila al-thawra*, 63.

sentences for the protests ranging from three and a half to seventeen and a half years' imprisonment. A number of these PCOT political prisoners were released by presidential pardon in June 2000.

The party's leadership were visible victims of regime repression. Mohamed Kilani, a spokesperson for PCOT and the editor of the group's newspaper *al-Badil*, was arrested in January 1995. He had been in hiding since November 1992, when he had been sentenced in absentia with other PCOT members on charges of belonging to an unauthorized association and holding unauthorized meetings in Gabes. He received a sentence of two years and six months at that time, and another ten months when he was tried again for the same charges in January 1993. After being apprehended in 1995, he received two sentences totaling seven years. The first sentence of two years upheld the earlier charges. The second sentence of five years resulted from a separate trial in April 1995, in which Kilani was charged with supporting a "terrorist organization" for allegedly possessing a leaflet produced by an unauthorized Islamist group in 1991.[38] Kilani was released by presidential pardon on November 6, 1995, on the eighth anniversary of Ben Ali coming to power. At the time, he was serving a sentence of eight years and seven months.

PCOT leader Hammami, who was also the director of *al-Badil*, was arguably the most persecuted member of the group and experienced near constant repression throughout the 1990s and 2000s. He experienced terrible torture under Bourgiba. As early as 1991, Hammami was sentenced to two and a half years imprisonment for publishing articles critical of the government in *al-Badil*. He was arrested again on February 14, 1994. Hammami had been in hiding since November 1992 and had received in absentia a sentence of four years and nine months imprisonment. He was retried in April 1994 and sentenced to four years and one month in jail. At the same time, Hammami was also charged with carrying a false identity card and assaulting two of the three armed police who arrested him, and sentenced to a total of eight years and seven months. This sentence was commuted by presidential pardon in November 1995. When Hammami

---

38. The leaflet included a cartoon of a former minister of the interior with bloody hands, a dagger in his belt, and a body laying at his feet. The minister was depicted walking free from a "commission of inquiry" made up of individuals in Western dress. The leaflet was allegedly found by police in Kilani's house when they searched his home while he was in hiding. It was believed to have been produced in 1991 by an illegal Islamist organization, most likely Ennahda, when Mohamed Kilani was the editor of *al-Badil*. See Amnesty International, "Fear of Unfair Trial: Mohamed Kilani, Tunisia" (AI Index: MDE 30/03/95) February 6, 1995.

was again sought out by police in connection with the 1998 trial of PCOT student members just a few weeks later, he and three other high-ranking members went back into hiding, reemerging in February 2002 after significant harassment of their immediate and extended families.[39] Hammami had been sentenced in absentia to nine years and three months imprisonment for membership in PCOT during the 1998 trial. In March 2002, the appeal court reduced Hammami's sentence to three years two months.[40] He was released September 4, 2002, due to significant health complications but did not find a reprieve from repression. Hammami was physically assaulted by police in front of the Kairouan office of the Tunisian Human Rights League (*Ligue Tunisienne des Droits de l'Homme*) in November 2004. In September 2009, he and his wife were assaulted by police at the Tunis airport because of an interview he gave while abroad. In October of the same year, Hammami was blocked from traveling to a meeting of political opposition in France. In the last days of a panicked and rapidly fading regime, Ben Ali's presidential guard arrested Hammami and another activist, Mohamed Mzem, who happened to be at Hammami's home on January 12, for speaking about PCOT and the escalating protest to international media outlets. The two men were held incommunicado at the Ministry of the Interior until Ben Ali's departure two days later.

Center-left opposition groups were similarly repressed. Leadership of the CPR, which would become the most prominent center-left party to survive the dictatorship, were victims of regime repression. Cofounder Ben Amor's car was vandalized by police in 2004. He was detained in December 2007 and explicitly warned to cease all political and human rights activities with CPR and the non-governmental organization *L'Association Internationale de Soutien aux Prisonniers Politiques* (AISPP). Another CPR cofounder Mohamed Abbou was arrested in March 2005 for disseminating "false" information, libeling Tunisia's judiciary, and inciting the public to disobey the laws after publishing an article denouncing torture on an

39. "Hamma Hammami: Chronology of Repression." https://web.archive.org/web/2011 0706085820/http://gewerkschafterinnen.amnesty.at/Hamma.Hammami/chronology.html. The other high-ranking members included Ammar Amroussia, Abdel Madour, and Samir Taamallah.

40. Amnesty International, "Tunisia: Fear of torture/Possible arrests/Possible prisoners of conscience," (AI Index: MDE 30/006/2002) February 4, 2002, https://www.amnesty.org/download/Documents/120000/mde300062002en.pdf. See also related updates from Amnesty International.

opposition website, www.Tunisnews.net. He was sentenced to a three-and-a-half-year term of imprisonment in April. Abbou served twenty-eight months of his sentence before being granted a conditional release by presidential pardon in July 2007, along with twenty-one other political prisoners, to mark the 50th anniversary of the Republic of Tunisia.[41]

Moncef Marzouki, another of CPR's founders, was repressed prior to the establishment of the party in 2002. He was a politician, human rights activist, and a presidential candidate for the 1994 contest. Marzouki was arrested in March 1994[42] and charged with "spreading false information liable to disturb public order" and "insulting judiciary authorities" due to a mistranslation in one of his answers during an interview with a Spanish newspaper. Marzouki was detained for four months and released on bail on July 13, 1994, though the charges against him were not dropped. His passport was confiscated, briefly returned in 1995, and then confiscated again in 1996. Marzouki was also demoted from his position as head of the public health department in Sousse hospital. Further, his brother and nephew were detained on several occasions as a means of intimidation, and his lawyer, Najib Hosni, was also arrested, seemingly for no other reason than their proximity to Marzouki. Marzouki was rearrested in 1999 and his earlier trial was revived. In December 2000, he was sentenced to a one-year imprisonment. Shortly thereafter, he moved into exile in France in 2002 after near constant harassment by police and the confiscation of his official documents.

### Legalized Opposition

Not even members of legalized opposition groups were spared from repression by the Ben Ali regime. Boujema Remili, a leading figure of the Ettajdid movement, was arrested on March 21, 1994, after giving an interview to a foreign news agency in which he talked about alleged irregularities in the recent elections. He was released on bail a week later but eventually

41. Amnesty International, "Urgent Action In Focus: Mohammed Abbou—'We need the world's solidarity'" (AI Index: ACT 60/018/2007) September 2007, https://www.amnesty.org/download/Documents/56000/act600182007en.pdf.

42. The only other person who had announced his intention to stand against President Ben Ali in the March 1994 elections, lawyer Abderrahmane Hani, was also detained. Hani was arrested on February 15, 1994, and held on charges of "setting up an unauthorized association and spreading false information." He was released on bail on April 23, 1994, reportedly after asking for presidential pardon. He was later tried and convicted, and received a suspended prison sentence of eight months.

received a sentence of eight months (suspended) for "spreading false information." Lassad Zitouni, a leading member of the PSL Party, was barred from leaving Tunisia in May 1998 because of an outstanding case against him, about which he had never been informed.

On April 15, 1994, Mustapha Ben Jaafar, Ettakatol's Secretary General, was arrested, interrogated for several hours, and threatened with prosecution for setting up an illegal organization. In November 1994 of the same year, Ben Jaafar was prevented from leaving the country as he was going to attend a medical conference abroad; his passport was confiscated and returned to him a year later. It was later confiscated again and never returned. He was subsequently demoted from his position as the head of the radiology department in a hospital in Tunis, and his new meaningless position included an office overlooking the April 9th prison, where political prisoners were held.[43] In 1997, Ben Jaafar was revealed to be on a travel ban in connection with his 1994 detention, though the incident had not resulted in any formal charges.[44] In October 1999, Ben Jaafar was detained and interrogated for five hours at a police station in the Tunis suburb of Carthage, facing charges of maintaining an "unrecognized association." Leading Ettakatol member Khemais Ksila had his passport confiscated in August 1995 to prevent him from participating in human rights and other political activities outside Tunisia. During the same period, his telephone was repeatedly intercepted and disconnected. In September 1997, Ksila made a public statement announcing a hunger strike protesting the restrictions imposed on him by Tunisian authorities and was arrested. In February 1998, Ksila was sentenced to three years' imprisonment on charges of outrage to public order, spreading false information, and inciting citizens to break the law, and was fined TND 1,200. He was released in September 1999, having served two years of his three-year sentence. After 2002, when Ettakatol was legalized, Ben Jaafar remarked that "the only thing that changed was that we no longer had to go down to the police station."

43. Mustapha Ben Jaafar, *Un Si Long Chemin Vers la Démocratie* (Tunis, Tunisia: Editions Nirvana, 2014). Also Mustapha Ben Jaafar. Interview with the author. January 16, 2017. Tunis, Tunisia.

44. Human Rights Watch's 1999 World Report (available at https://www.hrw.org/legacy/worldreport99/mideast/tunisia.html) noted that Ben Jaafar and human rights activist Sihem Ben Sedrine had been placed on a travel ban in late 1997, after having their passports seized in 1994 and 1995, respectively. Neither had been charged with a crime and were only made aware of the ban through a report issued to European parliamentarians about judicial complicity into false, politically motivated criminal investigations.

Instead, the police came to them, maintaining constant surveillance of the party headquarters rather than detaining its leaders.[45]

Even the loyal opposition, formed from splits within the ruling party, faced repression during this period. On October 8, 1995, the political bureau of MDS published an open letter criticizing the president's behavior and the political environment he was creating. MDS Secretary General Mohammed Mouada was arrested the next day and charged with "secret and compromising relations with a foreign state." Mouada was charged under articles of the Tunisian Penal Code concerning threats to the external security of the state, two of which would permit the use of the death penalty. Ultimately, he was sentenced to a total of eleven years' imprisonment. MDS vice president and parliament member Khemais Chammari was also arrested in connection to the open letter and was sentenced to five years' imprisonment on charges of "disclosing a national secret to a foreign power."[46] Both men were conditionally released in December 1995, though they were kept under constant surveillance by authorities. Mouada was placed under house arrest between April and July 1996. He was rearrested in 2001 after he issued a manifesto cosigned with Ennahda leader Ghannouchi in which they agreed to set up a "patriotic and democratic front based on the defense of public freedoms" and announced their rejection of the "institutional candidacy" of Ben Ali for the next presidential election in 2004. He was sent back to the April 9th prison in Tunis to serve the nine remaining years of the sentence he received in 1996.

During the last decade of the Ben Ali period, the regime exploited increased international attention to local jihadi threats to further clamp down on remaining opposition, expanding on its already extreme repressive behaviors. In December 2003, the Tunisian parliament passed expansive domestic terrorism laws as part of its partnership with the United States in the "War on Terror." The text of the laws updated the definition of terrorism to include nearly any form of opposition against the regime. This development essentially legalized the regime's ongoing use of repression,

---

45. Mustapha Ben Jaafar. Interview with the author. January 16, 2017. Tunis, Tunisia.

46. Amnesty International speculated that this charge may have been related to Chammari's consistent refusal to stop his political and human rights work, including his involvement in the case against Tunisian human rights activist Frej Fenniche. Fenniche had been charged with possessing documents deemed to be damaging to national interests. At the time of his arrest, he allegedly had in his possession letters from Chammari which described the human rights situation in Tunisia and which were intended for participants in a human rights meeting in Montpellier, France. The letters included information about the judicial investigation into Mouada's case.

increasing its ability to limit mobilized opposition and ban newly forming political parties.[47] Under the new laws, the targets of state repression expanded to include personal enemies of the president's second wife,
Leila Trabelsi, and her family as they accumulated wealth through deliberate and rampant cronyism.[48] The regime arrested roughly four thousand
people between 2003 and the December 2010 uprising under the new
terrorism law.[49]

## REPRESSION IN EGYPT, 1981–2011

The Mubarak regime employed a targeted repressive environment against
its opposition. Other scholars have similarly referred to the system as a
"divided structure of contestation,"[50] wherein some parties were permitted to operate legally and participate in electoral contests, while others
were excluded. In my typology, I do not focus on a party's legal status
or electoral participation, but rather on its de facto position vis-á-vis the
repressive behavior of the state. Repression under the Mubarak regime targeted one opposition party, while tolerating some parties, and co-opting
others. Between 1981 and 2011, the regime overwhelmingly repressed the
Brotherhood while it permitted leftist organizations to exist and co-opted
center secular parties. The targeted repression against the Brotherhood
was visible in the differential treatment to which the organization was subjected, measured by sheer number of arrests, the regularity of repressive
waves, and the severity of the regime's legal strategy.

On October 6, 1981, a militant from *al-Gihad* assassinated Egypt's
third president, Anwar Sadat. The assassination occurred during a military
parade and Mubarak, then vice president, had been sitting at Sadat's side,
suffering minor injuries as a result of the attack. Mubarak was sworn in as
president on October 14. Upon taking office, Mubarak initially oversaw a
security crackdown on those suspected of involvement in the assassination,
and more than four thousand people were arrested during the first few

47. Lynn Welchman, "Anti-Terrorism Law and Policy in Arab States," in *Global Anti-Terrorism Law and Policy*, ed. Victor V. Ramraj et al. (Cambridge: Cambridge University Press, 2012).

48. Bob Rijkers, Caroline L. Freund, and Antonio Nucifora, "All in the Family: State Capture in Tunisia," *World Bank Policy Research Working Paper* 6810 (2014).

49. According to internal records held by *L'Association Internationale de Soutien aux Prison-niers Politiques* (AISPP).

50. Lust, *Structuring Conflict in the Arab World: Incumbents, Opponents, and Institutions.*

weeks of his presidency.[51] Mubarak then pursued a policy of accommodation and tolerance towards political opposition during the early years
of his rule. He released in stages members of the opposition imprisoned
in 1981 and 1982, and promised true political pluralism, holding regular
presidential and legislative elections beginning in 1984. However, by the
end of Mubarak's first decade in power, the president soon reverted to
the tried-and-true Egyptian policy of dividing and conquering the opposition. While Mubarak permitted the existence of fully co-opted parties and
superficial competition within limits, he also targeted the Muslim Brotherhood as a pillar of a repressive policy to control the mobilization of political
opposition.

### Co-opted Opposition

The main co-opted opposition parties under Mubarak were the New Wafd
and Gabha Parties, as well as the leftist Tagammu Party. While these parties
initially sought to establish themselves as effective independent opposition groups, they later became co-opted and compromised by the state,
becoming a loyal opposition that was permitted to contest elections and
serve in parliament—though only as "yes men." The absences of repression
and harassment against these parties' members and leaders, the parties'
free contestation of elections (limited only in terms of the upper bounds
of representation), and party leaders' involvement in government bodies
demonstrated the parties' co-opted status under Mubarak.

Under Mubarak, the New Wafd Party returned to Egyptian political
life after facing repression under Nasser[52] and Sadat.[53] In 1984, Egyptian
courts unfroze the party's membership on an appeal, and the party began
the publication of its daily newspaper, also titled *al-Wafd*, the content of

51. Amnesty International, "Amnesty International Report 1984" (AI Index: POL 10/00
04/1984), May 1, 1984, 328–332. Available at https://www.amnesty.org/download/Documents
/POL1000041984ENGLISH.PDF.

52. With the founding of the republic, the Wafd Party was repressed under Nasser after
all political parties were banned in 1954. Raymond A. Hinnebusch, "The Reemergence of the
Wafd Party: Glimpses of the Liberal Opposition in Egypt," *International Journal of Middle East
Studies* 16, no. 1 (1984): 102 described this period of the Wafd's history as follows: "Nasir [*sic*]
forged a broad cross-class base for his new state, embracing—and balancing—most of Egypt's
social forces. The leaders of Egypt's greatest political party found themselves excluded, subject
to 'political isolation,' imprisonment, and the expropriation of their property."

53. In May 1978, the regime staged a referendum in which voters were forced to approve
restrictions on political liberties, including a provision which banned individuals who had "cor-
rupted political life before the 1952 revolution," a thinly veiled threat to Wafd leadership. The
party voted to disband instead of waiting for arrests. Ibid., 117.

which was uncritical towards the regime. In legislative elections held the same year, New Wafd–dominated lists (in combination with Muslim Brotherhood candidates) won 15.1 percent of the vote and fifty-eight seats in parliament. In 1987, the party ran on its own lists, winning 10.9 percent of the vote and thirty-five seats. The New Wafd boycotted the 1990 elections along with the Socialist Labor and the Liberal Socialist parties in protest to an amended electoral law passed by referendum in October 1990, which party leadership claimed would violate free elections. During the four legislative elections held between 1995 and 2010, the party won an average of six seats. In addition, the New Wafd fielded a candidate in the first multi-candidate presidential election, held in 2005. The aftermath of the election further demonstrates Wafd's preferential treatment. While other candidates were arrested following their participation in the contest, the Wafd's candidate Numan Gomaa was not. The party did not face arrests or similar pressures under Mubarak.

While the Wafd became co-opted over time, the leftist Tagammu Party was essentially co-opted from its inception and by design. As noted above, the party initially began as the left-wing current of the ruling ASU. The faction became an independent party upon the dissolution of the ASU in 1978 but continued to have many members of the ASU in key positions of influence. Under Sadat, high-ranking members were arrested after the party applied for legal recognition, and it temporarily ceased publication of *al-Ahali*, as Sadat viewed the left as his main political challenge.[54] However, under Mubarak, Tagammu was permitted to participate in politics relatively freely and did not face state repression. The party ran lists in the 1984 and 1987 legislative elections, though it won no more than 4.2 percent of the vote and failed to secure a single seat. Tagammu placed second in the 1990 elections, which the majority of opposition parties boycotted and won six seats. The party held between two and six seats for the remainder of the Mubarak era.

Finally, Gabha quickly received its legal accreditation from the Parties Committee after its founding in 2007. Gabha was founded by regime loyalists, and its leadership maintained close ties to the regime, not only serving in government positions under Mubarak but also enjoying personal relationships with his family. For example, founder al-Ghazali Harb served on a five-person committee in charge of establishing a presidential library with

---

54. Husein Abdel Razik, *Al-Ahali: Sahifa taht al-hisar* (Cairo: Dar al-'Alam al-Thalith, 1994), 79–81.

the president's son in the late 2000s. Gamal, who al-Ghazali Harb described as "polite," later asked the politician to join the NDP's Policies Committee.[55] Gabha members faced very little pressure and were not subject to arrest.

### Tolerated Opposition

While Sadat systematically targeted leftist opposition,[56] Mubarak tolerated the left to a much greater extent. This is not to say that the left totally escaped repression, but rather that the nature of this repression differed from previous treatment, and from the treatment of targeted groups (outlined in the following section). The regime utilized reactive repression against leftist groups, moving in response to demonstrations either supporting the working-class movement, unionists, and students, or visible protests such as those against foreign policy issues including the 1991 Gulf War, the Palestinian *Intifada*, and the 2003 American invasion of Iraq. The majority of arrests of leftist oppositions lasted a few days, though these detainees were tortured in detention centers before being released, often without charge. Sometimes, longer holding periods lasted between fifteen days and a month. Many members of the left were arrested once or twice under Mubarak, in a shift from the Sadat era. Known leftist leaders were repressed more regularly than rank-and-file members. For example, Karama leader Sayyid al-Toukhy was arrested at least eight times under Mubarak,[57] while fellow Karama leader Hamdeen Sabahi was arrested seventeen times under Sadat and Mubarak in response to various incidents of political activism. A third Karama leader, leftist intellectual Amin Iskandar, was arrested between seven and ten times under Sadat and Mubarak.[58] Other leftists were arrested for participating in protests. Liberal activist Farid Zahran of what became the Egyptian Social Democratic Party (ESDP) was arrested for participating in protests supporting the Intifada and was similarly held for a few days.[59]

55. Osama al-Ghazali Harb. Interview with the author. February 7, 2018. Cairo, Egypt.

56. Raymond William Baker, *Sadat and After: Struggles for Egypt's Political Soul* (Harvard University Press, 1990), 123.

57. Sayyid al-Toukhy. Interview with author. January 31, 2018. Cairo, Egypt. This included arrests while he was a student in the mid-1980s, and then in 1989, 1991, 1993, 1995, 1997, 2002, and 2003.

58. Amin Iskandar. Interview with the author. February 3, 2018. Cairo, Egypt.

59. https://www.hrw.org/news/2001/09/26/egypt-abduction-detention-publisher-corde mned.

There are two major moments of repression under Mubarak that leftists remember collectively, regardless of their individual group affiliation.
In 1989, protesters affiliated with leftist groups joined workers in a demonstration against conditions at Egypt's largest steel plant, located in Helwan.
The Central Security Forces broke up the strike with force, killing one hundred leftists and detaining a total of six hundred people. Fifty-two people
were arrested and accused of advocating communism, an outlawed ideology, and seeking to overthrow the government. Those detained suffered
significant torture by police.[60]

The second incident occurred in 1997. At that time, the Mubarak regime
reversed the land rent freezes put in place by Nasser to the detriment of
Egypt's 900,000 tenant farmers, who along with their families accounted
for roughly 10 percent of the Egyptian population.[61] Those affected organized protests that devolved into riots and armed clashes between tenants
and landlords. Leftists joined the protests in solidarity with the agricultural
workers. More than 5,000 farmers were detained over the course of these
events, which came to be known as "the Peasants' Battle against the Landlords and Tenants Law." The regime also arrested between twenty-five and
forty leftists, including Hamdeen Sabahi and Kamal Khalil from the Workers Democratic Party and the Revolutionary Socialists, charging them with
inciting protest and torturing them in jail.

Leaders of secular parties were also repressed when they crossed the red
lines clearly delineated by the state. After the 2005 presidential elections,
the second-place candidate became the victim of state repression. Ghad
Party candidate Ayman Nour was imprisoned on January 29, 2005, on allegations of forgery in forming his party. He was released on health grounds
on February 18, 2009, having served almost his entire sentence. The red
line Nour had crossed was not contesting the presidential elections; the
other candidate from the loyal Gabha Party had not been arrested. Instead,
Nour had offended the state by taking advantage of his increased celebrity
by publicly criticizing human rights violations in Egypt to international
audiences.[62]

60. Human Rights Watch, "Behind Closed Doors: Torture and Detention in Egypt," July
1992, available at https://www.hrw.org/sites/default/files/reports/Egypt927.pdf.

61. Douglas Jehl, "Egypt's Farmers Resist End of Freeze on Rents," *New York Times*, December 27, 1997.

62. This is similar to the case of Saad Eddin Ibrahim, a Cairo-based independent political
activist and founder of the Ibn Khaldoun Center for Development Studies, a think tank working
on human rights, civil society, and minority rights. Though he had established the center in 1988,
was often critical of the regime, and participated in various protests against foreign policy issues,

In summary, the leftist opposition was tolerated, but not co-opted, by the Mubarak regime and did not totally escape harassment. Yet the regime's treatment of these groups was markedly less severe than that of the Brotherhood, described in the next section. Repression against tolerated groups was *reactive*, responding to provocations but not actively seeking eradication. Typically, the regime would arrest leaders or notable members to head off further mobilization, holding them in detention centers for a few days or weeks rather than imposing heavy prison sentences. When members of the tolerated opposition were subject to prosecution, they were tried in criminal courts instead of the military courts reserved for the targeted opposition.

### Targeted Opposition

Targeted repression was not an invention of the Mubarak regime. Instead, it has been the dominant strategy of state control in Egypt over the past century. Although the target of this repression has sometimes changed, as during Sadat's campaign against leftists, the Muslim Brotherhood has been the primary target of state repression since Egypt's independence.

In July 1952, a group of junior military officers, known as the Free Officers, overthrew Egypt's constitutional monarchy. Though the Free Officers and the Muslim Brotherhood worked together closely to oppose the monarchy before the coup, the Brotherhood soon became the first target of brutal state repression in the new republic. The Brotherhood was banned in January 1954 after violent clashes between university student supporters and the police. In October of the same year, a Muslim Brotherhood member attempted to assassinate President Gamal Abdel Nasser. In response, Nasser initiated what was—until 2013—the largest political crackdown in the modern history of Egypt.[63] Between 1954 and 1971, the Brotherhood was the main target of the Nasser regime, a period which the organization refers to as *al-mihna* (the ordeal).

During the *mihna* period, regime repression against the Brotherhood occurred in two waves. In the first wave, six leaders of the Brotherhood were hanged, roughly 1,100 were given various prison sentences, and a large group of Brotherhood supporters and low-ranking members were

---

Ibrahim was only arrested in 2000 and prosecuted for, among other charges, defaming Egypt's image abroad. He was cleared of charges and released in 2003, though the state retried him in 2003 and found Ibrahim guilty of the same crime. Ibrahim spent 2003–2010 in self-imposed exile in Istanbul due to security and health concerns related to his previous imprisonment.

63. Said K. Aburish, *Nasser, the Last Arab* (New York: St.Martin's Press, 2004), 54.

incarcerated without charges, in relation to an assassination attempt.[64] The second wave of persecution began in 1965, following another Brotherhood-related assassination attempt. The second repressive wave resulted in the arrests of hundreds of Brotherhood members. While serving a sentence of twenty-five years of hard labor resulting from a conviction during the first wave of repression against the Muslim Brotherhood, ideologue Sayyid Qutb wrote his most influential tract, *Ma'alim fil-Tariq* (*Signposts Along the Path*), first published in 1964 but informally distributed and circulated among Brotherhood members for many years previously. In the book, he called for an armed jihad (struggle) against Nasser's secular regime, which he declared *jahili* (ignorant or un-Islamic). A Brotherhood off-shoot, dubbed "Organization 1965" in court documents, sought to follow the directive Qutb laid out in his text. The organization was formed in 1957 by Brotherhood activists, many of whom had been newly released from jail. Their plot to overthrow the regime was discovered by security police in 1965, and the focus of the roundup quickly expanded from those involved in the assassination and coup attempt to a much wider circle of Brothers. Qutb was hanged on August 29, 1966, for treason against the state.

Nasser's successor, Sadat, defined his rule as a "correction of the revolution," and shifted the regime's treatment of the Brotherhood. The "correction" included a number of policy reversals, including a purge of Nasserists and socialists from posts in the upper echelons of government and the ruling party. Sadat, far less charismatic than Nasser, sought legitimacy and authority by invoking religious themes and values, presenting himself as the "Believer-President." The shifts in regime policy and legitimation strategy led Sadat to grant a general amnesty to the Brotherhood, release its members from prison in stages between 1971 and March 1975, and encourage those Brothers in exile abroad in Gulf countries to return home. Sadat viewed the Brotherhood as a counterweight to the Nasserist left, which he considered the "great challenge to his authority" and which he targeted as such.[65] In 1976, Sadat granted leading positions in the ASU and the assembly to Brotherhood members, including Salih Abu Ruqayaq. In the same year, the regime permitted the Brotherhood to resume publishing its long-banned monthly magazine, *al-Da'wa*.[66] The relationship between

---

64. Richard Paul Mitchell, *The Society of the Muslim Brothers* (Oxford: Oxford University Press, 1993), 160–162.

65. Kassem, *Egyptian Politics: The Dynamics of Authoritarian Rule*.

66. Erika Post, "Egypt's Elections," *MERIP Middle East Report* 147 (1987): 18–19.

the Brotherhood and Sadat remained collegial through the 1970s. The Brotherhood became critical of the Sadat regime only toward the decade's end, first in response to the economic and social inequality caused by his economic liberalization (*infitah*) policies, and then in response to his visit to Jerusalem in 1977, which culminated in a peace treaty with Israel in 1979.

Upon taking power, Mubarak initially pursued a policy of accommodation towards the Brotherhood, in line with the policy of general amnesty initiated by the change in ruler. Mubarak released all Brotherhood political prisoners arrested under Sadat during the 1981 campaign, as well as permitting the Brotherhood to reoccupy its downtown Cairo headquarters and resume publication of its periodicals.[67] However, as the Brotherhood demonstrated its ability to challenge the regime, the government's repressive approach reverted to patterns of targeting the organization. The Brotherhood increasingly threatened the regime on three fronts: in parliament, in the country's strong professional associations and syndicates, and in the streets.

First, the Brotherhood won eight seats in alliance with the secular Wafd Party and thirty-six seats in alliance with the Liberal and Socialist Labor parties during the 1984 and 1987 elections, respectively, for the 360-member People's Assembly. Second, the Brotherhood worked to establish a presence and get its members elected to leadership roles within the country's strong professional associations and syndicates.[68] By 1990, it held political control of the professional syndicates for doctors, engineers, dentists, merchants, and pharmacists, and in September 1992, it won a majority of seats in the bar association. Third, the Brotherhood proved adept at public displays of strength and mobilizational capabilities. The Brotherhood was vocal in its opposition and organized protests against the regime's participation in the October 1991 Arab-Israeli Madrid peace talks. The organization also quickly mobilized to assist victims in downtown Cairo

67. With the passage of time and benefit of hindsight, analysts have reflected on why Mubarak allowed this policy during this period of regime consolidation. One reasoned that, "[c]onvinced that the Brotherhood posed no real threat, the regime continued to overlook its growing presence" (Diaa Rashwan, "A Trial at the Polls," *Al-Ahram Weekly*, 1995, 2). Another summarized the gentleman's agreement between the state and its Islamist opposition as follows: "the government turned a blind eye to Islamist grassroots power. In return, the Islamists did not confront state corruption and inefficiency." Ahmed Abdalla, "Egypt's Islamists and the State: From Complicity to Confrontation," *Middle East Report* 23 (1993).

68. Sana Abed-Kotob, "The Accommodationists Speak: Goals and Strategies of the Muslim Brotherhood in Egypt," *International Journal of Middle East Studies* 27, no. 3 (1995): 321–339.

during the 1992 earthquake, putting the government's 36-hour response (due to the earthquake's occurring on a weekend) to shame.

In the mid-1990s, "after more than a decade of toleration, the government launched a major counteroffensive against the Muslim Brotherhood, arresting many of its most dynamic leaders and hammering away at its reputation by condemning it as an 'illegal organization with ties to extremist groups.'"[69] The targeted approach taken by the Mubarak regime combined media campaigns, which labeled the group a terrorist organization operating with or financing radical segments of the violent Islamic movement,[70] and waves of targeted arrests of Brotherhood leadership and prominent members.

Arrests began to occur regularly, both preemptively, as a means of collecting information on the organization, and in response to Brotherhood-organized mass mobilization of various kinds. The most well-known example of preemptive arrests against the group was the Salsabil affair. In February 1992, security forces raided the offices of the Salsabil computer company owned by prominent Muslim Brotherhood members Khairat al-Shater and Hassan Malek. The information obtained during the raid was later used to arrest eleven Brotherhood leaders in December of the same year. The regime also began to pass legislative initiatives specifically aimed at curtailing Brotherhood influence in professional syndicates,[71] and was aided in this effort by an emergency law that had been in place for all but a few months since 1967. The law granted the executive extraordinary powers intended for times of war and granted legal permission for violations of citizens' rights and freedoms, which the regime invoked during preemptive arrests of Brotherhood leadership.[72]

As an example of the regime responding to Brotherhood mobilization, twenty Brothers and eighty Brotherhood-affiliated children were arrested after a four-day recreational camp in Alexandria held by the organization

69. Carrie Rosefsky Wickham, *Mobilizing Islam: The Muslim Brotherhood in Egypt* (New York: Columbia University Press, 2002), 3.

70. The media campaigns included articles in Egypt's semi-official newspapers and magazines like *al-Akhbar*, *Rose al-Yusuf*, and *al-Mussawar*, with statements issued by high-level ministers insinuating or claiming direct links between the organization and militant Islamist groups. As early as April 1989, then-Interior Minister Zaki Badr called the Muslim Brotherhood terrorists in a highly publicized press conference.

71. Joel Campagna, "From Accommodation to Confrontation: The Muslim Brotherhood in the Mubarak Years," *Journal of International Affairs* 50, no. 1 (1996): 294–296.

72. Brownlee, "The Decline of Pluralism in Mubarak's Egypt."

without permission from the Interior Ministry in August 1989.[73] In October 1991, after the Brotherhood organized a number of large protests demonstrating against the Madrid peace talks, 185 individuals were arrested including fifteen known Brotherhood leaders. Between 1992 and 1994, Brotherhood leaders were regularly arrested after staging demonstrations that supported the plight of Muslims in Bosnia-Herzegovina, and protested the death of Islamist lawyer Abdel Harith Madani while in police custody, among other causes. The charges levied against the organization were "calling for agitation," "holding contacts with foreign elements," "giving to foreign news agencies statements and reports designed to create confusion, incite citizens, and to distort Egypt's image abroad," and "financing terrorism."[74]

Targeted arrests against the Brotherhood were most evident during election season. Repression was particularly severe surrounding the semi-competitive elections to the lower house of Egypt's bicameral parliament held every five years.[75] Repression of the Brotherhood was notably heavy-handed during the 1995 and 2000 elections.[76] In 1995, 1,392 Islamist campaign workers, supporters, and poll-watchers were arrested, along with over one thousand Muslim Brotherhood candidates.[77] This campaign against the organization may have been exacerbated by a June 1995 assassination attempt on Mubarak while in Addis Ababa, which implicated the Sudanese Muslim Brotherhood. In retaliation, the regime arrested 81 of the Brotherhood's leading activists and tried them in a special military tribunal.

73. Egyptian Organization for Human Rights, "A New Series of Arbitrary Arrests in Egypt," 1989.

74. Campagna, "Accommodation to Confrontation."

75. Other elections also occurred at regular intervals during this time period but were even less competitive. For example, presidential elections were held in 1981, 1987, 1993, 1999, and 2005—though only the 2005 contest included more than one candidate. Elections for the upper house of parliament, known as the Shura Council, were tightly controlled, and rarely saw more than a few seats go to non-NDP candidates. Held every three years between 1983 and 2010, each of these contests put 88 of the council's 264 seats up for election, with another 44 appointed by the president. Municipal elections followed a similar schedule to the legislative elections, but were competitive only within the ruling party (Blaydes, *Elections and Distributive Politics in Mubarak's Egypt*).

76. Al-Awadi, *In Pursuit of Legitimacy.*

77. Al-Lajna al-Wataniyya al-Misriyya li-Mutaba'a al-Intikhabat al Barlamaniyya, "Taqrir," *MERIP Middle East Report* 147 (1987): 2–3. See also the Egyptian Organization of Human Rights, "Democracy Jeopardized: The Egyptian Organization of Human Rights' Account of the Egyptian Parliamentary Elections of 1995," 1996.

The 2000 elections were held in three stages between October and November. 49 of 161 Brotherhood candidates were arrested ahead of the first round of elections. During the second round of the elections, 1,400 individuals were arrested, of which more than one thousand were Brotherhood supporters detained to prevent them from reaching the polling stations.[78] Ahead of the 2005 elections, during which the Brotherhood won an unprecedented eighty-eight seats, the International Crisis Group reported that eight hundred Brotherhood members, including some prominent top leaders, had been arrested, though the Muslim Brotherhood claimed that the real number exceeded two thousand. Those arrested included Mahmoud Ezzat, the organization's Secretary General and the most senior figure arrested since 1996.[79]

The Brotherhood's major electoral showing during the 2005 elections marked a final wave of repression against the group under Mubarak and mirrored earlier repressive efforts.[80] What was particularly notable about the 2005 period was that activism by both secular and Islamist opposition had reached a new level in what became known as the "Cairo Spring." Despite the broad mobilization, the regime continued to overwhelmingly target the Brotherhood with repression. Though the group had faced significant difficulties convening and operating since 1995, the International Crisis Group noted a "quantitative and qualitative change," describing this period as "the most widespread campaign against the group since the 1960s, even if the level of repression is far less and its aim is to control and contain rather than eradicate the group," as it had been under Nasser.[81]

Following the 2005 elections, the regime re-initiated a press campaign publicizing the dangers of the group and its possible linkage with militants. It also resumed mass arrests again in earnest. Between March and June 2006, while the Brotherhood led demonstrations in support of judges

78. Carrie Rosefsky Wickham, *The Muslim Brotherhood: Evolution of an Islamist Movement* (Princeton, NJ: Princeton University Press, 2013), 97.

79. International Crisis Group, "Egypt's Muslim Brothers: Confrontation or Integration?" June 18, 2008 (76), 1. Available at https://d2071andvip0wj.cloudfront.net/76-egypt-s-muslim -brothers-confrontation-or-integration.pdf.

80. This crackdown may have also been facilitated by international political developments. In 2006, Hamas, the Palestinian branch of the Brotherhood, did very well during the first round of the Palestinian parliamentary elections. In addition, following a peak post-9/11, and frightened by the outcomes of both the 2005 Egyptian and 2006 Palestinian parliamentary elections, which were deemed to be more free and fair than previous contests, international pressure for democratization in the Middle East had subsided.

81. International Crisis Group, 2008, 9.

put on trial for their role in reporting electoral fraud, 850 Muslim Brothers were detained, and the "al-Azhar militia" incident led to the arrest of 140 Muslim Brothers in December 2006.[82] Several hundred Muslim Brothers were arrested before and during the June 2007 Shura Council elections, which resulted in the organization failing to win a single seat.[83] Ahead of the April 2008 municipal elections, 830 potential Brotherhood candidates and their supporters were arrested, and only 498 out of 5,754 MB candidates were able to register due to administrative and police obstruction.[84] During the November 2010 parliamentary elections, held on the eve of the 2011 uprising, the regime maintained this pattern of media campaigns against the Brotherhood and arrested almost four hundred Brotherhood candidates and supporters. The majority of parties including the Brotherhood boycotted the contest.

Reports of repression from domestic and international observers during this period noted that the regime was systematic. The regime intimidated Brotherhood members and suspected Brotherhood voters, conducted illegal search and seizure of campaign offices, and arbitrarily arrested known Brothers or those suspected to be related to the organization. Between 2008 and 2010, the regime not only focused on visible leadership but also arrested many middle-ranking members across the country, confiscating their belongings and banning them from leaving the country.[85] Internal Brotherhood statistics maintained by al-Shater's office recorded that during the last decade of Mubarak's rule, roughly 100,000 arrests had been carried out against the 30,000 members of the group. This figure averaged three arrests per active member.[86]

## Conclusion

This chapter has outlined the ways in which the political opposition was repressed under successive regimes in Egypt and Tunisia, justifying the categorization of each case as targeted or widespread. My treatment of Egypt as a case of targeted repression against the Muslim Brotherhood does not deny that others, both private citizens and political activists, suffered from

82. Samer Shehata and Joshua Stacher, "The Brotherhood Goes to Parliament," *Middle East Report* 240 (2006): 32.

83. International Crisis Group, 2008, 10.

84. ikhwanweb.com, March 12, 2007.

85. Khalil al-Anani, *Inside the Muslim Brotherhood: Religion, Identity, and Politics* (Oxford University Press, 2016), 140–141.

86. Husayn al-Qazzaz. Interview with the author. June 15, 2016. Istanbul, Turkey.

multiple forms of repression under Mubarak. Rather, aggregate data suggest that a divide-and-conquer approach defined the regime's efforts to control the opposition, and that this repression disproportionately targeted the Muslim Brotherhood. Egypt's targeted repression of the Brotherhood stands in stark contrast to repression in Tunisia, where the Ben Ali regime severely repressed all mobilized opposition groups alike. In the following two chapters, I demonstrate the implications of this variation in repressive regimes for polarization among opposition actors in Egypt and Tunisia.

# PART III

# Repression, Identity, and Polarization

# 5

# Repression and Polarization in Tunisia, 1987–2010

The variation in repressive regimes between Egypt and Tunisia, outlined in detail in chapter 4, had major implications for the level of political polarization among opposition groups in each country, over time and at the moment of transition in 2010–2011. In this and the following chapter, I document how repression altered levels of affective and preference polarization among the opposition by creating either divisive or bridging political identities through the psychological, social, and organizational mechanisms theorized in chapter 2. This chapter focuses on repression and polarization of opposition in Tunisia during the Ben Ali regime, which lasted from 1987 through the 2010–2011 uprising. First, I document the existence of a widespread repressive environment which created common experiences of repression among jailed and exiled opposition members. I then provide evidence of the three mechanisms—psychological, social, and organizational—through which widespread repression created a bridging political identity among opposition groups in Tunisia. Finally, I link the development of this political identity with decreasing political polarization among the opposition, manifested in increasingly positive affect between groups as well as in less divergence in political preferences among groups.

## Common Experiences of Widespread Repression

While individual members of the opposition under Ben Ali were repressed during different time periods and for different lengths of time, there were a number of commonalities across individuals' experiences created by a widespread repressive environment. As early as 1994, the widespread nature of repression under Ben Ali was apparent to the opposition. Drawing on interviews with this community, Amnesty International reported,

> The campaign of repression against [Ennahda] signaled the beginning of the end of the short-lived acceptance by the authorities of any opposition or criticism and the increasingly systematic targeting of opponents and critics from across the political spectrum. In the past eight years, thousands have been detained for political reasons. Although most of the victims have been supporters and suspected sympathizers of al-Nahda, supporters and suspected sympathizers of the PCOT and other tendencies across the political spectrum, including leaders of the *Mouvement des Democrates Socialistes* (MDS), the largest legal opposition party, have suffered the same fate. In addition, relatives and friends of political opponents, not themselves involved in political activities, as well as human rights activists who defended the rights of these victims, have also been targeted. By 1993–1994, it became increasingly clear, including to those in the human rights movement and in the political opposition in Tunisia who had been silent about, or supported, the repression against the Islamists, that what had been presented by the authorities as a necessary measure to "protect democracy"—namely the repression of the Islamist opposition—was in fact a campaign to stamp out all opposition or dissent.[1]

The similarities across individual experiences of repression are striking: no matter when the repression during the Ben Ali period occurred, the content was nearly identical. Taken together, these experiences reveal a consistency to the manner in which the regime physically injured and psychologically harassed its opposition across time, across national space, and across opposition groups.

1. Amnesty International, "Human Rights Defenders in the Line of Fire" (AI Index: MDE 30/20/98) November 1, 1998, available at https://www.refworld.org/docid/3ae6a9a918.html.

The repressed opposition contained a portion of the Tunisian opposition that lived in exile from the country under Ben Ali. Exile typically resulted when opposition members fled other types of repression and feared for their or their family's safety upon return to the country, rather than through official banishment. The opposition community in exile was smaller than the group in prison, most likely numbering in the hundreds or possibly low thousands, but was politically significant as it included a number of high-profile leaders of opposition groups. For example, Ennahda's Rachid Ghannouchi had been released from jail in May 1987 and soon after left for Europe through Algeria due to health issues that had worsened in prison. He was granted political asylum by the United Kingdom in 1993 and remained in London until the 2010–2011 uprising. In the early 2000s, Moncef Marzouki moved into exile in France after near constant harassment by the police and a politically motivated legal campaign by the regime following his presidential bid in 1994 and decades of human rights activism. He cofounded the CPR while abroad. Many leaders of other major opposition groups similarly concentrated in a handful of Western European countries, namely France (where they understood the language and were surrounded by other Tunisians), Germany, and Switzerland. In spaces of exile, opposition members had similar experiences. They were considered outsiders, as Muslim migrants from North Africa, and were largely confined to religious, neighborhood, and educational communities that reflected this background. Though they were physically far from Tunisia, the opposition continued to be regularly monitored by what appeared to be Tunisian security agents posted to local embassies, as remembered during my interviews with these individuals.

For those members of the opposition who were cycled through the Tunisian legal and penal system, political prisoners could be arrested by any one of five state policing bodies: the National Security Police (*Sûreté Nationale*), the national guard (*Garde Nationale*), the judicial police, the Office of Territorial Surveillance (*Direction de la Surveillance du Territoire*), and the Public Order Brigade (*Brigade d'Ordre Publique*, or BOP). These institutions fell under the jurisdiction of either the Ministry of the Interior or the Ministry of Justice. The presidential guard, which reported directly to the president and his inner circle, was also sometimes involved in arrests of well-known opposition members. Arrests typically occurred at night by plainclothes officers who did not show identification or warrants. In addition to executing the arrest, the police searched homes, confiscated private property, and harassed family members.

Political prisoners were first held in a local police or national guard station, and then transferred to holding cells in the Ministry of the Interior, located in downtown Tunis. The Tunisian Criminal Procedure Code refers to this practice to *garde á vue*, or incommunicado, detention. Incommunicado detention occurred before a formal charge was issued. During this period, lawyers could not access their clients and families were left in the dark about the whereabouts of the detainee. In November 1987, incommunicado detention was legally limited to a ten-day maximum, though the state regularly violated this provision. During the 1989–1991 crackdown on Ennahda, detainees were kept garde à vue between thirty and fifty days, and PCOT members arrested in 1997 reported being held for over two weeks.[2]

Families of detainees speculated that the incommunicado period was extended by police to hide the physical evidence of torture, the worst of which political prisoners experienced during this detention. Torture was not an insolated incident, but rather "the pillar of an overall institutional mechanism."[3] Commonly reported methods of torture included beatings on the body and feet, electric shocks, and burning skin with cigarettes. One method became known as *poulet róti*, or "roasted chicken," where a detainee was tied to a horizontal pole by his hands and feet and suspended for long periods of time. Detainees also reported being subjected to a process approximating water-boarding and referred to as *baño*: the victim was suspended by his ankles from a pulley and his head was repeatedly plunged into a bucket of dirty water. Mock executions were also employed as a torture tactic. While physical and psychological torture was a near universal experience, interrogation for information, ostensibly the purpose of harsh treatment, only sometimes followed. This suggested that instead of using harsh repressive techniques to extract credible information, torture was instead used "to create an atmosphere of terror" among political detainees in an effort to break their commitment to political opposition.[4]

Once a charge was formally levied, detainees were transferred to a prison. At this point, political prisoners were given access to their lawyers and

2. The details in this and the previous paragraph were recounted to me time and again by different members of the opposition who had been arrested by the regime. See also Amnesty International, "Tunisia: Prolonged Incommunicado Detention and Torture" (AI Index: MDE 30/04/92) March 1992, available at https://www.amnesty.org/download/Documents/192000/mde300041992en.pdf.

3. Jebnoun, *Rogue Elephants*, 114.

4. Amnesty International, "Tunisia: Prolonged Incommunicado Detention and Torture," March 1992, 13.

families. Political prisoners were concentrated in two of Tunisia's twenty-seven overcrowded prisons, the Borj er-Roumi prison in Bizerte and the April 9th prison in Tunis. Political prisoners serving lengthy senten-ces were arbitrarily rotated through a number of prisons as an additional form of psychological torture, and to inconvenience their families during permitted visits. Ennahda's Lareydh was transferred among seven prisons during his fourteen years in prison. Sadok Chourou, also a high-ranking member of Ennahda, was often transferred between prisons during his eighteen years in prison without warning to him or his family. During his 2005 trial, CPR's Abbou was transferred from a prison in Tunis to one in Le Kef, a three-hour drive from the capital, his family, and his attorneys.[5] When PCOT's Hamma Hammami undertook a hunger strike to protest conditions during an arrest in 1994, he was transferred from Sousse prison, to Messadine prison, and finally to the April 9th prison in Tunis, where he was held in solitary confinement with a constant chain around his foot and denied access to his lawyers. His family was denied access to him for over a week and told he was being punished for the hunger strike, while he was then further rotated through the Kasserine, Mahdia, and Nadhour prisons.[6]

Torture in prison occurred less frequently than torture during incom-municado detention, but it took a more sexually explicit form.[7] While common-law prisoners were generally only tortured when they were first detained, political prisoners might also experience torture during impris-onment. Lotfi Hammami, a PCOT member arrested in 1998, reported that while in prison, a guard tied a rope to his penis and then pulled.[8] In addition, common-law prisoners were often weaponized to rape political prisoners in shared cells. In a more extreme example, a man accused of being a sympathizer—rather than a member or leader—of Ennahda was

5. Amnesty International, "Urgent Action In Focus: Mohammed Abbou—'We need the world's solidarity,'" September 2007, 2.

6. Amnesty International, "Health Concern/Torture" (AI Index: MDE 30/06/1994) February 22, 1994, available at https://www.amnesty.org/download/Documents/180000/mde300061994en.pdf, and related updates.

7. McCarthy documents a similar development in his interviews with Ennahda activists (Rory McCarthy, *Inside Tunisia's Al-Nahda: Between Politics and Preaching* (Cambridge University Press, 2018), 76).

8. Amnesty International, "Fear of torture or ill-treatment/Fear of further possible arrests/Prisoners of conscience and new concern: Health concern" (AI Index: MDE 30/17/98) June 25, 1998, available at https://www.amnesty.org/download/Documents/156000/mde300171998en.pdf.

arrested in 1990, convicted in the mass trials of 1992, and sentenced to six-teen years eight months imprisonment. He spent the majority of his prison sentence in communal imprisonment, where he was one of four political prisoners in a cell housing 110 inmates at the Borj er-Roumi prison. In June 2004, he was moved to a *siloun*, a solitary confinement punishment cell, as the result of an incident in the prison. The prison guards then placed four common-law prisoners in his cell and one proceeded to rape the political prisoner with the help of the others. The common-law prisoners were then let out of the cell while the injured political prisoner was left unattended for six days, strongly suggesting this attack was condoned or orchestrated by prison administration.[9]

The torment of persecuted opposition members did not end once they were formally released from prison. Former political prisoners experienced post-detention life similarly and were subjected to a wide range of arbitrary restrictions collectively known as *contrôle administratif* (in English, administrative control). Articles 23 and 24 of the Tunisian Penal Code gave the state the right to determine the location of residence for former political prisoners for a certain period of time as part of criminal sentencing. In addition, authorities could legally prohibit a former political prisoner from leaving an assigned location without permission and arbitrarily revise that location. While these terms were legally required to be included in the initial sentencing, they often were not imposed until a prisoner was released. These terms were rarely conveyed to prisoners in writing and could change or be extended without warning.[10] Ninety percent of former political prisoners were subjected to excessive administrative control following their release, according to estimates obtained from human rights organizations.[11]

Although administrative control was legally limited to dictating the physical location of prisoners after their release, in practice it included a continuation of surveillance, physical threats, and other arbitrary restrictions of movement by local representatives of the country's coercive institutions. One such practice required former political prisoners to check

9. Human Rights Watch, "Tunisia—Crushing the Person, Crushing a Movement: The Solitary Confinement of Political Prisoners," (17.4) April 2005, 28. Available at https://www.hrw.org/reports/2005/tunisia0405/tunisia0405.pdf.

10. Human Rights Watch, "A Larger Prison: Repression of Former Political Prisoners in Tunisia," March 24, 2010, available at https://www.hrw.org/report/2010/03/24/larger-prison/larger-prison.

11. Hibou, *Force of Obedience*, 5.

in at a police station multiple times per day or week. Authorities kept confiscated identity documents and passports, which prevented former prisoners from finding employment or receiving state-subsidized medical care for injuries and illnesses, many of which they acquired from torture while in state custody. Former political prisoners were similarly prevented from traveling abroad where they might find employment or seek private medical care. In addition, political prisoners were often granted "conditional" releases. Under the Tunisian penal system, a conditional release indicated that a political prisoner could be re-imprisoned without a trial before expiration of their sentences for unspecified misconduct.

Two examples help to elucidate the nature of administrative control, and how it both impeded political prisoners from resuming normal activities as well as extended many of the repressive experiences from prison. After he completed a sixteen-year and four-month jail sentence, the terms of release for Ennahda's Jebali included an additional sentence of a five-year administrative control period during which he was confined to his home city of Sousse. Jebali as well as his immediate and extended family were under near constant surveillance from State Security and National Guard officers, both while in the family home and on the street. He and his wife's applications for passports were denied, and their inquiries into the applications went unanswered. Jebali was quoted in an Amnesty International report as saying, "since I am not allowed to move, to travel, to work, I am confined in a prison smaller than the one I left for an illusion of freedom."[12] A second example comes from the experience of CPR's Abbou. After serving twenty-eight months of his sentence, Abbou was granted a conditional release July 27, 2007. Between the date of his early release and the original termination of his sentence in August 2008, Abbou was turned back from the airport three times while attempting to travel to human rights conferences abroad, despite the absence of any written orders. After August 2008, he was turned back at least four more times. When Abbou moved around within the country, he was followed closely by plainclothes policemen.[13]

12. Amnesty International, "Freed but Not Free: Tunisia's Former Political Prisoners" (AI Index: MDE 30/003/2010) March 2010, available at http://www.amnesty.org/en/library/asset/MDE30/003/2010/en/11495e9c-da2b-4af1-98bc-67b5b7c97c76/mde300032010en.pdf.

13. Mohamed Abbou, *Maqalat qabla ath-thawra* (Tunisia: Sotepa Graphic, 2014), 48–50. See also Human Rights Watch, "A Larger Prison: Repression of Former Political Prisoners in Tunisia," March 24, 2010, 18.

## PSYCHOLOGICAL EFFECTS OF WIDESPREAD REPRESSION

The empirical record of repression in Tunisia demonstrates that multiple groups were repressed. As outlined in chapter 2, I argue that repression influenced political group identities, and ultimately polarization, among groups through three reinforcing mechanisms, psychological, social, and organizational in nature. Most important is the psychological mechanism through which repression created awareness among the opposition of their membership in a larger group with common characteristics and experiences. Perceptions of these shared experiences created a sense of what characteristics defined the opposition and who could rightfully be considered part of this group. In other words, whether or not the opposition *perceived* themselves as having been repressed together—whether repressive experiences provided information about other opposition groups, created a feeling of entitativity, and whether this shifted over time as repression became increasingly ubiquitous in Tunisia—is an important component of the psychological mechanism through which repression creates political identities.

Recollections and documentation of historical developments demonstrate that a perception of a collective opposition jointly defined by experiences of regime repression developed over time. Initially, the way in which the regime repressed Ennahda gave the opposition information suggesting a lower level of bridging opposition-level entitativity, or a system in which individual opposition groups were important. Though the atmosphere during the advent of the Ben Ali regime was generally described as cordial, the way in which opposition members described other parties revealed a lack of identification as a unified opposition movement. Ennahda leadership felt that secular opposition kept their distance as the regime targeted Islamist opposition during the 1989–1991 roundup. Jebali noted that the secular opposition appeared to "sense Ennahda was in a rare truce with the regime and that one day conflict would arrive, and they retreated from us."[14] During my conversations about this period, there was little reference to "the opposition." Instead, members of the opposition referred to their own groups by name, suggesting that these were the most important reference groups for these individuals at the time.

But over time, as repression became more ubiquitous, and the opposition gained more direct experience with repression and acquired

---

14. Hamadi Jebali. Interview with the author. December 10, 2014. Sousse, Tunisia.

information about the broader repressive and political environment, perceptions shifted, from lower-level, individual opposition groupness towards a higher-level, bridging collective groupness. Beginning in 1999, jailed leadership of Ennahda emerged from the prison period with a stronger perception of a broader opposition movement being victimized by the regime having learned more information about other opposition movements. During my conversations about the late Ben Ali regime, individuals spoke more about "the opposition" as a cohesive entity. One Ennahda leader characterized repression as a threat to the democratic movement, not simply the Islamist movement. Mourou said following the repression of the 1990s and first half of the 2000s, "the opposition collectively felt the danger from the regime was one danger: it was the lack of freedom. All of us had been affected by it." Ennahda leaders felt that secular opposition groups had also changed their approach towards Islamists following heavy regime repression, seeing Ennahda as part of their group in the "us" of the opposition versus "them" of the regime. Mourou felt that slowly,

> People came to sympathize with us. The regime continued to blame us for [Islamist] violence in the country when we couldn't possibly be responsible for it; our entire organization was scattered or in jail. Some finally asked, why is [the regime] violating these people's freedom? They came to realize that the regime was worse than the Islamists. After all, it was the regime that was violating people's freedom, not us.[15]

As a result of the information provided by repression, Islamists increasingly learned that they were not the regime's only victims. The narrative put forward by Ennahda about the brutal regime campaign targeting the movement in the early 1990s places it within a larger framework of widespread repression. Leader Rachid al-Ghannouchi said, "after [Ben Ali] attacked the Islamists, he attacked secularists. Anyone who demanded freedom, he struck at them."[16] Mourou similarly explained, "the regime used different tactics to first hurt the Islamists and then others. He first repressed the Islamists, and then anyone who disobeyed him."[17] Lareydh said, "repression happened against those who looked like [Ben Ali] from the left, those who looked like him from the nationalists, those who were like him from the ruling party. He struck [Islamists] the hardest but he also rotated

15. Abdelfattah Mourou. Interview with the author. January 16, 2017. Tunis, Tunisia.

16. Rachid al-Ghannouchi. Interview with the author. November 19, 2014. Tunis, Tunisia.

17. Abdelfattah Mourou. Interview with the author. January 16, 2017. Tunis, Tunisia.

through, and then targeted leftists and nationalists."[18] Ennahda's leadership understood that the broader opposition had been repressed because it watched the regime arrest these groups, and then suffered with them.

Similar developments occurred with the perceptions of secular opposition leaders. Ettajdid leader Brahim described the group as historically being among "the strongest opponents" of mixing religion and politics and fervently against some of the tenets in Ennahda's political program. The group had long remained hesitant to a formal agreement with Islamists; as he Brahim said, "opposition to Ben 'Ali did not require a [formal] political alliance in order to unite against repression and dictatorship. There were a wide range of viable alternatives available to us for resistance, and we didn't want to accept that kind of formal commitment" in the 1980s and early 1990s. In addition, the group's leadership maintained that any democratic movement "had to remain civil and secular," and it was unclear how they would do this in partnership with Islamists. However, by 2005, as the political landscape continued to be limited and repressed, Ettajdid had "become more open to negotiations and compromise with our fellow oppressed opposition." Islamists were now included as fellow opposition, demonstrating a shift in the way Brahim thought about those included in the bridging identity group of "opposition."[19]

When asked to describe repression under the Ben Ali regime, members of the former opposition consistently characterized it as a regime that harassed all opposition, though they also noted that this shifted over time. For example, Brahim from the Ettajdid Movement said, "we all went to jail, one after the other."[20] Ben Amor from CPR said that during the 1990s the regime "arrested most of the political activists and put them in jail. The regime started targeting opposition or activist without choosing."[21] Chebbi of PDP similarly described the environment as follows: "if someone was in the opposition, his only place was in prison or in exile."[22]

Over time, secular opposition members increasingly learned that while everyone suffered, Islamists "got it much, much, much worse," in the words of Brahim. Ben Jaafar noted that the Islamists had a "special place" under the generally repressive Ben Ali regime. Marzouki of CPR painted a similar picture. He mentioned that fellow secularist opposition members Chebbi

18. Ali Lareydh. Interview with the author. December 18, 2014. Tunis, Tunisia.

19. Ahmed Brahim. Interview with the author. December 2, 2014. Tunis, Tunisia.

20. Ahmed Brahim. Interview with the author. December 2, 2014. Tunis, Tunisia.

21. Samir Ben Amor. Interview with the author. November 28, 2014. Tunis, Tunisia.

22. Ahmed Najib Chebbi. Interview with the author. January 19, 2017. Tunis, Tunisia.

of PDP and Ben Jaafar of Ettakatol, both of whom he considered "close friends," had suffered "similar fates" to him in terms of treatment by the Ben Ali regime. However, the regime's repression of Islamists was at a different level: "when you compare what happened to the Islamists, my treatment was not that harsh. Yes, I have been arrested, I have received death threats, but I haven't been subjected to torture. I can't say my experience was like the Islamists, because they lost everything."[23] Despite variation in the severity of their treatment, the opposition's reflections demonstrate the increasing identification as a victimized group of democratic opposition.

## SOCIAL EFFECTS OF WIDESPREAD REPRESSION

Second, repression affected group identities through a social mechanism in spaces occupied by opposition members abroad and in Tunisia's prisons. Repression significantly altered the composition of opposition members' social surroundings, forcing certain kinds of exposure and interaction, and bringing certain groups into close and specific contact. The socialization effects of repression are evident in the shared and overlapping repressive experiences of members of different opposition groups when they were imprisoned or exiled in the same physical places or arrested during the same roundups.

In exile, the Tunisian opposition shared space. Being in exile permitted a freer mingling with other members of their own opposition groups—but more importantly, with members of other opposition groups. Indeed, exile facilitated social interaction with other Tunisians in social spaces, such as cafes and restaurants, Muslim community spaces related to local mosques, and schools that children attended together. This kind of reinforced community is not uncommon to migrant communities in foreign countries.[24] These interactions took a political bend when the Tunisians that interacted were from the opposition and were forced abroad for similar political reasons. Shared exile experiences and spaces facilitated exposure to others' political ideas as well as political conversations.

Similar social overlap unfolded in prison spaces. There, prisoners of different ideological stripes shared physical space. Between the early 1990s

---

23. Moncef Marzouki. Interview with the author. January 11, 2017. Tunis, Tunisia.

24. Careja and Emmenegger, "Making Democratic Citizens: The Effects of Migration Experience on Political Attitudes in Central and Eastern Europe."

and 2004, roughly 500 political prisoners were kept in solitary confinement, but the vast majority were held in communal cells. The overcrowding of prisons as well as individual cells may have further facilitated the sharing of physical space. The April 9th prison through which political prisoners rotated was initially built to accommodate 900 inmates but housed nearly 5,000 prisoners at the height of its use in the mid-2000s, when the proportion of the Tunisia population in prison was reportedly the fourth highest globally with 252 prisoners per 100,000 citizens.[25] While creating horrific hygienic conditions, these patterns of imprisonment also created specific social conditions for political prisoners. Prisoners shared a cell for days, months, and years with tens and even hundreds of other cellmates. The shared nature of prison experience among the opposition may have also been aided by mild improvements in the treatment of prisoners beginning in 1996. Previously, prison officials appeared to fear permitting political prisoners, particularly those of the Islamist persuasion, to congregate for group activities. However, after a series of hunger strikes,[26] political prisoners won the right to eat and pray in groups. As a result, political activists jailed during this period had more opportunities to socialize and communicate with prisoners from other cells from within their own group, but more importantly with political prisoners of other ideological persuasions.[27]

Many of an individual's cellmates were drawn from members of the general prisoner population. But more important for the political importance of prison were the ways in which prison forced close interaction between members of different opposition groups and movements. Many political prisoners were isolated from the general population of common-law prisoners and held in small-group isolation. The practice confined a small number of prisoners (typically four) also being held on political charges to one cell. This limited their exposure to other inmates and the general prisoner population but created bonds with their immediate fellow cellmates. When I asked about their time in prison, former political prisoners often mentioned other members of the opposition from different parties and of different ideologies whom they had met while imprisoned. Members of different groups were jailed together in the same cell and intermingled communal prison spaces, such as during prayer or meal times. Leftists

25. McCarthy, *Inside Al-Nahda*, 70; Wolf, *Political Islam*, 81.

26. McCarthy, *Inside Al-Nahda*, 84–87, powerfully describes the emergence of hunger strikes as a political tactic as a way in which prisoners "retook control of their bodies."

27. Human Rights Watch, "Tunisia: Long-term Solitary Confinement of Political Prisoners," (16.3) July 2004, available at https://www.hrw.org/reports/2004/tunisia0704/tunisia0704.pdf.

imprisoned during the early 1990s as part of the crackdown on university campuses mentioned meeting Ennahda activists,[28] while Ennahda leadership said they sometimes overlapped with the leaders of secular groups. Samir Dilou, currently a member of the executive committee of Ennahda, was arrested for participating in opposition mobilization as a UGET student leader in 1991. He described meeting activists from secular groups, including names such as Khemais Ksila and Abdel Latif Mekki as well as Hamadi Jebali. During our conversation, Dilou showed me a picture taken of him in his cell with a camera smuggled into the prison. The picture shows him in a cell with about ten other prisoners, none of whom were from Ennahda.[29] The small-group isolation configuration limited prisoners' exposure to the entire prison population, but forced them to interact with each other quite intimately. McCarthy similarly documents how Nour, a Nahdawi prisoner held in Sousse, was randomly assigned to share a cell with Hamma Hammami, a leader of the PCOT. The author writes that "from their shared experience of repression, they crossed what would have been an unbridgeable divide." In an interview, Nour described his relationship with Hammami: "we told each other stories about the failures of our society. I couldn't believe how kind he was. There was no ideological battle because we were in the same boat, facing the same difficulties. There were values that we shared."[30]

The social interaction caused by prisons extended beyond the prisoners themselves to their wives and families as well. Prison authorities tightly controlled visits and made them very difficult to undertake. Families of political prisoners were forced to wait in long lines and in visiting facilities and so interacted in these spaces. In this way, "on the day of prison visits large groups of mothers, wives, and sisters met at the prison and spent several hours talking, spreading news, offering reassurance, and reinforcing community bonds."[31] These forced interactions among opposition families may have had a similar effect to prison and exile on political prisoners, increasing contact as well as the exchange of ideas and stories focused on similar experiences.

The way in which the Tunisian regime treated political prisoners, in prison and in exile, facilitated certain patterns of interaction and socializing among opposition groups, and even extended to the relatives and

28. Samir Ben Amor. Interview with the author. November 28, 2014. Tunis, Tunisia.

29. Samir Dilou. Interview with the author. November 17, 2014. Tunis, Tunisia.

30. Ibid., 83.

31. McCarthy, *Inside Al-Nahda*, 92. Similar stories were recounted to me during my interviews.

acquaintances of political prisoners. Within a widespread repressive environment, members of different opposition groups were forcible exposed to each other during long and harsh prison terms or in exiled spaces, becoming more familiar with each other and in turn engaging in conversation and even constructive political debate.

## ORGANIZATIONAL EFFECTS OF WIDESPREAD REPRESSION

In addition to altering political identities through psychological and social mechanisms, repression can also change the organizational structure of affected opposition groups. And in Tunisia, repression altered the organization of individual opposition groups and the broader Tunisian opposition movement. In short, widespread repression simultaneously forced the fragmentation of individual groups' organizational structures (i.e., *within* group effects) and the strengthening of non-political party organizations focused on more general principles of reform and resistance such as human rights abuses, arbitrary detention, and democratic reforms (i.e., *across* group effects).

First, repression weakened individual group organizations by creating double party structures. Opposition groups struggled to survive under the regime's heavy-handed repression by adapting parallel leadership and party structures. The regime crackdown on Ennahda in the late 1980s and early 1990s led to the duplication of its Tunisian leadership structure among exiled leaders in Europe. This was no easy task, as Ennahda exiles came to be dispersed through over seventy countries and faced severe travel restrictions, financial difficulties, and continued surveillance by Tunisian intelligence agents. In 1987, Ennahda created a Political Bureau and communications office in Paris, and added an Executive Bureau in 1989 headed by Ghannouchi from London. The European branch of the movement was charged with tasks important to the movement in exile, such as publicizing the group's plight, gaining asylum status for movement members abroad, and mobilizing international opinion against the Ben Ali regime. Ennahda's European leadership held a major party congress in Germany in 1992 and elected a Shura Council in an effort to continue the movement's political activities.[32] Many of the foreign organization's activities duplicated and replaced the political function of the domestic organization. During

32. Wolf, *Political Islam*, 87–89.

this same period, Sadok Chourou served as the movement's leader within Tunisia, where a similar hierarchy and division of labor among political, economic, and social bureaus had been developed since the movement's inception in 1981.

The duplication of its organizational structures shaped Ennahda into a more diffuse organization than in the past and ultimately weakened the movement structurally. Other scholars have noted how this permitted the development of rival factions and internal divisions, a lack of within-group coordination, and a major communication gap between domestic and international leadership.[33] This resulted in a period during which there was no active representation of Ennahda on the ground in Tunis, as the party's only visible leadership was located abroad. However, this changed once Ennahda leadership were released from prison in the mid-2000s. At that time, senior activists such as Jebali and Abdelhamid Jlassi reestablished the domestic Executive Bureau began to reconstitute the group through small meetings in parts of the country where the group was popular. However, because the domestic leadership remained weakened and without visible widespread popular support, the shifting of leadership from the European to Tunisian leadership structures was postponed: as Ennahda leader Lareydh said, "we did not have the means yet. So instead we decided to have two power bases, one official in London, and one undeclared in Tunis."[34] Other opposition groups similarly developed dual centers and structures of command as a result of the regime's harsh tactics. CPR's leadership was split, with Marzouki in France and the majority of other cofounders located in Tunisia.

The increasing diffuse nature of opposition groups' structures may have played into the development of organizations mobilizing on broader political themes. The Tunisian League of Human Rights (in French, *Ligue Tunisienne des Droits de l'Homme*; known by the acronym LDTH) was founded in 1976 and played an increasingly important and public role in promoting general issues of human rights abuses and the necessity of legitimate democratic reform as repression increased in the early 1990s. While the organization was carefully monitored, it was never fully outlawed, though it unfortunately became ineffective once it was co-opted by the regime

---

33. Ibid., chapter 4; Francesco Cavatorta and Fabio Merone, "Moderation through Exclusion? The Journey of the Tunisian Ennahda from Fundamentalist to Conservative Party," *Democratization* 20, no. 5 (2013): 857–875.

34. As quoted in Wolf, *Political Islam*, 115.

in 1994.[35] LDTH Founder Mustapha Ben Jaafar described it as becoming "something important, not something that divided us" in that it provided space for jointly repressed opposition groups to mobilize more strongly together on issues that affected all groups.[36]

The weakened parties and dual structures of command enabled those in exile to develop two key cross-group initiatives in the 2000s: the 2003 *Appel de Tunis* (Call from Tunis) and the 2005 *Collectif du 18 October* (both of which will be discussed in more detail in a following section). Exiles were more easily and regularly in contact with other groups located abroad than with their partners in Tunisia due to physical proximity. The diffuse nature of these organizations, in combination with the social circles and relatively free environment created by exile, facilitated the coming together of these groups in mobilizing on political issues of concern across opposition groups of various ideologies.

———

Through a psychological mechanism, shared experiences of repression provided information about the political world regarding which groups were being harmed by the regime, laying a foundation for bridging identity in which a broader victimized opposition served as the core of that identity's content. Both parts of the victimized opposition increasingly became aware of the suffering of competing groups, and social and organizational developments reinforced acknowledgement of other opposition groups as fellow victims of a larger collective in a fight against the regime. Through a combination of psychological, social, and organizational mechanisms, repression facilitated the creation of a unique bridging political identity in which shared victimhood and continued struggle against a highly repressive regime unified individual opposition groups into a broader opposition movement.

## Affective Polarization among the Tunisian Opposition

The opposition identity which developed over time through the psychological, social, and organizational mechanisms detailed above was accompanied by corresponding shifts in political polarization. First, the development and strengthening of an identity as a broader opposition led to

35. Ibid., 99.
36. Mustapha Ben Jaafar. Interview with the author. January 16, 2017. Tunis, Tunisia.

a decrease in affective polarization, or increasingly positive feelings and less dislike among opposition groups, over time. With the advent of the Ben Ali regime, identity divisions created high levels of affective distance between parties. The initial moments of the new regime in the late 1980s were described as cautiously cordial; groups sometimes coordinated small demonstrations against the regime, and often held meetings or sittings (*jalasat*) with each other. But in a moment when Ennahda was being heavily targeted by the regime, Nahdawi feelings about this period went beyond the observation of the simple defection of support from the left. Instead, the feeling that secular opposition had either tacitly or explicitly supported repression of the group is pervasive in Nahdawi narratives of the 1989–1991 period. Dilou reflected that "the other opposition parties were silent or conspired with the regime" during the crackdown.[37] Mourou went further and used stronger language:

> In the beginning of the Ben Ali period, [the secular opposition] was afraid of Islamists because of our popularity, and bit by bit they agreed to the parts of Ben Ali's program which struck at Islamists. The left was persuaded that the ban on Islamists was just; it supported the secular political program being undertaken by the RCD because the same program was being advanced by leftists and secularists. The left claimed [that we were] against secularism and political liberties [and that we had some] secret, evil plan against the rights of women and children. Because of this, they came to use government agencies to repress Islamists, because they themselves were unable to fight us.[38]

This description suggests that Ennahda leadership felt distrustful of their secular counterparts during the early periods of the Ben Ali regime, conflating the left as at least tacitly and possibly explicitly supportive of the regime's repression of the Islamist movement. The regime's early repressive tactics had not only created an identity division, but also engendered negative feelings between the two ideological sides of the opposition.

A particularly moving anecdote from Ennahda leader Ali Lareydh is demonstrative of shifts in affect between secular and Islamist opposition groups followed collective experiences of repression. As a known leader of Ennahda, Lareydh had been imprisoned from 1990 to 2004 and spent much of that time in solitary confinement. He was imprisoned during major

37. Samir Dilou. Interview with the author. November 17, 2014. Tunis, Tunisia.
38. Abdelfattah Mourou. Interview with the author. January 16, 2017.

events like the dissolution of the Soviet Union, the advent of the internet, the 9/11 attacks, and domestic developments in Tunisia. He had had few people to talk to about his feelings or thoughts regarding these events, which he described as being particularly torturous for someone "cerebral" like himself. A few days after Lareydh was released, Ahmed Najib Chebbi, Maya Jribi, and other members of the PDP came to visit him at his house. They began what he referred to as "a political discussion." Because of his limited access to newspapers, television, other people, and other politicians, Lareydh told them that he felt distant from what had occurred in Tunisia and in the world during his imprisonment. He felt that his opinion was "strange" and he "did not have confidence in himself or [his] perception of the situation in Tunisia." Lareydh continued,

> They stayed with me for hours, explaining what had happened and what was currently happening in Tunisia as well as popular reactions to [these events]. They knew that for a period I had been far away from developments in Tunis and I wanted to hear their opinions and understand the details they told me, as people who had not been in jail for 14 years. They told me these things as if I had been a member of their party sitting in their office ... what I mean by this is that there was no longer anything that divided us at all.[39]

The visit was more than just paying respect to a man who had suffered tremendously, though it was also that. The conversation was an example of different opposition groups treating each other as fellow victims and evincing positive affect towards the broader opposition movement despite their origins from opposite sides of the political spectrum. Members of the PDP treated Lareydh like one of their own.

When I later asked Chebbi about this encounter, he said, "it was very important to me to visit him. The solidarity between us already existed before he was released." Chebbi recalled that he often went to visit political prisoners when they were released from prison and would also visit those who were in exile when he traveled abroad. This camaraderie is evidence of positive affect between Chebbi and other members of the opposition, regardless of ideological persuasion. Though Chebbi was not repressed under Ben Ali, he had suffered eleven years in prison as a leftist and student activist under Bourguiba. This experience helped him to understand what released prisoners might be feeling after such an ordeal and what they

---

39. Ali Lareydh. Interview with the author. December 18, 2014. Tunis, Tunisia.

might need, and to view them as both fellow victims and potential partners. Moreover, regarding the 1989 National Pact and the left's support for it, Chebbi said he "never understood it myself," stating political mobilization was a fundamental right. Following the crackdown on Ennahda between 1989 and 1991, Chebbi recalled that "as a politician, as an intellectual, and as a lawyer, I felt that I had to stand up against this repressive campaign towards the Islamists. I saw that democracy would either be for all of us, or it would not be for any of us. We could not be divided." He publicly criticized the regime for the actions it took towards Ennahda: "I didn't defend their ideas, which I largely disagreed with, but I did defend their rights."[40]

Even repressed members of the ruling party began to demonstrate more positive affect towards Islamists, whom the Ben Ali regime had actively demonized as enemies of the state. Mohamed Mzali was the Secretary General of the RCD and also served as prime minister under Bourguiba between 1980 and 1986. As the country witnessed strikes and riots related to price increases at the end of the Bourguiba regime, the president laid the blame on Mzali, dismissed him from the ruling party, and replaced him as prime minister with Rachif Sfar, previously the Minister of Finance. Mzali left the country for France and was sentenced in absentia to four years imprisonment and fifteen years hard labor in a politically charged case against him. In 1991, he published his own account of the ordeal under Bourguiba and accused Ben Ali of being just as dictatorial as his predecessor. In that book, Mzali described Islamist ideas as "legitimate in a country whose inhabitants are Muslim" and categorized Ennahda as consisting, "for the most part, of men of honor, pacifists and democrats."[41] Mzali and exiled Ennahda leadership, along with former Bourguiba-era minister and PUP founder Ahmed Ben Salah exiled under Ben Ali in 1989, jointly issued a statement that criticized Ben Ali and called for a national alliance against him later that year, and issued a similar declaration in 1995.

The emergence of CPR was an important development related to increasingly positive affect among the Tunisian opposition. CPR was founded in 2001, following the widespread repression of the 1990s, with Marzouki, a former political prisoner, as an influential cofounder. As early as 1994, Marzouki reached out to Ennahda leadership after having been granted exile in France following his imprisonment. He had always

---

40. Ahmed Najib Chebbi. Interview with the author. January 19, 2017. Tunis, Tunisia.
41. Mohamed Mzali, *Túnez: qué porvenir?* (Paris: Publisud, 1991).

been more sympathetic than some towards Ennahda because his father had been a sympathizer and he grew up in the south of Tunis, where Ennahda enjoyed extensive support. However, after his traumatic experience during the presidential elections, he publicly called on Tunisians from abroad to "forget about the divide between secularists and Islamists, and instead focus on the divide between democrats and non-democrats."[42] This was indicative of increased empathy; Marzouki articulated positive affect towards Ennahda, in that he considered them to be a part of the "democrats" group, in opposition to the "non-democrats" of the regime. In 2002, CPR worked to mobilize an opposition campaign against a constitutional referendum proposed by the president. While some members of the extreme left were against including Islamists in the campaign, CPR actively opposed this position. Fathi Jerbi, one of the party's founders, said that CPR leadership felt that "no one has the right to exclude anyone else … Ennahda was a victim of the Ben Ali regime, and so we stood for the rights of the organization in the name of democracy and the interests of the Tunisia people."[43]

Relatedly, secular groups' discourse about two initiatives in the early 2000s (the substance of which is discussed in more detail in the following section) points to increasingly positive affect between groups as central to sustained agreement among the opposition. The parties involved in these initiatives were convinced of the value of true political pluralism and inclusion of all opposition forces that accepted non-violent reform, directly citing decades of repression that eventually touched all opposition groups as the reason for commitment to pluralism. Repression was an important precursor to getting everyone around the same table, literally and figuratively. CPR's Ben Amor said that sustained repression under Ben Ali "brought us together and forced us to recognize each other."[44] Ben Jaafar of Ettakatol similarly observed that by 2005 there was "mutual acceptance" among the opposition. He continued,

> human rights was an important unifier among the opposition. It was the most important issue. Without basic freedom, how can you talk about anything else, political or otherwise? We felt that human rights and political freedoms were points of agreement, because the entire political spectrum had been a victim of the regime's repression and had their

42. As quoted in Wolf, *Political Islam*, 101.
43. Fathi Jerbi. Interview with the author. November 13, 2014. Tunis, Tunisia.
44. Samir Ben Amor. Interview with the author. November 28, 2014. Tunis, Tunisia.

freedoms violated. We had a desire and a willingness to talk to the others as common victims.[45]

PDP's Chebbi also cited a common experience of repression as shaping the way in which different groups of different ideologies approached undertaking reform:

> Repression helped to bring together the opposition, absolutely (*bi-kul ta'kid*). There was a common interest in changing the environment.... This basic defense was not so much mutual love, but rather a shared common interest. Defending the opposition as a group created a unified perspective without ideological differences or politicized cracks. And this coming together was one of the main reasons the Collectif succeeded. Our authority came from our coming together.[46]

Positive affect between groups should not be understood as true affection or friendship (though that certainly existed between individual members of the opposition), but rather positive feelings that facilitated whether or not these individuals could work together and compromise on major issues.

Chebbi noted that the Collectif was preceded by two important developments. First, the international environment had essentially permitted Ben Ali to continue heavy repression of political opposition; the combination of international economic support for the regime and the global "War on Terror" following 9/11 indicated to the regime that it would not be punished for domestic abuses of power. Chebbi said that while long-term detentions were less frequent, more regular repression "became stronger and affected all opposition members until even sitting in a cafe was prohibited. It became nearly absolute." While standard theories of repression suggest this increase should have dissuaded the opposition from working together, it appears it created a tipping point: instead, it spurred them to "become more" as a united movement.[47] Second, the detention and trial of Mohamed Abbou brought together a number of political leaders from different ideological backgrounds. Although political prisoners had previously supported each other by protesting on each other's behalf, this arrest proved significantly more momentous, perhaps because of CPR's

45. Mustapha Ben Jaafar. Interview with the author. January 16, 2017. Tunis, Tunisia.
46. Ahmed Najib Chebbi. Interview with the author. January 19, 2017. Tunis, Tunisia.
47. Ahmed Najib Chebbi. Interview with the author. January 19, 2017. Tunis, Tunisia.

middle position with regards to political ideology. Forty-five lawyers from different political affiliations, many of them opposition members themselves, worked together to have him released. According to Chebbi, this was an important moment of coordinated support that coalesced into a "unified movement." This coming together was driven by increasingly positive affect resulting from the strengthening of a collective identity among groups.

The unity the opposition displayed during the Collectif threatened the Ben Ali regime, and it increased pressure to try to fracture the cohesion. However, the affective and preference convergence the agreement signaled was unmistakable, and was the first true agreement between secularist and Islamist opposition about a common set of principles and a common vision for the identity of a democratic Tunisian state. CPR's Ben Amor said that the party felt that division among the opposition only aided the regime: "the dictatorship wanted to divert the conversation among [the opposition], until we put the issue of democracy, of oversight, or corruption to rest. The regime tried to transform the political struggle into an ideological one, and we weren't interested in that kind of fight."[48] The opposition was stronger when unified and focused on commonalities in their political agendas, and secular politicians considered Islamists part of the opposition movement despite differences in motivating ideologies.

## Preference Polarization among the Tunisian Opposition

The increase in positive affect among the Tunisian opposition was accompanied by a decrease in difference in preferences, resulting in lower levels of political polarization among the Tunisian opposition over time. Parties increasingly demonstrated agreement on central political issues. Two types of political developments provide evidence that the Tunisian opposition became less polarized between the late 1980s and the 2010–2011 uprising on policy preferences related to the nature of the state that would result from successful reform or overthrow of the regime, the central political divide. First, party platforms, manifestos, and official statements issued by parties ahead of electoral contests and after party congresses demonstrated convergence on central issues of state identity. Second, formal agreements among opposition parties demonstrated similar convergence on central issues of state identity.

---

48. Samir Ben Amor. Interview with the author. November 28, 2014. Tunis, Tunisia.

## OFFICIAL POSITIONS

Ahead of Tunisia's 1989 parliamentary elections, any party that wished to participate was required to sign the 1988 National Pact introduced by the regime. The document was intended to be a call for consensus and outlined the regime's vision of increased pluralism, political participation, and protection of human rights. The text included concessions to both secular and Islamist opposition groups: for the secularists, it included a commitment to the Personal Status Code which enshrined a secular notion of women's equality, and for the Islamists it included a provision for establishing freedom of opinion and association within the context of the law with rhetorical nods to Islam as a frame of reference.[49] However, an accompanying document also explicitly stated that it was the responsibility of the state—and not religious scholars or institutions—to "watch over the noble values of Islam."[50] Despite this phrase, Ennahda (then under the MTI name) represented by Noureddine Bhiri, joined all other significant opposition parties in signing the document.[51] Signatories assumed their agreement to the pact guaranteed the right to participate in the 1989 parliamentary elections and further democratization of the country as outlined in the document.

However, over the following year, Ben Ali moved to ban Ennahda as a party based on religion. Competing opposition parties' reaction to this move and their subsequent political platforms revealed policy preference divides over the appropriate role of religion in politics. The majority of secular parties stated that their position was that political Islam is in inherent contradiction to democracy and religion had no place in Tunisian politics.[52] The parties thus supported the regime's denial of Ennahda's democratic right to participate as a policy congruent to their platforms.[53] Parties' platforms similarly indicated strong secular preferences with regards to religion and politics. As a splinter of the ruling party, the MDS's platform differed little from that of the RCD's and proclaimed Tunisia as a strong, secular state. The political platforms put forward by the PSP and the PUP leftist

49. Christopher Alexander, *Tunisia: Stability and Reform in the Modern Maghreb* (New York: Routledge, 2010), 53.

50. Hibou, (*Force of Obedience*, 15, 158) notes that this was "a clause most MTI followers disapproved of, yet were open to compromise on."

51. Aliya Alani, *Al-Islamiyun al-Tunisiyun min al-Muʻarada ila al-hukm: al-Nashaʼ, al-Tatawwur, al-Afaq* (Tunis: Sharikat al-ʻAmal, 2014), 225; Hibou, *Force of Obedience*, 15, 158.

52. Al-Madini, *Tarikh al-Muʻarida al-Tunsiyya min al-nishaʼ ila al-thawra*, 260.

53. Haugbolle and Cavatorta, "Will the Real Tunisian Opposition Please Stand Up? Opposition Coordination Failures under Authoritarian Constraints," 334.

parties in the 1989 parliamentary elections included strong language against religion in political and public life, asserting the secular and civil nature of the Tunisian state and framing the legitimation for legislation and reform projects rooted in secular principles. In addition, the documents made reference to and indicated support for the ban put forward by the regime on parties formed on the basis of religion, as part of a larger commitment to a secular public sphere. A vocal exception was Ahmed Najib Chebbi, Secretary General of the RSP (later PDP), who publicly defended legalization as a democratic right no matter how conservative the party's political positions and charged that the "regime was exploiting the divisions of the opposition to weaken and marginalize it."[54]

In contrast, Ennahda's platform indicated preferences which remained true to the Islamic reform commitments of its June 1981 party-founding manifesto. Despite being legally banned from officially participating in the 1989 elections, Ennahda ran independents unified under a political platform. The platform rearticulated the main points of the 1981 manifesto, advocating wealth redistribution along regional lines and calling for the installation of genuine political pluralism through an "Islamic approach," suggesting the implementation of the Islamic shari'a although the document did not use this word specifically.[55] The 1989 platform called for a resurrection of the Islamic way of life in Tunisia and the renewal of Islamic thought through a return to more moral and religious values. In addition, the document outlined the party's main goals: the reconstruction of economic life on a more equitable basis, the end of single-party politics, the acceptance of political pluralism and democracy, and a limitation on Westernization and foreign influence.

Ennahda was forcibly absent from politics for the 1994 and 1999 elections and the organization did not issue formal political platforms during this period. However, it did make a number of public statements and issue documents following party congresses, most of which were held outside of Tunisia. Abdelfattah Mourou, the remaining Ennahda leader in Tunisia, declared that "the positions adopted by his party would be rooted in Tunisia's cultural heritage, including its Arab-Islamic traditions, which is similar to the stance laid out in Ennahda's 1989 political program."[56] But

54. Ahmed Najib Chebbi. Interview with the author. January 19, 2017. Tunis, Tunisia. See also al-Madini, *Tarikh al-Mu'arida al-Tunsiyya min al-nisha' ila al-thawra*, 241–242.

55. Alani, *Al-Islamiyun al-Tunisiyun min al-Mu'arada ila al-hukm: al-Nasha', al-Tatawwur, al-Afaq*, 229.

56. Wolf, *Political Islam*.

slowly, Ennahda began to move toward center on issues related to religion and politics. Exiled Ennahda leader Ghannouchi gradually refined his ideology while in London, developing a distinctive school of thought canonized in *al-Hurriyat al-'Amma fi al-Dawla al-Islamiyya* (*Public Liberties in the Islamic State*) published in 1993. In this text, Ghannouchi changed his position on the personal status code and expressed support for it. The nonviolence stance of Ennahda was not formalized until a 1995 party congress held in Switzerland. At that time, the Executive Bureau had officially put extremist leader Saleh Karker on leave to signal an abandonment of revolutionary tactics and violence. At its eight-party congress, the party published a declaration which stated that Ennahda is obligated to play a key role in promoting moderate ideology and safeguards against extremist and violent tendencies, and that the "closed political situation has negatively impacted the overall equality of social, economic, and cultural life." While Ennahda is often assumed to have held this position from its inception, it actually only developed during the mid-1990s.

Throughout the 1990's elections, the platforms and official statements of non-Islamist parties contesting elections were generally consistent. Each advanced a vision of a state whose legitimacy was derived from secular, humanist principles, and most called for a relatively moderate state role in imposing this vision on its citizens by limiting rights and freedoms. The PCOT did not issue political platforms since it was formally banned by the regime but its public statements were extreme in calling for a muscular secular state. Notably, Ettajdid wanted a stronger state role in imposing notions of secularism on the behaviors of citizens, limiting freedoms of worship and public displays of religion. These platforms collectively demonstrated the secular opposition's reform goals, which were focused on limiting state intervention into individual liberties, but indicated these rights were limited to secular notions of liberties of speech and press, and did not include rights related to freedom of worship or public displays of religion.

The 2002 emergence of CPR was a significant development for preference convergence for the Tunisian opposition, as the party's founding principles and platform reflect some of the changes that were occurring in the broader opposition. The leadership of the party included individuals from a wide array of ideologies, and the platform focused more on the form of opposition, the development of a democracy in a functional sense, and the importance of addressing fundamental human and political rights, rather than specifics about the identity of the Tunisian state. Prominent member Ben Amor described CPR's position as being "against division on the basis of ideology. Instead, we care about political divisions, meaning on the basis of the political program. What's your position with regards to reform? What's your position with regards to corruption? Anyone can work with us if they are a true democrat. We have found a joint platform with Hamma Hammami from the far left, and we have found a joint program with Rashid Ghannouchi from an Islamist party. We sort parties on the basis of politics, not ideology."[57]

By the 2004 elections, some leftist parties' platforms included language in which religious freedoms were noted as a type of individual liberty to be protected from state intervention. The additions included the CPR and Ettakatol parties, whose party platforms focused not only on secular liberties but also freedom of worship as part of a general freedom from state intervention. Similarly updated language in the PDP's platform moved the left closer to center on issues related to religion and politics. The language demonstrated a softening of positioning on state-enforced secularism, and provided space for freedom of individual religious practices and displays. Between the 1989 elections and the 2010 uprisings, the RCD's policy preferences were consistent. The ruling party issued political platforms of various lengths and forms ahead of elections, and in each it advanced a program that featured a secular state with a strong state role in the lives of citizens and room for encroachment on their individual freedoms.

After the revolution, parties' platforms had come to reflect changes in the distribution of policy preferences regarding religion and politics. The shift came from movement over time by both Islamist but more importantly secular opposition groups, and was driven by shifts in how groups conceptualized the state's role in enforcing either a combination or a separation of religion and politics (depending on the party's orientation), and protecting related individual liberties. Parties articulated a preference for state involvement in which state institutions protected differences in opinion and practices, rather than enforcing their own particular version of Islamism or secularism on the behavior of all citizens. For example, Ennahda's 2011 platform did cite Islam as the principal source of all legislation—but the reference to the religion as a whole rather than to shari'a specifically indicated that the party saw Islamic values as a guide, rather than as an exclusive legal code. In addition, the party supported a strong state role in promoting and enacting ideals of social justice, and again saw notions of social justice stemming from Islamic values rather than specific Islamic tenets

57. Samir Ben Amor. Interview with the author. November 28, 2014. Tunis, Tunisia.

that needed to be enacted. CPR's policy platform outlined a state in which liberal secular principles serve as the basis for legislation. The party envisioned a weaker state in which a strong civil society imposes limitations on the influence of religion, resulting in a state that does not interfere in the religious (or conversely, secular) rights of individual citizens. The political platforms for Ettakatol and PDP similarly cited secular principles as the basis for all legislation. Notably, the platforms did not mandate a strong state role in removing religion from public life, but rather saw the importance of a state strong enough to guarantee neutrality towards religion and individual religious rights. None of the main parties' platforms advocated an extreme division between religion and politics, or a total influence of religion on politics, but rather advanced a policy of a strong, centralized but neutral state that protected differences of opinion regarding these matters.

Ennahda leadership described the convergence of preference as an important development for an opposition that increasingly considered itself a cohesive group with similar priorities. In focusing less on differences in their ideological motivations, the opposition found common ground. Mourou said that by the 2000s, "there was no left platform. There was no Islamist platform. In that period, the political agenda focused on the lack of essential freedoms. We all had the same demands: free elections, freedom of expression, freedom to form parties, freedom of assembly."[58] Experiencing tremendous repression in an atmosphere of collective suffering appears to have strengthened the commitment of Ennahda leadership to issues of human rights. Reflecting on sixteen years' imprisonment, Jebali said, "If you were to ask me, Hamadi, were you broken by this [experience]? I would say no. My suffering made me more convinced of the importance of human rights, political liberties, and the democratic project."[59] In a 2009 interview, Sadok Chourou reflected on what the suffering of the group had meant for its political vision. He said, "during my time in prison, Ennahda had decided that the goal of its political work was to achieve a comprehensive and inclusive national reconciliation that restores political equilibrium and prevents a monopoly by any one party in deciding the fate of the country."[60]

58. Abdelfattah Mourou. Interview with the author. January 16, 2017.

59. Hamadi Jebali. Interview with the author. December 10, 2014. Sousse, Tunisia.

60. Sadok Chourou. Interview with *Islam Online.net*. Available at https://archive.islamonline.net/?p=402.

## COOPERATIVE INITIATIVES

As noted above, the opposition was significantly polarized about the role of religion in the state in 1989, and secular opposition largely supported the Ben Ali regime in its ban of Ennahda. Yet by the mid-2000s, Tunisia's opposition was significantly less polarized on issues related to religion and politics. In addition to changes in parties' preferences, this convergence was evident in a number of sustained cooperative initiatives beginning in 2003. The agreements were similar in text and tone and touched on a variety of shared political visions of individual liberties, human rights, and institutional protections. Most importantly, the agreements demonstrated convergence on matters related to religion, politics, and the identity of the Tunisian state.[61]

The first initiative was the 2003 *Appel de Tunis*. In May 2003, thirty-two members of the Tunisian opposition met secretly in Aix-en-Provence, France, to negotiate an agreement and present a common front to the Ben Ali regime. Participants included representatives from Tunisia's most influential and visible political movements, including Marzouki from CPR, Samir Dilou from Ennahda, Chebbi from the PDP, and Ben Jaafar from Ettakatol. On June 17, 27 of the participants signed a pact resulting from the meeting, the first formal and public agreement between secular and Islamist opposition groups. The document underscored the freedom of religion, the neutrality of mosques, and a pro-Palestine and pan-Arab position as points of agreement among the opposition. Notably, five participants did not sign the 2003 *Appel* agreement, including Ben Jaafar of Ettakatol and Chebbi from the PDP. The May 26th press release announcing the agreement lamented these defections, noting that they effectively split the opposition between legal movements based in Tunisia and illegal parties headed by leadership in exile. Chebbi subsequently explained his refusal as reflecting his party's reticence in overtly collaborating with Ennahda and inviting additional state repression. Ben Jaafar similarly noted that Ettakatol had only received formal accreditation as a legal opposition party in October 2002 and did not want to provoke the regime to revoke that status.[62]

---

61. These initiatives, and how they formed the basis of the consensus which emerged after the 2010–2011 uprising, are documented in detail in Laryssa Chomiak, *Deliberative Resistance: Dissent and Democracy in Tunisia* (Book manuscript, 2016).

62. Jaafar, *Un Si Long Chemin Vers la Démocratie*, 120. Both men also confirmed these sentiments to me during interviews in January 2017.

The second initiative was the 2005 *Collectif du 18 October,* which ulti-mately issued a document very similar to the 2003 *Appel.* The Collectif was a joint effort by legal and illegal opposition, both in Tunisia as well as in exile, with the aim of formulating a shared set of principles and reform demands around which to challenge the Ben Ali regime. The initiative drew its name from the day on which eight members of the opposition had announced a month-long hunger strike to protest state abuses related to freedom of expression and human rights. Six of the eight strikers had also participated in the 2003 *Appel de Tunis*—Chebbi from the PDP, Judge Mukhtar Yahiaoui, Aberraoud Ayadi from CPR, Samir Dilou from Ennahda, Mohamed Nouri from the International Association for the Support of Political Prison-ers, and Ayachi Hammami from the LDTH. These men were joined by Hamma Hammami, Secretary General of the PCOT, and Lotfi Hadj from the unrecognized Tunisian Union of Journalists.

In December, the strikers announced a political platform called the *Collectif du 18 October pour les Droits et les Libertés.* The content of the doc-ument mirrored many of the articles from the 2003 *Appel,* but went further by collecting additional signatures from individuals representing a more diverse array of parties and groups,[63] again agreeing to one set of reform principles for the first time. In addition to the core signatories from the 2003 document, the 2005 document included signatories from the PDP, Ettakatol, and the PCOT, thus fully incorporating Tunisia's leftist oppo-sition. However, while Abderraoud Ayadi and Fethi Jerbi signed the 2005 Collectif for CPR, Marzouki's name was absent from the final document. In February 2006, a coordinating committee was formed in Paris. It was led by ideologically mixed leadership from the PDP, CPR, and Ennahda.[64] Its founding document included signatures from representatives of CPR, Ennahda, Ettakatol, PCOT, and PDP, as well as smaller leftist parties.

The 2005 document included an entire section titled "Relations bet-ween Religion and the State" which focused on issues of religious freedom, national identity, and the state's future role in institutionalizing these ideas. Individual religious liberties were treated as central to reconciling a civil state with a religious orientation. The section begins by outlining general individual freedoms of conscience, but quickly turns to individual free-doms related to religion and beliefs such as religious rituals, practices, and

---

63. Mustapha Ben Jaafar. Interview with the author. January 16, 2017. Tunis, Tunisia.

64. Haugbolle and Cavatorta, "Will the Real Tunisian Opposition Please Stand Up? Opposi-tion Coordination Failures under Authoritarian Constraints."

teaching. The document states that freedom of choice over these matters is to be protected by the state, both in law and in practice. In addition, signatories agreed that the guarantee of these liberties was "not in the least in contradiction with the place and importance of Islam" in the Tunisian state. The vision strikes a balance between the independence of religion from the state, and the independence of the state from religion. The result was a democratic state that is "a civil state grounded in republican principles and respect for human rights" yet one which "must give special consideration to Islam … while avoiding any monopoly or any misuse of religion, as well as guaranteeing the right to practice any religion and belief in the effective implementation of religion and worship."

The Collectif was active for five years, from 2005 through the uprisings. In 2010, the Collectif published a volume entitled "Our Way Towards Democracy," in which the groups involved in the initiative articulated their agreed-upon democratic principles of governance and argued that they were not simply "a short-term political coalition, but a social project for society."[65] This reaffirmed that the parties had agreed on the kind of reform that should be put into action once the regime was overthrown. Importantly, the two cooperative agreements of the 2000s were not the result of changing political opportunity structures. In fact, political opportunities for the opposition were practically nonexistent at the time, and had certainly not changed significantly from previous periods. Indeed, repression remained widespread in its political targets and was increasing during this period as a result of the 2003 terror law and related domestic and international developments at the turn of the century. The cooperation thus was not the result of less repression, and did not appear to be strategic in order to better achieve progress on reform demands. As such, there was no apparent benefit to agreeing to these sets of principles in an environment where the prospects for participation and reform remained bleak.

## Conclusion

As the number and variety of Tunisian opposition groups repressed increased, these experiences became increasingly ubiquitous among the Tunisian opposition. The combination of psychological, social, and organizational effects from widespread repression created a bridging political identity among the Tunisian opposition. The shared trauma of widespread

---

65. Rachid al-Ghannouchi. Interview printed in *Financial Times*, January 18, 2011.

repression was an experience in which individuals' identification with their immediate opposition groups was not primed or made more salient, and through which individual groups came to identify with a larger collective of active opposition groups. The formation of this political identity facilitated two major developments marking the decrease of political polarization among the opposition. First, opposition parties demonstrated increasingly positive affect towards each other during the Ben Ali period. Put simply, opposition groups articulated more positive feelings about and towards each other over time. Second, the extent to which opposition parties differed in their preferences decreased—or said differently, the Tunisian opposition demonstrated increasing convergence on issues of high salience for political contestation. Party platforms, manifestos, and official statements issued by parties ahead of electoral contests demonstrate convergence on central issues of state identity and the official role of religion in Tunisia. Two major collaborative initiatives in the early 2000s solidified an agreement among opposition leaders about how religion and politics would be dealt with officially should authoritarianism end. Chapter 8 shows how the relatively low level of affective and preference polarization that resulted from the Ben Ali period was an important factor in the transition from authoritarianism following the 2010–2011 uprising. Less animosity and convergent preferences permitted the opposition to come to agreement on central issues of politics and policy during a potentially tumultuous yet critical moment of decision making.

The next chapter turns to Egypt, documenting how a repressive environment experienced very differently by competing opposition parties resulted in much higher levels of political polarization. Between 1981 and the 2011 uprising, repression targeted one opposition group while permitting others to exist in a much less restricted manner. Through similar psychological, social, and organizational mechanisms, targeted repression facilitated much higher levels of political polarization, with implications for the country's subsequent political transition.

# 6

# Repression and Polarization in Egypt, 1981-2011

This chapter focuses on repression and polarization of opposition in Egypt under the Mubarak regime, which lasted from 1981 through the 2011 uprising. First, I document the existence of a targeted repressive environment which created different experiences of repression among targeted and non-targeted groups. I then provide evidence of the three mechanisms—social, organizational, and psychological—through which widespread repression created divisive political identities among opposition groups in Egypt. Finally, I link the development of political identities with increasing political polarization among the opposition. This manifested in increasingly negative affect between the Muslim Brotherhood and other opposition groups, as well as increasing divergence in political preferences among opposition groups.

## Different Experiences of Repression in Egypt

The nature of repression under the Mubarak regime differed from that of the Ben Ali regime outlined in the previous chapter, in that the Mubarak regime relied on a targeted repressive approach meant to divide and conquer. But before getting into the opposition's experiences of repression under Mubarak, and how significantly this differed from the Tunisian opposition's experiences during the same time period under Ben Ali, it is worth noting that the Mubarak era began with a situation uncharacteristic to Egyptian politics, created through a final anomalous repressive wave carried out by Sadat. Like Mubarak, Sadat similarly contained Egyptian opposition through a "divide and rule" policy and targeted repression. However, the targets of repression were different from that of the Mubarak era; the Sadat regime instead repressed leftist and centrist secular opposition parties challenging or mobilizing within the ruling party instead of the Muslim Brotherhood.[1]

After the passage of the 1977 political parties law, two subsequent laws were passed that helped the regime to control opposition. First, Law 33 of 1978, titled "The Protection of the Internal Front and Social Piece," granted the Parties Committee the ability to punish individuals who were found to have contributed to the corruption of the country's political life, broadly defined. Second, Law 95 of 1980, titled "The Protection of Values from Shame" and known as the Law of Shame, permitted the Parties Committee to punish individuals who had criticized the president, the government, and its actions. Sadat used the former law to put pressure on the Wafd Party, labeling them old regime figures for their political participation pre-1952, and used the latter law against Tagammu for its criticism of the president's 1979 peace treaty with Israel. At the same time, Sadat permitted the Brotherhood to rebuild after severe repression under Nasser (to be discussed in more detail in a following section). Sadat increasingly incorporated themes of traditionalism and conservativism in his political rhetoric as his domestic legitimacy declined, even appointing conservative Brotherhood affiliates to his cabinet.[2]

However, in 1981, the Sadat regime diverged from Egypt's typical divided approach to the opposition and clamped down on all opposition, as an increasing number of groups mobilized to protest the president's economic policy and his peace treaty with Israel. In total, 1,536 opposition members were arrested. The arrests were immediately recognized by political actors as an anomaly. Former Free Officer and Tagammu leader Khaled Mohieddin described it as "the widest wave of arrests in the history of modern Egypt" which hit "all political wings."[3] Independent political activist and sociologist Saad Eddin Ibrahim similarly described the mixed nature of the political prisoner population at this moment:

1. Raymond A. Hinnebusch, "Egypt Under Sadat: Elites, Power Structure, and Political Change in a Post-Populist State," *Social Problems* 28, no. 4 (1981): 442–464.

2. Kassem, *Egyptian Politics: The Dynamics of Authoritarian Rule.*

3. Magdy Naseef, "Sadat's Final Act of Repression: The September 1981 Arrests of 1650 Egyptians was a 'Purge' of the Intelligentsia," *Index on Censorship* 11, no. 1 (1982): 37–39.

Some 1,600 public opponents were arrested and jailed within a twenty-four hour period starting on the night of 3 September 1981. This mass arrest included key figures along the entire political spectrum—from the extreme right to the extreme left; Muslim and Copts; men and women; all age groups from twenty to eighty years old; students, professors, journalists, writers, and other professionals. In a sense, and in one sensational strike, Sadat put Egypt's "political class" under arrest.[4]

Those arrested included the leadership of the Tagammu Party such as Mohammed Rifat al-Saeed, Sayyid Abd al-'Aal, Hussein Abdel Razik, and Farida al-Naqash; well-known communist activists such as Doctor Ismail Sabri Abdullah; long-time labor activist Kamal Aboul Eita; and Amin Iskandar, Hamdeen Sabahi, and Sayyid al-Toukhy, young Nasserists who would later form the leadership of the Karama Party. Even members of the long-loyal Wafd Party, most notably its leader Fouad Serag al-Din, were caught up in this repressive wave. In addition, the regime imprisoned more than 1,000 individuals affiliated with the Muslim Brotherhood, including its then Murshid (General Guide) Umar al-Tilmisani and a well-known affiliated preacher named 'Abd al-Hamid Ksihk.[5]

The Mubarak regime continued the Sadat policy of divide and rule, but switched targets, more regularly and more harshly repressing the Muslim Brotherhood as a matter of normal policy. As a result, opposition groups experienced repression differently under Mubarak. The regime did not repress co-opted groups, permitting them to operate relatively freely within the confines of the limited electoral system. Yet instead of relegating all other political opposition to prisons through long sentences, as did the Ben Ali regime, the Mubarak regime applied different approaches to tolerated and targeted opposition.

Waves of arrests against the Brotherhood could either be preemptive to gather information about the group, or reactive to Brotherhood-led mobilization. Brotherhood leader Khairat al-Shater described the two different forms of collective arrests targeting the Brotherhood during this period:

4. Saad Eddin Ibrahim, *Egypt, Islam and Democracy: Critical Essays* (American University in Cairo Press, 2002).

5. Abdel Azim Ramadan, "Fundamentalist Influence in Egypt: The Strategies of the Muslim Brotherhood and the Takfir groups," in *Fundamentalisms and the State: Remaking Polities, Economies and Militance*, ed. Martin E. Marty and R. Scott Apple by (University of Chicago Press, 1993), 172.

[The goal was] to create internal chaos within the Brotherhood, to scare its membership on all levels, by organizing continuous security raids. The raids took two forms. They were either tied to certain events—for example, the Brotherhood would organize a march or a demonstration, or put out a statement criticizing one of the tactics of the state, or perform well in the elections. Then the regime arrests a few members of the Council, a few members that were at the march. These [arrested individuals] normally serve three to four months in jail, and then they are released. The other, more organized and more tactical approach, was a programmed arrest that happens almost twice or three times a year, on vertical sections of the Brotherhood. Mubarak... consecutively arrested members each year. He arrested members from the guidance council, members who are governing different areas at the district level, and members from the grass-roots body of the organization.[6]

Al-Shater also recalled that during the late Mubarak era, particularly as the frequency of raids increased, "it was very common for nearly all members to have a ready-set bag of clothes and necessities by the door. They took it with them when they left the house every day, and every night their wives slept with clothes by the bed. If a raid came in they would need to dress quickly." While the regime often arrested Brotherhood members without warning, raids occurred regularly enough that they could be expected. In 2005, Amr Darrag, for example, was one of four leaders arrested at Essam al-Arian's house. The men were part of the group's political leadership and had gathered to have breakfast and plan for a press conference for the then General Guide of the Brotherhood, Mahdi Akef, a few days later, though the regime accused them of planning for protests that took place the same day.[7] Over the new few days mass arrests started and occurred in a similar manner, with security forces arresting members from their homes at early and late hours of the day.

Known Brotherhood leadership were the most targeted and harshly treated, which was evident in the regime's legal strategy. Beginning in 1995, the Mubarak regime referred a large number of Brotherhood leaders' cases to military tribunals. The regime had not used this tactic against political opposition since 1965 under Nasser, and the same tactic was not used against the handful of secular opposition leaders who were arrested during

6. Khairat al-Shater. Interview with Josh Stacher. March 24, 2011. Cairo, Egypt.
7. Amr Darrag. Interview with the author. June 13, 2016. Istanbul, Turkey.

the same time period.[8] Military tribunals could sentence those found guilty to sentences longer than regular courts could; typical judgments included three-, five-, seven-, and ten-year sentences and included hard labor. In 1995, eighty-one prominent and leading Brotherhood organizations, all "former parliamentarians, leading civic activists, or parliamentary candidates"[9] rounded up in arrests surrounding the elections, were referred for prosecution in two trials before the Supreme Military Court for the attempted assassination of Mubarak. On November 23, the court sentenced fifty-four defendants to prison terms ranging from three to five years with hard labor, in addition to ordering the closure of the Brotherhood's unofficial headquarters in Cairo and confiscating its publicly known funds.[10] In 2000, twenty Brotherhood members were tried by a military tribunal a few days ahead of the first round of elections. Among those detained in December 2006, forty-one high-ranking members, including Deputy General Guide and major Brotherhood financer Khairat al-Shater, were referred to a military tribunal to face charges of belonging to and funding an illegal organization, money laundering, and financing terrorism. On April 15, 2008, after ignoring two lower court decisions calling the trial illegal for trying civilians in a military court, the military tribunal returned a verdict in which al-Shater and Malek received sentences of seven years each, sixteen others received sentences between eighteen months and five years, and seven others who were tried in absentia were given ten-year sentences (the remaining fifteen were acquitted).[11]

The Mubarak regime's use of military tribunals resulted in longer sentences for Islamist leaders than they had faced before, and also longer sentences than the brief detentions of leftist opposition leaders. Many Muslim Brotherhood leaders endured continuous years in prison, in addition to short sentences on lesser charges. Between 1992 and 2011, al-Shater spent twelve years in jail on four different counts. Mohamed Badie, the group's murshid as of 2011, and Ezzat had each spent five years in prison after being

8. Al-Awadi, *In Pursuit of Legitimacy*. Writing in 1998, Kienle ("More than a Response to Islamism: The Political Deliberalization of Egypt in the 1990s," *Middle East Journal* (1998): 226) noted that "hitherto only alleged members of armed Islamist groups had been tried by military tribunals."

9. Campagna, "Accommodation to Confrontation," 279.

10. Wickham, *Mobilizing Islam*, 215; Mona el Ghobashy, "The Metamorphosis of the Egyptian Muslim Brothers," *International Journal of Middle East Studies* 37, no. 3 (2005): 373.

11. International Crisis Group, "Egypt's Muslim Brothers: Confrontation or Integration?" June 18, 2008 (76), 1. Available at https://d2071andvip0wj.cloudfront.net/76-egypt-s-muslim-brothers-confrontation-or-integration.pdf.

convicted in a military tribunal.[12] Many Brothers sentenced during the later military tribunals remained in prison through the 2011 uprisings.

The leftist experience of repression under Mubarak differed significantly from that of the Brotherhood. The regime's approach to permitted groups like the leftists was reactive and relied on short, repetitive arrests, sometimes holding individuals for hours or days in detention centers and failing to charge them before they were released. The years 1989 and 1997 (outlined in chapter 4) stood out as having an unusually heavy-handed response by the regime. The more regular course of action involved the arrest of a few group members for a short period of time following a demonstration.

Leftists were aware of how their treatment differed from repression under Sadat, and how their treatment differed from the Brotherhood. Farida Naqash of Tagammu was arrested three times under Sadat for being a member of the communist party, participating in a study group against Zionists, and for establishing the Egyptian Communist Party in 1975. Barring 1989, she noted that there were no big waves of arrests against the left under Mubarak, only small, limited, and reactive arrests: "when leftists protested, they would arrest a few of us and keep us for a few days. But there weren't any big campaigns."[13] Ahmed Fawzi of the ESDP was arrested only once under Mubarak for participating in a protest and released after a short detention in the *Amn al-Dawla*. His experience was similar to fellow leftists, who might be held for up to forty-five days without being put on trial or receiving a final judgment but were then released.[14]

Leftist parties' narratives of this time attest to the fact that the Brotherhood was targeted more regularly. One communist activist under Mubarak who was also a member of the ESDP after 2011 said that Mubarak generally dealt with leftists more "officially" than Sadat had. Torture was now less physically brutal and focused more on psychological games, and leftists were treated better than other political prisoners while in custody.[15] Iskandar described the treatment of the left under Mubarak similarly; his longest and worst prison experience was under Sadat, when he was severely tortured, whereas under Mubarak he suffered only brief detentions.[16] Abdel Razik of Tagammu served a total of six months in prison through a series

12. Khairat al-Shater. Interview with Josh Stacher. March 24, 2011. Cairo, Egypt.

13. Farida Naqash. Interview with the author. February 10, 2018. Cairo, Egypt.

14. Ahmed Fawzi. Interview with the author. February 4, 2018. Cairo, Egypt.

15. Interview with the author. January 22, 2018. Cairo, Egypt.

16. Amin Iskandar. Interview with the author. February 3, 2018. Cairo, Egypt.

of arrests in 1977 under Sadat, both for involvement in the Bread Riots and for being a communist sympathizer. But Mubarak, he said, "had a different style. There weren't any campaigns of communal arrests against leftists, like under Sadat. Instead there was a legal embargo foisted upon us by the political parties law. The law forbade the establishment of any party that wanted to organize people, and so we weren't able to organize in the factories, companies, or universities."[17] These men also noted how the Brotherhood had been tolerated and permitted to rebuild their social and political presence in the country under Sadat, while the left was being repressed most harshly during that period.

## PSYCHOLOGICAL EFFECTS OF REPRESSION

The historical record of repression in Egypt demonstrates that the Brotherhood was overwhelmingly the victim of state violence under Mubarak. But this history is only important insofar as members of the opposition *perceived* the differential treatment by the state. Members of leftist and center secular opposition described the Mubarak regime as a system that was quite closed generally, but which more heavily targeted the Brotherhood in a consistent manner.

The regime's shift to using military tribunals against the Brotherhood in 1995 felt like a particular betrayal for the group. Prior to this, the regime and the Brotherhood had both played by unspoken rules of the game, and the Brotherhood felt like the regime had "invented" military tribunals for civilians to punish the group unfairly.[18] As the repression of the Brotherhood progressed in the Mubarak era, the Brotherhood increasingly perceived itself to be a unique victim of the regime. Its narratives centrally featured a unique experience of isolated repression, evidence that the regime's divide-and-conquer approach succeeded in providing information about the differences between groups and creating increasingly divergent identities among the larger opposition.

A report titled "The Muslim Brotherhood and Mubarak: From Appeasement to Confrontation," issued in the early 2000s, is emblematic of this narrative.[19] The report claimed that the regime detained 40,000 members, levied seven military trials against the Brotherhood, and launched

17. Hussein Abdel Razik. Interview with the author. February 3, 2018. Cairo, Egypt.

18. Khairat al-Shater. Interview with Josh Stacher. March 24, 2011. Cairo, Egypt. Amr Darrag. Interview with the author. June 13, 2016. Istanbul, Turkey.

19. Accessed on *Ikhwan Wiki.*

systematic media campaigns intended to undermine the group's legitimacy, popularity, and success. The report claims that Mubarak used the organization as a "scarecrow," but goes even further in its language, claiming that by the hand of the regime "[the Brotherhood] has received consecutive blows and been subjected to the ugliest shades of injustice, abuse, and racism—like what happened in South Africa and America between those with white skin and [those with] black skin." Other parts of the report detail the Brotherhood's military trials of the 1990s and 2000s, including minute details of the harsh conditions facing Brothers while being held in jail. The documentation includes photographs of Brothers in handcuffs and prison jumpsuits, transcriptions of official documents related to the cases, the testimonies of those who were "unfairly" tried, and opinion pieces that condemn the justice system for its "systematic targeting" of the Brothers on "false accusations." Al-Shater similarly noted that waves of repression against the group "resulted in a feeling of oppression and being tied down."[20]

The psychological effects of targeted repression culminated in the immediate aftermath of the 2011 uprisings, when Brotherhood rhetoric revealed that the group felt itself to be the sole victims of the previous regime. On February 10, 2011, three days after Mubarak resigned, *al-Hayat* reported that an unnamed Muslim Brotherhood leader told the newspaper that the new period presented opportunities for achieving some of "our legitimate rights after lean years during which the group was repressed." In June 2012, Gamal al-Banna, brother of founder Hasan, said in an interview, "Brotherhood members alone have spent eighty years in prisons and in detention camps, because they alone wanted to reform Egyptian society."

The understanding among the left and secular opposition prior to the 2011 uprisings did acknowledge that the Brotherhood had been repressed more severely under the Mubarak regime. For example, Abdel Razik of Tagammu said, "the repressive campaigns focused on the Ikhwan, especially during the last days of the Mubarak era."[21] This was a common refrain. And while other interviewees repeated this sentiment, they immediately and without prompting followed up with information about the Sadat era, when they had been the victims of the regime and the Brotherhood had not suffered.

As noted in chapter 4, though it was overwhelmingly the Brotherhood which was pursued by regime repression, other individuals were

---

20. Khairat al-Shater. Interview with Josh Stacher. March 24, 2011. Cairo, Egypt.

21. Hussein Abdel Razik. Interview with the author. February 3, 2018. Cairo, Egypt.

intermittently targeted when they crossed the regime's red lines. One example is Ayman Nour of the Ghad Party. Nour suffered disproportionately to other members of the non-Islamist opposition. He described the "repression and harassment" used by the regime against him as treatment "typically reserved for the Muslim Brotherhood." He also noted in our interview that he was not tried in military court for his political infractions, as members of the Brotherhood were, but instead his case was brought to a "regular" civilian court, suggesting he was treated slightly better than the Islamist opposition.[22]

## SOCIAL EFFECTS OF REPRESSION

Targeted repression in Egypt contributed to increasingly divisive group identities in Egypt through a social mechanism that primarily occurred in the country's prisons. The way in which prisoners were separated and isolated forced socialization *within* groups rather than *between*. The beginning of the Mubarak era began with an anomalous situation, in which Sadat's 1981 assassination resulted in significant similarity in the treatment of the opposition by the regime and a physical overlap of the opposition in prison. In his memoirs, al-Tilmisani described how the Brothers mixed with Wafdist, Nasserite, and communist political prisoners in the same prison cells as well as in the lunchroom and other communal spaces in the prison during this period.[23] Male prisoners overlapped in the Qasr al-Ayni medical prison and in the Tora prison complex, which had been expanded following the Bread Riots. Female activists from leftist parties and female members of the Brotherhood shared space in the Qanatir prison.[24]

This was a unique moment for the Egyptian opposition; both before and after 1981, the regime treated leftists and Islamists differently and they were separated in repressive spaces as a matter of regular policy. The Mubarak regime separated political prisoners of different ideological persuasions, keeping Islamist and leftist opposition in separate prisons or in separate blocks of prisons. Due to the severity of the crimes they were charged with by the regime and their sentencing by military courts, Brotherhood members were concentrated in high-level-security prisons (*liman*), such as the

22. Ayman Nour. Interview with the author. February 11, 2017. Istanbul, Turkey.

23. Umar al-Tilmisani, *Dhikrayat LaMudhakkirat* (Dar al-Tiba's wa-al-Nasht al-Islamiya, 1985), 116.

24. Farida Naqash. Interview with the author. See also Margot Badran, "Speaking Straight: 'Four Women of Egypt,' " *Al Jadid Magazine* 4, no. 25 (1998).

maximum-security prison at Abu Za'bal and prisons located in the Tora complex southeast of Cairo. One Brotherhood leader remarked that in the late 2000s, maximum-security prisons were "crowded with Brothers."[25]

Tora was designated to hold criminal and political detainees, and the larger complex included a number of different buildings, including Tora Istiqbal, a receiving area for holding new prisoners until they could be assigned, and Tora al-Mahkoum. Brotherhood political prisoners were held in one of three prisons. Tora Agricultural Prison, referred to as *al-Mazra'a,* or the farm, had some of the best physical conditions and permited prisoners to move freely within its confined walls during daytime hours. This forum was reserved for higher-profile prisoners like Brotherhood leaders, who were given slightly better treatment and were tortured less than middle-ranking Brothers. Tora Liman was a maximum-security prison designated for prisoners sentenced to hard labor for serious crimes. In 1992, a commander of the Tora Liman described it as the "most secure and heavily guarded" prison because "the most important political prisoners are there."[26] Finally, the Scorpion Prison (*Sijn al-'Aqrab* in Arabic) was a site for "those deemed the most dangerous enemies of the state."[27] It was constructed in 1993 and known for excessively torturing prisoners; Brothers who were sentenced to this prison described it as a "nightmare."[28] The Scorpion Prison also served as a CIA rendition site under the Mubarak regime as early as 1995. These prison spaces were not only worse off than the spaces where secular opponents were held, but limited the composition of opposition groups' social circles largely to in-group members only.

When leftists were arrested by the Mubarak regime, they were held with other leftists in prison. Amin Iskandar, Hamdeen Sabahi, and Sayyid al-Toukhy from Karama were held with longtime labor activist Kamal Aboul Eita, Revolutionary Socialist founder Kamal Khalil, and others of similar ideological persuasions. As al-Toukhy described, "the leftists were always jailed together, and the Islamists were isolated. The Islamists were always in different prisons than us, like Tora and Abou Zabal, because they were tried

25. Amr Darrag. Interview with the author. June 13, 2016. Istanbul, Turkey. See also al-Anani, *Inside the Muslim Brotherhood: Religion, Identity, and Politics,* 110.

26. Human Rights Watch, "Prison Conditions in Egypt: A Filthy System," February 1993, available at https://www.hrw.org/sites/default/files/reports/Egypt932.pdf.

27. Human Rights Watch, "'We are in Tomb's: Abuses in Egypt's Scorpion Prison," September 28, 2016, available at https://www.hrw.org/report/2016/09/28/we-are-tombs/abuses-egypts-scorpion-prison.

28. Amr Darrag. Interview with the author. June 13, 2016. Istanbul, Turkey.

in court by the Mubarak regime for different offenses than us. The Brotherhood was mostly arrested for having a secret organization, things like that, while we were arrested because of demonstrations and protests. They were different issues, so we received different punishments."[29] Similarly, Karama co-founder Iskandar said he "was never kept with Brotherhood members while in prison."[30]

## ORGANIZATIONAL EFFECTS OF REPRESSION

In addition to altering patterns of opposition socializing, repression can also changed the organizational structure of targeted opposition groups. And indeed, structural and related behavioral changes occurred within the Brotherhood following targeted repression from the Mubarak regime, and the organization increasingly acted as one under siege. This influenced the way in which the organization saw itself, the extent to which it was exposed to competing opposition groups, and the extent to which it worked in cooperation with these groups. Shifts in structure and behavior reinforced the Brotherhood narrative of victimhood and strengthened group members' identification with the group at the expense of an identity linked with a broader collective opposition. These changes, undertaken in partial response to victimhood identity created through repression, also permitted hardliners to consolidate their power and influence within the organization.

Al-Anani's account of the Brotherhood's structure and its development under the Mubarak regime features identity heavily as an important component driving organizational developments, which in turn served to further strengthen members' identification with the group. The Brotherhood had long operated as an organization built on exclusive membership, indoctrination, and ideological socialization. Each level of the organization's tiered, hierarchical membership structure facilitates increasing levels of assimilation within the group. This organizational structure was designed to create a unique identity, which al-Anani refers to as *Ikhwanism*, and which is "responsible for implanting the movement's objectives, governing its internal dynamics, and reshaping the identity of its members." Identity defines the group: it regulates membership, sets the prerequisites for joining the movement, and lays out the criteria by which members differentiate

---

29. Sayyid al-Toukhy. Interview with author. January 31, 2018. Cairo, Egypt.
30. Amin Iskandar. Interview with the author. February 3, 2018. Cairo, Egypt.

themselves and in turn are recognized by others. The stronger and more intense the targeted repressive environment became, the more "victimhood" became more centrally incorporated into the Brotherhood identity. The structure of the Brotherhood facilitated this by creating members more strongly aligned with the Brotherhood's ideology, objectives, and norms as the exclusivity of Brotherhood identity became stronger.

The targeted repressive environment under Mubarak influenced the structure of the organization, with implications for the group's identity. The relationship between identity and structure is one of reciprocity. While the Brotherhood was always relatively successful at socializing loyal members from its inception, the organization further consolidated a distinct pattern of hierarchy, structure, and leadership under Mubarak in line with its increasing victim identity. This further forced the organization to adapt structurally in order to not only survive but to thrive under targeted repression. Indeed, during times of repression, the Brotherhood has tended to prioritize internal unity and survival at the expense of openness, transparency, and reform.[31] During repression, survival of the movement becomes the ultimate goal, and survival is ensured through a more exclusive system characterized by rigid rules, homogeneity of membership, and an authoritarian style of management.

These changes manifested in a number of ways as the organization transformed repression from a threat into a shared experience that could bind together members and foster allegiance and solidarity.[32] First, as the group's identity increasingly became one focused on victimhood, the organization became more exclusive in its membership selection, choosing members who were more strongly vetted and already demonstrated commitment to the organization, in the hopes they could be more heavily indoctrinated and prove to be very loyal members. In addition, leaders employed the *mihna* narrative to ensure members' commitment to the group, and it became an important component of socialization.

An already centralized decision-making process became further dominated by leadership and senior members by the reinforcement of the group's hierarchy under repression. Because the regime put significant pressure on the organization when it gathered in large numbers, including arresting senior leaders, the Brotherhood began to hold meetings in

31. Hossam Tammam, *Tahawwulat al-Ikhwan al-Muslimin* (Cairo: Maktabat Madbouli, 2010), 34.

32. Al-Anani, *Inside the Muslim Brotherhood: Religion, Identity, and Politics*, chapter 9.

secret and opted for smaller meetings of cells and remote voting instead of convening large meetings.[33] Internal processes became more secretive, and were only known to high-ranking leaders who had been members for long periods of time. The group's increasing focus on loyalty as central to membership and mobility, and increasing structural consolidation played into the hands of conservative elements that came to control the organization at the expense of the reformists in the late 2000s.

Scholars of the Brotherhood have noted at least two distinct generations within the organization. The "hardliner" generation (in Wickham's typology) or *al-tayyar al-tanzimi* (the organizational current in al-Anani's typology) held strict ideological beliefs and were primarily concerned with the organization's unity and survival. These men had left the country under the repression of Nasser, returned to Egypt in the 1980s, and were considered part of the *mihna* generation. It included Mustafa Masshur, Ma'mun al-Hudaybi, and Mahdi Akef, who would go on to become the Brotherhood's fifth, sixth, and seventh general guides. This group was reinforced by a slightly younger group of conservatives such as the Brotherhood's eighth General Guide Mohamed Badie, Mahmoud Ezzat, and Khairat al-Shater. In contrast, the "reformist" generation (in Wickham's typology 2013) or *al-tayyar al-'aml al-'amm* (the public activity current in al-Anani's typology) holds more progressive ideological views and seeks to integrate the Brotherhood into the mainstream Egyptian political process. This generation emerged in the relative openness of Sadat in the 1970s and held peak influence over the Brotherhood's behavior during the 1984 and 1987 parliamentary elections, during which the group cooperated and coordinated with other parties. The reformists were defined by names such as Abdelmoniem Aboul Fottouh, Essam al-Arian, Abul 'Ela Madi, Helmi al-Gazzar, and Ibrahim al-Za'farani, and were backed by moderate General Guide Umar al-Tilmisani.

The influence of the hardliner generation increased after the passing of al-Tilmisani, who successfully balanced these factions prior to his death in 1986. During the first half of the 1990s, the Brotherhood's conservative current solidified its grip on power by dominating the Guidance Bureau, Shura Council, and Administrative Offices, and arranging the election of one of their own, Mustafa Masshur, as the fifth General Guide. The conservative

---

33. Khairat al-Shater. Interview with Josh Stacher. March 24, 2011. Cairo, Egypt. See also Wickham, *Muslim Brotherhood*, 60.

movement within the party was spearheaded by al-Shater and Ezzat. Al-Shater had spent seven years in exile in Yemen, Saudi Arabia, Jordan, and the United Kingdom to avoid repression against the opposition following Sadat's assassination. In 1992, he was imprisoned for a year following the Salsabil case. He improved his standing in the Brotherhood between 1995 and 2000 by running the Brotherhood's business operations. Ezzat had joined the Brotherhood at a very young age and studied directly under Sayyid Qutb. He spent nine years between 1965 and 1975 in prison under Nasser, and was considered one of the Brotherhood's most conservative hardliners. Ezzat was elected to be a member of the Guidance Bureau in 1995, and then served as secretary general from 2004 to 2010.

In a group under siege, the suffering that the hardliners had endured and the extreme ideology they supported was respected and rewarded. Moreover, the "suffering of members enhanced their position within the organization because it demonstrated their level of sacrifice. Therefore those who have been frequently arrested or tortured tend to employ their oppression to reach leadership positions in the movement and gain respect from the rank and file."[34] The amount of suffering one had endured for the organization, rather than other merits, became an important component of qualifying for advancement within the organization. As the conservative faction gained control of the Brotherhood, it restructured the socialization process to further reward suffering on behalf of the group. Hardliner Ezzat took responsibility for the Students Section (which recruits new members from universities) and the Socialization Section (responsible for helping members internalize the MB ideology) to further instill these ideas in new members.

Under Mashhur's tenure and the dominance of the hardliner faction, the conservative leadership adopted an uncompromising stance toward the reformists, resulting in the Wasat splinter. Brotherhood leadership would not tolerate calls from reformists to implement reforms or share power. When reformists led by Abul 'Ela Madi and Esam Sultan failed to persuade leadership to establish a political party in the mid-1990s, they decided to take the initiative and do so themselves, establishing the Wasat Party. The Wasat Party was primarily concerned with ideological differences it had with the leadership, and secondly concerned with the inability of the organizational structure to accommodate reform. Mashhur forced Wasat Party

34. Al-Anani, *Inside the Muslim Brotherhood: Religion, Identity, and Politics.*

members to resign from the MB. The hardliner Brotherhood leadership exploited the targeted repressive environment under Mubarak to deflect any internal reform. Said Amr Darrag, "All the political behavior through-out this period (2000s) was the direct outcome of the preferences of the leadership of the Ikhwan ... they made a sort of paradigm as what to do, how to engage people, what the priorities are, and so on and so forth. They were never removed or distant from what the [Guidance] Bureau was telling them to do. [It was ...] very centralized, hierarchical."[35]

The final consolidation of the conservative movement's power over the Brotherhood began in 2008. That year, five new members joined the Guidance Bureau, the first time that new members had been elected to these positions since 1995. All five were from the conservative movement: Mohamed Saad al-Katatni, Saad al-Husseini, Mohei Hamed, Osama Naser, and Mohamed Abdel Rahman. Then in March 2009, Akef announced that he would step down as general guide at the end of his term in January 2010, citing health reasons and breaking with Brotherhood norms in which General Guides served two terms. Conservatives within the group called for an immediate election for the Guidance Bureau and a new General Guide, while reformists called for postponing elections until June 2010. The Shura Council intervened in the dispute and, because it was dominated by Ezzat allies, decided in favor of holding immediate elections. Mohamed Badie, a veteran member and a strict hardliner, was elected as the Brotherhood's eighth General Guide. In addition, the Guidance Bureau elected in 2009 was filled with hardliners. As al-Shater described, they had all been repressed by the Mubarak regime: "If you look at the current Irshad council [in 2011, elected in 2009], all council members have been jailed in Mubarak's era. None of them survived this era without jail time, some to very hard extents. The Murshid himself spent five years in a military tribunal. His first deputy, Mohamed Ezzat, spent five years in the same tribunal. The other members have all suffered through periodical arrests that ranged from three to six months."[36]

The combination of hardliners in charge and lack of democracy within the increasingly consolidated organization forced out reformists seeking to democratize the Brotherhood. The departure of the reformists for the Wasat Party in 2006 inadvertently further elevated and consolidated the

---

35. Amr Darrag. Interview with the author. June 13, 2016. Istanbul, Turkey.
36. Khairat al-Shater. Interview with Josh Stacher. March 24, 2011. Cairo, Egypt.

influence of the hardliners; those who had been repressed, who had a stronger identification with the Brotherhood, were more wary of the broader opposition, and held stronger group-related preferences. Many of the remaining reformists would depart the party immediately after the 2011 uprising, ensuring that the conservative leadership remained at the helm with significant influence over the organization as it entered a crucial period.

Repression, both in how it was directly experienced by the group as well as how influential leaders constructed it into a narrative of victimhood, is important for making sense of the Brotherhood's internal dynamics and its positions towards other groups. The Brotherhood was always designed to socialize loyal members, but as repression increased in-group identification and the organization became more internally cohesive at the expense of the broader opposition, its identity became more exclusive. Reflecting on the Brotherhood's identity before 2011, Darrag noted that "a significant part of the narrative of the Brotherhood prior to 2011 was the experience of these people in jail."

———

Through a psychological mechanism, different experiences of repression under the Mubarak regime provided the opposition with information about the political world, in which some groups were co-opted, some tolerated, and one repressed. This undermined the formation of a bridging opposition identity, and instead laid the foundation for an exclusive and hostile Brotherhood identity shaped by unique victimization at the hands of the regime. In combination with social mechanisms, wherein political prisoners were kept in separate spaces, and organizational mechanisms, wherein the Brotherhood's structure increasingly fueled and instilled the unique vicitimization narrative among its members, repression facilitated the creation and strengthening of unique political identities *within* different opposition groups, rather than one in which shared victimhood was a common feature *across* groups, as in Tunisia. My interviews with members of the co-opted and tolerated opposition, as well as with the Brotherhood, demonstrate that members of the opposition were aware of how differently competing groups were treated by the regime, and social and organizational developments further reinforced the division among these groups.

## Affective Polarization among the Egyptian Opposition

As I mentioned earlier, the Mubarak era began with an anomalous repressive situation. In September 1981, Sadat arrested nearly 1,600 members of the opposition. These individuals covered the ideological spectrum, including Islamists, leftists, and even regime loyalists. Though leftists had been targeted by the regime before, and Islamists would be targeted after, this period was different. The opposition experienced psychological similarities in their treatment, as well as a physical overlap in prisons, where they were held together for a couple of months. Members of the opposition who suffered together during this period do not directly cite this interactive experience as being a bonding one, or one in which they discussed politics and reached consensus on ideological differences.

There is evidence that this anomalous experience helped members of different opposition groups come to see each other more positively, as individuals also struggling against the regime, and thus the Mubarak era began with relatively more positive affect between opposition groups. In particular, the Brotherhood felt more connected to secular groups who were also mobilizing in opposition to the regime. Brotherhood General Guide Al-Tilmisani recalled the 1981 arrest as bringing together individuals from many different schools of thought and opinion: "There were those among the Communists who prayed with us." Further, he saw this as a more unified group of opposition, responding to a question about the possibility of Islamic and leftist forces with "anyone who calls for freedom is my ally and I am his." Al-Tilmisani even went so far as to describe members of the opposition as "extremely charming," referring by name to the prominent communist figure Doctor Ismail Sabri Abdullah and Waft Party leader Fuad Siraj al-Din Pasha.[37]

The shared repressive experience and strong(er) intergroup identification coincided with the beginning of a period of opposition unity. Mubarak released political prisoners arrested by Sadat in waves beginning in November 1981. He vowed to refrain from using repression against mobilized opposition, and reinstated regular and somewhat competitive elections. The Brotherhood entered the 1984 parliamentary elections in an alliance with the Wafd Party. In many ways, this partnership was strategic; the Brotherhood was legally barred from entering candidates in the election

---

37. Al-Tilmisani, *Dhikrayat La Mudhakkirat.*

and the Wafd was the strongest opposition party permitted in the contest. But in addition, the Brotherhood's experience with the Wafd Party in 1984 demonstrates that a stronger unified opposition identity and a willingness to work together as such preceded ideological change and increased affinity between the parties.

The Brotherhood and Wafd Party entered into an alliance, aided by comparatively stronger feelings of opposition identity, and only after did the Wafd Party update its position on religion and politics. The party had previously advocated a separation of religion and state, considering religion to be a personal matter. However, the party eventually yielded, and the 1984 platform called for the application of the Islamic shari'a as a main source of legislation. Party campaign materials held that Islam was both religion and state, and called for the Islamization of the mass media and educational institutions.[38] My interviews with active leadership and public Brotherhood narratives of this period point to the joint electoral lists as evidence of closeness between the Brotherhood and other opposition forces, not necessarily convergence and agreement in political preferences.

However, with the onset and continuation of targeted repression against the Muslim Brotherhood organization under the Mubarak regime in the 1990s, the Brotherhood experienced increasing in-group identification and decreasing identification with other groups. Targeted repression altered the group's identity, and the organization increasingly depicted itself as an isolated group, not identified with a broader opposition, unique in its victimization. As a result, the Brotherhood's affect towards secular opposition groups grew increasingly negative.

Brotherhood descriptions of the Mubarak period went so far as to accuse its secular opponents of actively supporting the regime in its systematic persecution of the group, demonstrating increasingly negative affect between groups. The Brotherhood narrative drew a firm boundary between its members who had suffered for their cause specifically and for democratization more generally, and members of the opposition groups who had been co-opted by the regime. For example, Gamal Heshmat, a member of the Shura Council who served in parliament and was jailed under Mubarak, noted that leftist and liberal opposition to the regime "also

---

38. Ramadan, "Fundamentalist Influence in Egypt: The Strategies of the Muslim Brotherhood and the Takfir groups," 172.

opposed the Brotherhood ... it even encouraged the security apparatus in its tyrannical goal. 'Progressives' in Egypt only wore the costume of progressivism." Moreover, Heshmat described the support of the secular opposition for the regime as follows: "they did what they did, and in the end, they don't feel a thing. They said, God is with you. Good luck while you're in jail. We're as far as we can be from you."[39] Amr Darrag similarly accused secular opposition of working with the regime: "What Mubarak did was to attract all others players to his camp. Even the opposition, those who are 'performing' opposition, were not actually far from the regime's agenda. The opposition was cooperating with state security, particularly the leftists."[40]

High-ranking members of the Brotherhood explicitly tied their unique identity of victimhood, and their increased identification with it, back to a number of inward-facing and defensive behaviors, which provide additional evidence of the lack of identification between the Brotherhood and the broader opposition. Darrag said, "part of the reason why some of the people in the Brotherhood were not capable of good communication is that they felt the others did not appreciate the kind of sacrifice [Brotherhood leaders] went through to maintain the protest movement" during this period. In these statements, the "others" were identified as non-Islamist members of the opposition, particularly those who were actively involved in the parliament and who might have benefited electorally from sidelining the Brotherhood. Brotherhood narratives of a divided opposition focused on a difference in identities, separating those who had suffered and paid a price for their political activism from those who had not, accusing the latter of co-optation and collusion with the regime.[41]

In contrast, secular opposition members remembered an increasingly bad relationship with the Brotherhood which resulted from less identification as a broader opposition movement. Secular opposition groups identified with groups of similar ideologies and described their relationships as positive and cooperative, despite a multiplicity of organizational representation. These individuals had been arrested and tortured together under Sadat, as part of the Egyptian Communist Party, the left of the ASU, or other leftist mobilization. This identification extended even to secular parties who had been co-opted by the regime, namely the Wafd,

39. Gamal Heshmat. Interview with the author. June 18, 2016. Istanbul, Turkey.
40. Amr Darrag. Interview with the author. June 13, 2016. Istanbul, Turkey.
41. Amr Darrag. Interview with the author. June 13, 2016. Istanbul, Turkey.

who they were able to think of as "partners in legitimate contestation of the regime."

Non-Islamist opposition noted increased affinity and cooperation with the Brotherhood at the beginning of the Mubarak era. In addition to the joint electoral lists between the Muslim Brotherhood and the more secular Wafd Party and Hizb al-ʿAmal, the opposition worked together in a formal committee (in Arabic *Lajnat al-Ahzab al-Muʿaridha*), an initiative which brought together members of political opposition parties, civil society, and the Brotherhood, notably including active participation from Umar al-Tilmisani, then the third General Guide of the Brotherhood. Abdel Razik, a leader of the Tagammu Party, noted that beginning in 1981, there were a number of unofficial fronts with the Brotherhood as united opposition against the regime on a number of limited issues such as democracy and the hegemony of the NDP.[42]

However, there was increasingly negative affect from secular opposition towards the Brotherhood. Secular opposition members accused the Brotherhood of allying with the Mubarak regime, pointing to the Brotherhood's significant representation in parliament, particularly in 2005, as evidence of collusion. Al-Toukhy of Karama labeled the relationship between the Brotherhood and the regime as one of "mutual exploitation: I use you, you use me." Secularists claimed that the Brotherhood had not only worked with the regime against them under Mubarak, but also under Nasser and Sadat, establishing a long historical narrative of divided contestation and co-optation, in which the left was the victim and the Brotherhood the regime's coconspirator. Farida Naqash of Tagammu described this long-term collaboration as follows:

> Nasser had tried to ally with the Brotherhood, but they tried to kill him. Sadat didn't learn this lesson. He released the Brotherhood from jail, and then they helped him immensely in repressing the left on university campuses. Sadat allied with the Brotherhood against the left, and … well, the ending is well known. Mubarak did the same thing. He also tried to ally with the Brotherhood against the left.

Some leftists further clarified that their public comments about human rights and political prisoners were not out of sympathy with the regime's worst victims (i.e., the Brotherhood) or any empathy with them as fellow victims; it was only meant to refer to groups with which they felt close and

42. Hussein Abdel Razik. Interview with the author. February 3, 2018. Cairo, Egypt.

positively. For example, Amin Iskandar, one of the Nasserist cofounders of Karama, wrote a piece about military trials for civilians. When I asked if this was a veiled critique of the state's repression of the Brotherhood, he responded vehemently that it was not: "My only point was that citizens should not be put in prison without a civil trial, and a fair one at that, with a fair defense and clear charges. My feelings about the Brotherhood are very negative. My political opinion is at the completely opposite end of the spectrum from the Brotherhood. I'm completely against political Islam. This country can't progress with a religious program, only a civil one. As I said, I am the most radically opposed to the Brotherhood."

As noted above, though it was overwhelmingly the Brotherhood which was pursued by regime repression, other individuals were intermittently targeted as well. One example is Nour of the Ghad Party, and the effect of his experience of repression is the exception that proves the rule in the case of Egypt. Nour suffered disproportionately to other members of the non-Islamist opposition; he described the "repression and harassment" used by the regime against him as tactics normally reserved for the Muslim Brotherhood. And compared to other non-Islamist opposition, Nour expressed more positive affect towards the Brotherhood as an important part of a larger collective opposition movement engaged in democratic reform:

> I believe that a progressive must recognize the right of the other to exist. I believe that Islamists are a part of political life in Egypt—not just the Brotherhood, all Islamists, and all Christians, and all communists, and all liberals … accepting the others, that's part of my principles. It is necessary that we maintain a position in line with our principles. It is not necessary that we are fully agreed with Islamists; we were not fully agreed with anyone, and opposed many often. But in the end, at a minimum, I recognize them, for in democratic principles, it is necessary that we respect each other.

His language about the Brotherhood suggests similar experiences of repression caused him to more closely identify with Brotherhood victims and feel more positive about the organization than other, less persecuted opposition. This does not suggest a formal alliance between Ghad and the Brotherhood, but rather a higher level of affinity and closeness than that experienced by other secular opposition.

## Preference Polarization among the Egyptian Opposition

In contrast to the decreasing preference polarization in Tunisia, the Egyptian opposition became more polarized between 1981 and the 2011 uprising on policy preferences related to the identity of the state that would result from successful reform or overthrow of the regime. This increasing divergence is captured, first, in how party platforms, manifestos, and official statements discussed central issues of state identity. The Brotherhood's preferences for religious influence over the state and the public sphere strengthened over time. Second, while some cooperative initiatives were broached during the later years of Mubarak, they never addressed central issues related to religion and politics for fear of internal fighting.

### OFFICIAL POSITIONS

In Egypt, there was relative agreement on issues of religion and politics among the active opposition in the 1980s. In the 1984 elections, the Brotherhood ran in an alliance with the Wafd Party and issued a joint statement as a common political platform. The Wafd's leadership was representative of small businessmen lacking personal connections to the regime, and the political platform centered around policies to decrease government corruption, linked with calls for increased democracy and budgetary transparency as part of the solution. Implementing the shari'a was a secondary concern in the platform, and the language outlined a plan in which strengthening the role of Islam in society was the primary means of achieving this rather than having state institutions enforce this. In 1987, the Brotherhood also ran in an alliance with the Socialist Labor Party and the Liberal Socialists Party, two other small Islamist parties, under the banner *Al-Islam Huwwa al-Hal* (Islam is the solution). The joint party platform included a section titled "The Application of the Shari'a" which specified that the implementation of Islamic law was not only the duty of individuals but also government institutions:

> The great work which is required in this direction is not the task of the legislator alone, but is an integrated task, parts of which the legislator carries and others which jurists, law professors, scientists, economic specialists, and trade and industry employees hold, as well as others. They are required to put forward learned, accurate effort and to apply a sharp eye to the circumstances of the times and the needs of the people.

During this early period of parliamentary participation, much of the Brotherhood's activity in parliament focused on the application of shari'a as well as clarifying and better implementing Article 2 of the constitution. Throughout parliamentary sessions in 1984 and 1985, the Brotherhood-Wafd bloc held several sessions in which high-ranking Brothers (including General Guide Umar al-Tilmisani) were invited to offer guidance.[43] A 1985 report stated that "a general consensus was reached in these [parliamentary] sessions on the necessity of applying the Shari'a in a gradual manner, beginning with the cleansing of existing laws, that is, the removal of elements in conflict with shari'a rulings."[44] The Brotherhood criticized the government on its slow pace of applying the shari'a and linked this behavior with other corrupt and undemocratic regime behaviors, finding support from other opposition groups in this critique.

As early as the 2000 platform, the Muslim Brotherhood articulated the group's collective preferences for a state with a stronger role in enforcing the shari'a.[45] As Wickham writes, "Islam and the 'fixed values of the nation' would hence serve as the ultimate reference point for the new political order, setting the outer limits of free expression and assembly."[46] The elections came on the heels of the last releases of those jailed during the 1995 military trials. In order to not antagonize the regime, the Brotherhood limited its numbers, contesting only 75 of 444 seats, and downplayed its religious discourse; it exchanged its normal controversial campaign slogan, "Islam is the solution," for the more universal "The Constitution is the Solution,"[47] though the Brotherhood's focus on this institution focused on its Islamic attributes.

However, at the same time, the organization's platform outlined preferences for stronger state enforcement of morality, political and economic reform, and freedoms defined by Islamic tenets and practice. The platform outlined preferences for state behavior including "giving the proponents of the *da'wa* the freedom to explain the principles and characteristics of Islam, the most important of which is its comprehensiveness as a guide to all aspects of life," "encouraging people to worship and to abide by good

---

43. Wickham, *Muslim Brotherhood*, 52.

44. 1985 Arab Strategic Report.

45. The preferences indeed guided the organization for the next five years: they were reiterated nearly verbatim during a conference outlining the Brotherhood's reform initiative in March 2004.

46. Wickham, *Muslim Brotherhood*, 106.

47. Shehata, *Islamists and Secularists in Egypt: Opposition, Conflict and Cooperation*, 55.

and upright morals," and "purifying the media of everything which violates the rulings of Islam and established norms." All "freedoms" were couched in language that framed them as providing space for individuals to practice their religion and promote Islamic reform, but implied a strong role for the state in actually mandating certain religious behaviors from citizens in working towards reform.

The 2000 platform also included a stronger role for state institutions than previously articulated. The judiciary would be given a mandate to "adjust the laws and cleanse them to hasten their conformity with the principles of shari'a," while the national education system would be charged with "the spread of religious values, moral principles, good examples, and national belonging" in accordance with Islamic values. Similarly, the platform articulated preferences for state control over media outlets in order to ensure proper content to deepen society's education of and commitment to Islamic values and principles. As Wickham continues, "To 'rebuild the Egyptian person,' it suggests, the levels of the state—such as its control over education, the media, and the mosques—must be employed to spread Islamic beliefs and values."[48] The Brotherhood's preference for any successful reform was increasingly to create a strong state in order to promote Islamic values and behaviors, as defined by the organization.

Increased polarization among political parties, and the continued movement of the Brotherhood, on preferences regarding the salient axis of competition were most evident after 2005. Between 2005 and the 2011 uprising, both the Brotherhood's officially issued as well as its unofficially leaked political platforms articulated the party's strong Islamist preferences for a state in which Islam featured prominently as the basis for laws, and both the state and religious institutions played strong roles in advancing the particular version of Islamism outlined in these documents. The 2005 electoral program stated, "Islam is in need of a state that will institute it and protect it and abide by its teachings," diverging from previous platforms that prioritized reforming society as a path towards Islamic reform. The platform rejected the notion of direct clerical control but did articulate the party's notion of the state's strong role in implementing shari'a:

> The state in Islam is a lay state which implements shari'a and God's limits ... the civic nature of the state deprives it of any sanctity but it must nonetheless abide by the principles of Islam, for Islam has

---

48. Wickham, *Muslim Brothehood*, 107.

prescribed certain limits and rights. It is a state that blends religion and politics without either separation or merger.

In 2007, the Brotherhood issued a party platform that diverged from previous documents. A number of leaked drafts were circulated in the months before, and were similar to official party documents from the early 2000s. The document was not prepared in anticipation of applying to the Political Parties Committee for legal status, but rather was intended to clarify and signal its preference positioning to the electorate. Similar to previous platforms, the content focused on strengthening state institutions to best implement Article 2 of the amended constitution, which delineated to what extent shari'a was the source of legislation. Where the document diverged from previous positions was increasing the role of non-state institutions in aiding this task. Although Brotherhood leadership had previously emphasized that they "rejected the idea of a country ruled by religious authorities, preferring a state of institutions, with laws passed by an elected parliament but conforming to shari'a,"[49] the platform outlined a vision of religious institutional oversight for legislation. The document introduced the idea of a Higher Ulema Council, advanced as an elected body of clerics who were charged with playing an advisory role in reviewing pending and existing legislation and offering non-binding suggestions to reform these in better accordance with shari'a. The body was intended to be separate from al-Azhar, but to play the role the institution should have served had it not become co-opted by the regime. This new feature of the party's platform articulated the group's preference for an increased role for religious institutions in more effectively implementing shari'a, and marked a new preference for stronger non-state institutions to assist in this goal.

The Muslim Brotherhood issued a final party platform ahead of the 2010 elections. The program outlined the party's accomplishments in parliament over the past five years, and focused on its achievements in further incorporating the values and principles of shari'a into legislation. The freedoms the party credited itself with achieving were in line with the Islamic versions of freedom of expression and worship articulated in previous platforms. The 2010 platform called for the continuation of this program, in addition to outlining a strong role for state institutions in implementing shari'a as well

---

49. Mohammed Habib. Interview published on *Ikhwan Online*, January 18, 2007.

as Islamicizing society. In a section titled "Religious Leadership," the platform continued with the change noted in the 2007 party platform, in calling for a religious body with an advisory role over existing and pending legislation. This role was assigned to al-Azhar rather than a new institution; however, al-Azhar was to be constrained by a number of democratizing reforms including selecting the Grand Imam and the Center for Islamic Research (a council of senior scholars) by election. These reforms would permit the institution to play an important legislative role in addition to its religious and educational functions, and were intended to free it from the control of the Mubarak regime in order to be more effective.

Between 1981 and 2011, secularist opposition movements were relatively stable in their preferences for the nature of the state resulting from any successful reform. After an initial shift away from articulating preferences for shari'a as the basis of legislation while in partnership with the Muslim Brotherhood, the Wafd Party remained committed to a civil secular state that respected the private right of individuals to practice their religion while maintaining a secular public sphere, with a moderate role for the state in enforcing these notions. Tagammu articulated a similar platform with a slightly stronger but still somewhat moderate role for the state in enforcing secular public and political spheres. More extreme leftists articulated a vision of a robust secular state that "guarantees the equality of men and women, in wages and in rights," as well as freedom of belief. These positions persisted throughout the 1990s, and shifted as later platforms articulated a stronger state role in imposing secular notions of legitimacy and regulating religious behavior in the 2005 elections. The cumulative effect of changes in party preferences and positioning, largely driven by changes from the Brotherhood, was a highly polarized society on the eve of the 2011 uprisings. While both Islamist and secularist opposition desired change and reform of the existing regime and state, they differed significantly in their preferences over what that state would look like, how it would derive its legitimacy, and how strongly it could legally intervene in citizens' lives with regards to religion and politics.

Ghad Party leader Nour succinctly summarizes developments with regards to preference polarization among the opposition: "during the Mubarak era, [the opposition] knew what we didn't want. After Mubarak, we couldn't agree on what we did want."[50]

---

50. Ayman Nour. Interview with the author. February 11, 2017. Istanbul, Turkey.

## COOPERATIVE INITIATIVES

During the late 2000s, an often-repeated claim in academic and policy work on the Brotherhood was that the organization was moderating politically.[51] These arguments left the term "moderation" undefined[52] but mainly pointed to two main behaviors: increased cooperation with competing opposition groups and the incorporation of democratic rhetoric into its official statements and platforms.

In terms of increased cooperation, the Brotherhood worked with other opposition forces to organize a number of events between 2000 and 2003, such as protests in support of the Palestinian Intifada (including the Egyptian Popular Committee in Support of the Palestinian Intifada) and in opposition to the American invasion of Iraq (including a major protest held in Cairo Stadium in 2003). During a 2005 referendum on direct presidential elections, the Brotherhood joined a boycott called for by other opposition parties. The Brotherhood participated in *at-Tahaluf al-Watani min ajl al-Islah wal-Taghyir* (The National Coalition for Reform and Change), a coalition of parties and civil society organizations committed to reforming the Egyptian political system. The organization also cooperated with initiatives put forward by *Kefaya* (meaning enough in Arabic), a grassroots political movement building on the Egyptian Popular Committee in Solidarity with the Intifada (EPSCI) and which protested political corruption, economic stagnation, and the possibility of Mubarak's son Gamal inheriting the presidency. In addition, the organization increasingly articulated a commitment to democratic values of political, gender, and social pluralism in its public statements. In 1994, the organization published a book containing statements highlighting its progressive positions on political pluralism and women's political rights, and a 1995 statement similarly reaffirmed its commitment to the rights of non-Muslims, human rights issues, and a non-violent approach to politics.[53] Following the 1995 crackdown on the group, the Brotherhood announced its intention to form a formal political party that was civic in nature with guiding principles derived from Islam, and stated that the party would be open to all Egyptians including Coptic Christians.

---

51. For example, see Ghobashy, "The Metamorphosis of the Egyptian Muslim Brothers."

52. Schwedler, "Can Islamists Become Moderates? Rethinking the Inclusion-Moderation Hypothesis."

53. Shehata, *Islamists and Secularists in Egypt: Opposition, Conflict and Cooperation*, 62.

However, a closer reading of this time period demonstrates that simul-
taneous to these developments, the Brotherhood's central policy preferences—on issues of religion, politics, and state identity—were becoming
more distant from those of competing opposition groups. The Brotherhood did increasingly articulate a public commitment to democratic values
and non-violent contestation of the regime, but this was not an indication
of a development in ideology or a change in approach towards democratic
contestation; indeed, the group had maintained a non-violent reformist
approach to politics since the 1950s. Rather, the statements appear to have
been repeatedly issued in response to continued targeted state repression
against the group, which the regime publicly legitimized through a narrative linking the Brotherhood to terrorist organizations. And where the
Egyptian opposition did demonstrate some agreement, it was only over
peripheral policy issues related to international issues, or general themes
of protest and reform.

Even in instances of seeming cooperation, the Brotherhood's participation was tenuous; the group often remained on the sidelines or backed out
of agreements and events, sometimes at the last minute, for fear that the
group would be singularly targeted for these cooperative initiatives with
further arrests and imprisonments. Ultimately, the National Coalition and
Kefaya initiatives failed to establish any robust and enduring cross-partisan
alliance, or to resolve central issues of disagreement. The Islamists who
were involved were not directly affiliated with the Brotherhood; the two
notable Islamists included in the initiative had either left for the Wasat Party
or had formally left any Brotherhood-related organization.[54] As George
Ishaq, a leader of the Kefaya movement, remarked when asked whether the
two sides had resolved their differences on the issue of shari'a, he replied
that the issue "never came up" (*lam tutrah*); the discussion of contentious
issues was reserved for a later time.[55] Al-Toukhy from the Karama Party
noted that the opposition could cooperate on tangential issues: "we always
tried to unite around commonly held positions, but the Islamists had completely different ideas about economics, about peasants, all stemming from
their ideas about religion and politics. We believed in widespread social justice, while they believed in the idea of *zakat* and private charity. We had
very different ideas with regards to the role of religion. And according to

54. Amin Iskandar. Interview with the author. February 3, 2018. Cairo, Egypt.
55. Wickham, *Muslim Brotherhood*, 115.

Islamists, if you're a communist, you're a *kafir*."[56] Differences with regards to religion and politics appeared to preclude any real dialogue on a number of topics.

While cooperative developments among the opposition in the 2000s were undoubtedly meaningful, they were also unrelated to parties' central policy preferences and issues, and the salient issues of contestation in Egypt. As a result, they did not represent a decrease in polarization among the opposition groups on the most contentious axis of contestation, that of religion and politics. This was ultimately the salient axis of differentiation and competition—how to define the nature of the state with regards to religion and politics, and how to enforce this amendment as part of a larger program of reform. The political opposition was increasingly polarized on this dimension of competition over the course of Mubarak's rule, with the movement of the Muslim Brotherhood doing much of the work of polarization. The party was not moderating on its key policy preference of incorporating Islam into politics during this time period. Rather, the Brotherhood was slowly articulating policy preferences for a future state with a stronger role for religion in politics, and was becoming more distant from those of competing opposition groups, particularly after 2005.

## Conclusion

The targeted repressive environment under Mubarak left a divided opposition. There was no common identity as a unified opposition, and as a result, the opposition in Egypt was left highly polarized both in terms of affect and preferences. Individuals in the opposition under Mubarak—including both secularists and leftists as well as Brotherhood members—perceived that they were operating in a repressive environment that most affected the Muslim Brotherhood. This is in stark contrast to the way in which a widespread repressive environment in Tunisia resulted in a less polarized opposition.

56. Sayyid al-Toukhy. Interview with author. January 31, 2018. Cairo, Egypt.

# 7

# Identity and Polarization in the Lab

This chapter presents the motivation, design, and results of lab experimental tests of how repression conditions political polarization through identity.[1] The effects of shared trauma on group identification and polarization are well-established in the psychological literature. Here, I test for the relationship between repression and political identities to establish the central psychological mechanism through which repression conditions polarization. To do this, I designed an experiment in a controlled lab environment to observe, measure, and make causal inferences about the psychological mechanism underpinning my theory.

## Justification for Lab Experimental Design

As I noted in the introductory chapter, the book relies on mixed methods combining complementary qualitative and quantitative data and analyses. I incorporated a lab experimental set-up for a number of logistical and ethical reasons. Perhaps most importantly, the controlled experimental set-up provides more complete leverage on issues of endogeneity, external validity, and generalizability than the observational data presented elsewhere in the book. Further, the experimental set-up eliminates potential confounding factors present in observational data from consideration by testing the

1. A modified version of this chapter appeared in *World Politics* 72.2 (2020): 291–334.

theory in a controlled environment. These factors include regime characteristics, such as strategic choice of repressive strategy. Though I do not
subscribe to the idea that repression is a fully strategic choice by a regime,
as discussed in more detail in chapters 3 and 4, this is often the assumption
made by scholars and thus one I needed to be able to account for in my argument. Additional factors included potential confounders such as relative
group size, pre-existing relationships between groups, or selection issues
with regards to group membership in real-world cases. The set-up also
gave me control over the repressive content to which respondents would
be exposed, and permitted a full debriefing by enumerators to ensure participants understood the imaginary nature of the scenario and could raise
any issues or concerns that resulted from participation.

While a laboratory is a controlled environment, the broader cultural and
social context determines the validity of the experimental scenario for the
participants. I chose Tunisia as the country site for the experiments because
it is a context in which the content of the repressive primes is both relevant
and realistic. Primes about repression should be expected to be most believable in a context where politically motivated repression has previously been
employed by the state. In Tunisia, respondents were likely to have real-
world reference points for political repression because of the country's long
and widespread experience with it under its two previous authoritarian
presidents.[2] Although state repression has significantly decreased since the
2011 uprisings, it remains a salient political topic.[3] Because Tunisia has a
legacy of widespread repression (documented in chapter 5), I could real-
istically manipulate information about the targets of state repression. As
such, Tunisia's widespread repressive history might actually provide a hard
test of my theory, given that respondents may have internalized this history.
In Egypt, where repression has been highly correlated with specific political groups at different times, respondents may have been less receptive
to manipulation that disagreed with their knowledge of historical repression. In addition, the state of politics in Egypt in recent years has created
a difficult environment for conducting research, and I was unwilling to
jeopardize the safety of a host institution and participants, or to put myself

2. Elizabeth R. Nugent, "Personal Exposure to Repression and Political Preferences: Evidence from Tunisia," Working Paper, 2019.

3. Amnesty International, *Tunisia: Severe Restrictions on Liberty and Movement Latest
Symptoms of Repressive Emergency Law.* June 2016, available at https://www.amnesty.org/en/
latest/news/2016/03/tunisia-severe-restrictions-on-liberty-and-movement-latest-symptoms-of-
repressive-emergency-law/.

at risk. While the repression treatment is randomized at the individual level, measurements occur at the group level, similar to how repression occurs in the real world. Individuals experience repression, but as a result of their group membership rather than individual traits, and this ultimately has implications for outcomes aggregated at the group level.[4]

## EXPERIMENTAL PROCEDURE

To conduct the experiments, I worked in partnership with an independent research company based in Tunis. The lab experiments were conducted with a sample of 434 Tunisian adult citizens between May 13 and 20, 2016. Each respondent was paired with a Tunisian enumerator who read the instrument to the respondent and filled out answers on a tablet computer.[5] After being asked a number of questions recording basic demographic information, recruited respondents were told they had been randomly assigned to a fictitious group called the Tunisian Organization for Social Dignity, a group with like-minded individuals. In addition to learning their group assignment, respondents were also told about a rival peer group, the Tunisian Forum for Freedom and Social Justice. The below text was read to each respondent, and the bracketed text was randomized across participants:

> Since 2011, many organizations working on political issues have been created. Based on your answers to the previous questions, you have been assigned to The Tunisian Organization for Social Dignity with other individuals who have the same opinions and ideas as you do in terms of [policies pertaining to matters of religion and politics/policies pertaining to economic matters]. The group holds events, debates, and conferences about political and social issues affecting Tunisians on [matters of religion and politics/economic matters]. In addition, the group mobilizes its members to demonstrate for causes the group supports.

> Your group, The Tunisian Organization for Social Dignity, is a very popular one and membership is highly exclusive. It has a number of peer

4. Francisco Gutiérrez-Sanín and Elisabeth Jean Wood, "What Should We Mean by 'Pattern of Political Violence'? Repertoire, Targeting, Frequency, and Technique," *Perspectives on Politics* 15, no. 1 (2017): 20–41.

5. More information on the organization of the experiment is included in the book's appendix.

*organizations including The Tunisian Forum for Freedom and Social Jus-*
*tice, which runs similar events but whose members hold different opinions*
*about [religion and politics policies/economic policies] from yours.*

*Please keep your membership in The Tunisian Organization for Social*
*Dignity group in mind as you proceed with the tasks ahead of you.*

The set-up of the experiment requires three points of clarification. First, the group names—the Tunisian Organization for Social Dignity and the Tunisian Forum for Freedom and Social Justice—were chosen to represent a generic name similar to those used by organizations which have formed in Tunisia during the period of liberalization following the 2011 revolution. Names similarly invoking themes of social justice and political equality have been used by groups that mobilize on a number of political, social, and economic causes, and which are both secular and Islamist in their orientation. To the best of my knowledge, these two specific names were not in use at the time.

Second, I chose to use a meaningful characteristic—common pre-ferences—as the basis for group membership rather than generic identifiers such as Groups A and B or Teams Red and Blue used in the minimal group paradigm.[6] Countless studies have demonstrated that individuals do meaningfully identify with randomly assigned and contentless groups in lab experimental settings; however, it was unclear to me what individu-als' group-related preferences would be in these situations beyond simple material group interests, or how these preferences might be altered or updated. Assigning membership to a group with more content than the typ-ical minimal group was intended to capture movement in political opinions related to that group membership later in the experiment.

Third, I assigned respondents to one of two types of groups: one based on economic policy preferences, or one based on policy preferences related to religion and politics. This was a deliberate choice to determine whether group membership defined by similar preferences regarding reli-gion and politics was different or whether group members were affected differently by repressive conditions than members of economic-preference based groups. Lipset and Rokkan observed that "systems will come under much heavier strain if the main lines of cleavage are over morals and the nature of human destiny than if they concern such mundane and negotiable matters as the prices of commodities, the rights of debtors and creditors,

6. Tajfel et al., "Social Categorization and Intergroup Behaviour."

wages and profits, and the ownership of property."[7] Their observation suggests that differences in certain preferences, especially those related to economics and tangible material trade-offs, may be more malleable or easier to find compromise over than philosophical differences with less clear, concrete solutions. However, because the same patterns emerged from initial analyses of both types of groups, I pool data from the two group assignments for my analyses.

Respondents then completed a priming task in which they were asked to brainstorm about the group to which they were assigned. This task was intended to increase the salience of this group in each respondent's mind before continuing with the experiment. Respondents were asked to describe the policies, slogans, activities, and other members of the group to the enumerator. The answers to the priming questions are beyond the scope of this chapter, but demonstrated that respondents understood their group assignment, found it believable, and could construct a group narrative consistent with their assignment. For example, one respondent assigned to the religious group treatment, and who identified herself as highly in support of the statement, "the government and parliament should enact legislation according to Islamic law" in pre-treatment questions, described her in-group as consisting of like-minded individuals similarly invested in a state combining religion and politics, and her out-group as consisting of individuals highly supportive of secularization policies.

Next, respondents were randomly assigned to one of three repressive treatments: one of which served as an active control, a second which primed a widespread repressive environment, or a third which primed a targeted repressive environment against the respondent's assigned group. The treatment consisted of informational primes, which included facts about Tunisia's current emergency law, and varied only in terms of the policies' targets. The control text below was read to all participants, while the widespread and targeted treatment groups received a second paragraph of information as follows:

CONTROL: *As you may know, the Tunisian government extended the state of emergency for three months on March 22, 2016. The emergency measure allows the government to ban any type of strike or gathering. However, over the past few months, various groups have been involved*

---

7. Lipset and Rokkan, "Cleavage Structures, Party Systems, and Voter Alignments: An Introduction," 94.

*in organizing events to denounce terrorism and participating in strikes demanding security and protection in the country.*

WIDESPREAD: Control text + *The police claim that the events violate the terms of the state of emergency, and are placing all groups, including your group, The Tunisian Organization for Social Dignity, as well as The Tunisian Forum for Freedom and Social Justice, under investigation to determine whether they have been involved in planning or participating in these events. Until the investigation is concluded, the groups will not be able to hold meetings or host events, and members will be put under surveillance. The police maintain the right to arrest group members pending the results of the investigation.*

TARGETED: Control text + *The police claim that the events violate the terms of the state of emergency, and are placing your group, The Tunisian Organization for Social Dignity, under investigation to determine whether it has been involved in planning or participating in these events. Until the investigation is concluded, the group will not be able to hold meetings or host events, and members will be put under surveillance. The police maintain the right to arrest group members pending the results of the investigation.*

## OUTCOME VARIABLES

In order to test both components of my two-stage theory, I measured in- and out-group identification, and affective and preference polarization, in questions following the repressive condition assignment. To measure in-group identification, respondents were asked six questions about the strength of their identification with the group to which they had been assigned. These questions were adapted from a battery of social identity questions known as the Identification with a Psychological Group (IDPG) scale.[8] This is a standard battery used for determining individuals' level of identification with a number of social and political groups.[9] The question read, "I'd like to ask you a few questions about your feelings about other members of and your membership in the Tunisian Organization for

---

8. Fred A. Mael and Lois E. Tetrick, "Identifying Organizational Identification," *Educational and Psychological Measurement* 52, no. 4 (1989): 813–824.

9. Marilynn B. Brewer and Michael D. Silver, "Group Distinctiveness, Social Identity, and Collective Mobilization," in *Self, Identity, and Social Movement*, ed. Sheldon Stryker et al. (Minneapolis: University of Minnesota Press, 2000).

Social Dignity. On a scale of 1 to 10, where 1 is 'absolutely disagree' and 10 is 'absolutely agree,' to what extent do you agree with the following statements?"

1. When someone criticizes the Tunisian Organization for Social Dignity, it feels like a personal insult.
2. I am very interested in what others think about the Tunisian Organization for Social Dignity.
3. When I talk about the Tunisian Organization for Social Dignity, I would usually say "we" rather than "they."
4. The Tunisian Organization for Social Dignity's successes are my successes.
5. When someone praises the Tunisian Organization for Social Dignity, it feels like a personal compliment.
6. If a story in the media criticized the Tunisian Organization for Social Dignity, I would feel embarrassed.

Respondents were asked the same questions about the Tunisian Forum for Freedom and Social Justice, their out-group. Recorded responses to the questions loaded onto one factor, and thus were summed and rescaled to range between 10 to 100 for ease of interpretation.[10]

To measure affective polarization, respondents were asked three questions about members of the Tunisian Forum for Freedom and Justice, the group to which they had *not* been assigned. These questions were designed to capture their feelings towards the out-group with regards to trust, empathy, and cooperation. The question read, "I'd like to ask you a few questions about your feelings about the other social organization we mentioned before but to which you do not belong, the Tunisian Forum for Freedom and Social Justice. On a scale of 1 to 10, where 1 is 'absolutely disagree' and 10 is 'absolutely agree,' to what extent do you agree with the following statements?"

1. How much do you trust members of the Tunisian Forum for Freedom and Social Justice?
2. How much do you empathize with members of the Tunisian Forum for Freedom and Social Justice?
3. How willing would you be to cooperate with members of the Tunisian Forum for Freedom and Social Justice?

10. Cronbach's $\alpha = .75$ for the in-group questions and .69 for the out-group questions, using responses only from the control (i.e., non-treated) group.

Recorded responses to the questions loaded onto one factor, and thus were summed and rescaled to range between 10 to 100 for ease of interpretation.[11]

To measure preference polarization, respondents were asked their opinions on a number of policies, but were told the average opinion of the out-group *before* reporting their level of agreement. The questions posed to respondents varied based on their group assignment. Respondents who were assigned to a group with people of similar opinions on economic policies received the following three questions:

1. The government should privatize more public companies, like SONEDE and STEG.[12] For comparison, the average member of the other group, The Tunisian Forum for Freedom and Social Justice, answered 7.
2. The government should impose both a wage cap as well as a minimum wage to ensure equality of income. For comparison, the average member of the other group, The Tunisian Forum for Freedom and Social Justice, answered 3.
3. The government should increase taxes on the wealthy in order to increase spending on social welfare programs. For comparison, the average member of the other group, The Tunisian Forum for Freedom and Social Justice, answered 5.

Meanwhile, respondents who were assigned to a group of people with similar opinions on policies related to religion and politics received the following three questions:

1. The Tunisian government should prioritize legislation that preserves the Islamic heritage of the state. For comparison, the average member of the other group, The Tunisian Forum for Freedom and Social Justice, answered 7.
2. The parliament should enact personal status laws according to Islamic law. For comparison, the average member of the other group, The Tunisian Forum for Freedom and Social Justice, answered 3.

11. Cronbach's $\alpha = .76$, using responses only from the control group.

12. SONEDE stands for *Sociéte Nationale d'Exploitation et de Distribution des Eaux*, a national water supply authority founded in 1968 under the supervision of the Ministry of Agriculture. STEG is the Tunisian Company of Electricity and Gas; *Société Tunisienne de l'Electricité et du Gaz* is a public electric company founded in 1962.

3. The government should mandate the separation of religion from politics. For comparison, the average member of the other group, The Tunisian Forum for Freedom and Social Justice, answered 5.

Principal component analysis revealed that the three questions asked in each of the group assignments loaded onto one factor. I pool results across the three questions for each type of group, constructing a dependent variable measuring the respondent's average distance from the out-group's position across the three questions.[13]

## HYPOTHESES

I posited earlier a two-stage psychological process through which repression influences processes of polarization, which leads to four hypotheses to be tested by the experiment. The first two hypotheses concern the relationship between the repressive treatment group and distance from the out-group, measured by questions capturing both affective and preference polarization. The last two hypotheses speak to the centrality of group identification as the mechanism through which different repressive environments alter levels of polarization per the theory. My hypotheses, all constructed relative to the control, are as follows:

Hypothesis 1a (affective polarization): *Lower* levels of positive feelings towards the out-group will be observed in the *targeted* treatment group, while *higher* levels of positive feelings towards the out-group will be observed in the *widespread* treatment group.

Hypothesis 1b (preference polarization): *Larger* distances from the stated preferences from the out-group will be observed in the *targeted* treatment group, while *smaller* distances from the stated preferences from the out-group will be observed in the *widespread* treatment group.

Hypothesis 2a (in-group identification): *Higher* levels of in-group identification will be observed in the *targeted* treatment group, while *lower* levels of in-group identification will be observed in the *widespread* treatment group.

---

13. Because the internal reliability was not remarkably high for these indexes (Cronbach's $\alpha = .44$ for the economic questions; Cronbach's $\alpha = .63$ for the religious questions), I also ran separate regressions disaggregating the three components into separate variables, and the same pattern holds.

Hypothesis 2b (out-group identification): *Lower* levels of out-group identification will be observed in the *targeted* treatment group, while *higher* levels of out-group identification will be observed in the *widespread* treatment group.

## Results

Observed values support hypotheses 1a and 1b: priming widespread repressive environments fosters less polarization, or distance from the out-group in either affect or policy preferences, than priming the control and targeted repressive environments. Figure 7.1 displays the average treatment effect on positive affect towards the out-group measured by the three-item index, across treatment groups. Positive affect towards the out-group is highest in the widespread treatment group; while this is not significantly different from the control ($p = .12$), it is in the expected direction. On a scale of 10 to 100, the control group reported an average of 62.79 on the out-group affect index, the widespread treatment group reported an average of 67.19, and the targeted treatment group reported an average of 61.85. The difference in positive affect towards the out-group is significant between the widespread and targeted treatment ($p = .05$).

Figure 7.1 also displays the marginal treatment effect in terms of the average distance from the out-group's preferences by treatment group. I standardized this measurement to measure observed distance from the out-group as a percentage of total possible distance. The widespread treatment group is closest to the out-group, and significantly more so than not only the targeted treatment group but also the control. The control was an average of 70.72 percent of the total distance away from the out-group, while the widespread treatment group was an average of 55.2 percent and the targeted treatment group an average of 76.7 percent.

In addition, observed values support hypothesis 2a: in-group identification is significantly lower in the widespread treatment condition and significantly higher in the targeted treatment condition when compared with the control, as demonstrated in figure 7.2. Respondents in the control, widespread, and targeted treatment groups reported average levels of in-group identification of 66.3, 61.11, and 76.79, respectively, on a scale of 10 to 100. Similarly, observed values provide some support for hypothesis 2b: out-group identification is lower in the targeted treatment group condition ($p = .06$), though the widespread treatment group is not statistically different from the control. Respondents in the control, widespread, and targeted

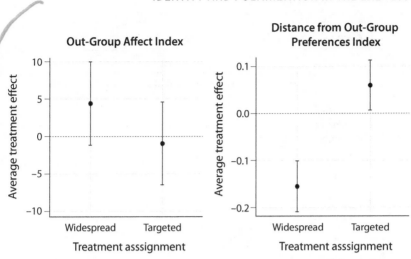

FIGURE 7.1. Affective and Preference Polarization by Treatment Group

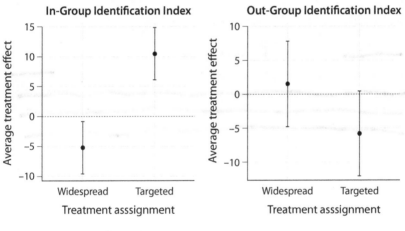

FIGURE 7.2. Group Identification by Treatment Group

treatment groups reported average levels of out-group identification of 55.54, 57.05, and 49.74 respectively, on a scale of 10 to 100.

## FURTHER MECHANISM TESTS

Descriptive results demonstrate that treatment assignment predicts levels of in-group identification and levels of polarization as expected. However, beyond simple observable differences by primed repressive environment, I posit that repression alters levels of polarization *through* shifts in group

TABLE 7.1. Group Identification and Positive Affect towards Out-Group

| | Dependent variable | | | |
|---|---|---|---|---|
| | Positive affect towards out-group | | | |
| | (1) | (2) | (3) | (4) |
| In-Group identification | −0.059 (0.054) | −0.073 (0.058) | | |
| Out-Group identification | | | 0.558*** (0.036) | 0.546*** (0.037) |
| Covariates | | ✓ | | ✓ |
| Constant | 67.749*** (3.571) | 75.096*** (10.409) | 34.489*** (2.270) | 42.667*** (8.695) |
| Observations | 415 | 404 | 396 | 386 |
| $R^2$ | 0.002 | 0.051 | 0.363 | 0.389 |

Note: *p < 0.1; **p < 0.05; ***p < 0.01

identification. Correlations demonstrate that the relationships are in the predicted direction for thinking about a mediated relationship. There is a negative relationship between in-group identification and positive feelings towards the out-group, while there is a significant and positive relationship between out-group identification and positive feelings towards the out-group (see table 7.1). Regression results also demonstrate that there is a significant and positive relationship between higher levels of in-group identification and distance from the stated position of the out-group, and also a significant negative relationship between out-group identification and distance (see table 7.2). Similar patterns hold in models with and without covariates.[14]

I conducted an additional analysis to test whether increased in-group identification may plausibly mediate the relationship between repressive environment and polarization per the mechanism outlined in my theory. This approach is outlined by Baron and Kenny and is particularly helpful for thinking about mediation in a setting where the variable has not been directly manipulated.[15] Here, the independent variable is treatment assignment, the mediator is group identification, and the dependent variable is

14. See the appendix for additional information on which covariates were included in the models.

15. Reuben M. Baron and Davjd A. Kenny, "The Moderator-Mediator Variable Distinction in Social Psychological Research—Conceptual, Strategic, and Statistical Considerations," *Journal of Personality and Social Psychology* 51, no. 6 (1986): 1173–1182.

TABLE 7.2. Group Identification and Distance from Out-Group Preferences

| | Dependent variable | | | |
|---|---|---|---|---|
| | Distance from out-group preferences | | | |
| | (1) | (2) | (3) | (4) |
| In-Group identification | 0.003*** | 0.003*** | | |
| | (0.001) | (0.001) | | |
| Out-Group identification | | | −0.002*** | −0.002*** |
| | | | (0.0005) | (0.0005) |
| Covariates | | ✓ | | ✓ |
| Constant | 0.470*** | 0.487*** | 0.776*** | 0.799*** |
| | (0.041) | (0.092) | (0.030) | (0.085) |
| Observations | 417 | 407 | 394 | 385 |
| $R^2$ | 0.061 | 0.117 | 0.040 | 0.110 |

Note: $^*p < 0.1$; $^{**}p < 0.05$; $^{***}p < 0.01$

average affective or preference distance of the out-group. Again, the treatments are not significant for out-group feelings, but the relationship is in the expected direction (see table 7.3). Out-group identification is a strong predictor of out-group feelings and also reduces the size of the effect for the widespread treatment. When difference in preferences of the out-group is the dependent variable, in-group identification slightly mediates the effect of both treatments, as does out-group identification (see table 7.4). The size of the treatment effect decreases for the widespread treatments, and the significance of the treatment effect of the targeted prime loses significance and magnitude, when in-group identification is added to the regression.

## Conclusion

This chapter provides evidence in support of the importance of the psychological mechanism through which the repression that defines authoritarian regimes affects processes of polarization in these systems, drawing on central insights from social psychology on the causes and consequences of group identification. Repression affects how actors come to identify themselves, shaping related affect and the distribution of preferences among political groups. Repressive environments either target repression at a specific opposition group, or are pervasive and affect all opposition groups. Targeted repression, following the logic of divide and conquer, increases

**TABLE 7.3.** Treatment Assignment, Group Identification, and Positive Affect towards Out-Group

| | Dependent variable | | | |
| --- | --- | --- | --- | --- |
| | Positive affect towards out-group | | | |
| | (1) | (2) | (3) | (4) |
| Widespread treatment | 3.181 (2.994) | 2.416 (2.977) | 0.523 (2.450) | 0.432 (2.576) |
| Targeted treatment | −0.694 (2.765) | −1.244 (2.973) | 0.774 (2.492) | −0.270 (2.717) |
| In-Group identification | | −0.049 (0.065) | | 0.053 (0.058) |
| Out-Group identification | | | 0.547*** (0.038) | 0.553*** (0.040) |
| Covariates | ✓ | ✓ | ✓ | ✓ |
| Constant | 67.705*** (9.735) | 73.038*** (10.417) | 42.338*** (8.694) | 38.484*** (9.567) |
| Observations | 417 | 404 | 386 | 375 |
| $R^2$ | 0.046 | 0.055 | 0.389 | 0.388 |

*Note:* *p < 0.1; **p < 0.05; ***p < 0.01

**TABLE 7.4.** Treatment Assignment, Group Identification, and Distance from Out-Group Preferences

| | Dependent variable | | | |
| --- | --- | --- | --- | --- |
| | Distance from out-group preferences | | | |
| | (1) | (2) | (3) | (4) |
| Widespread treatment | −0.154*** (0.028) | −0.150*** (0.028) | −0.147*** (0.029) | −0.145*** (0.029) |
| Targeted treatment | 0.063** (0.027) | 0.047* (0.028) | 0.063** (0.028) | 0.052* (0.029) |
| In-Group identification | | 0.001** (0.001) | | 0.001* (0.001) |
| Out-Group identification | | | −0.002*** (0.0004) | −0.001*** (0.0005) |
| Covariates | ✓ | ✓ | ✓ | ✓ |
| Constant | 0.746*** (0.089) | 0.660*** (0.098) | 0.849*** (0.092) | 0.760*** (0.104) |
| Observations | 417 | 407 | 385 | 377 |
| $R^2$ | 0.191 | 0.217 | 0.232 | 0.246 |

*Note:* *p < 0.1; **p < 0.05; ***p < 0.01

polarization across the opposition. In contrast, widespread repression decreases within-group identification within opposition groups, which in turn decreases polarization among these groups. I tested the argument here with carefully designed lab experiments that nonetheless posed a hard test. Subtle priming of repressive environments against fictional groups, lasting only a few minutes and comprising a few lines of text, was able to create the hypothesized effects in the lab. Chapters 5 and 6 demonstrate that similar effects occurred in much greater magnitude over time in Egypt and Tunisia, as repression physically and psychologically affected individuals over the course of multiple years and even decades, and when these state-inflicted traumas target group memberships about which members care much more deeply and to which they more strongly relate. The next section turns to how the legacies of these experiences affected each country's democratic transition.

# PART IV

# After Authoritarianism

# 8

# Polarization during Democratic Transitions

The fourth and final section of the book returns to the transition period. Having established how different levels of polarization develop over time as a function of variation in repression, I now explore the central role played by polarization in elite decisions critical to the continued progression of an initial democratic transition towards consolidation. This chapter first revisits the literature on democratic transitions to highlight how polarization prevents the elite compromise and cooperation vital to success. Next, I examine the timeline of events between 2011 and 2014 in Tunisia and Egypt to explain how these transitions progressed differently, and document where affective and preference polarization contributed to the divergence. I focus on political developments related to the drafting and passing of a new constitution, holding first elections, and creating a transitional justice campaign to highlight differences across the two transitions. High levels of polarization derailed Egypt's transition, while significantly more agreement in Tunisia facilitated cooperation and compromise during the same processes. However, as with any social phenomenon, the divergence in these transitions is likely influenced by multiple factors. While affective and preference polarization among elite actors clearly played a major role in this divergence, I also note where other factors, such as structural predecessors, continued protests, the emergence of new political actors, and ongoing events in other countries, were important for political developments.

## CONTINGENCY AND SUCCESSFUL DEMOCRATIC TRANSITIONS

History attests that moments of regime instability do not always lead to successful transitions and consolidated democracy. An oft-cited definition of transition labels it as "the interval between one political regime and another... delimited, on the one side, by the launching of the process of dissolution of an authoritarian regime and, on the other, by the installation of some form of democracy, the return to some form of authoritarian rule, or the emergence of a revolutionary alternative."[1] The definition reveals the multitude of outcomes that can result from a destabilized regime, rather than automatic progression from the initial phase of transition to consolidation.

Much ink has been spilled by scholars seeking to understand what determines the success of a democratic transition. A dominant set of explanations focuses on the explanatory power of structure: the nature of pre-existing socio-economic institutions facilitates the successful consolidation of a democratic transition. Here, aggregate phenomena, such as levels of economic development and accompanying levels of urbanization, wealth, and education, facilitated by large historical processes of technological innovation and industrialization, create institutions that are thought to promote democracy[2] and to increase the likelihood of a successful democratic transition and consolidation.[3] Generally higher scores, particularly on measurements of economic development, provide more fertile ground for democracy to take hold.[4] Particular formations of these scores, such as a certain kind of capital[5] or class distribution,[6] make certain environments

1. O'Donnell, Schmitter, and Arnson, *Conclusions*, 6.

2. Seymour M. Lipset, "Some Social Requisites of Democracy: Economic Development and Political Legitimacy," *American Political Science Review* 53, no. 1 (1969): 69–105; Dietrich Rueschemeyer, Evelyne Huber Stephens, and John D. Stephens, *Capitalist Development and Democracy* (Chicago: University of Chicago Press, 1992).

3. Carles Boix and Susan C. Stokes, "Endogenous Democratization," *World Politics* 55, no. 4 (2003): 517–549; David L. Epstein et al., "Democratic Transitions," *American Journal of Political Science* 50, no. 3 (2006): 551–569; Ryan Kennedy, "The Contradiction of Modernization: A Conditional Model of Endogenous Democratization," *Journal of Politics* 72, no. 3 (2010): 785–798.

4. Larry Diamond, *Developing Democracy: Toward Consolidation* (Baltimore: Johns Hopkins University Press, 1999).

5. Huntington, "Will More Countries Become Democratic?"; Carles Boix, *Democracy and Redistribution* (New York: Cambridge University Press, 2003).

6. Barrington Moore, *Social Origins of Dictatorship and Democracy: Lord and peasant in the making of the modern world* (Boston: Beacon Press, 1993).

more conducive to democratic consolidation. These structures and the interests they create are then reflected in actors'—particularly elite actors'—behavior.[7]

The benefits of the structural approach are many. The approach uses concrete and enduring features of society that can be easily observed, described, and measured in individual countries, and then compared across cases. Yet structural arguments may be better characterized as pre-conditions or pre-requisites, rather than causes, of democratization and democratic consolidation; they increase the possibility of democratization once the process is initiated, and may be necessary but are not sufficient or deterministic of the success of a transition. For one, successful democratization and consolidation have occurred at various levels of development and modernization, failing in contexts where structural theories would predict success and vice versa.[8] In addition, it is unclear exactly how structural conditions affect democratic consolidation: a number of linking steps and mechanisms must be assumed in these arguments. For example, to convincingly demonstrate that the level of development and the existence of a robust middle class facilitates democratic consolidation, a cross-national study must demonstrate that universally, "members of this class share a common political interest, that they act cohesively to express it, and perhaps most important, that they possess political instruments—like business associations or political parties—through which to aggregate preferences." This is a standard that few historical examples and academic studies meet. Structural theories thus may be helpful for generalizing important pre-conditions that are correlated with the success of democratic consolidation, but they do not adequately explain how these factors matter during moments of transition. As such, a structural approach

is useful in explaining no more than the outer parameters of political transitions. For example, it may help to answer whether an old authoritarian regime will endure, or help to predict the kind of political equilibrium that will prevail after a transition is over. But a structural approach can never account for the cut and thrust of events during interludes between regimes, or play more than a partial role in foreseeing

7. Lipset and Rokkan, "Cleavage Structures, Party Systems, and Voter Alignments: An Introduction."

8. Adam Przeworski and Fernando Limongi, "Modernization: Theories and Facts," *World Politics* 49, no. 2 (1997): 155–183.

whether any given transition attempt will result in the installation of a democratic government.[9]

In contrast, explanations of contingency focus on political developments during critical moments of democratic transition and the decisions made by elite actors charged with navigating a transition. In these types of explanations, the progression of a transition is not predetermined but rather directly dependent on compromise and cooperation by elite actors during the moment of transition.[10] As Best writes, "in these [transitional] moments, the fate of societies and politics depends on the willingness and ability to bring about comprehensive elite settlements which avoid the use of violence and the outbreak of outright civil war and which forge an agreement on the basic design of a new institutional order for the power system of a given society and polity."[11] A seminal article by Rustow similarly argues that in crucial moments of transition regarding the course, substance, and procedures of a new regime, "a small circle of leaders is likely to play a disproportionate role."[12] While structural explanations look to long-developing historical processes, contingent explanations focus on the short term, and the success of democratic transitions depends on decisions made by humans suffering from imperfect information, high amounts of pressure, and heightened passions during moments of significant consequence.[13]

The extent to which the political actors comprising an interim government dislike each other and disagree with each other has important implications for whether they can reach agreement about the process, substance, and nature of a democratic transition. The broader argument I make in this book links polarization during transitions with preceding repressive conditions, with a specific focus on the repressive nature of that context: the level of polarization during the critical transition period is conditioned by repressive experiences in the previous period under electoral authoritarianism. This approach resonates with the concept of "structured contingency"

9. Michael Bratton and Nicholas van de Walle, *Democratic Experiments in Africa: Regime Transitions in Comparative Perspective* (New York: Cambridge University Press, 1997), 22–23.

10. Kitschelt, "Political Regime Change: Structure and Process-driven Explanations?"; Schmitter, "Transitology: The Science or the Art of Democratization?"; Mainwaring, O'Donnell, and Valenzuela, *Issues in Democratic Consolidation: The New South American Democracies in Comparative Perspective.*

11. Heinrich Best, "Transitions, Transformations, and the Role of Elites," *Historical Social Research* 35, no. 2 (2010): 11.

12. Rustow, "Transitions to Democracy," 356.

13. See also Higley and Lengyel, *Elites after State Socialism: Theories and Analysis*; Higley and Burton, *Elite Foundations of Liberal Democracy.*

during transitions.[14] Here, individuals' preferences and related behaviors are conditioned by the context in which they are formed, and the choices made by political actors are typically rooted in "antecedent historical conditions."[15] More concisely, "people can make their own history, even if not under conditions of their own choosing."[16] Studies of structured contingency place high explanatory value on how preceding institutional arrangements under authoritarianism condition decisions during transitions by altering the expected payoffs from each choice. I think similarly and situate this book within the structured contingency theories of democratic transition—but add identity as an additional constraining factor.

## PROVISIONAL GOVERNMENTS AND DEMOCRATIC TRANSITIONS

The provisional government, or the interim body which governs during a transition, is an important institution in explanations of contingency. Countries undergoing a transition experience a period between the collapse of the old regime and the establishment of a new order, and it is this period which is led by interim governments. By definition, this provisional body's authority is transitional and its legitimacy temporary.[17] Though the provisional government is equally important in all transitions, its composition varies by transition type. During the Third Wave transitions, authoritarian regimes negotiated either their full exit or increased liberalization as a means of survival in the face of economic, social, and political turmoil, and so regime actors exerted a heavy influence on the transition period. In these transitions by extrication, negotiation, and pact- or bargain-making, provisional governments included both members of the regime and the democratic opposition.[18]

But provisional governments need not include incumbents. Transition by rupture leads to a different kind of interim government than pacted

14. Terry Lynn Karl, "Dilemmas of Democratization in Latin America," *Comparative Politics* 23, no. 1 (1990): 1–21.

15. James Mahoney, *The Legacies of Liberalism: Path Dependence and Political Regimes in Central America* (Johns Hopkins University Press, 2001).

16. Bratton and van de Walle, *Democratic Experiments in Africa: Regime Transitions in Comparative Perspective*, 45.

17. Yossi Shain and Juan J. Linz, "Introduction," in *Between States: Interim Governments in Democratic Transitions*, ed. Yossi Shain and Juan J. Linz (Cambridge University Press, 1995), 4.

18. O'Donnell, Schmitter, and Arnson, *Conclusions*, 19.

transition. Rapid mass mobilization constitutes a different form of democratization and the rupture it causes can quickly and forcefully remove the authoritarian leader and ruling party from power: the leader may flee or resign, and the ruling party may disband either by legal fiat or through the collapse of the party structure. In these cases, former regime actors are largely absent from the transition period, and the provisional government is instead dominated by the democratic opposition.[19] Power is divided based on a formula either arrived at through negotiations among potential participants or dictated by election results.

To successfully navigate a transition and facilitate democratic consolidation, a provisional government must implement meaningful reforms that change the function of state institutions and the nature of the government. In order to do so, provisional governments must undertake three main tasks: drafting and passing a new constitution, scheduling and holding foundational elections, and deciding the course of justice for authoritarian legacies of human rights abuse.[20]

First, the provisional government must *issue a new constitution*. Constitutions serve different functions in authoritarian and democratic contexts. In authoritarian contexts, constitutions are at best blueprints, and more likely window dressing, in the words of Ginsburg and Simpser.[21] When a constitution serves as a blueprint, the text is aspirational; it does not describe the legal and political system as it is but as it might be. Window dressing occurs when the text of the constitution diverges significantly from actual political practice. Both of these types of constitutions are common to authoritarian regimes, particularly in the contemporary era. Constitutions are central institutions for the survival of regimes in nondemocratic contexts. They fail to protect individual citizens' political rights and fail to limit the government's power—and often formally enshrine and legalize its undemocratic behavior. Constitutions solidify the regime by enshrining favorable solutions to the problems of authoritarian governance, such as the coordination of multiple political institutions and actors, the control

19. Rustow, "Transitions to Democracy"; Loxton, *Authoritarian Successor Parties Worldwide: A Framework For Analysis*; Haggard and Kaufman, *The Political Economy of Democratic Transitions*.

20. Shain and Linz ("Introduction," 5) add a fourth and related task for provisional governments, that of delineating a country's foreign relations.

21. Tom Ginsburg and Alberto Simpser ("Introduction," in *Constitutions in Authoritarian Regimes*, ed. Tom Ginsburg and Alberto Simpser (Cambridge University Press, 2013)) provide this terminology.

of subordinates and opposition, and the elicitation of cooperation from subjects.[22] In contrast, constitutions are important and respected documents in democracies, approaching an operation manual, in Ginsburg and Simper's typology. Similar to authoritarian regimes, constitutions in democratic contexts coordinate multiple political institutions central to all types of governance, but also constrain the executive through a balance power. Constitutions are followed more closely to the letter in democratic contexts; they establish the government's popular source of legitimacy and thus serve as the basis on which citizens hold their representatives accountable. Because of the different function a constitution serves in an authoritarian regime versus a democratic one, it is necessary for the provisional government to issue a new binding document institutionalizing checks and balances against executive power to facilitate a successful democratic transition.

Second, the provisional government must *schedule, plan, and hold transitional elections.* Transitional elections may include both the first elections for a constituent assembly, as well as the first elections for a representative body charged with conducting regular political governance, such as a parliament. The first regular elections are often conditional on the passage of a constitution as well as the determination of electoral law, so the timing and order can vary.[23] Similar to constitutions, elections need to be reformed significantly in order to function democratically rather than in facilitating the survival of authoritarian regimes. The comparative political literature offers us two views of elections in democratic contexts. In the mandate model, elections are intended to serve as a mechanism through which voters select good policies or politicians who are expected to produce good policies. In the accountability model, elections serve as a sanctioning device through which voters hold governments responsible for the outcomes of their past policies.[24]

22. Hilton L. Root, "Tying the King's Hands: Credible Commitments and Royal Fiscal Policy During the Old Regime," *Rationality and Society* 1, no. 2 (1989): 240–258; Robert Barros, *Constitutionalism and Dictatorship: Pinochet, the Junta, and the 1980 Constitution* (Cambridge University Press, 2002); Roger B.Myerson, "The Autocrat's Credibility Problem and Foundations of the Constitutional State," *American Political Science Review* 102, no. 1 (2008): 125–139; Tamir Moustafa, "Law and courts in authoritarian regimes," *Annual Review of Law and Social Science* 10 (2014): 281–299; Clara Boulianne Lagacé and Jennifer Gandhi, *Authoritarian Institutions* (New York: Routledge, 2015).

23. Shain and Linz, "Introduction," 9–10.

24. Adam Przeworski, Susan C. Stokes, and Bernard Manin, *Democracy, Accountability, and Representation* (Cambridge University Press, 1999).

However, elections serve a drastically different function in authoritarian contexts.[25] First, elections serve to establish a regularized method to share power and distribute limited state spoils among ruling party elites. Second, elections serve to provide information to the ruling party about supporters and opponents of the regime, including their location and density. Third, elections disseminate information to the mass public about the regime's strength and popularity. Finally, elections persuade opposition parties and candidates to work within existing institutions rather than challenging them through extralegal or extra-political forms. Regimes manipulate electoral outcomes to their benefit both through overt fraud, manufacturing electoral results,[26] as well as through a more subtle erosion of elections' representative and accountability functions through coercion and clientelism.[27]

The nature and quality of elections is an important measurement used to distinguish democratic regimes from non-democratic ones.[28] During a successful transition, a provisional government must first uproot the previous system which undermined the democratic nature and competitiveness of elections. Next, a provisional government must establish new formal electoral institutions and rules that guarantee the transparency of voting and party finances, increase uncertainty over the outcome of elections, and proportionately distribute power among competing actors.[29] Reforming the electoral system requires a collaborative decision by those in charge regarding how power will be distributed among competitors. As such, the nature, shape, and timing of foundational elections depend heavily on the provisional government's ability to cooperate and compromise. The successful conclusion of negotiations and scheduling of elections signals that "the question of institutional legitimacy is, at least in principle [if not in

25. Beatriz Magaloni, *Voting for Autocracy: Hegemonic Party Survival and its Demise in Mexico* (New York: Cambridge University Press, 2006); Blaydes, *Elections and Distributive Politics in Mubarak's Egypt.*

26. Posusney, "Multi-party Elections in the Arab World: Institutional Engineering and Oppositional Strategies."

27. Ellen Lust, "Competitive Clientelism in the Middle East," *Journal of Democracy* 20, no. 3 (2009): 122–135.

28. Linz and Stepan, *Problems of Democratic Transition and Consolidation: Southern Europe, South America, and Post-Communist Europe*; Joseph A. Schumpeter, *Socialism, Capitalism and Democracy* (Harper/Brothers, 1942); Nancy Bermeo, "On Democratic Backsliding," *Journal of Democracy* 27, no. 1 (2016): 5–19; Ellen Lust and David Waldner, "Unwelcome Change: Understanding, Evaluating, and Extending Theories of Democratic Backsliding," *US Agency for International Development* 11 (2015).

29. Shain and Linz, "Introduction," 17.

practice], settled"[30] among political actors, and helps to advance the transition towards consolidation.

Finally, the provisional government must *determine the path of transitional justice*. In transitions from authoritarianism, where state violations of citizens' rights were the norm, political actors need to collectively decide how to hold the old regime accountable—essentially, whether and how to even the score with their predecessors. There is not necessarily one particular form the policy must take to be effective, but rather all actors need to agree on the content and the appropriateness of the action taken to make sense of the past in an effort to move forward.[31] First, the provisional government needs to determine the identity of those responsible for the old order. This is important for the nature of the transition going forward; whether "the old guard [should] be treated as potential coalition partners or as criminals" delineates the scope of potential coalition partners and future elected officials.[32] Second, the provisional government must decide whether and how they will reconfigure the authoritarian institutions that did the repressing and corruption of the old regime, either keeping them intact with additional oversight or dissolving them to create new institutions. Third, the provisional government must decide whether they will hold accountable individuals who undertook repression and or relegate blame to "the system." Relatedly, the provisional government must decide whether former leaders, bureaucrats, and political prisoners of the old regime will be amnestied and permitted to participate in politics once again. Decisions made about transitional justice have important downstream consequences, in that they determine the "degree of political openness in the future democracy, including respect for human rights and willingness to eradicate the legacies of the old regime."[33]

## POLARIZATION AND DEMOCRATIC TRANSITIONS

Making decisions and implementing reforms in the three areas delineated above is of the utmost consequence for democratic transitions and the

30. Shain and Linz, "Introduction," 13–14.

31. Mark Arenhövel, "Democratization and Transitional Justice," *Democratisation* 15, no. 3 (2008): 570–587.

32. Shain and Linz, "Introduction," 42–43. The authors note that Poland is an example of "burying the past and exacting no retribution from individuals for the abuses of communism, [including even] the endemic criminality of the Communist-run secret police."

33. Ibid., 4.

nature of the state which follows.[34] Political actors' (in)ability to compromise on issues of substance and procedure have clear and measurable effects on the progression of a democratic transition; failing to successfully reform a constitution, hold first elections, and decide if and how to hold the previous regime accountable for violations of human rights makes it highly likely that a potential democratic transition will be derailed and result in authoritarian reentrenchment.[35] The extent to which those groups forming the provisional government are polarized determines whether it is able to accomplish these difficult tasks. Affective and preferential differences can prevent certain coalitions from forming and certain agreements from being reached. In short, polarization is "a problem since it convinces each side that their position is right and the opponent's is wrong; this makes compromise and negotiation less likely."[36]

First, polarization can affect the processes and outcomes of constitution drafting. The constitution-drafting process is led by an assembly of representatives from political parties. If parties are highly polarized, they may fail to adopt processes that value contribution and support from all participants. For example, a constitution-drafting body may be constructed such that a dominant party controls the creation of the text, or require less than full consensus of the body to approve the final document. As a result, the text may end up reflecting partisan political interests "at the expense of democratic-liberal principles."[37] A highly polarized provisional government is less likely to find compromise not only on the procedures guiding the constitution-drafting process but also on the central issues to be enshrined in the resulting document. In moments of transition, political actors "have to construct an entirely new socio-political edifice, and

34. Rustow, "Transitions to Democracy"; O'Donnell, Schmitter, and Arnson, *Conclusions*; Di Palma, *To Craft Democracies*; Kitschelt, "Political Regime Change: Structure and Process-driven Explanations?"; Schmitter, "Transitology: The Science or the Art of Democratization?"; Mainwaring, O'Donnell, and Valenzuela, *Issues in Democratic Consolidation: The New South American Democracies in Comparative Perspective*; Higley and Lengyel, *Elites after State Socialism: Theories and Analysis*; Higley and Burton, *Elite Foundations of Liberal Democracy*.

35. Huntington, "Will More Countries Become Democratic?"; Haggard and Kaufman, *The Political Economy of Democratic Transitions*; Linz and Stepan, *Problems of Democratic Transition and Consolidation: Southern Europe, South America, and Post-Communist Europe*; Kitschelt et al., *Post-Communist Party Systems: Competition, Representation, and Inter-party Cooperation*; McFaul, "The Fourth Wave of Democracy and Dictatorship: Noncooperative Transitions in the Postcommunist World"; Brownlee, Masoud, and Reynolds, *The Arab Spring*.

36. Eric L. Hirsch, "Generating Commitment Among Students," in *The Social Movements Reader: Cases and Concepts*, ed. Jeff Goodwin and James M. Jasper (John Wiley & Sons, 2009), 97.

37. Shain and Linz, "Introduction," 85.

thus debates surrounding the (re)definition of the state, as well as the relationship between citizen and state, figure prominently" in constitution drafting.[38] Highly polarized actors are more likely to fail in finding consensus on these highly charged issues.

Next, polarization can affect the process and nature of the first democratic elections. Di Palma[39] argues for quick elections at all costs to quicken the pace of transitions, while Huntington[40] maintains that speedy elections may hinder long-term democratic practices and stability if they facilitate imperfect contests. While we might assume that more polarized actors will take longer to find agreement, and this will increase the length of time that passes between the fall of the old regime and the establishment of new electoral norms, there is actually no academic consensus about the ideal timing of first elections.[41] What is important is that all participants feel satisfied with the timing of the elections: the setting of a date is likely to enhance the possibility of a successful transition "only if perceived as fair by other contending groups."[42] More polarized actors are less likely to feel this way. If actors dislike each other or perceive their preferences to be radically different, they are more likely to feel that the choice of a date is biased and favors their competition. This is particularly true of actors who feel less powerful or prepared. Groups that are dissatisfied with the decision may actively seek to delay the elections or undermine their democratic legitimacy, perhaps derailing the transition process.

Levels of polarization among actors may also affect the nature of elections by influencing the kinds of electoral institutions chosen by those negotiating. If actors are highly polarized, they are more likely to choose systems that reflect this polarization, favoring winner-take-all type rules which can be easily manipulated by the strongest among them.[43] Meanwhile, if actors are less polarized, they are more likely to choose a system that exerts limits on the executive and fairly balances power between multiple parties, in a manner which truly reforms the previous authoritarian regime. Ultimately, the extent to which parties like each other and agree on principles is important for what kinds of electoral institutions they choose. These early

---

38. Chomiak, *Deliberative Resistance: Dissent and Democracy in Tunisia*, 14.

39. Di Palma, *To Craft Democracies*.

40. Huntington, *The Third Wave: Democratization in the Late Twentieth Century*.

41. Shain and Linz, "Introduction," 76.

42. Ibid., 42.

43. Posusney, "Multi-party Elections in the Arab World: Institutional Engineering and Oppositional Strategies."

decisions have downstream effects for the immediate transition as well as the relationship between the legislative and executive branches, the role of political parties, and the nature of political life under the next regime.

Finally, polarization can affect how provisional governments decide questions of transitional justice. The provisional government has both the responsibility and the discretion to decide who is labeled a victim of the old regime and thus worthy of compensation as well as the nature of that compensation. The interim government also determines who, if anyone, should be held accountable for the indiscretions of the old regime. These decisions might influence characteristics such as whether a formal transitional justice process is established, who is in charge of the process, whether the process is public, and how extensive the process will be. If the interim government is polarized, it may be less likely to hold the regime accountable, given that transitional justice may be perceived to benefit certain actors at the expense of others. In contrast, if the democratic opposition is less polarized, it may be able to come together in an interim government, find agreement on what to do with regards to transitional justice, and then move forward with carrying out these difficult tasks. Decisions made by the interim government with regards to transitional justice ultimately determines "whether the country reaches the stage when a general declaration of human rights is recognized and certain freedoms are assured,"[44] ideals and safeguards that are as central to democracy as free and fair elections.

## Polarization during the Arab Spring Transitions

In this section, I provide concrete examples of how comparative levels of affective and preference polarization among the democratic opposition factored into divergent transition trajectories and outcomes in Egypt and Tunisia. Guided by the existing literature synthesized above, I focus on key developments during a transition period: the drafting and passage of a new constitution, holding first elections, and the creation of a transitional justice initiative. Because these three tasks are often intertwined throughout the transition period, the following sections read as a narrative, rather than as separate discussions of developments pertaining to each component. In short, high levels of polarization derailed Egypt's transition, while significantly more agreement in Tunisia facilitated cooperation and compromise surrounding the same processes.

---

44. Shain and Linz, "Introduction."

At the outset of the transition, Egypt and Tunisia inherited different repressive legacies. Descriptive data of the repressive histories of politicians elected to the 2011 Tunisian National Constituent Assembly and the 2012 Egyptian Constituent Assembly demonstrate how variation in the countries' repressive histories manifested among elite leadership during the transition, presented in figure 8.1. "Repressed" indicates that the member was either arrested or exiled under the previous authoritarian regime. In Tunisia, multiple parties had multiple members repressed during the Ben Ali era, while in Egypt, experiences of repression under Mubarak highly concentrated among members of the Brotherhood-affiliated FJP.

Relatedly, the political systems in Egypt and Tunisia were differently polarized in preferences following the 2011 uprisings, demonstrated in figure 8.2. Although religion and politics was the salient division in both countries, the distribution of elite preferences was different in Egypt and Tunisia, with Egypt emerging more polarized and Tunisia demonstrating a centrist tendency.[45] While these data do not capture affective polarization and group identification, they begin a narrative of how different repressive legacies contributed to the divergent transitional outcomes witnessed in Tunisia and Egypt.

## THE TUNISIAN TRANSITION, 2010–2014

Most narratives of the Arab Spring uprisings begin with the events of December 17, 2010. On that day, Mohammed Bouazizi, a fruit vendor in Sidi Bouzid, Tunisia, set himself on fire in front of a local municipal office.[46] He succumbed to his injuries on January 4, 2011. The self-immolation was a response to an incident in which police confiscated his cart because he lacked a permit, physically harmed him when he resisted arrest, and then refused to hear his official complaint. The act quickly came to represent an act of defiance against declining economic conditions, unrestrained police corruption and violence, and rampant un- and under-employment. Protests began the same day in Sidi Bouzid, then spread to Tunisia's other economically disenfranchised interior regions, such as Kairouan, Sfax, and Ben Guerdane, and to Tunis, the capital. Over the next two weeks, formal

45. See the book's appendix for information on how political platforms issued by the parties were coded for this visual representation.

46. Elizabeth Cummings, *The Spark That Lit the Flame: The Creation, Deployment, and Deconstruction of the Story of Mohammed Bouazizi and the Arab Spring* (2015).

## 2012 Egyptian Constituent Assembly
Members previously repressed encircled in black

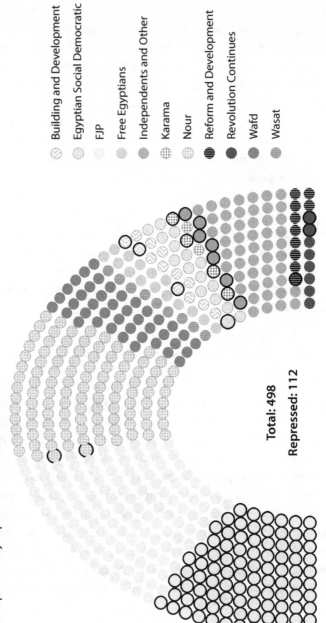

Total: 498
Repressed: 112

Building and Development
Egyptian Social Democratic
FJP
Free Egyptians
Independents and Other
Karama
Nour
Reform and Development
Revolution Continues
Wafd
Wasat

# 2011 Tunisia National Constituent Assembly

Members previously repressed encircled in black

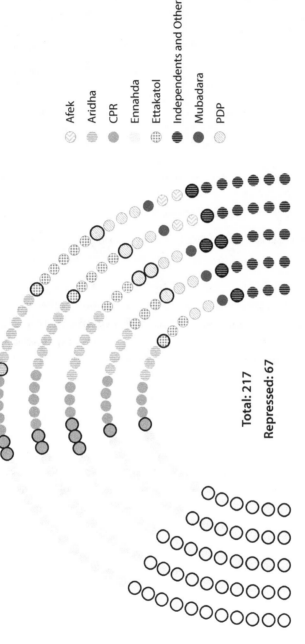

Afek
Aridha
CPR
Ennahda
Ettakatol
Independents and Other
Mubadara
PDP

Total: 217
Repressed: 67

FIGURE 8.1. Repressive Histories of Political Elites in Egypt and Tunisia, 2011–2012

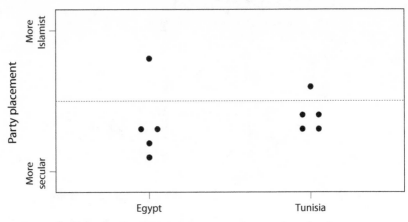

FIGURE 8.2. Comparative Party Polarization in Egypt and Tunisia, 2011

bodies such as the Tunisian Federation of Labor Unions (known by its French acronym, UGTT) and informal groups of the unemployed organized protests, rallies and strikes.[47] Police initially responded with low levels of violence, but between January 8 and 12, reports of attacks on unarmed protesters incited nationwide protests.[48] Ben Ali appeared on television several times in the hopes of restoring order. He first condemned the protests, then imposed a state of emergency and dismissed the government. Finally, he announced a number of concessions to protesters' demands and promised not to seek reelection in 2014.

On January 14, Prime Minister Mohammed Ghannouchi[49] announced Ben Ali's resignation. The next day, then-speaker of parliament Fouad Mebazaa assumed the presidency in accordance with the constitution and directed Ghannouchi to form a unity government. Protests (later referred to as Qasba I and Qasba II) continued, though this time their targets were

47. M. Omri, "No Ordinary Union: UGTT and the Tunisian Path to Revolution and Transition," *Workers of the World: International Journal on Strikes and Social Conflict* 1, no. 7 (2015): 14–29.

48. Regular police forces continued to be charged with maintaining the peace and protecting the regime in the face of mounting protests. The national military waited until after Ben Ali resigned to assume control of security issues in the country (Risa Brooks, "Abandoned at the Palace: Why the Tunisian Military Defected from the Ben Ali Regime in January 2011," *Journal of Strategic Studies* 36, no. 2 (2013)).

49. He has no relation with Ennahda's Rachid Ghannouchi.

not Ben Ali's regime but rather the interim government and the perceived continuation of RCD rule. The continued mobilization forced a cabinet reshuffle on January 27 and the replacement of Ghannouchi with Beji Caid Essebsi, foreign minister under Bourguiba and speaker of parliament under Ben Ali, on February 27. In March, interim president Mebazaa dissolved the existing legislature and announced that a new constitution would be drafted by a National Constituent Assembly (NCA) to be elected shortly. In April 2011, Essebsi formed a technocratic government to govern the country until the NCA elections could be held. Meanwhile, the Ministry of the Interior announced the dissolution of the State Security Administration, a central repressive institution under Ben Ali, and a constitutional court dissolved the RCD.

Cooperation among the former opposition began early in the transition process. Ghannouchi's first unity government included several members of opposition parties legally recognized by the former regime, including Ahmed Najib Chebbi of PDP, Mustafa Ben Jaafar of Ettakatol, and Ahmad Brahim of Ettajdid. On February 15, a coalition of twenty-eight opposition parties and civil society groups came together to form the National Council to Protest the Revolution (*al-Majlis al-Watani li-Himayat al-Thawra*). This included Ennahda and the PCOT, as well as civil society groups such as the UGTT, Tunisian Judges Association, Tunisian Journalist Syndicate, National Lawyers Association, and Tunisian Association for Combating Torture.[50] In March, members of the council were invited by the government to join the Higher Committee for Political Reform (*al-Lajna al-'Ulya lil-Islah al-Siyasi*). This was a body of legal experts headed by legal scholar Yadh Ben Achour tasked with dismantling Ben Ali's government apparatus. The body was later subsumed into a new organization called the High Commission for the Fulfillment of Revolution's Goals, Political Reform, and Democratic Transition (*al-Hay'a al-'Ulya li-Tahqiq Ahdaf al-Thawra wal-Islah al-Siyasi wal-Intiqal ad-Dimuqrati*, or the HCFRG). The HCFRG became a central pillar of the interim government, bringing together representatives of political parties, civil society groups, families of martyrs killed during the uprising, and the country's twenty-four governors.[51] At its peak, the high commission had 155 members representing interests "from the far

50. I find the inclusion of the last organization very interesting, as it is less overtly political than the other civil society groups involved. In hindsight, I believe it to be an early indication of the influence of the country's repressive history and the importance of addressing it during the transition.

51. Duncan Pickard, "Challenges to Legitimate Governance in Post-Revolution Tunisia," in *North Africa's Arab Spring* (Routledge, 2013), 141–156.

right to the far left."[52] Among other accomplishments, the HCFRG proposed a law, later enacted by the government, that banned RCD members from holding office for ten years, and it selected the sixteen members of an independent, non-partisan elections committee.

The existence of representative organizations does not imply a completely smooth transition with total agreement between parties. Early disagreement emerged around the timing of the NCA elections suggesting that some level of negative affect existed between political parties after the revolution. Party leaders disagreed about when to hold elections, which were first scheduled for July but were eventually postponed by the electoral commission until October. Many members from the former opposition, such as leaders from Ennahda, CPR, Ettajdid, and PDP, opposed delaying the elections for fear that instability caused by political, economic, and security issues would overcome the progress already achieved by the revolution. Others, notably leadership from small parties both new and old, considered the delay necessary to counter the organizational advantage they believed Ennahda would have over other parties. PCOT issued a statement in which it claimed that the true disagreement about the elections was not about the timeline but its nature: "it is between those who want it to be free and democratic and clean ... and those who think of nothing but getting to the throne, even if this requires accepting elections that don't fulfill the conditions necessary to provide citizens with free democratic choice."[53]

Trepidation over the possibility of Islamist domination similarly permeated debates about the length of the NCA's mandate. In September 2011, a coalition of fifty secular and leftist parties including the PDP proposed that the NCA's term should be limited to six months. These groups were concerned that Islamists would overpower them in early elections, receive a majority in the Constituent Assembly, and thus dictate the terms of the new constitution and the transition more generally. In response, Ennahda, CPR, and several other parties drawn from the former opposition formed the October 23rd Coalition and stated that they would reject any attempt to limit the incoming assembly's sovereignty. Political actors ultimately overcame this impasse with a compromise. Under the guidance of the Ben Achour Commission, the parties signed a Democratic Transition

52. Brownlee, Masoud, and Reynolds, *The Arab Spring*, 132.
53. Cited in Brownlee, Masoud, and Reynolds, *The Arab Spring*, 134.

Declaration which defended the autonomy of the NCA to "determine the new structure of public authority" and to elect a president, while also establishing that the assembly's term would not exceed a year. The document both defended the sovereignty of the NCA as an institution, pleasing Ennahda's leadership, and also allayed the concerns of those who feared Islamist domination by limiting the length of its mandate. The agreement demonstrated that while some negative affect existed, it was not so extreme as to prevent these parties from coming together.

Elections for the 217-seat assembly were held on October 23, 2011. The majority of parties that won seats in these elections were previously active as the democratic opposition. Through a closed list, proportional representation system, Ennahda won 37.04 percent of the vote and eighty-nine seats. Former opposition parties with more secular programs, namely CPR, PDP, and Ettakatol, also made a good showing. Others from the democratic opposition competed in the elections and won a handful of seats. The Democratic Modernist Pole (in Arabic *Al-Qutb ad-Dimuqrati al-Hadathi*), a coalition of four political parties and five citizen initiatives, was led by the Ettajdid Movement. Similarly, the PCOT won three seats led by Secretary General Hamma Hammami. The People's Movement brought together a number of intellectuals, academics, and activists from the democratic opposition, many of whom had mobilized against the previous regime as students, and won two seats under the unifying banner of "freedom, socialism, unity." The party's first Secretary General, Mohamed Brahmi, founded the Nasserist Unionist Movement after leaving his position as a leader of the Arab Progressive Unionist Students in 2005.

New parties emerged to compete with the established opposition. The Popular Petition (*Al-Aridha ash-Sha'biyya*) placed third in the constituent elections and won twenty-six seats. It was founded in March 2011 by Mohamed Hechmi Hamdi, owner of satellite television channel *Al Mustakillah*, and won seats representing the interior of the country on a campaign mixing vague messages of Islamism and populism. Afek Tounes was founded in the same month by businessman Yassine Brahim as a center-right party focused on secularism and defense civil liberties. The party won four seats. In addition, Kamel Morjane, a businessman and former defense and foreign minister under Ben Ali, founded the National Destourian Initiative (*al-Moubadra*) in April 2011. The party won five seats running on a platform overtly supporting the representation of former RCD members in post-revolutionary politics.

**TABLE 8.1.** National Constituent Assembly Election Results (Tunisia, 2011)

| Party | % of vote | Seat share |
|---|---|---|
| Ennahda | 37.04 | 89 |
| CPR | 8.71 | 29 |
| Popular Petition | 6.74 | 26 |
| Ettakatol | 7.03 | 20 |
| PDP | 3.94 | 16 |
| The Initiative | 3.19 | 5 |
| Democratic Modernist Pole | 2.79 | 5 |
| Afek Tounes | 1.89 | 4 |
| Tunisian Workers Communist Party | 1.57 | 3 |
| People's Movement | 0.75 | 2 |

After the conclusion of the election, Ennahda reached a power-sharing agreement in which the party's leadership would form the cabinet, a member of CPR would be elected president, and a member of Ettakatol would be the chairman of the Constituent Assembly. Moncef Marzouki of CPR was elected president, with 155 votes in favor, 3 against, and 42 abstentions, and Mustapha Ben Jaafar of Ettakatol was elected chairman. Marzouki then appointed Hamadi Jebali of Ennahda as prime minister. This so-called "Troika" government demonstrated that preference polarization was low, and that former opposition parties had similar political ideas. As CPR member Samir Ben Amor noted, there was no formal cooperation during the elections, but afterwards a conversation occurred between parties "who are close in their programs and their ideas" to form a government. As Ettakatol's Ben Jaafar said, "in my opinion, [previous initiatives such as October 18] were the pretext for when we [meaning, the secular opposition] discussed the constitution with the Islamists. We were already 97 or 96 percent in agreement."

The Islamist-secular divide was the axis of division during deliberations over the new constitution. Six 22-person committees were formed and each was tasked with a principle component of the constitution. The makeup of the committees mirrored the distribution of power in the larger assembly: in each committee, Ennahda received nine seats, CPR received three, and Ettakatol received two, while coalitions of parties and independents divided the remaining seats.[54] An early draft of the constitution revealed disagreement among the negotiating parties. For example, the preamble spoke of "enhancing [Tunisia's] cultural and civilizational affiliation to the Arab Islamic nation," which enraged secular politicians who sought a constitution which explicitly established the secular and civil nature of the state. In addition, the early draft used language that referred to differences in the responsibilities of men and women. This article would have been in violation of Tunisia's long-standing personal status law, which guaranteed legal gender equality. In addition, it suggested to secular politicians that Ennahda was attempting to enshrine an Islamic approach to gender differences in the country's highest legal document. In response, representatives of different secular trends boycotted a national dialogue called by Marzouki, and formed two party initiatives. First, a coalition of small leftist parties united under the banner of the Popular Front. A second party called Nidaa Tounes was founded by former middle-ranking members of the RCD on an explicitly anti-Islamist platform. Many parliament members from smaller secular parties joined Nidaa Tounes when it formed to combat Ennahda's influence over the constitution and course of the transition. Nidaa's rhetoric towards Ennahda was inflammatory, referring to the group as "terrorists," labeling those who worked with Ennahda as "traitors," and describing the constitution as "having an *Ikhwani* flavor."[55]

By the beginning of 2013, the constitution process was at a standstill. The NCA had extended its mandate but had not yet produced agreement on a document to govern the country. Secular politicians unaligned with Ennahda were unhappy about the text of the draft constitution, and felt like they had no power to influence any changes due to their relatively weak position in the NCA. During this political crisis, two prominent secular politicians were assassinated. A hardliner Salafist group named *Ansar al-Shari'a* was widely believed to be behind the murder of Chokri Belaid on February 6 and Mohamed Brahmi on July 25. In the aftermath of Brahmi's death, dozens of leftists withdrew from the Constituent Assembly in protest to what they stated was the government's failure to deal with major security issues related to Islamic terrorism. Brahmi's funeral on July 27 descended into mass protests and an occupation of the Qasbah. A large coalition of leftists, led by the Popular Front, united around a demand for the NCA to complete its work by a firm deadline. Interestingly, the group

---

54. Brownlee, Masoud, and Reynolds, *The Arab Spring*, 140–141.

55. Abdel Aziz Kotti. Interview with the author. September 24, 2014. Tunis, Tunisia.

did not request that the Constituent Assembly be disbanded, but rather requested that they work harder to bring the initial phase of the transition to a close.

In late summer, a quartet of civil society organizations—the UGTT, the Tunisian Confederation of Industry, Trade, and Handicrafts, the Tunisian Human Rights League (LTDH), and the Tunisian Order of Lawyers—called for negotiations to get the Constituent Assembly back on track and organized a National Dialogue. On September 17, the quartet issued a roadmap with four main items that all parties had to agree to in order to participate: the replacement of the current Ennahda-dominated government by an independent, technocratic government; fixed dates for parliamentary and presidential elections; an agreement to preserve national identity in the new constitution, recognizing Tunisia's secular *and* Islamic heritage; and deadlines for agreed upon steps necessary for the transition to a democratic government. Twenty-one parties agreed to these terms. By December, the National Dialogue had produced an agreement on steps to move forward with the political transition.[56]

The political process proceeded in fits and starts, but ultimately continued on a forward trajectory. Constituent Assembly members who had been active in the opposition before the revolution noted the importance of previous agreements for guiding debates during the constitutional proceedings, and as the foundation which ultimately brought groups with different opinions back to the negotiating table during the 2013 National Dialogue. Ettakatol's Mouldi Riahi noted that the human rights issues over which they had established agreement during the 2003 and 2005 collective initiatives were "exactly the same rights enshrined in the constitution."[57] Marzouki similarly noted that the conversation which began in 2003 "set the path" for what came after 2010. He cited "procedural disagreements rather than identity issues" as the reasons behind the stalled constitution-drafting process and CPR's abstention from the National Dialogue.[58]

In addition to low levels of preference polarization, the way in which politicians described their rivals, revealed affect between the groups had

---

56. The National Dialogue Quartet, formerly little known outside of Tunisia, burst into the global spotlight when it was awarded the 2015 Nobel Peace Prize for its efforts in building this consensus.

57. Mouldi Riahi. Interview with the author. September 16, 2014. Tunis, Tunisia.

58. Moncef Marzouki. Interview with the author. January 11, 2017. Tunis, Tunisia. See also Maryam Ben Salem, "The National Dialogue, Collusive Transactions and Government Legitimacy in Tunisia," *International Spectator* 51, no. 1 (2016): 102.

changed dramatically from the late 1980s. Individuals of different ideological persuasions considered each other partners in resistance, particularly among those politicians drawn from the former opposition to the regime. What divisions did exist were described as being indicative of pluralism, as Ennahda's Ali Lareydh said:

> During the National Dialogue, we were open to cooperating with any party that truly believed in freedom and democracy. Democracy brings together different types of people and ideas. If you disagree with us on the status of women, or our economic program, or whatever, you can agree with our position on freedom. It improves the conversation to have differences of opinion. When we sit and talk about common interests, the differences between us are ones that encourage diversity.[59]

Similarly, former opposition members described political divisions as being, in the words of Ben Amor of CPR, "the residue of the dictatorship: the former regimes preferred approach was to create ideological competition and division to control society and the opposition."[60] In a similar vein, Abbou noted that "people found democratic freedoms more important than religious divisions," and this ultimately benefited the National Dialogue.[61] While the formal representation held by some secular parties drawn from the democratic opposition was limited, and thus their agreement was not essential for many tasks, the actions of their leaders and members were nonetheless important during the transition process. For example, it was important that Ettajdid's Brahim and PCOT's Hammami lent their support to the NCA and the constitution-drafting process. Their public statements and ability to mobilize supporters against the government was tantamount to having a veto over the transition process. The assassinations of leftists Belaid and Brahmi, both from the People's Movement, could have quickly caused a political crisis. But instead, elite actors followed through on a commitment to return to the negotiating table.

Members of the former opposition collectively felt that the entire country was better off moving forward, which required passing a constitution that protected individual liberties of all sorts, and that returning to the previous system would be catastrophic. Central to this sentiment was a feeling

---

59. Ali Lareydh. Interview with the author. December 18, 2014. Tunis, Tunisia.
60. Samir Ben Amor. Interview with the author. November 28, 2014. Tunis, Tunisia.
61. Mohamed Abbou. Interview with the author. October 1, 2014. Tunis, Tunisia.

of collective victimhood, and an agreement on the fundamental importance of human rights. Ben Jaafar of Ettakatol said, "those who suffered from tyranny have an awareness that we passed through a distinct moment, one we survived but that can't return." He continued,

> Experiencing tyranny had an important effect on the transition. The subject of freedom—in all respects, without any constraints, now or ever—became something that was not up for discussion. We worked together because we only had two choices: we could either return to what happened before the revolution, or we could move forward. Things will be better than before. They have to be.[62]

Ennahda's Ghannouchi articulated a similar point: "We didn't want tyranny to return to our country. We don't want to [become] like those who enslaved and imprisoned us. We don't want another generation founded in blood."[63]

Voting on the new constitution began on January 3, 2014. The final document incorporated mentions of Islam as the religion and culture of the Tunisian people while also establishing a state role for protecting freedom of religious worship and expression. Ennahda led the compromise over enshrining shari'a as the basis for legislation and legitimacy; it dropped its insistence that the new constitution refer to Islamic law as "a" or "the" primary source of legislation. Speaking on behalf of Ennahda to *Radio Mosaique*, Larayedh said the party had "decided to retain the first clause of the previous constitution without change. We want the unity of our people and do not want divisions," reversing previous public statements by Ennahda leadership. The constitution established the new republic as a "civil" state but identified its religion as Islam and expressed the Tunisian "people's commitment to the teachings of Islam … from our enlightened reformist movements that are based on the foundations of our Islamic-Arab identity." Article 6 designated the state as the "guardian of religion," and guaranteed citizens' freedoms of conscience, belief, and exercise of religious practices, as well as the political neutrality of places of worship.

On January 26, 2014, the Constituent Assembly adopted Tunisia's new constitution by a vote of 200 to 12, with 4 abstentions. The potentially divisive articles on state identity, the relationship between religion and politics, and gender equality each passed with a clear majority. Earlier in the month,

62. Mustapha Ben Jaafar. Interview with the author. January 16, 2017. Tunis, Tunisia.
63. Rachid Ghannouchi. Interview with the author. November 19, 2014. Tunis, Tunisia.

Lareydh was replaced with Mehdi Jomaa, a non-partisan engineer and former Minister of Industry. This paved the way for parliamentary elections in
October 2014 and a presidential election in December 2014, both of which
were held without incident.

In addition to first elections and the constitution, political actors at the
helm of Tunisia's transition were also charged with deciding on the nature
and course of transitional justice. The first attempt to address issues of
transitional justice began with an ad hoc commission, with the mandate
to investigate deaths caused by the state between December 2010 and the
first elections in October 2011, and the establishment of the Ministry of
Human Rights and Justice in December 2011. In December 2013, Tunisia's
Transitional Justice Law, titled the "Organic Law on Establishing and Organizing Transitional Justice," was passed and disbanded the first commission
and the ministry. The law established the Truth and Dignity Commission (known by the acronym of its name in French, IVD), which would
become the country's official and enduring transitional justice body headed
by Sihem Ben Sedrine, a journalist and human rights activist who herself
had been a victim of repression under the previous regime. The purpose
of the IVD was to document past abuses by the state since 1955, to provide
reparations to victims, and to pursue criminal accountability for serious and
systematic economic, social, and political crimes of two highly repressive
authoritarian regimes, as well as the end of the French colonial period.

While the IVD was highly successful in many regards and remains unpar-
alleled in the region, its progress was not without significant conflict and
setbacks. The Ministries of the Interior and Defense refused to cooperate
with the IVD despite its legal mandate and denied commission members
access to state police and military tribunal archives and refused to summon
current and former employees for questioning. As the country faced severe
economic and security crises in 2013, many political figures expressed the
need to address the current weakness of the state instead of analyzing the
past. In September 2017, the Tunisian parliament voted overwhelmingly
in favor of a controversial reconciliation law put forward by President Beji
Caid Essebsi. The law offered an alternative—and decidedly less punitive—
approach to transitional justice, granting amnesty to those accused of being
involved in state corruption. In March 2018, the parliament voted not to
extend the IVD's mandate for the one-year period permitted by law to
continue its transitional justice work.

The most visible and vehement objections to the IVD and a comprehensive transitional justice process was led by members of Nidaa Tounes,

the party with the strongest ties to the old regime. During his 2014 presidential campaign, Essebsi's criticism of transitional justice was a central part of his platform. At this final campaign event, he declared that Tunisia needs to "smile and be hopeful again and not talk of the past" in order to move forward with the transition.[64] In October 2018, Nidaa Tounes and splinter party Machrouu Tounes left parliament and announced a boycott of all parliamentary work until the IVD ceased operations and withdrew the cases it had referred to court. The threat of being held accountable for the behavior of the ousted regime appeared to mobilize these parties to undermine the commission.

Ennahda was implicated in these public protests because it had entered a governing alliance with Nidaa following the 2014 parliamentary and presidential elections. Party leadership denounced the reconciliation bill, but then supported it. Ghannouchi had first called for a "purge" of the Ministries of the Interior and Defense, and later switched to backing the bill.[65] Ennahda parliament members refused to vote to end the IVD's mandate in late 2018, though Ghannouchi called for the contrary at his party's general congress. The party often demonstrated it was "more inclined to protect the bipartisan balance with Nidaa Tounes than to pursue transitional justice,"[66] appearing to prioritize stability and consensus over justice. At the same time, Nidaa members charged that IVD's leader Ben Sedrine was unfairly serving the interests of Ennahda to the detriment of other political players, for example, by giving supposed priority to cases investigating abuses against Islamist militants. In addition, Ennahda leaders spoke about the importance of information as the primary purpose of transitional justice. Ennahda's Lareydh said, "I see the goal of the IVD not as retribution, but rather as an attempt to understand the nation's past. We were forbidden to talk or write about topics of repression, torture, and killing by the state in Tunisia. We need a reconciliation process so we could learn and understand."[67]

Ultimately, the IVD was largely successful because it had the tacit backing of the former democratic opposition. By the end of its mandate in June

64. Eric Reidy. "Tunisia Transitional Justice Faces Obstacles." *Al-Jazeera* January 1, 2015. http://aje.io/3t7n.

65. Walid al-Talili and Basma Barakat. "Ghannouchi Calls on Parliament to Approve General Amnesty for Perpetrators of the Ben Ali Regime's Violations." *Al-'Araby* October 27 2018.

66. Fatim-Zohra El Malki. "Tunisia's Partisan Path to Transitional Justice." *Carnegie Endowment for International Peace*. https://carnegieendowment.org/sada/68206.

67. Ali Lareydh. Interview with the author. December 18, 2014. Tunis, Tunisia.

2016, the commission had received 62,544 complaints and had held listening sessions to collect additional information for nearly 27,000 files, documenting the ubiquity of repressive experiences among Tunisian citizens. Local press closely follows reports and statements issued by the organization, and public hearings of select testimony were broadcast on national television. In 2018, the IVD referred thirty cases of enforced disappearance, extrajudicial execution, death under torture, excessive use of force against peaceful protests during the 2010–2011 uprising, and presented its final report on live television in December of that year.[68] Included in the final report were recommendations for institutional and legislative reforms as well as a national reparation plan to compensate victims financially.

## THE EGYPTIAN TRANSITION, 2011-2014

As events unfolded in Tunisia in early 2011, activists in Egypt called for similar protests against worsening economic conditions, government corruption, and Mubarak's rule. January 25 is a national holiday to commemorate the contributions of the police forces. Protest organizers reclaimed the day for a demonstration against police brutality and regime corruption. Thousands of Egyptians marched in Cairo, Alexandria, the Nile Delta cities of Mansoura and Tanta, the cities of Aswan and Assiut in Upper Egypt, Suez, and Port Said. This began eighteen days of sustained protest. The number of protesters increased significantly on Friday, January 28, known as the "Day of Rage," as hundreds of thousands demonstrated in Egypt's major cities following Friday prayer. The regime initially responded to the protests with brute force and teargas, beating and arresting protesters. The regime also arrested members of the leading opposition movement the Muslim Brotherhood, despite the fact that the organization publicly stated they were not the organizers behind the events and did not participate in early protests. The regime responded to later increases in protest mobilization by shutting down Internet service and mobile phone text messages, replacing regular police forces with the military, and imposing a curfew. On February 2, the regime escalated violence against protesters significantly— even after the military announced it would not fire on civilian protesters on January 31. Pro-Mubarak demonstrators targeted journalists, and, in what became known as the "Battle of the Camel," plainclothes policemen

68. As of the end of 2019, the president of Tunisia had not yet formally accepted the findings of the IVD, the final step of the process.

rode into Tahrir Square on camels and horses to attack unarmed protesters. Mubarak appeared on television a number of times, first pledging to form a new government, then promising not to seek another term in the next elections and additional reforms, all the while asking protesters to return to normal and becoming increasingly defiant about not stepping down. The increase in violence from the regime and pro-regime violence fueled further mobilization. On the evening of Thursday, February 10, protests again grew in anticipation of Mubarak's rumored impending resignation and ahead of a call for more protests on Friday.

On February 11, General Omar Suleiman announced Mubarak's resignation, and that the Supreme Council of Egyptian Armed Forces (SCAF) would assume leadership of the country. Two days later, SCAF dissolved the parliament, elected in December 2010 in highly controlled elections, and suspended the constitution. On February 15, SCAF announced the formation of an eight-person committee to amend the constitution and create a roadmap for a transition to a democratic government. The committee included Tariq Bishri, an independent Islamist intellectual, three members of the Supreme Constitutional Court, two Cairo University law professors, and a single politician: Subhi Saleh, a member of the Muslim Brotherhood who had represented Alexandria in the Egyptian parliament from 2005 to 2010. Two weeks later, the committee announced nine amendments to the constitution. The most consequential was Article 189, which specified that a new constitution would be written by a 100-member committee chosen by an elected parliament. On March 19, the amendments were approved in a national referendum with 77 percent of votes amidst a 41 percent turnout.

During March and April 2011, SCAF granted a number of concessions to protesters' demands in an effort to clear the streets of continued demonstrations. Ahmed Shafiq, appointed prime minister during the interim period but viewed as a remnant of the old regime, resigned, and both the NDP and the State Security Investigation Service were dissolved. However, SCAF rule, even if temporary, presented more continuity with the Mubarak regime than change. On March 30, SCAF replaced the constitution created by committee and approved by the Egyptian public with a constitutional declaration of fifty-three new articles. Taken together, the articles granted SCAF full legislative and executive powers until elections could be held.[69]

---

69. Brownlee, Masoud, and Reynolds, *The Arab Spring*, 109.

During the early days of the transition, there was some hope for collaboration between the former opposition under the Mubarak regime. In June 2011, twenty-eight parties including the Brotherhood, the New Wafd, Tagammu, and several other new and old parties formed the Democratic Alliance, a joint electoral list for the upcoming parliamentary elections. While they intended to continue the cooperation and unity of the eighteen days of protest which ousted Mubarak, old divisions reemerged quickly. The Democratic Alliance quickly failed in its unifying purpose and cleaved along ideological lines, leaving the Brotherhood's newly formed Freedom and Justice Party (FJP) at the head of a list dominated by Islamists and conservatives. Publicly, SCAF worked to resolve differences between the two camps. Behind the scenes, it exploited divisions between politicians when it was useful, similar to the previous regime. During the early days of the transition, SCAF often met with different camps separately.[70] Later, secular politicians pointed to early cooperation between the Brotherhood and SCAF as evidence that they were working together to derail the transition, while Brotherhood leaders claimed it was leftists and liberals who were working with the regime.[71] In addition, SCAF intervened in the constitution-drafting process and appeared to pick favorites. In November 2011, SCAF released the Silmi document, twenty-two articles that would guide the constitution writing process ahead of the elections. SCAF claimed the document made concessions both to Islamists and secular opposition. However, the text suggested otherwise: it declared Egypt to be a civil, democratic state and specified the makeup of the 100-person Constituent Assembly in a manner which constrained the Brotherhood's ability to influence its composition. Secular politicians enthusiastically supported the document, thought it was withdrawn due to large protests against it during the same month.

Elections for the 498 elected seats of the People's Assembly of Egypt were held between November 28, 2011 and January 11, 2012. SCAF had instituted a hybrid system in which two-thirds of the legislature's seats were chosen in a closed list proportional representation, and the remaining third was elected through a majoritarian system. Similar to Tunisia, the majority of parties that fared well in the elections had been active before the 2011 uprising as part of the democratic opposition. The Democratic Alliance,

70. David D. Kirkpatrick, *Into the Hands of the Soldiers: Freedom and Chaos in Egypt and the Middle East* (Penguin Books, 2019).

71. Amr Darrag. Interview with the author. June 13, 2016. Istanbul, Turkey.

led by the Brotherhood's FJP, won 37.5 percent of the vote. This resulted in a breakdown of 213 seats awarded to the FJP and 22 "allies" that remained in the Democratic Alliance, including 9 independents and 6 members of the Dignity Party. The Wasat Party, formed as a split from the Brotherhood in 1996, won 10 seats. Members of the democratic opposition mobilizing on secular platforms also won a number of seats. The New Wafd won 9.2 percent of the vote and 41 seats. Meanwhile, the Egyptian Bloc included a number of members from democratic opposition party Tagammu and activists formalized in the Egyptian Social Democratic Party. The coalition won 35 seats.

In addition to the familiar faces, the elections saw a number of new entrants. Most notably, the Islamic bloc, led by the newly formed Salafi *al-Nour* Party and composed of Islamist parties, took a surprise second place finish with 27.8 percent of the vote. Prior to the 2011 uprising, Egypt's Salafi organizations abstained from politics, but decided to take advantage of the shifting political landscape after the uprising to represent their interests. This led to Islamist groups comprising 70 percent of the parliamentary seats, as shown in table 8.2, a percentage that complicated debates about the constitution later on. The new faces also included a number of secular parties. The Free Egyptians Party was founded in April 2011 by Naguib Sawiris, a Coptic billionaire businessman who is chairman of Orascom Telecom Media and Technology Holding SAE. The party brought together a number of prominent businessmen, intellectuals, and academics on liberal economic and social policy issues. The Egyptian Social Democratic Party (ESDP) merged two small pre-revolutionary parties with independent progressives communists, and other leftist activists. In addition, a number of smaller parties formed the Revolution Continues Alliance. The Socialist Popular Alliance Party, the Freedom Egypt Party, and the Equality and Development Party all formed after the uprisings and mobilized on secular themes related to social justice, corruption, and youth representation.

Presidential elections followed six months after the parliamentary election. Shaken by the revelation of overwhelming support for the Brotherhood and the Salafi Nour Party, SCAF appointed Kamal al-Ganzuri, who had served as prime minister under Mubarak from 1996 to 1999, as interim prime minister in December 2011. In February 2012, Mubarak remnant Shafiq announced his candidacy for the presidency. Brotherhood leadership feared these developments signaled the return of the old regime, prompting General Guide Mohammed Badie to retract the Brotherhood's

**TABLE 8.2.** People's Assembly of Egypt Election Results (Egypt, 2012)

| Party | Percentage of national vote | Seat share |
|---|---|---|
| Democratic Alliance | 37.5 | 235 |
| *Freedom and Justice Party* | | *213* |
| *Dignity Party* | | *6* |
| *Ghad al-Thawra Party* | | *2* |
| *Civilization Party* | | *2* |
| *Islamic Labor Party* | | *1* |
| *Egyptian Arab Socialist Party* | | *1* |
| *Egyptian Reform Party* | | *1* |
| *Affiliated independents* | | *9* |
| Islamic Bloc | 27.8 | 123 |
| *Nour Party* | | *107* |
| *Building and Development Party* | | *13* |
| *Authenticity Party* | | *3* |
| New Wafd Party | 9.2 | 41 |
| Egyptian Bloc | 8.9 | 35 |
| *Egyptian Social Democratic Party* | | *16* |
| *Free Egyptians Party* | | *15* |
| *Progressive Unionist Party* | | *4* |
| Wasat Party | 3.7 | 10 |
| Revolution Continues Alliance | 2.8 | 9 |
| *Socialist Popular Alliance Party* | | *7* |
| *Freedom Egypt Party* | | *1* |
| *Equality and Development Party* | | *1* |
| Reform and Development Party | 2.2 | 9 |
| Freedom Party | 1.9 | 4 |
| National Party of Egypt | 1.6 | 5 |
| Conservative Party | 1.0 | 1 |
| Egyptian Citizen Party | 0.9 | 5 |
| Democratic Peace Party | 0.9 | 1 |
| Justice Party | 0.7 | 1 |
| Arab Egyptian Unity Party | 0.6 | 1 |
| Union Party | 0.5 | 2 |

earlier pledge not to field a presidential candidate. The FJP first nominated Khairat al-Shater, but he was disqualified for his arrests under Mubarak. The FJP's final candidate, Mohamed Morsi, went on to win the presidency in a runoff election against Shafiq in June 2012.

During the week between the elections and the SCAF's announcement of the final results, Morsi called a conference, later known as the "Fairmont Summit," in downtown Cairo to "discuss developments and changes in the political scene and the steps to be taken in the fact of current challenges." The conference was staged essentially to issue a number of promises from the Brotherhood's leadership in an effort to assure non-Islamists that they would be part of decision making during the transition period. Morsi promised to include "all national trends" on his presidential team, to appoint a "national salvation government" headed by a prime minister who was a "political independent," and "to strive for balance in forming the constituent assembly, in order to guarantee the writing of a constitution for all Egyptians." However, Morsi quickly disappointed his peers: non-Islamists were dismayed by his decision to replace Ganzuri with Hesham Qandil, and by the continued dominance of Brotherhood members and allies in Morsi's new cabinet. He also forced Defense Minister Hussayn al-Tantawi and army chief of staff Sami Anan to resign after Islamist militants killed sixteen people in the Sinai in August 2012. Morsi's decisions, made with consultation with top FJP and Brotherhood leadership, demonstrated that the Brotherhood was unwilling to work with other political groups as partners, and perhaps suggested negative feelings between the groups.

Per the constitutional articles issued by SCAF, the parliament elected between November 2011 and January 2012 was required to form a Constituent Assembly to draft and approve a permanent constitution. With the plurality of seats in the new parliament, the FJP led the formation of the assembly. A first, 100-member Constituent Assembly was elected by the FJP-led parliament in March 2012. The assembly was criticized for being unbalanced and unrepresentative; while only 38 of the 50 parliamentary members of the Constituent Assembly were members of the FJP and Nour Parties, in line with the party's representation in parliament, opponents pointed to a total of 66 Islamist-leaning members. Only 75 of 100 members attended the assembly. Members from leftist and social democratic parties including the Free Egyptians Party, the Socialist Popular Alliance, the Dignity Party, the Social Democrats, the Tagammu Party, the New Wafd, and the Freedom Egypt Party boycotted the election to determine the makeup of the Constituent Assembly.[72] On April 10, the assembly was dissolved by a decree from Cairo's Supreme Administrative Court on the grounds that it violated a March 2011 Constitutional Decree, which stated that parliament members were responsible for electing the Constituent Assembly but could not elect themselves to that body. Even after the assembly was dissolved on legal grounds, members of the secular opposition followed through with filing an additional suit about the legality of the body out of fear that it might permanently enshrine a strong role for Islamic religious law in the new constitution.

Leftists and liberals described the Brotherhood as "power hungry,"[73] beginning with their support for early parliamentary elections which left secular trends at an organizational disadvantage, and continuing with their decision to amend the constitution largely by itself rather than through a coalition. After the parliamentary elections, the Brotherhood felt it had received a mandate from the Egyptian people, and as a result, it had the right to dictate the course of the transition and the constitution-drafting process. Leftists accused them of "not playing by the rules of the game," as Ahmed Fawzi explained:

They were pushing to gain more ground. In most of the meetings that I attended with the Muslim Brotherhood, it was about showing their strengths. They said, "We are the majority, we have a large number of Islamists around," and in any kind of debate or discussion we use to have with them, they would say, "Ok, fine. Let's go back to the people, and find out what they want." And they knew, of course, that the majority was with them at that time. They said, They have been in Egypt for almost 90 years, or 85 years at that time, and they have been suffering. They are the majority. The western world keeps demanding democracy, democracy, and so by democracy they came to power. They absolutely felt entitled.[74]

Secular politicians were picking up on feelings the Brotherhood later admitted having at the time. The Brotherhood's Amr Darrag said,

72. "Al-Libiraliyin fi al-Barliman al-Masri Yansajibun min Jalasat al-Dustur al-Jadida," *Al-Wasat*, March 24, 2016, http://www.alwasatnews.com/news/645567.html.

73. Mohamed Gabr. Interview with the author. February 11, 2018. Cairo, Egypt. Osama Ghazali Harb described this sentiment with the Egyptian colloquialism, *"hamout fi power."* Interview with the author. February 7, 2018. Cairo, Egypt.

74. Ahmed Fawzi. Interview with the author. February 4, 2018. Cairo, Egypt.

Our motive was to establish democracy. We used to say that it wasn't our fault that we had been working for so long. We paid the price. Our opponents were on TV saying, "these people have been here for 80 years and we just arrived. We're not established so it's not fair to have elections now." So we wait for another 80 years? How much longer will we wait? There are feelings within the Muslim Brotherhood that we paid a very high price. [Other opposition] didn't have a wide base of support, so we felt that they did not have the right to impose what they wanted. If we're in a democracy, and we are the majority, it's our right to govern . . . . Our opponents should allow for the Brotherhood's role in history. We paid a high price before 2011.[75]

However, the fear of an Islamist dominated party was not simply based on the importance of fair and transparent procedures. More than this, leftist and secularists faced what Mohamed Gabr called an "existential fear."[76] Liberals called the Brotherhood's vision for Egypt "totally contradictory with the Egyptian national character,"[77] which, they claimed, respected pluralism of religion and the secular division of religion and politics. As Karama's Sayyid al-Toukhy described, the Brotherhood "held the presidency and the majority in parliament, and then they took over the constitutional council. They tried to leave a religious imprint on the new state, but the revolution had called for a modern civil democratic state. The Brotherhood was extremely opposed to this idea."[78] Two additional factors may have further pushed the FJP to adopt more extreme behaviors and positions than it might have done otherwise. First, hardliners within the party gained power as more moderate factions, such as those led by Aboul Fotouh and the youth movement, left for newly formed opposition parties. This process mimicked changes following the departure of the middle generation of Brothers to form the Wasat Party in the mid-1990s.[79] Second, the presence of Salafi Islamist party Nour in parliament forced the Brotherhood to take more conservative positions than they might have otherwise.

The first assembly was dissolved. On June 7, 2012, parliament members, each of the major parties, and SCAF reached an agreement on the

75. Amr Darrag. Interview with the author. June 13, 2016. Istanbul, Turkey.

76. Mohamed Gabr. Interview with the author. February 11, 2018. Cairo, Egypt.

77. Amin Iskandar. Interview with the author. February 3, 2018. Cairo, Egypt.

78. Sayyid al-Toukhy. Interview with the author. January 31, 2018. Cairo, Egypt.

79. Wickham, "The Path to Moderation: Strategy and Learning in the Formation of Egypt's *Wasat Party.*"

composition of a new assembly.[80] The new assembly was to be composed of thirty-nine members of parliament (divided according to parliamentary proportions), six judges, nine legal experts, thirteen union leaders, and twenty-one public figures, in addition to one member of the armed forces, one member of the police, and one member of the justice ministry. Five additional seats would be filled through appointments by al-Azhar University and four by the Coptic Orthodox Church. Because sixty-one of the non-parliamentary seats were allotted to individuals who might be affiliated with political parties and movements, the agreement further outlined the ways in which these seats could be divided up to result in a 50-50 split between Islamists and non-Islamists, according to statements by Mohie al-Din, vice president of the secular Ghad al-Thawra Party. Importantly, the percentage of seats held by the FJP in the assembly was in proportional to its publicly mandated power as dictated by recent election results. In addition to outlining the division of power, this agreement was important because it indicated that the constitution draft process "was specified, understood, and agreed to by all 22 parties, despite what the opposition" later claimed in 2012.[81]

When the list of suggested names for the assembly was approved by parliament on June 12, fifty-seven MPs walked out and refused to participate in the process, claiming that the Brotherhood was attempting to secure a voting majority of Islamists through the appointment of Islamist-leaning independents. Members of Egypt's major political parties, including the Egyptian Bloc, the Revolution Continues Alliance, the Wafd Party, the Hurriyah Party, the Socialist Party, the Alliance Party, the Egyptian-Arabic Union Party, and the Egyptian Citizen Party as well as several independents, participated in the walkout.[82] While many leftist members had legitimate concerns about the constitution-drafting process, they also withdrew from the assembly before exhausting debate and discussion options, and refused to return after repeated official invitations from the FJP.

The second assembly was as fraught as the first. The body again faced legal charges regarding the parliamentary membership of some of its

80. Bethany Bell. "Egypt parties end deadlock over constitutional panel." *BBC*, June 8, 2012. https://www.bbc.com/news/world-middle-east-18360403.

81. Mohamed Elmasry. "Unpacking Anti-Muslim Brotherhood Discourse." *Jadaliyya*, June 28, 2013. http://www.jadaliyya.com/Details/28855.

82. Marina Ottaway. "Egypt: Death of the Constituent Assembly?" *Carnegie Endowment for International Peace*, June 13, 2012. https://carnegieendowment.org/2012/06/13/egypt-death -of-constituent-assembly-pub-48501.

members and for being unrepresentative, but decisions by the Supreme Administrative Court were delayed such that the assembly continued its work through the fall. On November 22, 2012, Morsi issued a constitutional declaration in which he declared the presidency autonomous and immune from the authority of the judiciary pending the approval of a new constitution. Morsi's declaration "provided a focal point around which previously scattered liberals, leftists, and Mubarak supporters could coalesce":[83] two days later, liberals and leftists formed the National Salvation front and demanded a new government of national unity. From the first referendum, many secular politicians had feared Brotherhood domination, but it was Morsi's election and the way he and the Brotherhood handled his presidency that served as a unifying point for non-Brotherhood forces.

During a marathon session held on November 29, 2012, to pass the constitution, twenty-one members of the elected body and seven members of the alternate list withdrew, again citing Islamist domination of the process and criticizing ambiguous language on human rights and freedoms of expression. Only eighty-five members, including members of the alternate list, of the 100-person body attended the marathon session, but that number fulfilled the minimum attendance requirement to hold the vote. The assembly then issued a 234-article draft constitution. The document, again criticized as the product of an Islamist-dominated assembly, was approved by 65 percent of voters in a low turnout referendum (33 percent) and signed into law by Morsi on December 26. During this period, dueling protests were carried out by Brotherhood supporters and opponents.

One journalist observed, "the process of drafting it was more controversial than the text itself."[84] As Ayman Nour said, "we really agreed on 80 percent of the issues. But the 20 percent was the sticking point. There was no structure for disagreement, just like there was none for agreement."[85] Other secular opponents and newspapers pointed to the final text of Article 2 and Article 4 as evidence of the Muslim Brotherhood's undue influence on the document and monopolization of a key component of the transition. The final text of Article 2 read, "Islam is the religion of the state and Arabic is its official language. The principles of Islamic shariʿa are

83. Brownlee, Masoud, and Reynolds, *The Arab Spring*.

84. Kristen Chick. "Why is Egypt's draft constitution so controversial?" *Christian Science Monitor*, November 30, 2012. https://www.csmonitor.com/World/Middle-East/2012/1130/Why-is-Egypt-s-draft-constitution-so-controversial.

85. Ayman Nour. Interview with the author. February 11, 2017. Istanbul, Turkey.

the principal source of legislation." A second article, Article 219, titled "Principles of an Islamic shari'a," included a conservative interpretation but was in fact introduced by members of the Nour Party. The article specified that "principles of the Islamic shari'a" included "general evidence, foundational rules, rules of jurisprudence, and credible sources accepted in Sunni doctrines and by the larger community." In addition, Article 4 upheld al-Azhar as an independent, fiscally autonomous Islamic institution and also included language that stipulated it should hold sway over matters of religion.[86] Taken together, the entire process betrayed severe levels of distrust, discord, and inability to cooperate among the Islamist and non-Islamist members of the assembly.

Morsi's brief tenure saw enormous tension between Islamists and non-Islamists, most dramatically captured in the public disagreements surrounding the constitution. Taken together, there was neither an opportunity nor a desire for compromise among politicians during the Egyptian transition. Both affective and preference polarization hindered cooperation and compromise. Secular and Islamist groups fundamentally disliked each other and struggled to build trust. In addition, the Brotherhood terrified its secular opponents because their visions for the future of Egypt differed so dramatically, yet the Brotherhood had the power to carry out its vision without compromise.

In early 2013, a grassroots movement called *Tamarod* ("rebellion") emerged in opposition to Morsi. The group outlined a petition demanding early presidential elections to replace Morsi, and sought to collect fifteen million signatures by the first anniversary of his inauguration. The petition drive soon morphed into large protests on June 30. On July 3, Minister of Defense Sisi—surrounded by some of the country's most prominent political and religious leaders, in a symbol of their support for military intervention—announced that Egypt's first democratically elected president had "failed to meet and conform to the demands of the people," and had been "removed from office."

While the protests that led to Morsi's ouster were widely supported and based on a year of real policy failures under his leadership, the military exploited the widespread frustration with Morsi and the Brotherhood's Freedom and Justice Party to declare open season on the Brotherhood and its supporters. Subsequent investigations revealed that the military may

---

86. The text reads, "Al-Azhar's Council of senior scholars is to be consulted in matters relating to Islamic shari'a."

have financed and co-opted Tamarod.[87] When removing Morsi as president, SCAF suspended the constitution passed under Morsi and installed an interim government, officially presided over by senior jurist Adly Mansour but with the military at the helm. In August, at least 648 people (probably closer to 1000) were killed and thousands more were injured when the military used force to clear protesters demonstrating in support of Morsi in Cairo's Rabaa al-Adaweya and al-Nahda squares, according to official estimates.[88]

It was not until after the coup that issues of transitional justice were formally addressed. Prior to that, some members of the old regime had been tried in courts. However, these criminal prosecutions were generally private and were highly manipulated. Most of those who were found guilty of abuses would eventually have their convictions overturned or their sentences shortened significantly. In addition, there appeared to be a lack of political will for transitional justice because holding the former regime accountable would have further privileged the Brotherhood in a political arena which they were already dominating.[89]

In July 2013, interim president Adly Mansour appointed Judge Mohamed Amin al-Mahdi as the country's Minister of Transitional Justice and National Reconciliation. During the same month, the organizers of the June 30 protests invited Egyptian politicians of all stripes to attend a meeting of the National Reconciliation and Transitional Justice committee, to be held at the presidential palace and ostensibly with Mansour's approval. In attendance at the first meeting called on July 24 were Wafd Party Chairman Al-Sayed al-Badawy, Chairman of the Reform and Development Misruna Party Mohamed Anwar Sadat, head of the Egyptian Social Democratic Party Mohamed Aboul Ghar, Free Egyptians Party head Ahmed Saeed, and Mohamed Sami of the Dignity Party.[90]

87. Sheera Frenkel and Maged Atef. "How Egypt's Rebel Movement Helped Pave The Way for A Sisi Presidency." *Buzzfeed News*, April 15, 2014. https://www.buzzfeednews.com/article/sheerafrenkel/how-egypts-rebel-movement-helped-pave-the-way-for-a-sisi-pre.

88. Omar Shakir. "All According to Plan: The Rab'a Massacre and Mass Killings of Protesters in Egypt." *Human Rights Watch*, August 12, 2014. https://www.hrw.org/report/2014/08/12/all-according-plan/raba-massacre-and-mass-killings-protesters-egypt.

89. Noha Aboueldahab. "Transitional Justice Policy in Authoritarian Contexts: The Case of Egypt." *Brookings Institution*, October 19, 2017. https://www.brookings.edu/research/transitional-justice-policy-in-authoritarian-contexts-the-case-of-egypt/.

90. Attendance at the meeting was reported in the state-affiliated newspaper, *al-Ahram*.

The Brotherhood issued a statement through a spokesperson announcing it would boycott the event, and proclaimed "there cannot be reconciliation when blood is being shed."[91] Abdel Moneim Aboul Fotouh, a former Brotherhood member and then head of centrist party *Misr al-Qawiyya*, similarly expressed his opposition to the meeting on Twitter, writing that "the military coup government that failed to stop the daily bloodshed detains tens of peaceful protesters and surrounds media and closes its channel; what reconciliation is it calling for?" While the Islamist focus remained on justice for abuses under Mubarak prior to 2011 as well as the state's ongoing roundup of Brotherhood leaders, members, and sympathizers, secular political actors' notion of transitional justice instead wanted retribution for human rights abuses committed by the Morsi administration. Tamarod called for national reconciliation, but further specified that process as "the arrest of all Brotherhood leaders who encouraged the killing of innocent people."[92] The divergence in the groups' responses reveal different notions among political groups of who constituted the oppressors and the victims during the transition period.

In the aftermath of the coup, SCAF ordered Mansour to form a new 50-member Constituent Assembly, which included only two Islamists, to draft a new constitution. A referendum on a newly amended constitution and presidential elections were both held in 2014. Their results signaled the reinstallation of the country's pre-2011 electoral authoritarianism: 98.1 percent of voters approved the constitution presented by the military, and the de facto president, Field Marshal Abdel Fattah al-Sisi, won over 95 percent of the vote against a single, weak opponent.

Secular politicians reacted to the crackdown on the Brotherhood in a number of different ways. In essence, they blamed the Brotherhood for its own repression. In the view of one of the founders of the secular al-Adl Party, the Brotherhood had tried to dominate the political scene from the beginning of the transition, "and the way they managed the situation in June 2013 reinforced this belief. That was the key element for understanding what happened. Everything else was a reaction to their dominance within

91. Nourhan Dakroury, "First National Reconciliation and Transitional Justice Meeting." *Daily News Egypt*, July 24, 2013, http://www.dailynewsegypt.com/2013/07/24/first-national -reconciliation-and-transitional-justice-meeting/.

92. Rawan Ezzat. "Tamarod to Hold National Reconciliation Dialogue." *Daily News Egypt*, July 23, 2013. https://www.dailynewsegypt.com/2013/07/23/tamarod-to-hold-national -reconciliation-dialogue/.

state institutions."[93] Many secular politicians also sought to distance them-selves from the Brotherhood and apologized publicly for cooperating with the FJP after the revolution. Iskandar, a leader of the Karama Party who served in the Constituent Assembly and parliament, regretted his coop-eration with the Brotherhood, calling it "the period in my history that I wish I could forget." Iskandar appeared on television a number of times after the coup and apologized, saying the party had made a mistake, and that "political Islam, whether from the Brotherhood, the Salafist, or the Jihadist, can't build the future of Egypt. This country can't progress except with a civil program. As I have said, I am the most radically opposed to the Brotherhood."[94] Members of the Gabha and Ghad Parties said that they had only joined the 2011 Democratic Alliance because they were small parties and hoped to win more seats that way. Other regime loyalists claimed the organization "had no popularity in society" and "was not missed from the political scene" once removed.[95]

The crackdown on the Brotherhood beginning in 2013 may serve to strengthen the Brotherhood's narrative of exclusive victimhood and may perhaps produce yet another generation of hardliners within the organiza-tion. As of 2017, it did not appear that the Egyptian people were becoming more sympathetic towards the Brotherhood; instead, the Brotherhood was left feeling victimized and helpless once again. In the words of Mohamed Gabr,

> this is worse than the *mihna* period, because they are not only being victimized by the regime but the entire population. It's going to take a lot of time for this wound to heal. As other Egyptians are starting to see the depth of the abyss [under Sisi], how dark things are, they're start-ing to talk to the Brotherhood. But there's bitterness on both sides as well. I would call myself a centrist, but even I cannot forget how the miscalculations of the leadership led to the current moment in Egypt. Our paths have been very different, and that's why we're not very close. In the coming years, that will be even more evident. We won't have lived in exile. We won't have gone to jail. Some of us are going through strug-gles of our own [as a result of the 2011 uprising], but not on the same

93. Mohamed Gabr. Interview with the author. February 11, 2018. Cairo, Egypt.
94. Amin Iskandar. Interview with the author. February 3, 2018. Cairo, Egypt.
95. Osama Ghazali Harb. Interview with the author. February 7, 2018. Cairo, Egypt.

level. I would think the effects of Rabaa will be felt for anywhere from the next 20 to 50 years.[96]

## Conclusion

The transition period proceeded very differently in Egypt and Tunisia. While both Islamist parties won similar mandates in 2011–2012, the FJP used its plurality to push through a constitution despite the walkout of the secular opposition. Although this was technically in accordance with legal requirements, it created additional tension in an already polarized political sphere. Though Tunisia's constitution writing process was not without its problems, Ennahda deliberately sought out other parties and included alternative voices to create a constitution that was widely supported by all political factions.

While not the singularly important causal variable, polarization made a central contribution in explaining the divergent behavior among the countries' leadership. The high levels of political polarization in Egypt decreased the possibility of agreement regarding constitutional reform, holding democratic elections, and carrying out transitional justice between actors during a critical moment, and ultimately facilitated the country's descent into authoritarian reentrenchment. In addition, the July 2013 coup was aided in no small way by the polarization and division among political elites; secular elites supported the anti-Morsi protest and the military intervention, providing civilian backing and justifying the military's intervention as not ideal but necessary to preserve democracy. Their support was driven not only by dislike and distrust of the Brotherhood but also severe disagreement with the FJP's political preferences and policy initiatives. Meanwhile in Tunisia, less polarization among elites on critical policy issues and greater camaraderie, born of shared experiences of repression, allowed politicians to stay the course of democratization. Ultimately, they passed an inclusive constitution and turned to focus on the next steps of democratic consolidation, holding second elections and tackling reforms to address the long-term economic and security challenges inherent in post-authoritarian political systems.

96. Mohamed Gabr. Interview with the author. February 11, 2018. Cairo, Egypt.

# 9

# Conclusion

As I finish writing this book in late 2019, the contrast between Egypt and Tunisia could not be starker. In May 2018, Tunisia held long-delayed municipal elections, the first local contests since the uprising and which solidified post-revolutionary reform at the local level. Forty-five thousand candidates contested seats across 350 municipalities. After President Beji Caid Essebsi died in July 2019, presidential elections were scheduled and held early, with Kais Saied, an independent candidate and professor of constitutional law, winning the final runoff in October. Local and international observers concluded that both sets of elections were generally competitive and credible. There were, of course, complaints and concerns, such as low voter turnout, high levels of voter distrust in the system and in political elites, and the increasing monopolization of the party system by Ennahda and Nidaa Tounes, the only two parties capable of running nationwide campaigns. But overall, the elections were a success and marked a major milestone towards continued democratic consolidation. All parties respected formal agreements and the ballot box, and demonstrated commitment to democratic norms and procedures as the only game in town. Voters celebrated electoral outcomes on the main boulevard of downtown Tunis unfettered by police.

During the previous December, Tunisia's Truth and Dignity Commission presented its final report, drawing on over 62,000 complaints filed by Tunisian citizens against the state for human rights abuses committed since 1955. The closing conference was broadcasted on national television.

It began with the national anthem, and then Sihem Ben Sedrine, head of the commission and herself once a victim of state repression, offered some remarks. Despite the somber tone of the inquiry and the many difficulties the commission had faced since its inception five years earlier, Ben Sedrine celebrated the accomplishments of the commission and its success in carrying out its mandate to document past abuses by the state, to determine and provide reparations to victims, and to pursue criminal accountability for serious and systematic crimes committed by the state against its citizens and its opposition. She continued,

> The machinery of oppression and despotism did not distinguish between victims. It did not distinguish between those who are left-leaning, those who are Islamists, those who are in labor unions or those in the marginalized regions. This machinery indiscriminately repressed all of the sons and daughters of Tunisia, all of its citizens without distinction.

As she spoke, the camera panned over the faces of those in the audience—Ennahda's Samir Dilou and Rachid Ghannouchi seated next to Issam Chebbi of the PDP, Hamma Hammami and his wife Radhia Nasroui, Mustapha Ben Jaafar of Ettakatol—seemingly confirming the diversity of the state's victims. These victims then became the politicians who navigated the country through its first years of transition, for better and for worse. While the transition has been far from perfect, its leaders have achieved significant progress and demonstrated remarkable unity of purpose.

Meanwhile, the fall of 2019 saw yet further authoritarian reentrenchment in Egypt as the Sisi regime continued to reestablish its control and consolidate itself following the destabilization of the 2011 uprising and its aftermath.[1] Small protests broke out in September 2019 in response to allegations of corruption against Sisi and the military, and the regime arrested nearly four thousand people.[2] The heavy-handed response was typical for a regime that had baptized itself in blood. In the aftermath of the 2013 coup that overthrew president Mohamed Morsi, Egyptian security forces

---

1. Stacher Joshua, *Watermelon Democracy: Egypt's Turbulent Transition* (Syracuse University Press 2020) argues that Sisi's style of rule may constitute a new form of authoritarianism, rather than a reentrenchment or continuation of previous authoritarianism.

2. According to statistics maintained by the Egyptian Center for Economic and Social Rights, available at https://docs.google.com/spreadsheets/d/1MtnmLXnma3Dalo8fdWddbTuuCdv -RscnrV6oUjIe2Tk/edit#gid=1611783327. Last accessed by author December 2, 2019.

killed at least one thousand pro-Morsi protesters[3] and jailed sixty thousand political prisoners in at least nineteen new prisons built to house them.[4]

The April 2018 presidential contests, saw General Abdel Fattah al-Sisi elected to a second term with 97 percent of the vote against one hand-picked candidate, surpassing even the most unfair and controlled contests of the Mubarak era. In the lead-up to the election, the regime observed "few boundaries on its untamed repression of all forms of dissent," jailing, deporting, or otherwise silencing any semblance of opposition.[5] At the end of 2019, many of those arrested for political behavior remain in state custody. Those who have been tried and sentenced in military courts continue to appeal harsh sentences while others continue to be held without official charges in violation of domestic and international law. The regime's consolidation strategy couples repression with legal reforms intended to further shore up its control. The Egyptian parliament recently passed constitutional amendments that increase the duration of a presidential term from four to six years, permit Sisi to seek reelection for another six-year term in 2024, undermine the independence of the judiciary, and further institutionalize the military as a major player in civilian governance.

Perhaps the only positive by-product of the Sisi regime's consolidation is that expansive repression may be redrawing the boundaries of identity among Islamist and secular political actors. In June 2019, Morsi fainted and died during a court appearance for politically motivated charges stemming from his escape from jail during the 2011 uprisings. In the same month, it was revealed that Gehad Haddad, a Brotherhood activist who is also the son of former national security advisor and Brotherhood leader Essam Haddad arrested in connection with the deposition of Morsi, was no longer able to walk unassisted due to harsh treatment in prison.[6]

The response to these events demonstrated that the tone towards the Brotherhood had changed, and those who once opposed the Brotherhood

3. Omar Shakir. "All According to Plan: The Rab'a Massacre and Mass Killings of Protesters in Egypt." *Human Rights Watch*, August 12, 2014. https://www.hrw.org/report/2014/08/12/all-according-plan/raba-massacre-and-mass-killings-protesters-egypt.

4. Arab Network for Human Rights, "There's room for everyone: Egypt's prisons before and after the January Revolution," 2016, available at http://anhri.net/?p=173465.

5. Human Rights Watch, "Egypt: Untamed Repression," January 19, 2018, available at https://www.hrw.org/news/2018/01/18/egypt-untamed-repression.

6. Human Rights Watch, "The Working Group on Egypt's Letter to Secretary of State Pompeo," June 20, 2019. https://www.hrw.org/news/2019/06/25/working-group-egypts-letter-secretary-state-pompeo#.

and supported the military's political intervention have found common ground in their mistreatment. Mohamed Baradei, a politician who had supported the coup but now found himself in exile, tweeted a blessing for Morsi and his family, and followed it with an emphatic rebuke of the current government's violence.[7] Secular activists similarly tweeted that regardless of one's political opinions, it was unconscionable to see the physical suffering of a 38-year-old man as the result of his imprisonment. At a September 2019 New York City protest held in solidarity with those protesting in Egypt, I watched organizers remove anti-Brotherhood slogans from posters prepared for the event. They said that this was a time for unity rather than division in facing the regime. While these are small actions, they suggest glimmers of increased unity among the opposition in a way that will could be meaningful for any future democratization in Egypt.

This shift in rhetoric parallels the change in the domestic repressive environment, from one targeting the Brotherhood to one affecting nearly all politically mobilized groups as the regime reconsolidates. Political prisoners from the secular opposition are now tried in military courts and held in highly repressive prison conditions, tactics once reserved for the Brotherhood alone. The regime has explicitly linked political activists of different persuasions; during the 2018 roundup, the regime fabricated a narrative of unlikely cooperation between leftists and the Brotherhood in order to levy charges carrying heavier punishment. As a result, groups of different ideological persuasions all feel they are victims of this regime, because its repression has come to affect all of them.

Without oversimplifying the culmination of many complex events and historical precedents, elite polarization is central to any explanation of the divergence between Egypt and Tunisia after the Arab Spring uprisings. Egyptian and Tunisian political parties emerged from the authoritarian period differently polarized in 2011, both in terms of affect towards competing groups as well as in political preferences. In Egypt, high levels of polarization prevented the cooperation and compromise necessary to successfully navigate the complexities of a democratic transition, while lower levels of polarization facilitated forward movement on political issues of central importance in Tunisia.

In the previous pages, I outlined an argument that endogenizes levels of polarization to collective experiences of repression through a two-step process. In the first step, repression conditions how opposition actors

7. https://twitter.com/ElBaradei/status/964429249003204610?s=20.

come to identify themselves through reinforcing social, organizational, and psychological mechanisms. In the second step, political identities shape levels of political polarization within a given system, following established cognitive and psychological processes of affective and preference polarization: if group identities are highly polarized, then group-related affect and preferences are similarly polarized. The nature of repression determines whether it exacerbates or ameliorates political polarization. Widespread experiences of repression decrease in-group identification, creating a substitute bridging identity as the groups targeted form a larger collective identity of victimized opposition sharing experiences of repression across multiple groups. In contrast, targeted experiences of repression heighten in-group identification within the singularly targeted group, as only in-group members share experiences of repression. The way in which the dynamics of repression influence political identities then conditions the level of polarization within a given political system. Where repression is widespread, the opposition becomes less polarized as identities and related affect and preferences converge over time. In a targeted repressive environment, heightened in-group identification for the targeted group contributes to increasing intergroup distance over time. The result is a more highly polarized political system.

The remainder of this chapter extends my argument in three different directions. First, I discuss other cases where my argument provides explanatory value for divergence in transitional outcomes using evidence from transitions in Algeria and Indonesia. Second, I conclude with further implications of elite polarization during democratic transitions, namely for mass polarization. Finally, I conclude by outlining potential research questions building on this book, highlighting the importance of identity and polarization as conditioned by repressive experiences in political developments across different political regime types.

## Beyond Egypt and Tunisia: Repression, Polarization, and Transition in Algeria and Indonesia

While the developments and outcomes I have traced in detail throughout this book are specific to the Egyptian and Tunisian contexts, the process contains universal elements that generalize beyond these two cases. In particular, the way in which repression conditions identities of political importance with implications for both levels of political polarization as well as the extent to which elite actors can compromise and cooperate during critical moments of transition is not unique to Egypt and Tunisia. Evidence from two additional countries—Algeria and Indonesia—suggest that these processes operate in similar ways in different temporal and national contexts.

Both Algeria and Indonesia faced uprisings and the potential of sudden transitions. In addition, both countries were politically divided along a similar salient cleavage, that of the Islamist-secular axis. With these additional cases, I do not mean to imply that my theory of repression and polarization only applies to political systems which are divided along conceptions of religion and state, only to reduce the number of dimensions along which these cases differ from each other and from the cases analyzed in the book. Moreover, whether Islamist and non-Islamist actors can compromise, and under what conditions, is at the center of questions surrounding Islamist democracy. Indonesia represents an additional case of widespread repression, a more unified opposition identity, low levels of polarization, and ultimately a successful initial transition period, similar to Tunisia. In contrast, Algeria represents an additional case of targeted repression, an opposition fragmented in terms of identity, highly polarized, and a return to authoritarianism, similar to Egypt.

The shadow case studies that follow rely primarily on secondary sources. The broad national-level indicators outlined here are consistent with the expectations of the theory. A more thorough investigation would rely on interviews with the actors, careful reading of memoirs, and additional qualitative evidence, similar to the in-depth case studies which precede this section.

## ALGERIA, 1988–1992

In October 1988, Algeria witnessed riots described as the most serious since the country's independence from the French. The riots were youth led and focused on economic issues, such as rising prices, high rates of unemployment, and measures of austerity introduced by the government following years of economic crisis resulting from a drop in oil prices. Economic concerns were coupled with discontent at regime corruption and the pace of political reform. To quell the riots, the military assumed control of the police and staged a heavy-handed intervention against protesters. The use of torture against detainees was reported to be widespread and resulted in approximately five hundred civilian deaths and one thousand wounded.

In the face of mounting domestic pressure, President Chadli Bendjedid, who had assumed power in 1979, called for a transition towards multiparty democracy as a survival strategy. Algeria's first multiparty legislative elections began on December 26, 1991. However, the military intervened between the first and second rounds after it appeared that Islamist party *Front Islamique du Salut* (FIS) would win a nearly two-thirds majority of seats, essentially cancelling the elections. Previously, the FIS won 54 percent in municipal elections in the country's first multiparty municipal elections held in June 1990. Fears emerged from the military and other political parties that Islamists would hold the requisite majority needed to change the constitution in addition to having near absolute power at all levels of government. These fears were further stoked by public disagreements between the military and FIS surrounding support for Iraq and Kuwait during the January 1991 Gulf War, which culminated in an FIS-led general strike and the declaration of a state of emergency in June.

The military annulment of the elections on January 11, 1992 marked the beginning of the country's descent into a civil war. The decree announcing the cancellation of the elections simultaneously forced the resignation of President Bendjedid and installed exiled opposition leader Mohamed Boudiaf, who was assassinated a few months later. The regime immediately clamped down on the FIS, officially dissolving the organization on March 4. By the army's account, five thousand FIS members were arrested, while its leader Abdelkader Hachani put the total closer to forty thousand. The number overwhelmed Algeria's prison capacity, so the regime established prison camps for the overflow in the Sahara desert.[8] Those FIS activists that remained free became guerrilla fighters, retreating to the mountains of northern Algeria to fight against the state. As a result, guerrilla tactics and an urban-rural division defined the conflict. The bombing of the Algiers airport in August 1992 and a steady assassination of French-speaking academics, intellectuals, writers, journalists, and medical doctors furthered the conflict's descent into a civil war that would not end until 2002.

How did a moment of liberalization and potential democratic transition end so disastrously? If the dynamics documented in this book have any explanatory power for Algeria, we should expect to observe a targeted repressive environment under authoritarianism, as well as high levels of affective and preference polarization and a lack of cooperation among the opposition during the transition.

8. Gilles Kepel, *Jihad: The Trail of Political Islam* (IB Tauris, 2006), 258.

Prior to the events of 1988 that eventually led to civil war, repression under President Bendjedid and his predecessor, Houari Boumédiéne, was targeted. The regime officially recognized a number of opposition parties ahead of the multiparty elections, but the nature of repression was "divide-and-rule,"[9] targeting Islamists and co-opting leftist parties. In the 1970s, the remnants of the Algerian Communist Party (*Parti de l'Avant Garde Socialiste*, or PAGS) were co-opted into the government. Pagsistes, as they were known, had opposed the ruling regime at independence and had been the victims of early state violence. In addition, the relationship between PAGS and the ruling party was tenuous when Bendjedid came to power and purged suspected pagsistes from the government as he shifted towards economic liberalization. However, during the 1980s, PAGS was integrated into the government to provide leftist credentials to the Boumédiéne regime's state-led development programs.

In contrast, "Islamists suffered the harshest repression"[10] under the successive regimes. Initially, the FIS was permitted to occupy a larger public and political role, particularly on university campuses, with the Bendjedid regime's tacit approval. Similar to the Sadat era in Egypt, the new regime considered Islamism to be a means through which to combat the increasingly assertive Berberist movement and leftist opponents originating from within the regime. At that time, high-profile Islamist opponents of Boumédiéne were released from prison, most notably Algeria's first president Ahmed Ben Bella who immediately left the country due to safety concerns. He would go on to found the *Mouvement pour la Démocratie en Algérie* (MDA), a moderate opposition party with a combination of Islamist and socialist leanings, in 1984. In addition, a number of figures seen as sympathetic to the Islamists' agenda were appointed to prominent government positions.

However, the regime's brief tolerance of Islamists was quickly rescinded in 1982, when the regime reacted with a heavy hand to quell violence on university campuses between Islamist and leftist students. Nearly four hundred Islamist supporters were arrested and one was sentenced to eight years' imprisonment for the manslaughter of Kamel Amzel, a leftist student who was fatally stabbed during the campus violence. The regime

9. Michael Willis, *The Islamist Challenge in Algeria: A Political History* (New York University Press, 1999), 121.

10. Yahia H. Zoubir, "The Painful Transition from Authoritarianism in Algeria," *Arab Studies Quarterly*, 1993, 86.

broadened the scope of the crackdown and made large-scale arrests including the three well-known members of Algeria's Islamist movement, Abdel-latif Soltani, Ahmed Sahnoun, and Abassi Madani, as well as members of Mustafa Bouyali's Algerian Islamic Armed Movement (MAIA), five of whom eventually received the death penalty. Though Algeria's Islamist movements differed in tactics and ideologies, and rarely worked together, the nature of repression lumped these organizations together as one threat. At the same time, the regime usurped control over Algerian mosques and imams in an attempt to squash Islamist oppositional mobilization.[11]

Algeria's opposition movements demonstrated a lack of cooperation and an inability to compromise on central issues during a crucial moment of potential democratic transition. The main opposition parties included the FIS, legally recognized in September 1989 under President Abassi Madani and his deputy Ali Belhadj; the MDA, a socialist party with Islamist leanings established by President Ben Bella; and the *Front des Forces Socialist* (FFS), a Berber social democratic and secularist political party headed by major opposition figure Hocine Ait Ahmed. In addition, the *Rassemblement pour la Culture et la Démocratie* (RCD) formed as a coalition of smaller parties and independents after the 1990 elections, though it won just two percent of the vote in the following legislative elections.

These parties were unwilling and unable to work together and did not present a united front against the regime. Initially, the MDA and FFS boycotted elections, as the parties' leadership complained they had not been given enough time to prepare for the contests. After the June 1990 municipal elections, some opposition parties that had fought separately against each other attempted to coordinate their efforts in the form of an alliance for the upcoming legislative elections. However, the so-called "Group of 8" never fully materialized, failing to launch due to majority differences in policy, strategy, and personality. Later, the RCD and PAGS parties "openly and unambiguously applauded the termination of the electoral process" following the military coup. UGTA leader Abdelhak BenHamouda, working in coordination with the FFS, was quoted as saying, "We are legalists, but if the institutions do not fulfill their functions, it is our duty to resist and to participate in all initiatives aimed at countering the advance of the Islamists."[12]

---

11. Willis, *The Islamist Challenge in Algeria: A Political History*, 132–133.
12. Ibid., 254.

High levels of affective and preference polarization foiled any potential democratic transition. Both affective and preference polarization contributed to a lack of cohesion and cooperation among opposition actors, which in turn facilitated military intervention into domestic politics as well as the country's eventual decline into civil war. The "militant secularism" of the RCA and FFS created fostered extremely negative affect towards Islamists, as secular groups were compelled "to back any candidate capable of defeating the Islamists of the FIS which it saw as a far greater threat to Algeria than the FLN. Such a fundamental division on strategy and who the main enemy of the proposed alliance should be, therefore, seemed to ensure that a common front between the parties could not be achieved." Secular opposition groups' affect towards Islamists also manifested in the idea of "one man, one vote, one time," suggesting that once the FIS came to power, it would not govern democratically and would not work with the country's other political actors. Similarly, leading FIS figure Abdelkader Hachani was quoted as saying that the elections had "demonstrated that there are only two parties, the party of God and the party of the Devil ... our fight is between Islamic purity and democratic impurity." FIS leader Belhadj's "hugely popular Friday sermons, which attracted up to 20,000 people each week, were full of denunciations of followers of other religions, liberals, foreign governments and leaders of other parties." FIS leadership similarly portrayed the RCD party as "an arch enemy of Islamism." The FIS appeared not even to recognize the right of non-Islamists to participate in political contestation, and often equated democracy with "unbelief." Ultimately, both secular and Islamist opposition felt extremely negatively and were full of distrust towards each other.[13]

In addition to high levels of affective polarization, the Algerian political scene was highly divided on preferences about the nature of reform, namely in whether it would have an Islamist or secular flavor. The main disagreements revolved around social, cultural, and educational issues, and how these would be enshrined in the constitution or implemented by the government. The FIS advocated conservative ideas about the role of women in society and the need to Islamicize and Arabize the secular and French-dominated education system, presenting a significant departure from the status quo of Algerian politics. When FIS leader Hachani spoke of the party's commitment to guaranteeing individual, collective, and press liberties, he included the conditions "in the framework of Islamic law" and

---

13. Willis, *The Islamist Challenge in Algeria: A Political History*, 145–147.

"in keeping with our Arabo-Islamic principles."[14] In contrast, secular parties such as the PAGS, RCD, and FFS "occupied a diametrically opposed position in the new party-political spectrum to that of FIS."[15]

More recently, Algeria witnessed protests during the 2011 Arab Spring uprising as well as protests spawned by President Abdelaziz Bouteflika's announcement that he would seek a fifth term in office, which have lasted from February through the end of 2019. It remains to be seen whether Algeria's ongoing protests will result in a meaningful democratization. Unfortunately, the high level of polarization among the elites who would navigate the difficult transition appears stacked against its success; by expert accounts, the Algerian political elite remain deeply fractured as a result of previous repression, and this is particularly so among those who are considered opposition rather than elite insiders.[16]

## INDONESIA, 1998–2004

On May 21, 1998, former general Suharto resigned after thirty-one years in office. More than three decades earlier, Suharto had taken advantage of the instability caused by a thwarted Communist coup to seize power for himself, for his Golkar Party, and for the Indonesian military. Suharto's resignation was the culmination of two years of mounting opposition. In 1996, opposition forces began to coalesce around the Indonesian Democratic Party (PDI) and its leader Megawati Sukarnoputri, the daughter of Indonesia's founding president, Sukarno. In July of that year, the military stepped in and brutally repressed demonstrations in support of Megawati, surrounding the headquarters of the PDI in Jakarta. Domestic opposition coincided with increasing international concern about the Indonesian government's human rights violations during its occupation of East Timor and the 1997 Asian financial crisis. In May 1998, massive rioting broke out across the country, which the military and police did not step in to control. Shortly thereafter, Suharto won reelection, but the result was considered to be so fraudulent that rioting escalated and student protesters occupied the parliament. The president then resigned, naming B. J. Habibie of the ruling party as his successor.

14. Ibid., 240

15. Ibid., 145.

16. Karim Mezran and Erin A. Neale, "Algerian Demonstrations: What they mean for the future of the elite and the country," *MENASource: Atlantic Council*, 2019,

Between 1999 and 2004, Indonesia held its first free and fair parliamentary elections, democratized its constitution, and eliminated the military's undemocratic participation in the electoral and legislative processes. Indonesia's political sphere was ideologically diverse: Islamists represented a substantial portion of the opposition, collectively garnering 37.5 percent of the vote in the 1999 elections, compared with 33.7 percent for the largest secular-nationalist opposition party and 22.4 percent for the former ruling party.[17] Despite their ideological differences, the opposition succeeded in pushing forward with the democratization process while resisting reactionary pressures from the armed forces. With the completion of its political transition, Indonesia became the largest Muslim-majority democracy in the world.

If the causal process outlined in this book played a role in Indonesia's transition, we should expect to observe a more widespread repressive environment under authoritarianism, relatively low polarization among the opposition, and cooperation during the transition, to force concessions from the military and to present a cohesive front to the remnants of the old regime.

Established in 1966, Suharto's New Order regime relied primarily on the strength of the armed forces and the cooperation of a narrow civilian elite. The regime created a widespread repressive environment, which affected all opposition parties and movements prior to the events of 1998. Suharto explicitly sought to eliminate mass participation from politics through pervasive state violence.[18] In 1965, General Suharto had established the KOPKAMTIB (*Komando Operasi Pemulihan Keamanan dan Ketertiban*, or Operational Command for the Restoration of Security and Order) to persecute the political left and to monitor suspected dissidents and former political prisoners. As president, Suharto relied on the KOPKAMTIB to physically eliminate leftists and to control the nationalist and Islamist opposition in his effort to impose ideological conformity on the entire population.

To control opposition parties, Suharto forced a merger which created two main opposition blocs as an early survival strategy, ensuring that Golkar never won less than 60 percent of the vote in elections. In January

17. Marcus Mietzner, *Military Politics, Islam, and the State in Indonesia: From Turbulent Transition to Democratic Consolidation* (Institute of Southeast Asian Studies, 2009), 259.

18. Edward Aspinall, *Opposing Suharto: Compromise, Resistance, and Regime Change in Indonesia* (Stanford University Press, 2005), chapter 1.

1973, four Islamist parties were forced to establish the Unity Development Party (PPP) while non-Islamist parties, including unrelated Christian and nationalist parties, were forced to merge into the Indonesian Democratic Party (PDI). The political result of Suharto's reign was the "systematic repression of all social forces and the imposition of a highly manipulated political structure."[19]

Repression effectively stifled direct anti-regime mobilization, but opposition forces nevertheless mounted a growing challenge to Suharto's rule from within societal and state institutions throughout the 1980s and '90s.[20] When mass demonstrations suddenly inaugurated Indonesia's transition to democracy in 1998, the former political opposition was thrust into a newly competitive electoral system. In addition to the former ruling party, Golkar, and the two legal opposition parties, PPP and PDI, members of the country's two largest Islamic organizations, the traditionalist Nahdlatul Ulama (NU) and the modernist Muhammadiyah, also competed for power in the transitional period.

Regardless of their ideological stance, these competing political actors co-existed within the tightly constrained arena of opposition politics. In their collective efforts to push the boundaries of tolerated resistance to the New Order, the mainstream opposition came to identify more closely together with related developments for affect and political preferences. Despite fierce political maneuvering and occasionally violent clashes between their supporters, the opposition generally maintained cordial relations. While the Islamists of the NU and Muhammadiyah had been excluded from party politics under Suharto, their leaders developed cordial relationships, suggesting relatively low affective polarization.[21] For example, NU and Muhammadiyah leaders, Abdurrahman Wahid and Amien Rais, had a public rapprochement in December 1996, suggesting "the possibility of their collaboration."[22] Meanwhile, Wahid and Megawati, second-round competitors in the country's first democratic presidential election in 1999, were described by Wahid's biographer as "old friends" before serving together as president and vice president, respectively.[23]

19. Carmel Budiardjo, "Militarism and Repression in Indonesia," *Third World Quarterly* 8, no. 4 (1986): 1219–1238.

20. Aspinall, *Opposing Suharto: Compromise, resistance, and regime change in Indonesia*, 3–4.

21. Mietzner, *Military Politics*, 275.

22. Greg Barton, *Abdurrahman Wahid, Muslim Democrat, Indonesian President: A View from the Inside* (Sydney: UNSW Press, 2002), 224.

23. Ibid., 19.

Perhaps the most significant factor in the success of the transition was the low level of preference polarization among the opposition regarding the nature of the state in its relation to religion. As in other Muslim-majority countries, Indonesia's transition triggered a major debate over the proper role of Islam in public life and how this would be enshrined in the constitution and in governing structures, which could have gravely undermined elite cooperation in the democratization process. Instead, non-Islamists and Islamists of both the traditionalist and the modernist tendencies embraced similar views about religious pluralism and low support for declaring Indonesia an Islamic state at the moment of transition.[24] The leaders of the NU and Muhammadiyah disagreed ideologically but had both stated their opposition to an Islamic state prior to the transition.[25]

Consistent with the main argument of this book, relatively low affective and preference polarization among the opposition contributed to successful cooperation during the transition period. Even before the 1998 uprising, there had been signs of cooperation among elements of the political opposition. One dissident movement, the Petition-of-50 Group, formed in 1980 to challenge the military's dual function and Suharto's claims to ideological hegemony. Consistently censored in the state-controlled media, the group failed to garner grassroots support, but its pronouncements in favor of multipartism and denunciations of Suharto's repressive excesses indicate the potential for cooperation among the opposition.

When the transition began in 1998, the political sphere was characterized by rivalries and jostling for political advantage, yet the former opposition managed to cooperate toward the goal of advancing the transition. On November 10, 1998, the four most prominent opposition leaders met at Ciganjur and agreed to an eight-point declaration of principles for the Reformasi (reform) movement, including a commitment to the principle of unity in diversity.[26] Despite a long-standing rivalry between the traditionalist and modernist tendencies within the Islamist movement, leaders of the two movements joined forces in 1999 to support the

---

24. Mirjam Künkler, "How Pluralist Democracy Became the Consensual Discourse among Secular and Nonsecular Muslims in Indonesia," in *Democracy and Islam in Indonesia*, ed. Mirjam Künkler and Alfred C. Stepan (Columbia University Press, 2013), 53–72.

25. Greg Barton, "Political Legitimacy in Indonesia: Islam, Democracy, and Good Governance," ed. John Kane, Hui-Chieh Loy, and Haig Patapan (New York: Palgrave Macmillan, 2011), 98.

26. Meredith L. Weiss, "What a Little Democracy Can Do: Comparing Trajectories of Reform in Malaysia and Indonesia," Democratisation 14, no. 1 (2007): 26–43.

presidential bid of Abdurrahman Wahid, the leader of the NU. Wahid's rival to the presidency, PDI leader Megawati, would initially serve as vice president, as their personal relations remained friendly. Although Wahid's imperious governing style would lead to his impeachment after only two years in office, Megawati garnered broad consensus support to serve out the remainder of Wahid's five-year term, completing the successful transition to democracy.

The case of Indonesia may also allay two concerns arising from the case selection of Tunisia and Egypt. First, Tunisia is a relatively small country, with a population of approximately ten million at the time of the 2010– 2011 uprising. This might lead to the critique that widespread repression was more feasible, or that politicians knew each other more intimately with the expected implications for cooperation and compromise, given the relatively small population. In contrast, Indonesia current has a population of 237.4 million, yet similar dynamics played out in this very large country. The Suharto regime undertook widespread repression (given the endowment of pre-independence coercive institutions), which manifested in significantly less affective and preference polarization at the moment of democratic transition.

Second, Egypt's military is often mentioned as a singularly important factor for why the country reverted to authoritarianism. Given the armed forces' large size, substantial economic interests, and close ties to Mubarak and the ruling party, military intervention to overturn Egypt's democratic opening might seem inevitable. Yet the case of Indonesia demonstrates that overturning a military-dominated regime is possible when elite polarization is low, enabling civilian cooperation to check the power of the military. At the moment of transition, the Indonesian military was comparable to Egypt's in terms of its regime ties, force strength, and political influence, and thus its reactionary potential. As in Mubarak's Egypt, politics under Suharto were heavily influenced by the armed forces. In fact, the Indonesian military may have been even more entangled with the regime and thus more invested in its survival than the Egyptian military. Military involvement in Indonesian politics was enshrined in the doctrine of *dwifungsi* (dual function), the idea that the armed forces should control the country's political and social affairs, alongside military and security matters.[27] Suharto cultivated his power through the military, using patronage to maintain military loyalty and appointing thousands of active and retired soldiers to fill

---

27. Harold A. Crouch, *The Army and Politics in Indonesia* (Cornell University Press, 1988).

the ranks of the civilian administration.[28] The Indonesian transition thus took place under the constant threat of military intervention. A dominant political force prior to the transition, the armed forces were forced to acknowledge democratic control in large part because civilian leaders were able to cooperate effectively.[29]

In sum, the Indonesian military thus had the political motivation and the strength to prevent Suharto's departure, but did not. Pairing the Indonesian case with Egypt and Tunisia suggests that a strategic opening, specifically in the form of polarization among non-regime opposition actors, is a necessary condition for the occurrence of a counter-revolutionary coup. The military must be able to pick off civilian elites who support a coup, and this is difficult to do when the opposition is cohesive and demonstrates low levels of polarization. Elite cooperation can be the critical factor in preventing the remilitarization of politics during the difficult transition process.

## Beyond Elites: Elite and Mass Polarization during Democratic Transitions

The book has focused on how polarization among elites organized into political groups, and how this polarization contributes to divergence in transitional outcomes, by conditioning the ability to cooperate and compromise. Here, I explore other channels through which elite polarization may help or hinder transitions. A question that naturally follows from a discussion of elite polarization is whether partisans of these parties are similarly polarized, and in what direction the causal arrow points between mass and elite polarization.

Public opinion collected after the uprisings suggests that partisans in Egypt were more polarized than those in Tunisia on matters of central importance to the transition, those related to religion and politics. The second wave of the Arab Barometer was conducted after the uprisings in 2011 and included two important questions about preferred regime type in both countries. The first question asked respondents about the nature of their preferred state, giving them the option to answer "a civil state" and "a religious state." Egyptian and Tunisian partisans overwhelmingly supported a civil state, at roughly 75 percent in both countries. A follow-up question probed into how respondents defined a civil state. Options

28. Budiardjo, "Militarism and Repression in Indonesia."
29. Mietzner, Military Politics, 6.

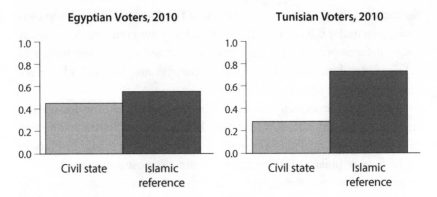

FIGURE 9.1. Voters' Preferences over the Nature of the State in Egypt and Tunisia, 2010 (Source: Arab Barometer)

included the same base definition: "a civil state is one in which the people are the source of power, and the state is governed by the constitution and the law with citizenship being the highest value irrespective of religion or race." Two further options continued, "Islam constitutes its cultural and civilizational frame of reference" or "secularism constitutes its cultural and civilizational background." Egyptian voters were significantly more polarized on this question than Tunisian voters, as demonstrated in figure 9.1. In Egypt, voters were nearly evenly split, divided 44.8 percent in support of a secular civil state and 55.1 percent in support of an Islamic frame of reference. In Tunisia, over 70 percent of voters agreed on an Islamic frame of reference, demonstrating significantly more agreement than Egyptian voters.[30]

These data raise a second question: is mass polarization a cause or a consequence of elite polarization? I side with those scholars who argue that polarization is a top-down process, whereby elites polarize first and then partisans follow. A review of existing studies by Fiorina and Abrams notes that there is "general agreement" that party sorting, and the mass

30. Data collected from the Transitional Governance Project (http://transitional governanceproject.org/) similarly demonstrates higher levels of polarization among Egyptian partisans compared with Tunisian partisans in 2011 using a different method. Respondents were asked to place both themselves and political parties on two axes of competition: the religious-secular and economic divides. With regards to religion and politics, voter self-placement demonstrated less polarization in Tunisia, clustered around a middle point, than in Egypt. Moreover, voters perceived parties to be more polarized on this axis in Egypt than in Tunisia. Voter and party placement on the traditional left-right axis did not demonstrate meaningful distinction between parties in either country.

polarization it implies, is driven by elites.[31] In a review on the study of polarization within the American context, Barber and Nolan Mccarty note that while there may be a feedback loop between parties and constituents, its existence has not been empirically tested or proven.[32] This finding further speaks to ideas embedded in the literature on elite cues and other elite heuristics voters utilize in making choices based on the preference positions of elites they trust or like in making and updating preferences.[33]

Data collected during a particularly momentous period in post-Mubarak Egypt suggests a similar process occurred in Egypt. In 2013, Amaney Jamal, Tarek Masoud, and I inadvertently implemented a survey and two pretests while tumultuous events further polarized Egyptian elites. We designed the survey to measure public opinion on unrelated political topics related to questions of repression and polarization. However, each iteration of the instrument included questions about party and voter placement. Two pretests were conducted on February 5 and 6, 2013, and between June 3 and 9, 2013. Each pretest sampled 400 different Egyptian adults in greater Cairo, encompassing the city of Cairo and the districts of Giza and Qalyub. The full survey, which included a nationally representative sample of 2,596 Egyptian adults, was completed between October 30 and December 5, 2013. For the following analyses, the nationally representative survey was subset to only include greater Cairo to more accurately compare the samples across time periods.

Two trends emerge from the data, though I note these are suggestive, not conclusive, given the small number of voters and the urban skew in the sample. First, voters appear to perceive when elite polarization occurs. All three instruments included the following question: "In politics, people often talk about "secular' and "religious'. Where would you place the following parties on a scale from 0 to 10, where 0 means "secular' and 10 means "religious'?" Figure 9.2 plots the average answer for respondents who reported voting in the 2011–2012 parliamentary elections for the six

31. Fiorina and Abrams, "Political polarization in the American Public," 581.

32. Michael Barber and Nolan McCarty, "Causes and Consequences of Political Polarization," in *Political Negotiation: A Handbook*, ed. Jane Mansbridge and Cathie to Martin (Washrington: Brookings Institution Press, 2015).

33. Jeffrey J. Mondak, "Candidate Perception in an Ambiguous World: Campaigns, cues, and inference processes." *American Journal of Political Science* 33, no. 4 (1989): 912–940; Lupia andMcCubbins, *The Democratic Dilemma: Can Citizens Learn What They Need to Know*?; Jeffrey J.Mondak, "Public Opinion and Heuristic Processing of Source Cues," *Political Behavior* 15, no. 2 (1993): 167–192.

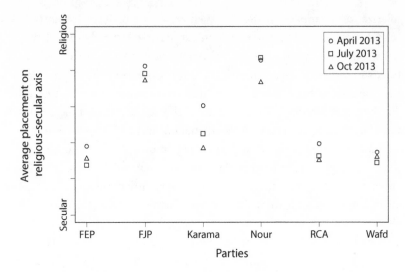

FIGURE 9.2. Party Placement in Egypt, 2013 (Source: Jamal, Masoud, and Nugent)

parties asked across the three surveys. Though the movement is some-what small, it does appear that voters perceive of polarization increasing among political parties during a tumultuous period. For example, the average placement of Islamist parties—namely, the FJP and Nour—was more distant from the placement of secular parties—the FEP, Karama, RCA, and Wafd—in October 2013 than earlier in the same year. This is evident in the average placement of secular parties increasing in distance from that of Islamists.

Second, voters appear to respond to elite polarization, and tend to place themselves further away from the parties for which they did not vote as they perceive polarization to be increasing. In addition to the question outlined in the previous paragraph, asking about party placement on the religious-secular divide, respondents were also asked to place themselves on the same axis. I limited the sample to those who voted in the 2011–2012 legislative elections, and further divided the sample into those who voted for secular parties and those who voted for the FJP in the elections.[34] Figure 9.3 plots the average distance from each party among secular and Islamist voters. Though there is a lot of noise, certain patterns emerge. For example, Islamist voters consistently place themselves closer to the FJP and Nour Parties, while secular voters place themselves closer to secular parties. In

34. I excluded Nour voters and placement for this analysis, given how their position with regards to both Islamism and the Muslim Brotherhood was complicated during this time period.

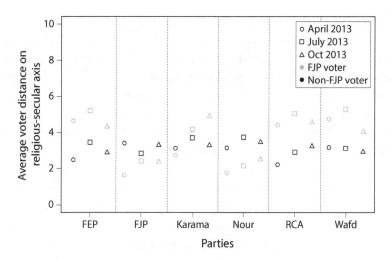

FIGURE 9.3. Party Placement in Egypt by Vote Choice, 2013 (Source: Jamal, Masoud, and Nugent)

addition, Islamist voters distance themselves from secular parties as polarization peaks in Egypt over the course of 2013. This trend is most evident for the Karama Party, but there is also a sharp increase in distance between Islamist and secular parties immediately after the 2013 coup. In combination, these data suggest that higher levels of mass polarization in Egypt than in Tunisia may have been an artifact of variation in elite polarization, rather than a cause of it.

In addition, established literature supports the idea that parties are not catering to the policy preferences of voters in moments of transition—and, indeed, may be shaping the electorate's preferences as well as the distribution of said preferences. The body of work on elections under authoritarian regimes suggests that individuals are not making choices about policies or politicians in these kinds of contests.[35] Rather, individuals vote either to accrue material benefits from opposition or ruling parties,[36] or to bravely signal disapproval of the regime.[37] This is not to say that individual policy

35. Jennifer Gandhi and Ellen Lust-Okar, "Authoritarian Institutions and the Survival of Autocrats," Annual Review of Political Science 12 (2009): 403–422

36. Magaloni, *Voting for Autocracy: Hegemonic Party Survival and its Demise in Mexico*; Susan C. Stokes, "Political Clientelism," in *The Oxford Handbook of Political Science* (2007); Lust, "Competitive Clientelism in the Middle East"; Blaydes, *Elections and Distributive Politics in Mubarak's Egypt*.

37. But see Carolina de Miguel, Amaney Jamal, andMark Tessler, "Elections in the Arab-World: WhyDo Citizens Turn Out?," *Comparative Political Studies* 48, no. 11 (2016): 1355–1388

preferences did not matter before 2011 in either of these countries, only that they were underdeveloped in systems where vote choice and political competition were not based on and did not offer substantive differences in policies by design of electoral authoritarianism.

This was reiterated to me during interviews with the political strategists of main parties in both countries, who revealed that parties were not primarily catering to voters during elections in the early transition period. While all parties issued political platforms articulating a set of policy preferences to voters, these references largely reflected those of the party's elite members and leadership rather than current or potential constituencies. Part of this was unfamiliarity with the electorate, particularly for newly formed or newly mobilizing parties.[38] Within the Muslim Brotherhood, drafting the 2011 platform was a top-down approach; the preferences of the Guidance Bureau were those articulated with little feedback even from lower levels of membership.[39]

The process had been similar before the uprisings. As early as March 1984, Umar al-Tilmisani was quoted in an interview as saying, "The only thing the Brotherhood cares about is the spread of its ideas."[40] In one particularly illuminating quote, Amr Darrag, a member of the political committee charged with drafting the Brotherhood's platforms, said, "Of course you want to attract people to elect you, definitely. But you don't just want any voters. You want voters who believe in your idea and are proponents of what you believe. These are the kinds of people you are interested in, and you want to spread these ideas so more people are convinced."[41] When opposition parties did utilize public opinion polling, questions included vote choice rather than support for specific policies.

---

for an analysis that takes seriously policy preferences as a motivation for voter turnout in authoritarian regimes.

38. Mohamed Nour. Interview with the author, May 25, 2012. Cairo, Egypt. Nour was a chief strategist for the Nour Party's parliamentary campaign in 2012.

39. Husayn al-Qazzaz. Interview with the author, June 15, 2016. Istanbul, Turkey. Al-Qazzaz was a long-term advisor to senior members of the Muslim Brotherhood, including President Morsi, and a close friend and confidant of Khairat al-Shater. Referring to the 2000s, he said that,"all the political behavior throughout this period was the direct outcome of the preferences of the leadership of the Ikhwan. There wasn't room for anyone to maneuver alone."

40. Wickham, *Muslim Brotherhood*, 49.

41. Amr Darrag. Interview with the author, June 13, 2016. Istanbul, Turkey. Darrag served as a member of the organization's political committee from 2002 to 2006, and was a founding member of the Muslim Brotherhood's Freedom and Justice Party.

## Beyond Transitions: Identity and Polarization in Democratic Politics

In the previous pages, I developed and tested an original theory of polarization under authoritarianism. In these contexts, the nature of state repression of opposition—i.e., whether it targets a specific group, or is more widespread—alters group members' level of in-group identification, in turn changing the perceived distance between groups, and ultimately shaping the level of affective and preference polarization among these groups through established processes of preference formation and group differentiation. In my story, the degree of polarization at the moment of potential democratic transition, as conditioned by the nature of repression in a given system, helps to explain why and when elites are able to compromise, cooperate, and continue the country's path towards democratic consolidation, and when polarized identities and preferences among elites facilitates the rapid reentrenchment of authoritarianism. My theory intends to expand our collective understanding of how authoritarian legacies set the sociological stage for transitions, and how these legacies can sow seeds among political actors that undermine democratic consolidation. I hope I have done so in a way that moves our collective understanding of polarization beyond explanations rooted in structure, strategy, or ideology.

Future work might expand the scope of analysis beyond authoritarian republics. First, scholars should investigate whether these processes occur in other types of authoritarian regimes. Monarchies have specific systems of legitimization in which the regime relies on more fractured opposition[42] and which thus witnesses relationships between the regime, repression, and other methods of control in a manner which systematically differs from republics. Additional contexts of inquiry might also include totalitarian regimes, where repression is widespread but much more violent. In these contexts, widespread victimization may ultimately create less polarized societies through the process outlined in this book.

Second, future work might also explore different kinds of transitions. In this book, I have focused on transitions by rupture, where the opposition is primarily in charge of navigating the early transition period, but similar dynamics may also exist in transitions where the regime is more present,

---

42. Lust-Okar and Jamal, "Rulers and Rules."

such as pacted or negotiated transitions.[43] Scholars might also investigate whether transitions from colonialism contain similar dynamics. In certain colonial contexts, some political groups were targeted with violence while others were co-opted by colonizing forces, and undoubtedly this affected the conflictual nature of political identities, the nature of the transition, and perhaps even the structures of post-colonial states with long-term implications for state violence and state collapse.[44]

Third, future research might compare whether similar dynamics exist in democratic contexts. I have focused here on authoritarian regimes because they are defined by repression of political opposition and are most likely cases to observe effects.[45] In contrast, democracies do not have the same relationship between state use of repression and control of political opposition, but many democratic regimes do sometimes use violence to maintain themselves against mobilized opposition. For example, democratic regimes often respond with violence to groups representing marginalized segments of society (such as students, racial and ethnic minority groups, immigrants, and women) and utilizing extrapolitical oppositional, mobilizational, and protest tactics. These state reactions may be less frequent or severe than commonplace behaviors in authoritarian contexts, but they are nonetheless coercive and may have the same effect on group identities, group-related preferences, and the relative placement of these preferences vis-à-vis other targeted and non-targeted groups. Studies of politics in the United States have more thoroughly incorporated the ideas I reference in this book, notably the importance of preference formation to the politicization, mobilization, and preference coherence of identity-based political groups. But scholars should continue to think about these processes outside of the United States and other consolidated democracies in the West.

Repression, polarization, and identity politics are global phenomena, and similar questions can and should be asked in different contexts. Scholars must recognize that political outcomes involving human actors are at least partially determined by the political identities of those actors. Our collective understanding of a wide variety of political developments must be

43. Rustow, "Transitions to Democracy"; O'Donnell, Schmitter, and Arnson, *Conclusions*; Alfred C. Stepan, *Democratizing Brazil: Problems of Transition and Consolidation* (New York: Oxford University Press, 1989).

44. Mahmood Mamdani, *When Victims Become Killers: Colonialism, Nativism, and the Genocide in Rwanda* (Princeton University Press, 2014) suggests this is a difficult yet fruitful avenue of research in post-colonial states.

45. Linz, *Totalitarian and Authoritarian Regimes*.

updated to reflect the central role of identity in creating and exacerbating disagreement. Political polarization is critical for the cooperative outcomes central not only to transitions from authoritarianism but also to politics in consolidated and consolidating democracies. Recognizing that polarization is a result of an iterative identity-based process in which repression features heavily may help leaders and populations to overcome seemingly impossible political divides.

# APPENDIX

## Institutional Review Board Approvals

My interviews were covered by protocol number 6889 approved by the Institutional Review Board at Princeton University. The experiments were covered by protocol number 7349 approved by the same board.

## Additional Information on Experiment

I conducted the lab expermients in partnership with One-to-One for Research and Polling, an independent research company based in Tunis. The lab experiments were conducted with a sample of 434 Tunisian adult citizens between May 13 to 20, 2016. No sessions were run on May 14 or May 15, as these days fell on the weekend. The first ten sessions ($n = 49$ respondents) were conducted at a small conference hall rented by my partner firm at the Yadis Ibn Khaldoun hotel, located at 30 Rue Kuwait in the Lafayette neighborhood of Tunis. Due to an unforeseen scheduling issue, the remaining seventy-nine sessions ($n = 385$ respondents) were conducted at a rented space located at 9 Avenue de Madrid in the Bab al-Khadra neighborhood of Tunis. The space is situated close to the *Place de la République* train station, commonly known as *Le Passage*, a busy central station on Avenue de la Liberté. The location of each respondent's session was controlled for in analyses and was not found to have any significant influence on the results. Experiments were conducted between 8:30 a.m. and 7:30 p.m. in order to recruit a diverse group of Tunisians passing through the busy neighborhood.

A rotating, mixed-gender team of four enumerators positioned themselves outside of the space to recruit participants. Recruited individuals were asked if they were willing to spend roughly thirty minutes completing an exercise about Tunisian society and were required to be over eighteen years old to participate. Potential participants were not told that they would be compensated for their time. A session began when five respondents had been recruited. Each respondent was paired with an enumerator who read the instrument to the respondent and filled out the answers on a tablet computer. Prior to fielding, I worked closely with a team of One-to-One staff to translate the instrument into Tunisian Arabic. During the experiments, I occupied a private office in the back of the rented space. I was not visible to participants but could check in with enumerators at the conclusion of each session.

I recruited "ordinary" Tunisian private citizens for logistical and ethical reasons. First, I believe the theory outlined above to be a generalizable process due to its robustness in social psychology and should occur with all types of individuals. A recent meta-analysis confirms that political scientists largely overstate the magnitude of elite-public gaps in decision making.[1] As such, participants drawn from the political elite are not necessary in experiments. In addition, Tunisian politicians were continuing to navigate the difficult political challenges of democratic transition during the period in which I conducted my experiments and I did not want to take up their valuable time.

The covariates included in regressions incorporate a number of attitudinal, demographic, and enumerator measurements. First, a respondent's relevant pre-treatment preferences were included; this was the respondent's level of agreement with the statement, "The government should take an active role in the economy instead of allowing for a free market economy," and the respondent's level of agreement with the statement, "The government and parliament should enact legislation according to Islamic law." In addition, a number of demographic controls were included. These variables captured the respondent's self-reported employment status, level of education, household income, and frequency of attendance at Friday prayer and Qur'an readership. Another set of covariates included pre-treatment "groupness" variables, including self-reported current group membership (coded as 1 if the respondent reported being a member of a political, social, or economic group) as well as levels of general trust. I also included enumerator gender and, if female, whether the enumerator wore a veil in order to control for related enumerator effects that may influence individual answers related to identification and trust.[2]

1. Joshua D. Kertzer, "Re-Assessing Elite-Public Gaps in Political Behavior," Working Paper, 2019.

2. Lisa Blaydes and Rachel M. Gillum, "Religiosity-of-interviewer Effects: Assessing the impact of veiled enumerators on survey response in Egypt," *Politics and Religion* 6, no. 3 (2013): 459–482.

In models using the pooled data, a dummy variable for group assignment was included (coded as 1 if the respondent was assigned to the religion and politics group), and all standard errors are clustered by the respondent's session.

## Coding of 2011 Party Platforms (figure 8.1)

In order to compare party platforms in Egypt and Tunisia, I devise a coding scheme to rank manifestos based on parties' stated policy preferences related to religion and politics. Similar to the Manifesto Project, I consider the manifestos, official statements, and platforms released during electoral competition to be parties' "only ... main authoritative policy statements and, therefore, as indicators of the parties' policy preferences at a given point in time."

The parties' political preferences related to religion and politics are shaped by debates about the politics of Islam and secularism in Muslim societies. I outline these complex concepts here in detail; it is important to correctly define them in order to correctly measure them and their political impact.[3] At the highest level of abstraction, secularism is situated at one end of the spectrum as the notion of separation between religion and politics. At the other end of the spectrum lies Islamism, the notion that the religion's tenets as outlined in the shari'a should serve as the basis of political legitimacy. Similar debates occur in non-Muslim societies between those seeking a total separation of religion and politics and those seeking a politics guided or influenced by Judaism, Christianity, or other religious ideologies. Here, I isolate Islam because I am specifically interested in the political ideologies and philosophies it has generated, and in notions of secularism contrasted against it. While Asad has argued that the secular and the religious exist as two distinct modes of being in the world, the real-world political application of these concepts is better thought of as a spectrum along which individuals and parties can have varying degrees of different preferences.[4]

In debates on secularism and Islamism, there are three main ways in which differences between these two different types of systems are manifested that can be summarized by answers to the *What?*, *Who?*, and

3. C. Christine Fair, Rebecca Littman, and Elizabeth R. Nugent, "Conceptions of Shari'a and Support for Militancy and Democratic Values: Evidence from Pakistan," *Political Science Research and Methods* 6, no. 3 (2018): 429–448.

4. Asad, *Formations of the Secular: Christianity, Islam, Modernity*.

*How?*[5] First, parties' preferences regarding religion and politics can differ in terms of the basis of legislation and guiding laws (*what* is being enforced in terms of religion and politics). This refers to whether the basis of law is secular principles, or Islamist and Qur'anic principles.

|        | Islamist                                              | Secularist                                                            |
|--------|-------------------------------------------------------|----------------------------------------------------------------------|
| High   | Strict interpretation of shari'a (total application)  | Strict interpretation of secularism (total division of religion and politics) |
| Medium | Some application of specific shari'a principles        | Some application of division of religion and politics                |
| Low    | Generally based on Islamic principles                 | Generally based on secular principles                                |

Second, parties' preferences regarding religion and politics can differ in terms of the role of religious institutions (a question of *who* is doing the enforcing). For secularists, this is the extent to which secular, state institutions have oversight over religious ones, while for Islamists, this is the extent to which religious institutions have oversight over political ones.

|        | Islamist                              | Secularist                            |
|--------|---------------------------------------|---------------------------------------|
| High   | Full religious institutional oversight | Full state institutional oversight    |
| Medium | Some religious institutional oversight | Some religious institutional oversight |
| Low    | Low religious institutional oversight  | Low state institutional oversight     |

Third, parties' preferences regarding religion and politics can differ in terms of the strength of state involvement in enforcing laws, grounded in religious or Islamic justification, answering the question of *how*. For secularists, this is the extent to which the state institutions can enforce the separation of religion and politics and how much it can infringe on individual liberties in doing so. Conversely for Islamists, this is the extent to which state institutions can force the integration or independence of religion into

---

5. Additional nuances that are secondary to this typology might include answers to the questions of *Where?* and *When?* for notions of secularism, most important for a mixed system in which certain kinds of laws only apply in certain times or places. In addition, another consideration would be *Whose?* interpretation of secularism or Islamism is applied within systems of law.

and over politics, and how much it can infringe on individual liberties in doing so.

|        | Islamist                                                     | Secularist                                                   |
|--------|--------------------------------------------------------------|--------------------------------------------------------------|
| High   | Strong state intervention                                    | Strong state intervention                                    |
| Medium | Some state intervention                                      | Some state intervention                                      |
| Low    | Low state intervention; focus on individual liberties and choice | Low state intervention; focus on individual liberties and choice |

These three components combine to form the following typology and coding scheme:

|               | Basis of law | Institutional oversight | Strength of state intervention |
|---------------|--------------|-------------------------|--------------------------------|
| *More Islamist* |              |                         |                                |
| 10            | High         | High                    | High                           |
| 9             |              | *2 High Scores*         |                                |
| 8             | Medium       | Medium                  | Medium                         |
| 7             |              | *2 Medium Scores*       |                                |
| 6             | Low          | Low                     | Low                            |
| 5             |              | *No mention of religion & politics* |                    |
| 4             | Low          | Low                     | Low                            |
| 3             |              | *2 Medium Scores*       |                                |
| 2             | Medium       | Medium                  | Medium                         |
| 1             |              | *2 High Scores*         |                                |
| 0             | High         | High                    | High                           |
| *More Secular* |              |                         |                                |

# BIBLIOGRAPHY

Abbou, Mohamed. *Majalat qabla ath-thawra*. Tunis: Sotepa Graphic, 2014.

Abdalla, Ahmed. "Egypt's Islamists and the State: From Complicity to Confrontation." *Middle East Report* 23 (1993).

Abed-Kotob, Sana. "The Accommodationists Speak: Goals and Strategies of the Muslim Brotherhood in Egypt." *International Journal of Middle East Studies* 27, no. 3 (1995): 321–339.

Abramowitz, Alan L. *The Disappearing Center: Engaged Citizens, Polarization, and American Democracy*. New Haven: Yale University Press, 2010.

Aburish, Said K. *Nasser, the Last Arab*. New York: St. Martin's Press, 2004.

Acemoglu, Daron, Simon Johnson, and James A. Robinson. "The Colonial Origins of Comparative Development: An Empirical Investigation." *National Bureau of Economic Research*, 2000.

Achen, Christopher H., and Larry M. Bartels. *Democracy for Realists: Why Elections Do Not Produce Responsive Government*. Princeton University Press, 2017.

Adams, James, and Zeynep Somer-Topcu. "Do Parties Adjust Their Policies in Response to Rival Parties' Policy Shifts? Spatial Theory and the Dynamics of Party Competition in Twenty-Five Postwar Democracies." *British Journal of Political Science* 39 (2009): 825–846.

Ahmed, Leila. *A Quiet Revolution*. New Haven: Yale University Press, 2012.

Alani, Aliya. *Al-Islamiyun al-Tunisiyun min al-Mu'arada ila al-hukm: al-Nasha', al-Tatawwur, al-Afaq*. Tunis: Sharikat al-'Amal, 2014.

Albrecht, Holger. "How Can Opposition Support Authoritarianism? Lessons from Egypt." *Democratization* 12, no. 3 (2006): 378–397.

———. "Political Opposition and Arab Authoritarianism: Some Conceptual Remarks." In *Contentious Politics in the Middle East: Political Opposition under Authoritarianism*, edited by Holger Albrecht, 17–33. Gainesville: University Press of Florida, 2010.

———. "The Myth of Coup-Proofing: Risk and Instances of Military Coups d'État in the Middle East and North Africa, 1950–2013." *Armed Forces & Society* 41, no. 4 (2015): 659–687.

Alexander, Christopher. *Tunisia: Stability and Reform in the Modern Maghreb*. New York: Routledge, 2010.

Allport, Gordon W. *The Nature of Prejudice*. Reading, Massachusetts: Addison-Wesley, 1979.

Anani, Khalil al-. *Inside the Muslim Brotherhood: Religion, Identity, and Politics*. Oxford University Press, 2016.

Anderson, David M., and David Killingray. "Consent, Coercion and Colonial Control: Policing the Empire, 1830–1940." In *Policing the Empire: Government, Authority, and Control, 1830–1940*, edited by David M. Anderson and David Killingray. Manchester University Press, 1991.

Anderson, Julie. *Intelligence and Democracy: A Russian case study of secret police transformation in the post-Soviet context*. PhD diss., City University of New York, 2008.

Anderson, Lisa. *The State and Social Transformation in Tunisia and Libya, 1830–1980*. Princeton: Princeton University Press, 1986.

Ansari, Hamied. *Egypt: The Stalled Society*. SUNY Press, 1986.

Arendt, Hannah. *The Origins of Totalitarianism*. New York: Harcourt, Brace/World, 1966.

Arenhövel, Mark. "Democratization and Transitional Justice." *Democratisation* 15, no. 3 (2008): 570–587.

Arnold, David. *Police Power and Colonial Rule: Madras, 1859–1947*. Oxford University Press, 1986.

Asad, Talal. *Formations of the Secular: Christianity, Islam, Modernity*. Stanford, California: Stanford University Press, 2003.

Aspinall, Edward. *Opposing Suharto: Compromise, Resistance, and Regime Change in Indonesia*. Stanford University Press, 2005.

Awadi, Hesham al-. *In Pursuit of Legitimacy: The Muslim Brothers and Mubarak, 1982–2000*. London: Taurus, 2004.

Badran, Margot. "Speaking Straight: Four Women of Egypt." *Al Jadid Magazine* 4, no. 25 (1998).

Badrawi, Malak. *Political Violence in Egypt 1910–1925: Secret Societies, Plots and Assassinations*. Routledge, 2014.

Baker, Raymond William. *Sadat and After: Struggles for Egypt's Political Soul*. Harvard University Press, 1990.

Balandier, Georges. *The Sociology of Black Africa: Social Dynamics in Central Africa*. New York: Praeger, 1970.

Balcells, Laia. "The Consequences of Victimization on Political Identities: Evidence from Spain." *Politics & Society* 40, no. 3 (2012): 311–347.

Balliet, Daniel, Junhui Wu, and Carsten K. W. De Dreu. "Ingroup Favoritism in Cooperation: A Meta Analysis." *Psychological Bulletin* 140, no. 6 (2014): 1556.

Barber, Michael, and Nolan McCarty. "Causes and Consequences of Political Polarization." In *Political Negotiation: A Handbook*, edited by Jane Mansbridge and Cathie Jo Martin. Washington: Brookings Institution Press, 2015.

Barclay, Fiona, Charlotte Ann Chopin, and Martin Evans. "Introduction: Settler Colonialism and French Algeria." *Settler Colonial Studies* 8, no. 2 (2018): 115–130.

Baron, Reuben M., and David A. Kenny. "The Moderator-Mediator Variable Distinction in Social Psychological Research—Conceptual, Strategic, and Statistical Considerations." *Journal of Personality and Social Psychology* 51, no. 6 (1986): 1173–1182.

Barros, Robert. *Constitutionalism and Dictatorship: Pinochet, the Junta, and the 1980 Constitution*. Cambridge University Press, 2002.

Barton, Greg. *Abdurrahman Wahid, Muslim Democrat, Indonesian President: A View from the Inside*. Sydney: UNSW Press, 2002.

———. "Political Legitimacy in Indonesia: Islam, Democracy, and Good Governance," edited by John Kane, Hui-Chieh Loy, and Haig Patapan, 85–104. New York: Palgrave Macmillan, 2011.

Bastian, Brock, Jolanda Jetten, and Laura J. Ferris. "Pain as Social Glue: Shared Pain Increases Cooperation." *Psychological Science*, 2014, 1–7.

Bayly, Christopher A. *Empire and Information: Intelligence Gathering and Social Communication in India, 1780–1870*. Cambridge: Cambridge University Press, 1999.

Beissinger, Mark R., Amaney A. Jamal, and Kevin Mazur. "Explaining Divergent Revolutionary Coalitions: Regime Strategies and the Structuring of Participation in the Tunisian and Egyptian Revolutions." *Comparative Politics* 48, no. 1 (2015): 1–24.

Bellin, Eva. "Reconsidering the Robustness of Authoritarianism in the Middle East: Lessons from the Arab Spring." *Comparative Politics* 44, no. 2 (2012): 127–149.

———. "The Robustness of Authoritarianism in the Middle East: Exceptionalism in Comparative Perspective." *Comparative Politics* 36, no. 2 (2004): 139–157.

Ben Salem, Maryam. "The National Dialogue, Collusive Transactions and Government Legitimacy in Tunisia." *International Spectator* 51, no. 1 (2016): 99–112.

Bennett, Andrew, and Jeffrey T. Checkel. *Process Tracing: From Metaphor to Analytic Tool.* Cambridge: Cambridge University Press, 2014.

Berger, Jonah, and Katherine L. Milkman. "What Makes Online Content Viral?" *Journal of Marketing Research* 2, no. 49 (2012): 192–205.

Bermeo, Nancy. "On Democratic Backsliding." *Journal of Democracy* 27, no. 1 (2016): 5–19.

Bernault, Florence. *A History of Prison and Confinement in Africa.* Portsmouth, New Hampshire: Heinemann, 2003.

Best, Heinrich. "Transitions, Transformations, and the Role of Elites." *Historical Social Research* 35, no. 2 (2010): 9–12.

Blanchard, Emmanuel. "French Colonial Police." In *Encyclopedia of Criminology and Criminal Justice,* edited by Gerben Bruinsma and David Weisburd, 1836–1846. New York: Springer, 2014.

Blaydes, Lisa. *Elections and Distributive Politics in Mubarak's Egypt.* New York: Cambridge University Press, 2011.

———. *State of Repression: Iraq under Saddam Hussein.* Princeton University Press, 2018.

Blaydes, Lisa, and Rachel M. Gillum. "Religiosity-of-interviewer Effects: Assessing the impact of veiled enumerators on survey response in Egypt." *Politics and Religion* 6, no. 3 (2013): 459–482.

Blondel, Jean, and Ferdinand Müller-Rommel. "Political Elites." In *The Oxford Handbook of Political Behavior,* edited by Russell J. Dalton and Hans-Dieter Klingemann. Oxford University Press, 2007.

Boix, Carles. *Democracy and Redistribution.* New York: Cambridge University Press, 2003.

Boix, Carles, and Susan C. Stokes. "Endogenous Democratization." *World Politics* 55, no. 4 (2003): 517–549.

Bougher, Lori D. "The Correlates of Discord: Identity, Issue Alignment, and Political Hostility in Polarized America." *Political Behavior* 39, no. 3 (2017): 731–762.

Bratton, Michael, and Nicholas van de Walle. *Democratic Experiments in Africa: Regime Transitions in Comparative Perspective.* New York: Cambridge University Press, 1997.

Brewer, Marilynn B. "When Contact is Not Enough: Social Identity and Intergroup Cooperation." *International Journal of Intercultural Relations* 20, nos. 3/4 (1996): 291–303.

Brewer, Marilynn B., and Michael D. Silver. "Group Distinctiveness, Social Identity, and Collective Mobilization." In *Self, Identity, and Social Movement,* edited by Sheldon Stryker, Timothy J. Owens, and Robert W. White. Minneapolis: University of Minnesota Press, 2000.

Brewer, Marilynn B., and Rupert J. Brown. "Intergroup Conflict." In *The Handbook of Social Psychology: Fourth Edition,* edited by Daniel T. Gilbert, Susan T. Fiske, and Gardner Lindzey, 554–594. Boston: McGraw-Hill, 1998.

Brewer, Michelle B. "Ingroup Bias in the Minimal Intergroup Situation: A Cognitive Motivational Analysis." *Psychological Bulletin* 82, no. 2 (1979): 475–482.

Brooks, Risa. "Abandoned at the Palace: Why the Tunisian Military Defected from the Ben Ali Regime in January 2011." *Journal of Strategic Studies* 36, no. 2 (2013): 205–220.

Brown, Nathan J. *When Victory Is Not an Option: Islamist Movements in Arab Politics.* Cornell University Press, 2012.

Brown, Nathan. "Brigands and State Building: The Invention of Banditry in Modern Egypt." *Comparative Studies in Society and History* 32, no. 2 (1990): 258–281.

Brown, N. R., P. J. Lee, M. Krsiak, F. G. Conrad, J. Havelka, and J. R. Reddon. "Living in History: How War, Terrorism, and Natural Disaster Affect the Organization of Autobiographical Memory." *Psychological Science* 20 (2009): 399–405.

Brownlee, Jason. *Authoritarianism in an Age of Democratization*. New York: Cambridge University Press, 2007.

———. "The Decline of Pluralism in Mubarak's Egypt." *Journal of Democracy* 13, no. 4 (2002): 6–14.

Brownlee, Jason, Tarek E. Masoud, and Andrew Reynolds. *The Arab Spring: Pathways of Repression and Reform*. New York: Oxford University Press, 2015.

Budiardjo, Carmel. "Militarism and Repression in Indonesia." *Third World Quarterly* 8, no. 4 (1986): 1219–1238.

Callahan, Mary. *Making Enemies: War and State-Building in Burma*. Ithaca: Cornell University Press, 2003.

Cammett, Melani, and Pauline Jones Luong. "Is There an Islamist Political Advantage?" *Annual Review of Political Science* 17 (2014): 187–206.

Campagna, Joel. "From Accommodation to Confrontation: The Muslim Brotherhood in the Mubarak Years." *Journal of International Affairs* 50, no. 1 (1996): 278–304.

Campbell, Angus, Philip Converse, Warren Miller, and Donald Stokes. *The American Voter*. New York: John Wiley, 1960.

Campbell, Donald T. "Common Fate, Similarity, and Other Indices of the State of Aggregates of Persons as Social Entities." *Behavioral Science* 1, no. 3 (1958): 14–25.

Campbell, Donald. *Ethnocentric and Other Altruistic Motives*. Lincoln, Nebraska: University of Nebraska Press, 1965.

Careja, Romana, and Patrick Emmenegger. "Making Democratic Citizens: The Effects of Migration Experience on Political Attitudes in Central and Eastern Europe." *Comparative Political Studies* 45, no. 7 (2012): 875–902.

Cavatorta, Francesco, and Fabio Merone. "Moderation through Exclusion? The Journey of the Tunisian Ennahda from Fundamentalist to Conservative Party." *Democratization* 20, no. 5 (2013): 857–875.

Chandra, Kanchan. *Constructivist Theories of Ethnic Politics*. New York: Oxford University Press, 2012.

Chauvet, Lisa, Flore Gubert, and Sandrine Mesplé-Somps. "Do Migrants Adopt New Political Attitudes from Abroad? Evidence using a multi-sited exit-poll survey during the 2013 Malian elections." *Comparative Migration Studies* 4, no. 1 (2016): 19.

Chomiak, Laryssa. *Deliberative Resistance: Dissent and Democracy in Tunisia*. Book manuscript, 2016.

Clark, Janine Astrid. "The Conditions of Islamist Moderation: Unpacking Cross-Ideological Cooperation in Jordan." *International Journal of Middle East Studies* 38, no. 4 (2006): 539–60.

Collier, David. "Understanding Process Tracing." *PS: Political Science and Politics* 44, no. 4 (2011): 823–830.

Collier, David, Henry R. Brady, and Jason Seawright. "Sources of Leverage in Causal Inference: Toward an Alternative View of Methodology." In *Rethinking Social Inquiry: Diverse Tools, Shared Standards*, edited by Henry E. Brady and David Collier. Lanham, Maryland: Rowman/Littlefield, 2010.

Collier, Ruth Berins. *Paths toward Democracy: The Working Class and Elites in Western Europe and South America*. Cambridge University Press, 1999.

Cook, Steven A. *Ruling But Not Governing: The Military and Political Development in Egypt, Algeria, and Turkey*. Baltimore: Johns Hopkins University Press, 2007.

Cox, Gary W. "Electoral Equilibria Under Alternative Voting Institutions." *American Journal of Political Science* 31, no. 1 (1987): 82–108.

Crouch, Harold A. *The Army and Politics in Indonesia*. Cornell University Press, 1988.

Crowder, Michael. "Indirect rule—French and British style." *Africa* 34, no. 3 (1964): 197–205.

Cummings, Elizabeth. *The Spark That Lit the Flame: The Creation, Deployment, and Deconstruction of the Story of Mohammed Bouazizi and the Arab Spring.* PhD diss., City University of New York 2015.

Davenport, Christian. *How Social Movements Die: Repression and Demobilization of the Republic of New Africa.* New York: Cambridge University Press, 2015.

———. "State Repression and Political Order." *Annual Review of Political Science* 10 (2007): 1–23.

de Miguel, Carolina, Amaney Jamal, and Mark Tessler. "Elections in the Arab World: Why Do Citizens Turn Out?" *Comparative Political Studies* 48, no. 11 (2016): 1355–1388.

Deegan-Krause, Kevin. "New Dimensions of Political Cleavage." In *Oxford Handbook of Political Science*, edited by R. Dalton and H.-D. Klingemann. Oxford: Oxford University Press, 2006.

Di Palma, Giuseppe. *To Craft Democracies: An Essay on Democratic Transitions.* University of California Press, 1990.

Diamond, Larry J. "Thinking about Hybrid Regimes." *Journal of Democracy* 13, no. 2 (2002): 21–35.

Diamond, Larry. *Developing Democracy: Toward Consolidation.* Baltimore: Johns Hopkins University Press, 1999.

Druckman, James N., and Arthur Lupia. "Preference Formation." *American Review of Political Science* 3, no. 1 (2000): 1–24.

Durkheim, Émile. *The Elementary Forms of Religious Life.* New York: Oxford University Press, 2001 (1912).

Eck, Kristine. "The Origins of Policing Institutions: Legacies of Colonial Insurgency." *Journal of Peace Research* 55, no. 2 (2018): 147–160.

Ellemers, Naomi, Russell Spears, and Bertjan Doosje. "Self and Social Identity." *Annual Review of Psychology* 53, no. 1 (2002): 161–186.

Ellis, Christopher, and James A. Stimson. *Ideology in America.* Cambridge University Press, 2012.

Epstein, David L., Robert Bates, Jack Goldstone, Ida Kristensen, and Sharyn O'Halloran. "Democratic Transitions." *American Journal of Political Science* 50, no. 3 (2006): 551–569.

Esposito, John L. *Islam and Politics.* Syracuse University Press, 1998.

Evans, Geoffrey, and Stephen Whitefield. "Explaining the Formation of Electoral Cleavages in Post-Communist Democracies." *Elections in Central and Eastern Europe: The First Wave*, 2000, 36–70.

Fair, C. Christine, Rebecca Littman, and Elizabeth R. Nugent. "Conceptions of Shari'a and Support for Militancy and Democratic Values: Evidence from Pakistan." *Political Science Research and Methods* 6, no. 3 (2018): 429–448.

Ferris, John. "Intelligence." In *The Origins of World War Two: The Debate Continues*, edited by Robert Boyce and Joseph A. Maiolo. Basingstoke: Palgrave, 2003.

Fiorina, Morris P., and Samuel L. Abrams. "Political Polarization in the American Public." *Annual Review of Political Science* 11 (2008): 563–588.

Free, Lloyd A., and Hadley Cantril. *Political Beliefs of Americans: A Study of Public Opinion.* Rutgers University Press, 1967.

Gandhi, Jennifer, and Ellen Lust-Okar. "Authoritarian Institutions and the Survival of Autocrats." *Annual Review of Political Science* 12 (2009): 403–422.

Geertz, Clifford. *The Interpretation of Cultures: Selected Essays.* New York: Basic Books, 1973.

George, Alexander L., and Timothy J. McKeown. "Case Studies and Theories of Organizational Decision Making." *Advances in Information Processing in Organizations* 2, no. 1 (1985): 21–58.

George, Alexander, and Andrew Bennett. *Case Studies and Theory Development in the Social Sciences.* Cambridge, MA: MIT Press, 2005.

Gerring, John. *Case Study Research: Principles and Practices.* New York: Cambridge University Press, 2007.

Ghobashy, Mona el-. "The Metamorphosis of the Egyptian Muslim Brothers." *International Journal of Middle East Studies* 37, no. 3 (2005): 373–395.

Gift, Thomas, and Daniel Krcmaric. "Democracy and Foreign Education." *Journal of Conflict Resolution*, 2015.

Ginsburg, Tom, and Alberto Simpser. "Introduction." In *Constitutions in Authoritarian Regimes*, edited by Tom Ginsburg and Alberto Simpser. Cambridge University Press, 2013.

Gordon, Joel. *Nasser's Blessed Movement: Egypt's Free Officers and the July Revolution*. Oxford University Press, 1992.

Greene, Steven. "Social Identity Theory and Party Identification." *Social Science Quarterly* 85, no. 1 (2004): 136–153.

Greenstein, Fred I. *Children and Politics*. New Haven: Yale University Press, 1969.

Greitens, Sheena Chestnut. *Dictators and their Secret Police: Coercive Institutions and State Violence*. New York: Cambridge University Press, 2016.

Grewal, Sharan, Amaney Jamal, Tarek Masoud, and Elizabeth R. Nugent. "Poverty and Divine Rewards: The Electoral Advantage of Islamist Politics Parties." *American Journal of Political Science*, 63.4 (2019): 859–874.

Gurr, Ted. *Why Men Rebel*. Princeton: Princeton University Press, 1970.

Gutiérrez-Sanín, Francisco, and Elisabeth Jean Wood. "What Should We Mean by 'Pattern of Political Violence'? Repertoire,Targeting, Frequency, and Technique." *Perspectives on Politics* 15, no. 1 (2017): 20–41.

Haggard, Stephan, and Robert R. Kaufman."Democratization During the Third Wave." *Annual Review of Political Science* 19 (2016): 125–144.

———. *The Political Economy of Democratic Transitions*. Princeton: Princeton University Press, 1995.

Haines, Herbert H. "Radical Flank Effects." *The Wiley-Blackwell Encyclopedia of Social and Political Movements*, 2013.

Hall, Peter A. "Historical Institutionalism in Rationalist and Sociological Perspective." In *Explaining Institutional Change: Ambiguity, Agency, and Power*, edited by James Mahoney and Kathleen Thelen, 204–224. New York: Cambridge University Press, 2010.

———. *Some Reflections on Preference Formation*. Memorandum for the Workshop on Rational Choice/Historical Institutionalism, 2000.

Harber, Kent D., and Dov J. Cohen. "The Emotional Broadcaster Theory of Social Sharing." *Journal of Language and Social Psychology* 4, no. 24 (2005): 382–400.

Hartnett, Allison Spencer, Nicholas J. Lotito, and Elizabeth R. Nugent. "The Origins of Coercive Institutions in the Middle East: Preliminary Evidence from Egypt." Working Paper, 2018.

Haugbolle, Rikke Hostrup, and Francesco Cavatorta. "Will the Real Tunisian Opposition Please Stand Up? Opposition Coordination Failures under Authoritarian Constraints." *British Journal of Middle Eastern Studies* 3, no. 38 (2011): 323–341.

Herbst, Jeffrey. *States and Power in Africa: Comparative Lessons in Authority and Control*. Princeton University Press, 2000.

Hibou, Béatrice. *The Force of Obedience: The Political Economy of Repression in Tunisia*.Malden, MA: Polity Press, 2011.

Higley, John, and Michael Burton. *Elite Foundations of Liberal Democracy*. Latham: Rowman & Littlefield, 2006.

Higley, John, and Gyorgy Lengyel. *Elites after State Socialism: Theories and Analysis*. Latham: Rowman & Littlefield, 2000.

Hinnebusch, Raymond A. "Egypt Under Sadat: Elites, Power Structure, and Political Change in a Post-Populist State." *Social Problems* 28, no. 4 (1981): 442–464.

———. "The Reemergence of the Wafd Party: Glimpses of the Liberal Opposition in Egypt." *International Journal of Middle East Studies* 16, no. 1 (1984): 99–121.

Hirsch, Eric L. "Generating Commitment Among Students." In *The Social Movements Reader: Cases and Concepts,* edited by Jeff Goodwin and James M. Jasper. John Wiley & Sons, 2009.

Hogg, Michael A., and John C. Turner. "Intergroup Behaviour, Self Stereotyping and the Salience of Social Categories." *British Journal of Social Psychology* 26 (1987): 325–340.

Holder, R. Clemente. "Egyptian Lawyer's Death Triggers Cairo Protests." *Washington Report on Middle East Affairs,* July/August (1994): 60–62.

Horowitz, Donald. *Ethnic Groups in Conflict.* Berkeley: University of California Press, 1985.

Horwitz, Murray, and Jacob M. Rabbie. "Individuality and Membership in the Intergroup System." In *Social Identity and Intergroup Relations,* edited by Henry Tajfel, 271–274. Cambridge: Cambridge University Press, 1982.

Howard, MarcMorje, and Philip G. Roessler. "Liberalizing Electoral Outcomes in Competitive Authoritarian Regimes." *American Journal of Political Science* 50, no. 2 (2006): 365–381.

Huntington, Samuel P. "Will More Countries Become Democratic?" *Political Science Quarterly* 99, no. 2 (1984): 193–218.

Huntington, Samuel. *The Third Wave: Democratization in the Late Twentieth Century.* Norman, Oklahoma: University of Oklahoma Press, 1993.

Hyman, Herbert. *Political Socialization.* New York: Free Press, 1959.

Ibrahim, Saad Eddin. *Egypt, Islam and Democracy: Critical Essays.* American University in Cairo Press, 2002.

Iskandar, Amin. *Al-Tanzim al-sirri li-Jamal 'Abd al-Nasir: Tali'at al-Ishtirakiyin: al-Mawlid, al-Masar, al-Masir.* Markaz Mahousa lil-Nashr, 2016.

Iyengar, Shanto, Gaurav Sood, and Yphtach Lelkes. "Affect, Not Ideology: A Social Identity Perspective on Polarization." *Public Opinion Quarterly* 76, no. 3 (2012): 405–431.

Iyengar, Shanto, and Sean J. Westwood. "Fear and Loathing Across Party Lines: New Evidence on Group Polarization." *American Journal of Political Science* 59, no. 3 (2015): 690–707.

Iyengar, Shanto, Yphtach Lelkes, Matthew Levendusky, Neil Malhotra, and Sean J. Westwood. "The Origins and Consequences of Affective Polarization in the United States." *Annual Review of Political Science,* 2018.

Jaafar, Mustapha Ben. *Un Si Long Chemin Vers la Démocratie.* Tunis, Tunisia: Editions Nirvana, 2014.

Jebnoun, Noureddine. *Tunisia's National Intelligence: Why "Rogue Elephants" Fail to Reform.* Washington, D. C.: New Academic Publishing, 2017.

Jones, Linda G. "Portrait of Rashid al-Ghannouchi." *Middle East Report* 153 (1988): 19–22.

Kalyvas, Stathis N. "Commitment Problems in Emerging Democracies: The Case of Religious Parties." *Comparative Politics,* 2000, 379–398.

Karl, Terry Lynn. "Dilemmas of Democratization in Latin America." *Comparative Politics* 23, no. 1 (1990): 1–21.

Kassem, Maye. *Egyptian Politics: The Dynamics of Authoritarian Rule.* Boulder, Colorado: Lynne Reiner, 2004.

Katznelson, Ira, and Barry R. Weingast. "Intersections Between Historical and Rational Choice Institutionalism." In *Preferences and Situations: Points of Intersection Between Historical and Rational Choice Institutionalism,* edited by Ira Katznelson and Barry R. Weingast. New York: Russell Sage Foundation, 2005.

Katznelson, Ira, and Aristide R. Zolberg. *Working-Class Formation: Nineteenth-century Patterns in Western Europe and the United States.* Princeton, NJ: Princeton University Press, 1986.

Kelly, Caroline. "Political Identity and Perceived Intragroup Homogeneity." *British Journal of Social Psychology* 28 (1989): 239–250.

Kennedy, Ryan. "The Contradiction of Modernization: A Conditional Model of Endogenous Democratization." *Journal of Politics* 72, no. 3 (2010): 785–798.

Kepel, Gilles. *Jihad: The Trail of Political Islam.* IB Tauris, 2006.

Kertzer, Joshua D. "Re-Assessing Elite-Public Gaps in Political Behavior." Working Paper, 2019.

Khalil, Andrea. "Tunisia's Women: Partners in Revolution." *Journal of North African Studies* 19, no. 2 (2014): 186–199.

Kienle, Eberhard. "More than a Response to Islamism: The Political Deliberalization of Egypt in the 1990s." *Middle East Journal*, 1998, 219–235.

Kirkpatrick, David D. *Into the Hands of the Soldiers: Freedom and Chaos in Egypt and the Middle East.* Penguin Books, 2019.

Kitschelt, Herbert. "Political Regime Change: Structure and Process-driven Explanations?" *American Political Science Review* 86, no. 4 (1992): 1028–1034.

Kitschelt, Herbert, Zdenka Mansfeldova, Radoslaw Markowski, and Gabor Toka. *Post-Communist Party Systems: Competition, Representation, and Inter-party Cooperation.* Cambridge: Cambridge University Press, 1999.

Korany, Baghat, Rex Brynen, and Paul Noble. *Political Liberalization and Democratization in the Arab World: Comparative Experiences, Volume 1.* Boulder, Colorado: Lynne Rienner Publishers, 1995.

Künkler, Mirjam. "How Pluralist Democracy Became the Consensual Discourse among Secular and Nonsecular Muslims in Indonesia." In *Democracy and Islam in Indonesia*, edited by Mirjam Künkler and Alfred C. Stepan, 53–72. Columbia University Press, 2013.

Lagacé, Clara Boulianne, and Jennifer Gandhi. *Authoritarian Institutions.* New York: Routledge, 2015.

Laitin, David D. *Identity in Formation: The Russian-Speaking Populations in the Near Abroad.* Ithaca, NY: Cornell University Press, 1998.

Levitsky, Steven, and Lucan Way. "The Rise of Competitive Authoritarianism." *Journal of Democracy* 2, no. 13 (2002): 51–65.

Linz, Juan J., and Alfred Stepan. *Problems of Democratic Transition and Consolidation: Southern Europe, South America, and Post-Communist Europe.* Johns Hopkins University Press, 1996.

Linz, Juan. *Totalitarian and Authoritarian Regimes.* New York: Lynne Rienner Publishers, 2000.

Lipset, Seymour M. "Some Social Requisites of Democracy: Economic Development and Political Legitimacy." *American Political Science Review* 53, no. 1 (1969): 69–105.

Lipset, Seymour M., and Stein Rokkan. "Cleavage Structures, Party Systems, and Voter Alignments: An Introduction." In *Party Systems and Voter Alignments: Cross-National Perspectives*, edited by Seymour M. Lipset and Stein Rokkan, 1–64. Toronto: Free Press, 1967.

Lotito, Nicholas J. *Soldiers and Societies in Revolt: Military Doctrine in the Arab Spring.* PhD diss., Columbia University, 2018.

Loxton, James. *Authoritarian Successor Parties Worldwide: A Framework For Analysis.* South Bend, IN: University of Notre Dame, Helen Kellogg Institute for International Studies, 2016.

Lupia, Arthur, and Mathew D. McCubbins. *The Democratic Dilemma: Can Citizens Learn What They Need to Know?* Cambridge: Cambridge University Press, 1998.

Lupu, Noam, and Leonid Peisakhin. "The Legacy of Political Violence across Generations." *American Journal of Political Science* 61, no. 4 (2017): 836–851.

Lupu, Noam, and Rachel Beatty Riedl. "Political Parties and Uncertainty in Developing Democracies." *Comparative Political Studies* 46, no. 11 (2013): 1339–1365.

Lust-Okar, Ellen, and Amaney Jamal. "Rulers and Rules: Reassessing the Influence of Regime Type on Electoral Law Formation." *Comparative Political Studies* 35, no. 2 (2002): 337–366.

Lust, Ellen. "Competitive Clientelism in the Middle East." *Journal of Democracy* 20, no. 3 (2009): 122–135.

————. *Structuring Conflict in the Arab World: Incumbents, Opponents, and Institutions.* Cambridge: Cambridge University Press, 2005.

Lust, Ellen, and David Waldner. "Unwelcome Change: Understanding, Evaluating, and Extending Theories of Democratic Backsliding." *US Agency for International Development* 11 (2015).

Mackie, David M. "Social Identification Effects in Group Polarization." *Journal of Personality and Social Psychology* 50 (1986): 720–728.

MacMaster, Neil. "Torture: From Algiers to Abu Ghraib." *Race and Class* 46, no. 2 (2004): 1–21.

Madini, Tawfiq al-. *Tarikh al-Mu'arida al-Tunsiyya min al-nisha' ila al-thawra.* Tunis: Sotupresse, 2012.

Mael, Fred A., and Lois E. Tetrick. "Identifying Organizational Identification." *Educational and Psychological Measurement* 52, no. 4 (1989): 813–824.

Magaloni, Beatriz. *Voting for Autocracy: Hegemonic Party Survival and its Demise in Mexico.* New York: Cambridge University Press, 2006.

Mahmood, Saba. *Politics of Piety: The Islamic Revival and the Feminist Subject.* Princeton University Press, 2011.

Mahoney, James. *The Legacies of Liberalism: Path Dependence and Political Regimes in Central America.* Johns Hopkins University Press, 2001.

Mahoney, James, and Kathleen Thelen. *Explaining Institutional Change: Ambiguity, Agency, and Power.* New York: Cambridge University Press, 2010.

Mainwaring, Scott. *Transitions to Democracy and Democratic Consolidation: Theoretical and Comparative Issues.* University of Notre Dame, Helen Kellogg Institute for International Studies, 1989.

Mainwaring, Scott, Guillermo O'Donnell, and J. Samuel Valenzuela. *Issues in Democratic Consolidation: The New South American Democracies in Comparative Perspective.* South Bend, Indiana: University of Notre Dame Press, 1992.

Malkki, Liisa H. *Purity and Exile: Violence, Memory, and National Cosmology among Hutu Refugees in Tanzania.* University of Chicago Press, 2012.

Mamdani, Mahmood. *When Victims Become Killers: Colonialism, Nativism, and the Genocide in Rwanda.* Princeton University Press, 2014.

Mansbach, Richard, and Edward Rhodes. "The National State and Identity Politics: State Institutionalisation and 'Markers' of National Identity." *Geopolitics* 12, no. 3 (2007): 426–458.

Mason, Lilliana. "'I Disrespectfully Agree': The Differential Effects of Partisan Sorting on Social and Issue Polarization." *American Journal of Political Science* 59, no. 1 (2015): 128–145.

Masoud, Tarek. *Counting Islam: Religion, Class, and Elections in Egypt.* New York: Cambridge University Press, 2014.

Matsuzaki, Reo. *Institutions by Imposition: Colonial Lessons for Contemporary State-building.* 2011.

McCarthy, Rory. *Inside Tunisia's Al-Nahda: Between Politics and Preaching.* Cambridge University Press, 2018.

McCarty, Nolan. "Measuring Legislative Preferences." In *The Oxford Handbook of the American Congress,* edited by George C. Edwards III, Frances E. Lee, and Eric Schickler. Oxford: Oxford University Press, 2011.

McCarty, Nolan, Keith T. Poole, and Howard Rosenthal. *Polarized America: The Dance of Ideology and Unequal Riches.* Cambridge: MIT Press, 2006.

McDevitt, Michael, and Steven Chaffee. "From Top-down to Trickle-up Influence: Revisiting Assumptions about the Family in Political Socialization." *Political Communication* 19, no. 3 (2002): 281–301.

McFaul, Michael. "The Fourth Wave of Democracy and Dictatorship: Noncooperative Transitions in the Postcommunist World." *World Politics* 54, no. 2 (2002): 212–244.

Méouchy, Nadine, and Peter Sluglett, eds. *The British and French Mandates in Comparative Perspectives (Les Mandats Français et Anglais dans une Perspective Comparative)*. Leiden: Brill, 2004.

Mezran, Karim, and Erin A. Neale. "Algerian Demonstrations: What they mean for the future of the elite and the country." *MENASource: Atlantic Council*, 2019.

Mietzner, Marcus. *Military Politics, Islam, and the State in Indonesia: From Turbulent Transition to Democratic Consolidation*. Institute of Southeast Asian Studies, 2009.

Miller, Arthur H., Patricia Gurin, Gerald Gurin, and Oksana Malanchuk. "Group Consciousness and Political Participation." *American Journal of Political Science* 25, no. 3 (1981): 494–511.

Mitchell, Richard Paul. *The Society of the Muslim Brothers*. Oxford: Oxford University Press, 1993.

Mondak, Jeffrey J. "Candidate Perception in an Ambiguous World: Campaigns, cues, and inference processes." *American Journal of Political Science* 33, no. 4 (1989): 912–940.

——. "Public Opinion and Heuristic Processing of Source Cues." *Political Behavior* 15, no. 2 (1993): 167–192.

Moore, Barrington. *Social Origins of Dictatorship and Democracy: Lord and Peasant in the Making of the Modern World*. Boston: Beacon Press, 1993.

Mosley, Layna. "Just Talk to People? Interviews in Contemporary Political Science." In *Interview Research in Political Science*, edited by Layna Mosley, 1–28. Ithaca, NY: Cornell University Press, 2013.

Moustafa, Tamir. "Law and courts in authoritarian regimes." *Annual Review of Law and Social Science* 10 (2014): 281–299.

Myerson, Roger B. "The Autocrat's Credibility Problem and Foundations of the Constitutional State." *American Political Science Review* 102, no. 1 (2008): 125–139.

Mzali, Mohamed. *Túnez: qué porvenir?* Paris: Publisud, 1991.

Naseef, Magdy. "Sadat's Final Act of Repression: The September 1981 Arrests of 1650 Egyptians was a 'Purge' of the Intelligentsia." *Index on Censorship* 11, no. 1 (1982): 37–39.

Nugent, Elizabeth R. "Personal Exposure to Repression and Political Preferences: Evidence from Tunisia." Working Paper, 2019.

O'Donnell, Guillermo, Philippe C. Schmitter, and Cynthia J. Arnson. *Transitions from Authoritarian Rule: Tentative Conclusions about Uncertain Democracies*. Johns Hopkins University Press, 2013 (1986).

O'Donnell, Guillermo, Philippe C. Schmitter, and Laurence Whitehead. *Transitions from Authoritarian Rule: Southern Europe*. Johns Hopkins University Press, 1986.

O'Keefe, Daniel J. *Persuasian: Theory and Research*. Safe: Oxford University Press, 1990.

Omri, M. "No Ordinary Union: UGTT and the Tunisian Path to Revolution and Transition." *Workers of the World: International Journal on Strikes and Social Conflict* 1, no. 7 (2015): 14–29.

Perry, Elizabeth J. *Patrolling the Revolution: Worker Militias, Citizenship, and the Modern Chinese State*. Lanham: Rowman/Littlefield, 2006.

Peters, Edward. *Torture*. New York: Basil Blackwell, 1985.

Pettigrew, Thomas F. "Intergroup Contact Theory." *Annual Review of Psychology* 49, no. 1 (1998): 65–85.

Pickard, Duncan. "Challenges to Legitimate Governance in Post-Revolution Tunisia." In *North Africa's Arab Spring*, 141–156. Routledge, 2013.

Pop-Eleches, Grigore, and Joshua A. Tucker. "Communism's Shadow: Postcommunist Legacies, Values, and Behavior." *Comparative Politics* 43, no. 4 (2011): 379–408.

Posner, Daniel N. *Institutions and Ethnic Politics in Africa*. New York: Cambridge University Press, 2005.

Post, Erika. "Egypt's Elections." *MERIP Middle East Report* 147 (1987): 18–19.

Posusney, Marsha Pripstein. "Multi-party Elections in the Arab World: Institutional Engineering and Oppositional Strategies." *Studies in Comparative and International Development* 36, no. 4 (2002): 34–62.

Przeworski, Adam. *Capitalism and Social Democracy.* Cambridge University Press, 1986.

——. *Democracy and the Market: Political and Economic Reforms in Eastern Europe and Latin America.* Cambridge: Cambridge University Press, 1991.

Przeworski, Adam, and Fernando Limongi. "Modernization: Theories and Facts." *World Politics* 49, no. 2 (1997): 155–183.

Przeworski, Adam, and John Sprague. *Paper Stones: A History of Electoral Socialism.* University of Chicago Press: Chicago, 1986.

Przeworski, Adam, Susan C. Stokes, and Bernard Manin. *Democracy, Accountability, and Representation.* Cambridge University Press, 1999.

Rabia, Amro Hashim. *Al-Ahzab al-Saghira wal-Nizam al-Hizbi fi Masr.* Cairo: Al-Ahram Center for Political and Strategic Studies, 2003.

Ramadan, Abdel Azim. "Fundamentalist Influence in Egypt: The Strategies of the Muslim Brotherhood and the Takfir groups." In *Fundamentalisms and the State: Remaking Politics, Economies and Militance,* edited by Martin E. Marty and R. Scott Apple by. University of Chicago Press, 1993.

Rashwan, Diaa. "A Trial at the Polls." *Al-Ahram Weekly,* 1995, 2.

Razik, Hussein Abdel. *Al-Ahali: Sahifa taht al-hisar.* Cairo: Dar al-'Alam al-Thalith, 1994.

Ricart-Huguet, Joan. "The Origins of Colonial Investments in Former British and French Africa." Working Paper, 2019.

Rijkers, Bob, Caroline L. Freund, and Antonio Nucifora. "All in the Family: State Capture in Tunisia." World Bank Policy Research Working Paper 6810 (2014).

Ritter, Daniel. *The Iron Cage of Liberalism: International Politics and Unarmed Revolutions in the Middle East and North Africa.* Oxford: Oxford University Press, 2015.

Robinson, Glenn E. "Defensive Democratization in Jordan." *International Journal of Middle East Studies* 30, no. 3 (1998): 387–410.

Rogowski, Jon C., and Joseph L. Sutherland. "How Ideology Fuels Affective Polarization." *Political Behavior* 38, no. 2 (2016): 485–508.

Root, Hilton L. "Tying the King's Hands: Credible Commitments and Royal Fiscal Policy During the Old Regime." *Rationality and Society* 1, no. 2 (1989): 240–258.

Rozenas, Arturas, Sebastian Schutte, and Yuri Zhukov. "The Political Legacy of Violence: The Long-Term Impact of Stalin's Repression in Ukraine." *Journal of Politics* 79, no. 4 (2017): 1147–1161.

Ruedy, John. *Modern Algeria: The Origins and Development of a Nation.* Bloomington: Indiana University Press, 1992.

Rueschemeyer, Dietrich, Evelyne Huber Stephens, and John D. Stephens. *Capitalist Development and Democracy.* Chicago: University of Chicago Press, 1992.

Rustow, Dankwart A. "Transitions to Democracy: Toward a Dynamic Model." *Comparative Politics* 2, no. 3 (1970): 337–363.

Sapiro, Virginia. "Not Your Parents' Political Socialization: Introduction for a New Generation." *Annual Review of Political Science* 7 (2004): 1–23.

Sartori, Giovanni. "Politics, Ideology, and Belief Systems." *American Political Science Review* 63, no. 2 (1969): 398–411.

Schedler, Andreas. *Electoral Authoritarianism: The Dynamics of Unfree Competition.* Boulder: Lynne Rienner Publishers, 2006.

——. "The Menu of Manipulation." *Journal of Democracy* 13, no. 2 (2002): 36–50.

Schmitter, Philippe C. "Transitology: The Science or the Art of Democratization?" In *The Consolidation of Democracy in Latin America*, edited by Joseph S. Tulchin and Bernice Romero, 11–41. Boulder, Colorado: Lynne Rienner, 1995.

Schuman, Howard, Robert F. Belli, and Katherine Bischoping. "The Generational Basis of Historical Knowledge." In *Collective Memories of Political Events: Social Psychological Perspectives*, edited by J. W. Pennebaker, D. Paez, and B. Rime. New York: Lawrence Erlbaum Publishers, 1997.

Schuman, Howard, and Jacqueline Scott. "Generations and Collective Memories." *American Sociological Review* 54, no. 3 (1989): 359–381.

Schumpeter, Joseph A. *Socialism, Capitalism and Democracy*. Harper/Brothers, 1942.

Schwedler, Jillian. "Can Islamists Become Moderates? Rethinking the Inclusion-Moderation Hypothesis." *World Politics* 63, no. 2f (2011): 347–376.

———. *Faith in Moderation: Islamist Parties in Jordan and Yemen*. Cambridge University Press, 2006.

Schwedler, Jillian, and Laryssa Chomiak. "And the Winner Is...: Authoritarian Elections in the Arab World." *Middle East Report*, 2006, 12–19.

Schwedler, Jillian, and Janine A. Clark. "Islamist-Leftist Cooperation in the Arab World." *ISIM Review* 18 (2006): 10–11.

Searing, Donald D. "The Comparative Study of Elite Socialization." *Comparative Politics Studies* 1, no. 4 (1969): 471–500.

Shain, Yossi, and Juan J. Linz. "Introduction." In *Between States: Interim Governments in Democratic Transitions*, edited by Yossi Shain and Juan J. Linz. Cambridge University Press, 1995.

Share, Donald. "Transitions to Democracy and Transition through Transaction." *Comparative Political Studies* 19, no. 4 (1987): 525–548.

Shehata, Deena. *Islamists and Secularists in Egypt: Opposition, Conflict and Cooperation*. London: Routledge, 2009.

Shehata, Samer, and Joshua Stacher. "The Brotherhood Goes to Parliament." *Middle East Report* 240 (2006): 32.

Shepsle, Kenneth A. "Rational Choice Institutionalism." In *The Oxford Handbook of Political Institutions*, edited by Sarah A. Binder, R.A.W. Rhodes, and Bert A. Rockman, 23–38. Oxford: Oxford University Press, 2006.

Sigelman, Lee, and SyngNam Yough. "Left-right Polarization in National Party Systems: A Cross-National Analysis." *Comparative Political Studies* 11, no. 3 (1978): 355–379.

Simon, Bernd. "Intragroup Differentiation in Terms of Ingroup and Outgroup Attributes." *European Journal of Social Psychology* 22 (1992): 407–413.

Sirrs, Owen L. *A History of the Egyptian Intelligence Service: A History of the Mukhabarat, 1910–2009*. Routledge, 2010.

Snow, David A., E. Burke Rochford Jr., Steven K. Worden, and Robert D. Benford. "Frame Alignment Processes, Micromobilization, and Movement Participation." *American Sociological Review*, 1986, 464–481.

Sperber, Dan, and Lawrence A. Hirschfeld. "The Cognitive Foundations of Cultural Stability and Diversity." *Trends in Cognitive Sciences* 8, no. 1 (2004): 40–46.

Stacher, Joshua. *Watermelon Democracy: Egypt's Turbulent Transition*. Syracuse University Press, 2020.

Stepan, Alfred C. *Democratizing Brazil: Problems of Transition and Consolidation*. New York: Oxford University Press, 1989.

Stokes, Susan C. "Political Clientelism." In *The Oxford Handbook of Political Science*. 2007.

Struch, Naomi, and Shalom H. Schwartz. "Intergroup Aggression: Its Predictors and Distinctness from In-group Bias." *Journal of Personality and Social Psychology* 56 (1989): 364–373.

Svolik, Milan W. *The Politics of Authoritarian Rule*. Cambridge: Cambridge University Press, 2012.

Tajfel, Henri, and John C. Turner. "An Integrative Theory of Intergroup Conflict." In *The Social Psychology of Intergroup Relations*, edited by William G. Austin and Stephen Worchel. Monterey, CA: Brooks/Cole, 1979.

———. "The Social Identity Theory of Intergroup Behavior." In *Psychology of Integroup Relations*, edited by Stephen Worchel and William G. Austin. Chicago: Nelson-Hall Publishers, 1986.

Tajfel, Henri, M. B. Billig, R. P. Bundy, and Claude Flament. "Social Categorization and Intergroup Behaviour." *European Journal of Social Psychology* 2, no. 1 (1971): 149–178.

Tammam, Hossam. *Tahawwalit al-Ikhwan al-Muslimin*. Cairo: Maktabat Madbouli, 2010.

Tarrow, Sidney. *Power in Movement: Social Movements and Contentious Politics*. Cambridge: Cambridge University Press, 1998.

Tauber, Eliezer. "Egyptian Secret Societies, 1911." *Middle Eastern Studies* 42, no. 3 (2006): 603–623.

Thomas, Martin. "Colonial States as Intelligence States: Security Policing and the Limits of Colonial Rule in France's Muslim Territories, 1920–40." *Journal of Strategic Studies* 28, no. 6 (2005): 1033–1060.

———. *Empires of Intelligence: Security Services and Colonial Disorder After 1914*. Berkeley: University of California Press, 2008.

———. "The Gendarmerie, Information Collection, and Colonial Violence in French North Africa Between the Wars." *Historical Reflections/Réflexions Historiques* 36, no. 2 (2010): 76–96.

———. *Violence and Colonial Order: Police, Workers and Protest in the European Colonial Empires, 1918–1940. Critical Perspectives on Empire*. Cambridge: Cambridge University Press, 2012.

Tignor, Robert L. *Modernisation and British Colonial Rule in Egypt, 1882–1914*. Princeton University Press, 1966.

Tilly, Charles. *Big Structures, Large Processes, Huge Comparisons*. New York: Russell Sage Foundation, 1984.

Tilmisani, Umar al-. *Dhikrayat LaMudhakkirat*. Dar al-Tiba'a wa-al-Nashr al-Islamiya, 1985.

Tollefson, Harold. *Policing Islam: The British Occupation of Egypt and the Anglo-Egyptian Struggle over Control of the Police, 1882–1914*. Greenwood Publishing Group, 1999.

Turner, John C. "Social Categorization and Social Discrimination in the Minimal Group Paradigm." In *Differentiation Between Social Groups: Studies in the Social Psychology of Intergroup Relations*, edited by Henry Tajfel, 101–140. London: Academic Press, 1978.

Ura, Joseph Daniel, and Christopher R. Ellis. "Partisan Moods: Polarization and the Dynamics of Mass Party Preferences." *Comparative Political Studies* 74, no. 1 (2011): 277–291.

van de Walle, Nicolas. "Tipping Games: When Do Opposition Parties Coalesce?" In *Electoral Authoritarianism: The Dynamics of Unfree Competition*, edited by Andreas Schedler. Boulder, Colorado: Lynne Rienner, 2006.

Wagner, Wolfgang, Nicole Kronberger, and Franz Seifert. "Collective Symbolic Coping with New Technology: Knowledge, Images, and Public Discourse." *British Journal of Social Psychology* 3, no. 41 (2002): 323–343.

Weiss, Meredith L. "What a Little Democracy Can Do: Comparing Trajectories of Reform in Malaysia and Indonesia." *Democratisation* 14, no. 1 (2007): 26–43.

Weitzer, Ronald J. *Transforming Settler States: Communal Conflict and Internal Security in Northern Ireland and Zimbabwe*. Berkeley: University of California Press, 1990.

Welchman, Lynn. "Anti-Terrorism Law and Policy in Arab States." In *Global Anti-Terrorism Law and Policy*, edited by Victor V. Ramraj, Michael Hor, Kent Roach, and George Williams. Cambridge: Cambridge University Press, 2012.

Wengraf, Tom. *Qualitative Research Interviewing: Biographic Narrative and Semi-Structured Methods*. London: Sage, 2001.

Wickham, Carrie Rosefsky. *Mobilizing Islam: TheMuslim Brotherhood in Egypt*. New York: Columbia University Press, 2002.

——. *The Muslim Brotherhood: Evolution of an Islamist Movement*. Princeton, NJ: Princeton University Press, 2013.

——. "The Path to Moderation: Strategy and Learning in the Formation of Egypt's *Wasat* Party." *Comparative Politics* 36, no. 2 (2004): 205–228.

Willis, Michael. *The Islamist Challenge in Algeria: A Political History*. New York University Press, 1999.

Wintrobe, Ronald. *The Political Economy of Dictatorship*. New York: Cambridge University Press, 1998.

Wolf, Anne. *Political Islam in Tunisia: The History of Ennahda*. Oxford University Press, 2017.

Wood, Elisabeth Jean. *Forging Democracy from Below: Insurgent Transitions in South Africa and El Salvador*. Cambridge University Press, 2000.

Zollner, Barbara. "Prison Talk: the Muslim Brotherhood's Internal Struggle during Gamal Abdel Nasser's Persecution, 1954 to 1971." *International Journal of Middle East Studies* 39, no. 3 (2007): 411–433.

Zoubir, Yahia H. "The Painful Transition from Authoritarianism in Algeria." *Arab Studies Quarterly*, 1993, 83–110.

# INDEX

## A NOTE ON THE TYPE

This book has been composed in Adobe Text and Gotham.
Adobe Text, designed by Robert Slimbach for Adobe,
bridges the gap between fifteenth- and sixteenth-century
calligraphic and eighteenth-century Modern styles.
Gotham, inspired by New York street signs, was designed
by Tobias Frere-Jones for Hoefler & Co.